FETTERED
FREEDOM

FETTERED
FREEDOM

Civil Liberties and the
Slavery Controversy
1830—1860

RUSSEL B. NYE

UNIVERSITY OF ILLINOIS PRESS
Urbana Chicago London

Illini Books edition, 1972

By permission from the Michigan State University Press
© 1963 by the Michigan State University Press
Manufactured in the United States of America
Library of Congress Catalog Card No. 63-17464

ISBN 0-252-00280-6

In Memory of

Charles Henry Nye
45th Wisconsin Vol. Rgt.
1862-1865

Loring James Nye
7th Wisconsin Vol. Rgt.
1861-1865

Contents

An Introductory Note

THIS STUDY is an attempt to show the reactions of the American people, during one central period and on one specific issue, to the civil liberties tradition. The period 1830-1860, considered both from the point of view of the political philosopher and the political scientist, was concerned with the discusson of the slavery question—with the definition and application of the term *freedom,* as it applied to Negroes, as it applied to white men, and eventually as it applied to Man. Before the era was terminated by war, the discussion expanded to include nearly all related terms and their legal and social applications. The nation was irrevocably split over what these terms meant and what their practice entailed.

The end of the eighteenth century saw the formulation and general acceptance in America of a political philosophy which laid great stress upon the freedom of the individual. Many influential thinkers believed that man was endowed at birth with certain inalienable rights, "naturally" and therefore divinely bestowed, rights which were reserved to him despite any contractual agreement entered into with a government. The theory itself had, it is true, little real justification in historical fact, but its adoption as a basis for action gave it a certain validity and made it a vital force in the development of society and politics. The natural rights philosophy could not be proved historically; pragmatically it could be proved by working it. The American experiment was one, perhaps the most important, of the practical applications of this theory.

The Founding Fathers spoke, therefore, in eighteenth-century fashion, of "inalienable rights," "the rights of man," and "natural rights," embodying them in the Constitution, the Declaration of Independence, and in the various bills of rights. The labels they used matter little; these rights themselves, sometimes vaguely and sometimes clearly expressed, have become that part of our native tradition known as "civil liberties," those freedoms belonging to the citizen as an individual and as a member of society. The common property and heritage of the American people, they may seem often distant from us, rarely to be considered unless attacked from within or without. Yet they are much more than simple safeguards. They are, as the late Carl Becker pointed out, "essential social processes" that make constitutional democracy possible and workable. Civil liberties are as important to the present, and to the future America, as they were to the eighteenth century that established them. Changes in society merely change their aspects and require new methods for protecting them.

Civil liberty is not a term difficult to define or discuss on a general or theoretical basis. The rulings of courts, both state and federal, the constitutions of the states and the nation, the individual's own awareness of his traditional and legal rights—all these provide sufficient familiarity with it in theory. More difficult are the establishment and limitation of the practical applications of the term. The question becomes, how far may the civil liberties of the individual be curtailed in the interests of a majority, for the good of society or of the individual? Legalistic interpretations in every instance do not give satisfactory answers, and the usual methods of compromise between individual and state do not always succeed. Free speech, for example, may be defined as the absence of governmental restraint upon the expression of ideas, and a beautifully constructed framework of logic may be pyramided upon that basic principle. Practice, however, demands a multitude of further definitions, some legally impeccable, some popularly endorsed, some mutually unacceptable to speaker and listener. One of the more interesting and important facets of history is the study of how the American people react, under pressure, to their belief in their own liberties.

An Introductory Note

The successful conclusion to the abolitionist crusade to free the slave, culminating in the Emancipation Proclamation of 1862, did not settle the argument over the civil liberties of the black man. Nor did the war which followed the abolition controversy, nor the adjustments of the difficult period of reconstruction, conclude the argument—indeed, as a greater perspective in time is reached, it is doubtful that it was settled at all so far as the civil liberties tradition is concerned.

The claim of the abolitionist that slavery threatened the liberty of the white man as well as that of the black disappeared with slavery. Yet we do not have, nearly a century after the close of the controversy, a more precise idea of what free speech, free press, and free thought mean, especially in regard to the Negro, than did Garrison or Goodell. The civil liberties tradition has grown and expanded, it is true. In practice, a set of standards has haphazardly evolved, and the abolitionists contributed significantly to that development, which is by no means finished. It is peculiar, in a society which was founded in revolution and which has progressed by change, that the rise of new ideas seems to be attended by difficulties and compromises in the reinterpretation of old ones. The struggle over civil liberties and abolition provides a case history of this American paradox.

It is not the aim of this study to draw parallels between the definition and treatment of civil liberties in the period of anti-slavery agitation and in the present; obviously, however, parallels do exist. If the house is ever again divided, civil liberties will once more inevitably be called into question, redefined, reconsidered, and reapplied. The America of Garrison and Calhoun, the America of today, and the America of tomorrow have at least this much in common, that they were, are, and will be concerned with the vital question of what constitutes civil liberties, who possesses them, how many of them may be possessed and used, and what means may be taken to protect or to infringe upon them.

* * * * *

As the first edition of this book went to press the question of civil rights, particularly as it related to those of the Negro citizen, had been projected into the forefront of public discussion by the report of the President's Commission on Civil Rights in 1948. In responding to the publisher's request for a new preface for the revised edition, I found, curiously enough, that the original version—now fifteen years old—was still exactly pertinent, and that there seemed to be no reason to change it. This fact, I believe, speaks for itself.

East Lansing, Michigan   Russel B. Nye
1948, 1963

FETTERED
FREEDOM

Slavery and Abolition—
the Backgrounds

I

NEITHER THE INSTITUTION of slavery nor its abolition became an important issue in the United States until the third decade of the nineteenth century. Antislavery agitation, mild in form and temperate in aim, had of course been known since colonial days, but it was not until after the formation of the Republic, and the enunciation of eighteenth-century ideals of liberty and equality, that serious attention was given to the slavery question.

The temper of the nation, North and South, was then prevailingly against the institution, though it was not a vital issue; the attempt to stop the slave trade, which met success in 1808, signalled the first national victory for the antislavery forces. After 1808, antislavery sentiment increased. State societies, beginning with Pennsylvania's in 1777, appeared in all states except New England and the deep South. Most of these favored colonization, gradual emancipation, or some kind of manumission scheme, since the immediate emancipation of slaves was usually deemed undesirable or impractical.

The American Convention for the Abolition of Slavery and Improving the Condition of the African Race, which began its meetings in 1794, was a vigorous force in propagating antislavery sentiment until its place was taken by the more influential American Colonization Society, founded in 1817, whose aim was to transport American Negro slaves to Africa after buying their freedom. The Society collected funds for many years, sponsored local societies, and founded the Liberia colony a few years later. By the late 'twenties, the growing sensitivity of the South to discussion of the slavery question brought an end to the era of goodwill. Antislavery sentiment seemed to be dying out, and although 251 colonization societies still remained in 1832, the scheme had lost much of its appeal. The policy of gradualism, which had characterized antislavery sentiment until 1830, no longer exerted an effective appeal after the opening of the aggressive phase of abolition.[1]

The abolition movement of the 'thirties was part of the great reform wave then sweeping the United States and Europe, a compound of idealism, liberalism, humanitarianism, and transcendentalism, a general movement which sought to perfect human institutions. "There is at hand," remarked William Ellery Channing in 1830, "a tendency and a power to exalt the people," founded on "devotion to the progress of the whole human race." Or, as Harriet Beecher Stowe phrased it in the preface to *Uncle Tom's Cabin*, "The hand of benevolence is everywhere stretched out, searching into abuses, righting wrongs, alleviating distresses, and bringing to the knowledge and sympathies of the world the lowly, oppressed, and the forgotten." Educational, religious, and penal reform; temperance crusades; struggles for women's rights, for peace, for health and serenity—all these indicated a suddenly renewed sense of social

[1] For treatments of early antislavery thought in America, see Henry Wilson, *History of the Rise and Fall of the Slave Power in America*, I:18-30; William Goodell, *Slavery and Antislavery*, pp. 152-170; Alice Adams, *The Neglected Period of Antislavery in the United States, 1808-1831;* and Thomas E. Drake, *Quakers and Slavery in America.*

responsibility toward the poor, the helpless, the wayward, and the slave, and reflected a significant change in the public attitude toward social problems. The abolition of Negro slavery, at first only one of these myriad reforms, bulked larger and larger until at the end it overshadowed all others. In it was encompassed the crusade to establish democracy according to the Declaration of Independence, to break the power of the dominant aristocratic class, to perfect the social order, and to apply Christianity to American life. Other reforms met success or failure and faded, only to merge with the greater issue of freedom versus oppression.[2]

The beginnings of "immediate" emancipation, more popularly referred to simply as abolition, may be dated approximately from the appearance of William Lloyd Garrison's *Liberator* in 1831.[3] "I stand," said Garrison in his first number, "for the immediate enfranchisement of our slave population." The idea of immediate freedom for the slave had its origin in British antislavery circles in the 'twenties, and was adopted by Garrison soon after. As interpreted by him, immediatism involved no really ordered or practical plan; it consisted of freeing Negro slaves, and that only. The various economic, social, and political problems incidental to their emancipation never caught his interest.

This "immediatist" doctrine, however, remained more or less

[2] For discussions of the relation of abolition to general reform, see A. B. Hart, *Slavery and Abolition*, 171-72; A. Y. Lloyd, *The Slavery Controversy*, 56-7; Avery Craven, *The Coming of the Civil War*, 134; and Clifford S. Griffin, "The Abolitionists and the Benevolent Societies," *Journal of Negro History* XLIV (July, 1959), 195-217. The background of reform is adequately treated in Harriet Martineau, *Society in America*, II, chapter IV; Merle Curti, *The Growth of American Thought*, chapters V-VII; and Alice F. Tyler, *Freedom's Ferment*. Louis Filler, *The Crusade Against Slavery*, is the best modern treatment of the movement; Dwight L. Dumond, *Antislavery: The Crusade for Freedom in America*, is an exhaustive treatment from the abolitionist point of view. Dumond's companion volume, *A Bibliography of Antislavery in America*, is the most complete listing of bibliographical items.

[3] *Niles' Register* began in 1834 to index "Abolitionism" as a separate item. For a discussion of the mutations of the term, see G. H. Barnes, *The Antislavery Impulse*, 31 ff.

Garrison's property. Non-Garrisonians (such as the New York group under the sponsorship of Arthur and Lewis Tappan and the western group under the leadership of Theodore Weld, James G. Birney, and others) perceived the difficulties inherent in Garrisonian immediatism and the impossibility of convincing the general public of its efficacy. The New York Anti Slavery Society, organized in 1833, officially adopted a modified version, "immediate emancipation, gradually accomplished," a compromise difficult to understand and equally difficult to publicize. The American Anti Slavery Society, organized later in the same year, adopted the New York doctrine. In the West, the Lane Seminary group, led by Theodore Weld, redefined the term as "gradual emancipation, immediately begun," a definition eventually accepted by the national society as meaning that "the slaves be at once delivered from the control of arbitrary and irresponsible power, and, like other men, put under the control of equitable laws, equitably administered."[4]

The Western doctrine did not mean, it was pointed out, simply turning the freed slave loose, colonizing him elsewhere, or investing him at once with political rights. It meant that legal control of the master over the slave should cease, that he was free to sell his labor in open market, and that he should be placed under "a benevolent and disinterested supervision" (presumably that of the state or federal government) until he was ready for "intellectual and moral equality with whites."[5] In effect, the Lane scheme was the older scheme of gradual emancipation augmented by new interpretations adapted from the Garrisonian and New York doctrines. The compromise did much to diminish public antipathy to the immediatists. It was

[4] A. A. Phelps, *Lectures on Slavery and Its Remedy*, 138.

[5] Minutes of the Lane Seminary Anti Slavery Society, Western Reserve Historical Society Collections, Cleveland, Ohio. Official explanations of the plan may be found in A. A. Phelps, *op. cit.*, 177-178, and LaRoy Sunderland, *The Anti Slavery Manual*, 79-80. Both are excellent sources of information concerning abolitionist principles during the early phases of the movement. It is interesting to note that none of the abolitionists made any proposals for reimbursing the slaveholder for the loss of his property by means of national or state funds.

argued, for example, that turning slave labor into free labor involved little more than a change of masters, of one type of slavery for another; that absorption of the slave into a free labor market would prove difficult; and that the plan would necessarily involve some type of forced Negro labor under supervision.[6] Yet despite its vagueness, the Western (or Lane) doctrine remained the popular version of immediatism for some years in non-Garrisonian circles. The greatest objection to its final adoption as official abolitionist doctrine was removed by the publication in 1838 of Thome and Kimball's *Emancipation in the West Indies,* which seemed to prove that emancipation could be successfully accomplished without difficulty or bloodshed; and that the freed slave, properly safeguarded, could be absorbed into free society with a minimum of dislocation.[7]

As the abolitionists slowly evolved a definition of their primary principle, so they organized national, state, and local societies to propagate it. Garrison's New England Anti Slavery Society, formed at Boston in 1832, at first led only a precarious existence while the New York City Anti Slavery Society, organized in the fall of 1833 under the Tappans' sponsorship, was hardly much stronger. A Philadelphia and a Providence group, and five small local societies in Ohio, made up the list of organized societies in 1833. To all these the New York Society issued an invitation to meet in Philadelphia for a national convention in December of 1833. After a three-day session, dominated by Garrison, some sixty delegates appointed a committee to draw up a constitution for a national body, the American Anti Slavery Society. By means of a complex system of interlocking directorates, control of the national, state, and local groups was vested in a small group of leading abolitionists, the committee secretaries and the agents—men such as Elizur Wright, Jr., Birney, Henry Stanton, Weld, J. G.

---

[6] Barnes, *op. cit.,* 101-103.

[7] See James G. Birney's explanations in the Cincinnati *Philanthropist,* November 25, 1836, and March 8, 1837; and Barnes, *op. cit.,* 138-139.

Whittier, Joshua Leavitt, William Goodell, Amos Phelps, and a few others.[8]

The most important function of the new national society was to spread the immediatist doctrine and organize support for it. Almost at once it began a pamphlet and periodical campaign, issuing five regular and numerous irregular publications. The establishment of new societies was left to the agents, who were especially trained and assigned to work in areas suited to their backgrounds and talents. From sixteen agents, the number was expanded in 1836 to seventy, the highest number, and in their wake a network of state and local societies, bound loosely to the national parent group, sprang up from Maine to Ohio. Before 1835, only Vermont and Massachusetts had state societies. By late 1836, Maine, New Hampshire, Ohio, New York, and Rhode Island had organized state groups and auxiliary locals. From a total of sixty societies in the nation in 1835, the number grew to more than a thousand in 1837, and by 1838 Birney calculated that there existed more than thirteen hundred, with 109,000 members.[9]

These societies clustered in well-defined areas, depending upon agents' routes, local conditions, and migrations. In New England they were concentrated in eastern Massachusetts, with others about the Connecticut river in the western part of the state, up the Merrimack valley into New Hampshire, and in

[8] For a study of the New England group, see Roman J. Zorn, "The New England Antislavery Society," *Journal of Negro History* XLIII (July, 1957), 157-76; and Lawrence Lader, *The Bold Brahmins: New England's War Against Slavery*. Whittier published his reminiscences of the famous meeting of 1833 forty years after, "The Antislavery Convention of 1833," *Atlantic Monthly* XXXIII (February, 1874), 166-72. A great deal of work remains to be done on the abolitionist activities of Northern Negroes. There were five Negroes on the first board of the American Anti Slavery Society, five on the executive Committee of the American and Foreign Anti Slavery Society, and a number of able Negro editors and lecturers; there were more than twenty Negro agents who toured Europe in behalf of the American abolition societies, and men such as Frederick Douglass, William Wells Brown, Charles Lenox Remond, and Theodore S. Wright were nationally-known speakers. See John Hope Franklin, *From Slavery to Freedom*, 246-50.

[9] *Correspondence Between F. H. Elmore and James G. Birney*, 7.

the vicinity of Portland, Maine. Connecticut and New Jersey both resisted abolitionism strongly, and little foothold was gained in either state for several years. The New England settlements, the area along the Mohawk, and the region south of Lake Ontario to Buffalo marked the abolitionist areas of New York outside of New York City. In Pennsylvania, the movement was strong around Quaker Philadelphia, and in the northwest and southwest portions of the state near Ohio. In Ohio, the Western Reserve was highly abolitionist, as were the southeast river towns and the areas bordering the Muskingum and Scioto rivers. Further West, in Indiana, Illinois, and Michigan, abolitionism showed little strength before 1845.[10]

State and local societies were usually patterned after the national organization, and some powerful ones, notably the New York and Ohio groups, published their own papers and sent out their own agents. In New England, young men's auxiliary societies were popular, and women's auxiliaries, nearly half of them in Massachusetts, became numerous enough in the late 'thirties to hold their own conventions. Juvenile societies were never very successful.

The history of the abolitionist societies is long and involved, marked by schisms, reorganizations, mergers, and both success and failure. Financial troubles plagued all of them,[11] and the control of the American Anti Slavery Society over state and local groups gradually loosened until the subsidiary societies became nearly autonomous and in some cases almost as powerful as the national group. Arguments over women's rights and

[10] Janet Wilson, "Early Antislavery Propaganda," *More Books: Bulletin of the Boston Public Library* XX (February, 1945), 51-52. This article with its predecessors, *ibid.*, XIX (November and December 1944), 343-361, 393-406, is a valuable source of information on the early organization of the American Anti Slavery Society. See also William Goodell, *op. cit.*, and William Birney, *James G. Birney and His Times*, Appendix C, 407-423, for histories of the organization of abolition groups. Birney's account of early antislavery thought in Ohio, 430-435, is interesting, and for an account of the movement in Indiana, see J. P. Dunn, *Indiana: A Redemption from Slavery.*

[11] For an explanation of abolitionist financing, see Benjamin Quarles, "Sources of Abolitionist Income," *Mississippi Valley Historical Review* XXXII (June, 1945), 63-77.

political action alienated the Garrison wing of the national society in 1840, and produced the rival American and Foreign Anti Slavery Society. After 1840, though both societies maintained an existence and published influential newspapers (The American Anti Slavery Society *The National Anti Slavery Standard,* and its rival *The National Era*), the center of abolition's influence and most of its leadership had passed into politics. By that time, however, the North had been subjected to thorough propagandizing, and the doctrine of immediatism, variously interpreted, had been widely disseminated.

The entry of the slavery issue into politics in the 1840's marked the second phase of the abolitionist movement. As early as 1834 Garrison expressed interest in some kind of political action, along with others such as C. C. Follen, William Goodell, Alvan Stewart, Myron Holley, Joshua Leavitt, Gerrit Smith, and Birney. The controversy over petitions and the mails, and the contemporary agitation for the abolition of slavery in the District of Columbia, put the abolitionists directly into national politics. The political phase of the abolition movement, culminating in the Liberty, Free Soil, and Republican parties, rested primarily on the Lane doctrine of immediatism with modifications, the accepted later version of abolitionism.[12] "Our business," said Gamaliel Bailey, one of the most astute and politically-minded of the group, "is to redeem the Federal Government from vassalage to the Slave Power, and all responsibility for slavery, and through its constitutional exercise, foster a sentiment of Liberty in the Slave States."[13]

The immediate emancipationists, or abolitionists as they were ordinarily called, formed only a small portion of the total antislavery group during the period, despite their eventual

---

[12] For discussions of abolition in politics, see W. B. Hesseltine, *A History of the South,* 260-273; A. B. Hart, *op. cit.,* 256-276; T. C. Smith, *The Liberty and Free Soil Parties in the Northwest;* and the biased but informative accounts of William Goodell, *op. cit.,* chapter XXXIX and Henry Wilson, *op. cit., in toto.* The disagreement over political methods between the political action group and the Garrison "no-voters" was a factor in the great schism of 1840 and the subsequent collapse of the national organization.

[13] *The National Era,* September 7, 1854.

dominance of it. Colonization still had many adherents, both North and South, until 1850. Some antislavery men favored colonization as the only plan with a chance of success; some proslavery men opposed it on the same grounds. Colonization was especially popular in the South, for it allowed a man to take a position against slavery that seemed morally right, without forcing any rearrangements of the social and economic patterns of Southern society. Other Southerners favored it as a means of getting rid of the free Negro without harming the institution of slavery, while certain abolitionists attacked it for precisely that reason.[14] Contributing also to the downfall of the colonization plan was its lack of practical success. In forty years of activity it transported about 11,000 Negroes at a cost of more than a million dollars; the birth rate replaced the number within a month. Merely to remove the four million slaves in the South, disregarding the renewal of the population by birth, was obviously a hopeless task, and an idea never seriously entertained by most antislavery thinkers.[15]

Various other methods of abolishing slavery received attention and met with little success. A small group, mostly Quaker, believed a boycott of slave-state products might force the South to consider emancipation.[16] Others believed that, if left alone, slavery might disappear from natural economic and biological

[14] Examples of pro-colonizationist thought, North and South, are "A New England Man," *An Attempt to Demonstrate the Practicability of Emancipating the Slaves . . . and of Removing Them from this Country;* Matthew Carey, *Letters on the Colonization Society . . .;* David Reese, *Letters to the Hon. William Jay;* Calvin Colton, *Colonization and Abolition Contrasted;* Henry Ruffner, *Address to the People of Western Virginia;* and David Christy, *African Colonization. . . .* The abolitionist attack on the colonizationists is represented by Garrison's *Thoughts on African Colonization . . .;* Elizur Wright, Jr., *The Sin of Slavery;* William Jay, *An Inquiry into the Characteristics and Tendencies of the American Colonization and American Anti Slavery Societies;* and James G. Birney, *Letter on Colonization, Addressed to the Reverend Thornton J. Mills.*

[15] A. B. Hart, *op. cit.,* 314. David Brion Davis, "The Emergence of Immediatism in British and American Antislavery Thought," *Mississippi Valley Historical Review* XLIX (Sept., 1962), 209-31, is an excellent summary.

[16] Lewis C. Gunn, *Address to Abolitionists . . .;* and Charles Marriott, *An Address to the Members of the Religious Society of Friends . . .* explain this plan.

causes.[17] William Ellery Channing believed that a slave might buy himself and his family, and under the sponsorship of a white guardian, educate himself to citizenship. Many other "self-emancipation" plans were offered.[18] Cassius Clay of Kentucky outlined a plan for the emancipation of all female slaves at 21 (thus providing freedom for their children), the purchase of existing slaves after 30 years through state-appropriated funds, the exile of present free Negroes, and the bestowal of the suffrage upon freed Negroes after a long period of preparation and education.[19] Henry Clay proposed a similar plan which combined the expatriation of free Negroes with gradual emancipation. These and other suggestions continued until 1860.[20]

Many individuals simply took an antislavery stand without committing themselves to a specific program. Opposing slavery on moral and religious grounds, they limited themselves to appeals to the consciences of slaveholders, trusting that in time the slave states themselves might emancipate their slaves in some yet unnamed fashion. Of these "philosophical" emancipationists, Francis Wayland and William Ellery Channing were the most prominent, although there were large numbers of others in both North and South. For example, Channing wrote in 1828: "We must first let the Southern states see we are their friends in the affair, that we sympathize with them, and from principles of patriotism and philanthropy are willing to share the toil and expense of abolishing slavery . . ."[21] Wayland served as president of the American Union for the

[17] See J. L. Baker, *Slavery* . . .; and Horace Bushnell, *The Census and Slavery*. . . .

[18] W. E. Channing, *Works*, II: 109-111. See also Marshall Hall, *Two-fold Slavery of the United States, with a Project for Self-Emancipation*, and John McDonough, *Self-Emancipation*. . . .

[19] *The Anti Slavery Bugle*, October 31, 1845.

[20] Calvin Colton, ed., *Works of Henry Clay*, III:346-352. See also Elihu Burritt, *A Plan of Brotherly Co-Partnership of the North and the South;* George Bush, *Aphorisms on Slavery and Abolition*, and Samuel Nott, *Slavery and the Remedy*.

[21] Letter to Daniel Webster, quoted by Hilary Herbert, *The Abolition Crusade and Its Consequences*, 47-48. Channing's *Slavery* explains his antislavery position in full.

Relief and Improvement of the Colored Race, formed in Boston in 1835, an organization that opposed neither abolition nor colonization, but objected to slavery on religious grounds.[22] However, despite the efforts of hundreds of such men of good will, there were no suggestions which seemed any more practicable, nor more acceptable to the South, than those of the immediatists, a fact which accrued to their advantage.[23]

The aims and principles of the "immediate" abolitionists were always fully and clearly expressed to the public.[24] They intended to appeal to the national conscience through fact and argument, to change public opinion, and thus to form a great body of Northern and Southern abolitionist sympathizers who would eventually, by legal means, abolish slavery at once. The exertion of political pressures, advocated by some and opposed by others, was to be a powerful tool in accomplishing this end; supported by popular sentiment, the Federal government would, they believed, find some legal means of abolition sanctioned by public approval.[25] The arguments by which the nation was to be convinced of the iniquity of slavery were religious, political, legal, moral, economic, ethical, and social. William Lloyd Garrison meant it quite literally when he said that slavery was "one of the strongholds of the devil—perhaps the strongest." Slavery, it was argued, was against Christianity,

[22] See the Union's *Exposition of the Objects and Plans.* . . .

[23] A. A. Phelps, *op. cit.*, 138-189, provides a valuable analysis of all current antislavery plans in relation to immediate abolition.

[24] For complete explanations of the abolitionist philosophy, see Charles Olcott, *Two Lectures on the Subjects of Slavery and Abolition, Compiled for the Special Use of Anti Slavery Lecturers and Debaters; The Constitution of the American Anti Slavery Society, with the Declaration of the National Anti Slavery Convention;* the American Anti Slavery Society's *Declaration of Sentiments;* The New York City Anti Slavery Society's *Address to the People of the City of New York;* and Wendell Phillips, "The Philosophy of the Abolition Movement," *Anti Slavery Tract No. 8.* For recent (and controversial) estimates of the abolitionists, see Merton L. Dillon, "The Failure of the American Abolitionists," *Journal of Southern History* XXV (May, 1959), 159-79; and especially David Donald, "Toward a Reconsideration of Abolitionists," *Lincoln Reconsidered: Essays on the Civil War Era* (New York, 1956).

[25] The Lane Seminary Anti Slavery Society Minutes, *op. cit.; The Anti Slavery Bugle,* May 11, 1849; and Wendell Phillips, *op. cit.,* 9-12.

constitutional rights, and common law; it violated moral and ethical law, and denied the natural rights philosophy of equality. As an economic system, it was wasteful, unjust, and productive of poverty.[26] Different abolitionists emphasized various aspects of the antislavery argument, but in general all agreed upon these objections to the institution of slavery.

"Immediatism" was opposed in the North throughout the period by the majority of antislavery sympathizers, until the approach of the Civil War forced a nominal agreement among the various schools of antislavery thought.[27] The colonizationists, gradual emancipationists, and temperate antislavery groups opposed the immediatists' methods, while the con-

[26] Good general expositions of the abolitionist argument may be found in Oliver Johnson, *An Address Delivered in the Congregational Church in Middlebury, Vermont;* LaRoy Sunderland, *op. cit.,* chapter XIX, "Abolitionists; Their Principles"; and the speech of Joshua Giddings, delivered in the House, January 12, 1859, titled "The Issue—Its History," reprinted in *The Anti Slavery Bugle,* February 5, 1859. Works treating the different aspects of the abolitionist argument are too numerous to cite, but comprehensive treatments of various abolition principles are: the moral and humanitarian argument, T. D. Weld, *American Slavery As It Is;* D. L. Child, *The Despotism of Freedom;* George Bourne, *Slavery Illustrated in Its Effects Upon Women and Domestic Society;* and G. W. Bassett, *Slavery Examined in the Light of Nature;* the religious argument, T. D. Weld, *The Bible Against Slavery;* James G. Birney, *Letters to Ministers and Elders;* J. Blanchard and N. Rice, *A Debate on Slavery . . .;* Charles Elliot, *The Bible and Slavery;* G. B. Cheever, *God Against Slavery;* and Richard Fuller and Francis Wayland, *Domestic Slavery . . . As a Scriptural Institution;* the legal and constitutional argument, G. W. F. Mellen, *An Argument on the Unconstitutionality of Slavery;* William Goodell, *Views of American Constitutional Law;* and Lysander Spooner, *The Unconstitutionality of Slavery;* the argument over political and civil rights, S. B. Treadwell, *American Liberties and American Slavery;* Horace Mann, *New Dangers to Freedom . . . ,* and Theodore Parker, *The Relation of Slavery to a Republican Form of Government;* the economic argument, G. M. Weston, *The Poor Whites of the South;* Daniel Goodloe, *The South and the North,* and H. C. Carey, *The North and the South.*

[27] For listings of the Northern objections to immediate abolition, see "Junius" (Calvin Colton) *Political Abolition;* "Aristides," "Thoughts on the Abolition Question," Newark, N. J., *Sentinel of Freedom,* January 22 to February 12, 1839; and E. P. Barrows, *A View of the American Slavery Question,* 106-146. The standard abolitionist replies are summarized in LaRoy Sunderland, *op. cit.,* ch. XXIII, "Objections Answered," and in A. A. Phelps, *op. cit.,* Lecture IV, "Objections Answered."

siderable Northern body of neutral and pro-Southern groups objected both to their methods and to their aims. The early abolitionists met strong resistance from nearly all established, conservative Northern interests. Even after the opening of the Civil War, Garrison admitted that "to be an Abolitionist is not to be with the multitude—on the side of the majority—in a popular and respectable position."[28]

Possibly the most common charge against the abolitionists was that their aggressiveness and belligerence encouraged disturbance and disorder. A public meeting in Rochester, New York, in 1833, accused the abolitionists of "exciting the feelings" of the populace, and agreed that the milder procedures of the colonizationists were much more worthy of support.[29] Abolitionists did not, it was said, "go to work like Christian gentlemen,"[30] and the accusation that abolition bred violence became a recurrent theme in anti-abolitionist propaganda. William Ellery Channing pleaded for a discussion of slavery that was "calm, general, and unmixed with personalities," and John Quincy Adams, attacking the American Anti Slavery Society in the House in 1839, charged it with "pouring oil into the summit of a smoking crater."[31] The trail of mobs left across the Northern states by abolition agents led to the common belief that they deliberately fomented disorder to gain sym-

[28] W. L. Garrison, "The Abolitionists and Their Relation to the War," *Pulpit and Rostrum*, No. VI (New York, 1862), 32. William Birney's analysis, *op. cit.*, 222-227, of the forces opposing abolition is interesting; Birney points out that church, state, business, and society all were predestined to object to the agitation of the slavery question. See also the accounts of the anti-abolition meetings in New England, carried by *The Liberator* during 1836-1837.

[29] *Niles' Register*, 45:210. Hezekiah Niles favored colonization; see *ibid.*, 45:167-168.

[30] Horace Bushnell, *A Discourse on the Slavery Question*, 17.

[31] William Ellery Channing, *Slavery*, 183, and Barnes, *op. cit.*, 165. Other typical attacks on abolitionist methods as productive of disorder are Elijah Barrows, Jr., *A View of the American Slavery Question*; W. E. Channing, *A Letter to the Abolitionists*; "A Northern Man" (Calvin Colton) *Abolition A Sedition*; Leonard Bacon, *Slavery Discussed in Occasional Essays*; and the Union Safety Committee, *Selections from the Speeches and Writings of Prominent Men in the United States on the Subject of Abolition and Agitation*.

13

pathy as martyrs, and their self-adopted label of "agitators" did nothing to dispel the impression.[32]

Closely related to this was the charge that the abolitionists were fanatic reformers, who intended to introduce not simply emancipation, but other strange and unsettling changes into the social order. The legislature of Ohio passed a resolution condemning them as "wild, delusive, and fanatical," and Roger Sherman expressed the common fear of their "extreme and intemperate zeal."[33] Mayor Otis of Boston called them "irresponsible revolutionaries," and the Catholic Boston *Pilot* wrote that "whenever you found an abolitionist," you would also find "an anti-hanging man, woman's rights man, an infidel frequently, bigoted Protestant always, a socialist, a red republican, a fanatical teetotaler, a believer in mesmerism, and Rochester rappings . . ."[34] The participation of prominent abolitionists in other reform movements, some close to the lunatic fringe, lent credence to the claim, and Garrison's excursions into "no-government" anarchy and anti-Sabbath crusades strengthened the popular fear of abolitionist fanaticism.[35] The New York *Day Book*, dedicating itself to battling "the mongrelism, social anarchy, and the total ruin of our country," spoke for many Northern conservatives in its opposition to abolitionism.[36]

Charges that the abolitionists were enemies of religious fidelity arose primarily from Garrison's notorious unorthodoxy, and although many within the movement disagreed with his views, his attitude was often accepted as characteristic of all

[32] See Catherine E. Beecher, *Essays upon Slavery* . . ., pp. 15-16, and J. G. Birney's reply, "Miss Beecher on the Slave Question," the Cincinnati *Philanthropist*, August 4, 1837. As late as 1853 the New York *Herald*, reprinted in *The Liberator*, September 30, repeated the charge.

[33] *Niles' Register*, 56:66, 410-411.

[34] *Ibid.*, 49:10-12, and M. H. Rice, *American Catholic Opinion in the Slavery Controversy*, 100.

[35] Excellent explanations of these are "The Garrisonians," "No-Voting and Disunion," and "The No-Voting Theory," in *The Anti Slavery Bugle*, September 6 and 13, 1851. See also "Reasons Against No-Voting," *ibid.*, November 1, 1851.

[36] Prospectus of the *Day Book*, R. G. Horton, *A Youth's History of the Great Civil War*, Appendix.

abolitionists.[37] Believing that unless the churches officially adopted an openly abolitionist stand they were actually aiding slavery, Garrison attacked each denomination which failed to do so, and eventually concluded that organized churches were useless and sinful. Garrisonian "comeoutcrism" (secession from all churches refusing to sanction abolitionism or to take an antislavery stand) gained a few adherents among leaders of the abolition movement and seriously weakened its appeal to Northern churches.[38] The Massachusetts Anti Slavery Society resolved that, "steeped in blood and pollution as that American church is, it becomes us to turn from it with loathing and abhorrence."[39] Benjamin Jones called the church "the refuge and hiding place of the slavery Monster," and both Parker Pillsbury and Wendell Phillips used equally violent names.[40]

The relationship of men from the Lane group (such as

[37] For Garrison's religious beliefs and his relations with the organized churches, see Oliver Johnson, *William Lloyd Garrison and His Times*, 67-98, 273-278, 363-371; and Russel B. Nye, *William Lloyd Garrison*, 83-4, 107-11, 136-38.

[38] See also J. G. Birney, *The American Churches, the Bulwarks of American Slavery*; S. S. Foster, *The Brotherhood of Thieves: A True Picture of the American Church and Clergy;* Parker Pillsbury, *The Church As It Is;* and William Goodell, *Come-Outerism: The Duty of Secession from a Corrupt Church*. The ethical and religious problems of slavery created some difficult problems for the religious and the churchly—see Wilson Smith, *Professors and Public Ethics* (Ithaca, 1956) ; Walter B. Posey, "The Slavery Question in the Presbyterian Church in the Old Southwest," *Journal of Southern History* XV (August, 1949) , 311-29; Walter B. Posey, "The Influence of Slavery upon the Methodist Church in the Early South and Southwest," *Mississippi Valley Historical Review* XVII (1930-31) , 530-32; Will F. Steeley, "The Established Churches and Slavery in Kentucky," *Register of the Kentucky Historical Society* LV (April, 1957) , 97-105; Hauser Winter, "The Division of Missouri Methodism in 1845," *Missouri Historical Review* XXXVIII (January, 1943) , 1-19.

[39] *The Anti Slavery Bugle*, February 19, 1853. The Michigan State Anti Slavery Convention, *ibid.*, October 30, 1852 and October 28, 1854, took a similar stand.

[40] Jones, *ibid.*, June 20, 1845. See also Gamaliel Bailey's "Abolition and the Methodist Episcopal Church," the Cincinnati *Philanthropist*, September 24, 1839. Pillsbury's and Phillips' addresses to the American Anti Slavery Society are found in *The Anti Slavery Bugle*, June 1, 1849, and Pillsbury's speech to the Western Anti Slavery Society, *ibid.*, September 27, 1851.

Weld, Thome, Stanton, Streeter, and Allan), both to the school of evangelism led by Charles G. Finney and to abolitionism, helped to foster the impression that abolitionism almost necessarily involved some kind of theological unorthodoxy. So did the centering of Western abolitionism at Oberlin, a school famed for its "heretical" doctrine of "perfectionism" in religion.[41] Though the established churches, after some dispute, eventually split over the abolition question, the anti-church doctrines of Garrison and others alienated a large portion of public opinion and helped materially to provide evidence to support anti-abolitionist claims. The Detroit *Free Press* believed that abolitionists were "Crazy men . . . , atheists . . . who denounce with utmost flippancy the Christian religion, Christian ministry, and the American Union," and the Reverend Henry Van Dyke of Brooklyn was certain that abolition "led, by a logical process, to utter infidelity."[42]

The fear of racial equality and amalgamation, raised by the possibility of the northward migration of freed Negroes, was a potent but less publicized factor in the anti-abolitionist argument.[43] Many antislavery sympathizers, such as William Woodbridge, a member of the Michigan Constitutional Convention, were willing to see the Negro freed, but could not accept "equality or amalgamation."[44] The attempt of the Massachusetts Anti Slavery Society to promote bi-racial schools in New

[41] Fuller explanations of the Oberlin doctrine are found in Barnes, *op. cit.*, 7-12, and R. S. Fletcher, *A History of Oberlin College*, I:223, 230-233.

[42] *The Liberator*, November 18 and December 2, 1853, and Henry Van Dyke, *The Character and Influence of Abolitionism* (New York, 1860), 28. A. A. Lyons, "Religious Defense of Slavery in the North," *Trinity College Historical Society Papers*, and William Goodell, *Slavery and Antislavery*, ch. XL, provide excellent summaries of the relations of the different denominations to abolition, while Rice, *op. cit.*, is a definitive treatment of the attitude of the Catholic Church. For an interesting summary of contemporary views, see "The Voice of the Pulpit," *The Anti Slavery Bugle*, July 19 and August 2, 1851.

[43] A complete exposition of the amalgamationist fear is that of A. T. Judson, *Remarks to the Jury, on the Trial of the Case, State vs. Prudence Crandall*.

[44] Letter to A. L. Porter, October 14, 1839, Woodbridge papers, Burton Collection, Detroit Public Library.

England in 1833, and its unsuccessful endeavor to secure repeal of the Massachusetts law forbidding mixed marriages, were taken as indications of general abolitionist policy.[45] The New York *Courier and Enquirer* agitated for the wider adoption of anti-miscegenation laws similar to those of Massachusetts, in view of the growing "abolition frenzy"; the Cleveland *Plain Dealer,* in the heart of the highly-abolitionized Western Reserve, pointed out that "this government is a government of *white* men . . ."; and the New York *Journal of Commerce* warned that abolition meant that "the men who are now slaves must be admitted to all the rights, privileges, and immunities, political, social, and religious" which belonged to white men.[46] The abolitionists' policy of treating the Negro with absolute equality, their cooperation with free Negro groups, and the presence in the movement of Negroes such as Frederick Douglass, Charles Remond, "Box" Brown, and others, heightened suspicions that they were integrationists, as they assuredly were.

Commercial interests in the North found much to object to in abolitionism.[47] Mayor Otis of Boston pointed out that if the Southern states were offended by antislavery agitation, they might boycott Northern products and completely upset trade relations—a forceful argument.[48] Southern threats to do exactly that frightened Northern business interests.[49] "The merchants, men of business, and men of property in this city should frown down the meetings of these madmen, if they would save themselves," editorialized the New York *Herald,*[50] and abolitionist threats to organize boycotts of slave-state products increased

[45] *The Liberator,* February 12, 19, and March 19, 1841

[46] *Ibid.,* February 20, 1836; the Cleveland *Plain Dealer,* April 11, 1856; and *The National Anti Slavery Standard,* September 17, 1846.

[47] Philip Foner's *Business and Slavery,* is a study of this aspect of Northern opposition to abolition. Also interesting is the contemporary analysis by Benjamin Jones, "Reformers—Conservatism," *The Anti Slavery Bugle,* January 1, 1847.

[48] *Niles' Register,* 49:11.

[49] *Ibid.,* 39:73, 77.

[50] *Ibid.,* 39:28. See also the New York *Journal of Commerce,* quoted by *The National Anti Slavery Standard,* November 7, 1850.

the merchants' fear of retaliatory Southern measures. Though antislavery leaders protested that a free Negro population in the South would actually mean a greater market for Northern goods,[51] they never fully succeeded in gaining the confidence of Northern commercial interests. In time, the political leaders of the abolition movement, by their assistance in obtaining a tariff, internal improvements, and a National Bank, convinced industrialists that their commercial interests ran parallel to those of antislavery. Abolition propaganda constantly reiterated the charge that slavery was a wasteful economic system, and the claim that abolition meant freer capital and more open markets in the South eventually gained some Northern commercial support.[52]

Another powerful anti-abolitionist argument was that their agitation had harmed the cause of the slave more than it had helped, by offending the South and by provoking the passage of more stringent laws governing slavery. Abraham Lincoln, for example, in 1837 signed a resolution stating that "the promulgation of abolition doctrines tends rather to increase than to abate its evils," and James Buchanan, addressing a Lancaster meeting in 1833, claimed that emancipation had been made much more difficult by Garrison and his followers.[53] The state of the slave and the antislavery sympathizer in the South after 1830 was said to be far worse than it had been before Garrison and his ilk had begun their work. As some said, "Whatever is done for the abolition of slavery must be done by time, by dispassionate argument, and by the slaveholder himself."[54] Related to this was the argument that

[51] See, for example, the argument of Cassius Clay, Horace Greeley, ed., *The Writings of Cassius M. Clay*, 357.

[52] Hesseltine, *op. cit.*, 266-68.

[53] Nicolay and Hay, *Abraham Lincoln, A History*, I:140, and *Niles' Register*, 55:90-93. Buchanan also warned of the "disgusting scenes" which might result from admitting Negroes to equality with white men and women.

[54] R. W. Bailey, *The Issue Presented in a Series of Letters on Slavery*, 35. A similar view is expressed in the report of the Committee of the Connecticut Legislature (1836), in the S. T. Mason papers, Burton Collection, Detroit Public Library.

slavery was the concern of the slave states alone, that interference from the North was, in the words of the Ohio State
Legislature, "unwise, unlawful, unconstitutional, and highly
criminal," or in those of the Indiana Legislature, "highly
reprehensible, unpatriotic, and injurious to the peace."[55]

Another powerful factor in inciting anti-abolitionist feeling
in the North was the disunionism that was widely prevalent in
abolition circles. The American Anti Slavery Society's *Declaration of Sentiments* in 1833 declared that the relation between
free and slave states must be instantly severed, and newspapers
warned that this policy, if followed, "must inevitably lead to
bloodshed, dis-union, and civil war . . . a horrid alternative to
slavery."[56] Ten years later the proposition had developed into
a full-fledged demand for the dissolution of any Union of free
and slave states. Garrison evolved the theory that the obligations imposed by the Constitution upon the people of the free
states in relation to slavery were immoral, and therefore not
to be acknowledged; by this reasoning disunion became a
moral necessity, and the Constitution itself between the states
"a covenant with death and an agreement with Hell."[57] The
Massachusetts Society refused to adopt the Garrisonian theory
in 1844, but the American Anti Slavery Society, after protracted debate, agreed to the principle later in the year, and
the New England Convention followed its lead. Though attacked by a good many abolitionist leaders, the disunion doctrine received endorsement in influential quarters after the

[55] *Niles' Register*, 57:378, and notation in the Woodbridge papers, Burton Collection, Detroit Public Library. Other expressions of this view are
found in the reply of Harrison Otis of Boston to a Southern correspondent, *Niles' Register*, 45:42-3, an excellent reflection of the New England
conservative view of abolition in 1831; in the speech of General Harrison
at Carthage, Indiana, in 1840, *ibid.*, 59:42-3; the resolution of Ewing of
Indiana in the House, 1839, *ibid.*, 56:15; and Calvin Colton, *Abolition a
Sedition, op. cit.*, 184-86.

[56] The Washington, D. C., *North American*, quoted by *The Liberator*,
November 15, 1834.

[57] Oliver Johnson, *William Lloyd Garrison . . .*, 335-36, and A. B. Hart,
op. cit., 252-254.

1850 Compromise, reaching its climax in the great disunion conventions of 1857 at Worcester, Massachusetts, and Cleveland.[58] The Union, said James Russell Lowell, no longer could be "stuck together with mouth glue," and "No Union with Slaveholders" became the slogan of abolitionists everywhere, ironically enough in the light of later justification of the Civil War as a means of preserving the Union.[59] Disunionism shocked the North, and contributed materially to Northerners' suspicion of abolitionist aims.[60]

The rise of the abolitionist argument against slavery coincided with the development of the Southern defense of it. Contrary to the claims of proslavery sympathizers, the South's justification of slavery was not provoked solely by the attack of the abolitionists on it. A proslavery philosophy had been forming for some time in response to a long-felt need to unify the white population of the South and to separate the social and economic classes along color lines, thus enabling the upper slaveholding classes and their adherents to control the political and economic life of the South by the "divide and rule" principle. At least part of the function of the proslavery argument arose from the need of the slaveholding class to adjust Southern thought to the conditions of slavery's existence, and to satisfy slaveholder and non-slaveholder alike of the propriety

[58] See the editorials of *The Anti Slavery Bugle*, February 18, March 24, 1848; Lowell and Wendell Phillips, in *The National Anti Slavery Standard*, March 21 and 28, 1850; C. E. Hodges, *Disunion Our Wisdom and Our Duty* (New York, 1855); *Anti Slavery Tract No. 11; The Proceedings of the State Disunion Convention, Held at Worcester, Mass. . . .*; and the reports of the disunion convention at Cleveland, *The Anti Slavery Bugle*, November 7 and 14, 1857.

[59] See Lowell's editorial, *The National Anti Slavery Standard*, March 7, 1850. Garrison removed *The Liberator's* anti-constitutional and disunion banner-head after the Civil War began, and explained his change of attitude by saying that when he refused to sustain the Constitution, "I had no idea I would live to see death and Hell secede. Hence it is that I am now with the Government to enable it to constitutionally stop the further ravages of death, and to extinguish the flames of Hell forever." "The Abolitionists and their Relation to the War," *op. cit.*, 46.

[60] See *The National Anti Slavery Standard*, February 15 and March 1, 1849, for the typical reactions of the New York *Herald* and the Batavia, N. Y., *Spirit of the Times*.

and necessity of the system.[61] Beginning in the 'twenties, the South was subjected to a thorough proslavery propagandizing.[62] Though the South generally came to feel that "the impertinent interference of Abolitionists . . . provoked us to argument and investigation,"[63] there is good reason to believe that if Garrison and his Northern followers had never existed, the proslavery philosophy would have developed no differently, though perhaps more slowly and with less unity.

The proslavery argument based its claims for the essential rightness of slavery on religious, social, political, economic, historical, and scientific grounds. The system, it was affirmed, had God-given Biblical sanction and historical justification. Socially and biologically demonstrated by the scientifically established inferiority of the Negro, slavery was held to be necessary by the plain facts of Southern existence. It had, first of all, legitimate Biblical sanction: it was consistent, the Charleston Union Presbytery resolved after protracted research, "with the precepts of patriarchs, apostles, and prophets." Slavery was also the best and safest way of life for the irresponsible and childlike Negro, for it provided him greater protection than any other system. William Gilmore Simms argued that

Indeed, the slave holders of the South, having the moral and animal guardianship of an ignorant and irresponsible people under their control, are the great moral conservators, in one powerful interest, of the entire world. . . . Providence has placed him in our hands, for his good, and has paid us from his labor for our guardianship.

[61] W. B. Hesseltine, "Some New Aspects of the Pro-Slavery Argument," *Journal of Negro History* XXI (January, 1936), 1-15; and Ralph E. Morrow, "The Proslavery Argument Revisited," *Mississippi Valley Historical Review* XLVIII (June, 1961), 79-95. See also Avery Craven, *Edmund Ruffin, Southerner*, 124-25, and W. E. Dodd, *The Cotton Kingdom*, 48-70.

[62] Alice Adams, *op. cit.*, 114, and Clement Eaton, *Freedom of Thought in the Old South*, 247.

[63] The Richmond *Enquirer*, October 17, 1857. For more recent statements of this point of view, see Beverly Munford, *Virginia's Attitude Toward Slavery and Secession*, 51-60, and A. Y. Lloyd, *The Slavery Controversy*, 124-215. Gamaliel Bailey's "The Fruits of Abolition," *The National Era*, August 23, 1855, and G. M. Weston's *The Progress of Slavery in the United States* are keen contemporary refutations of the Southern claim.

Slavery was, wrote another Southerner, the best "adjustment of the social and political relations of the races, consistent with the purest justice, commended by the highest expediency, and sanctioned by a comprehensive and enlightened humanity." By vesting control of government in the educated, wealthy class whose stake in society preordained stability, it avoided the disorders of a more widely dispersed democratic control; and by recognizing the inherent nature of class distinctions in society, provided a sound base for truly republican government. Seen in its true light, in the opinion of John C. Calhoun, slavery was "the most safe and stable basis for free institutions in the world." "Natural distinctions in society," wrote Dr. Samuel Cartwright of New Orleans in 1851, "is the rock on which American republicanism is built—built on any other foundation, it never has stood, and never can stand." And most of all, slavery was justified on the simple but tremendously effective argument that it was of vital necessity to the safety of the life as well as the civilization of the Southern white man.[64]

[64] The best summary of the proslavery argument is E. N. Elliott, ed., *Cotton is King and The Pro-Slavery Argument;* an earlier, less comprehensive edition was published in 1852 as *The Pro-Slavery Argument.* Particularly interesting is the pro and con of slavery as reviewed in the Virginia House of Delegates debates; see the summaries in "The Abolition of Negro Slavery," *American Quarterly Review* XI (September, 1832), 189-265, and *ibid.,* "Speech of Thomas Marshall" (December, 1832), 379-85. William Gilmore Simms' article, cited above, appeared as "Miss Martineau on Slavery," *Southern Literary Messenger* III (November, 1837), 641-57, and later in *The Pro-Slavery Argument.* The quotation following Simms' is from James D. Holcombe, "Is Slavery Consistent with Natural Law?" *Southern Literary Messenger* XXVII (December, 1858), 419; and Cartwright's from his article, "How to Save the Republic, and The Position of the South in the Union," *DeBow's Review* II (August, 1851), 186. William A. Smith, *Lectures on the Philosophy and Practice of Slavery* (Nashville, 1856) is a useful compendium of proslavery thought, while the best modern treatments are W. S. Jenkins, *Pro-Slavery Thought in the Old South,* and A. Y. Lloyd, *op. cit.* For studies of three tireless proslavery writers, see Otis Y. Skipper, "J.D.B. DeBow, the Man," *Journal of Southern History* X (October, 1944), 420-32; Herman C. Nixon, "J.D.B. DeBow, Publicist," *Southwestern Review* XX (1934-35), 212-22; Harold Wilson, "Basil Manly, Apologist for Slaveocracy," *Alabama Review* XV (January, 1962), 38-54; Lowell Harrison, "Thomas Roderick Dew, Philosopher of the Old South," *Virginia Magazine of History and Biography* LVII (October,

Southern arguments against the abolition of slavery ran parallel in some instances to Northern objections to the abolitionists' agitation of the issue. In order to defend slavery, it was necessary for the South to attempt to discredit the abolitionists as fanatics, infidels, and traitors, and to identify the slave system with the preservation of American principles.[65] Like many of their Northern counterparts, Southern defenders of slavery accused antislavery leaders of encouraging religious unorthodoxy, irresponsible agitation, and racial amalgamation. Since the Bible supported slavery, it was logical for the South to assume that the abolitionists, since they were attacking a Biblically-sanctioned institution, must necessarily be anti-Biblical.[66] Furthermore, they claimed, the confusions of free society naturally bred atheism, whereas the order and subordination of a slave society begot stability, "a belief in a Designer and Author of the order." Abolitionism was therefore simply a device to encourage religious infidelity.[67]

The fact that many prominent abolitionists were members of other reform movements led some Southerners to label them all as "criminal agitators," bent on destroying peace and or-

---

1949), 390-405; and Otis Skipper, *J.D.B. DeBow: Magazinist of the Old South.*

There were, of course, Southerners who recognized flaws in the slavery system; for two critics, see the letters of Dr. Francis Lieber of South Carolina College (who eventually was forced out of the South) and Judge Thomas R. R. Cobb of Georgia, whose *Inquiry into the Law of Negro Slavery in the United States of America,* published in 1858, suggested a number of legal revisions in the slave codes. For accounts of the slave system itself, as it was practiced in the South, consult D. R. Hundley's classic *Social Relations in Our Southern States* (New York, 1860), and among modern studies, chapters III and IV of Clement Eaton, *Growth of Southern Civilization 1789-1860;* Allan Nevins, *The Ordeal of the Union* I:412-98. A brilliant and provocative study of slavery from the point of view of social and institutional psychology is Stanley Elkins, *Slavery: A Problem in American Institutional and Intellectual Life.*

[65] Thorough expositions of Southern antiabolitionist thought are the anonymous *The South Vindicated from the Treason and Fanaticism of Northern Abolitionists,* and Henry F. James, *Abolition Unveiled.*

[66] *The Pro-Slavery Argument* (1852 ed.), 109, and *DeBow's Review* XXIII (July, 1857), 90.

[67] The Richmond *Enquirer,* quoted by *The Anti Slavery Bugle,* August 4, 1855, and Gamaliel Bailey, ed., *Facts for the People,* September 1, 1855.

der.[68] The Republican slogan in the 1856 campaign, thought the Richmond *Enquirer,* ought to be "free niggers, free women, free land, free love, and Frémont," and it pointed out that if the abolitionists had their way the "isms" of free society, the "lectures . . . against marriage, licentious philansteries, Oneida haunts of communism, agrarian doctrines and anti-rent practices, free love saloons, Mormon states and Quaker villages," would soon displace the "moral, religious, and law-abiding" ideals of American society.[69] George Fitzhugh reasoned that if slavery were wrong in principle, so then were all governmental institutions; abolitionists, therefore, in attacking slavery, attacked all human institutions as modifications of slavery.[70]

The more radical proslavery thinkers, by a somewhat circuitous argument, concluded that abolitionism was but one phase of a general attempt to loosen the social fabric, abolish social controls, and destroy the great Southern civilization based on slavery.[71] Agitation against slavery was not only dangerous to social equilibrium but an unconstitutional interference with the institutions of a sovereign state. The Petersburg, Virginia, *Express* summed it up by saying that the South desired nothing more than "the liberty to deal with the problem by her own people in her own way."[72] Abolitionism was, the North Carolina legislature resolved, ". . . a flagrant violation of the Constitution of the United States"; he who "seeks to interfere with slavery as it now exists in the Southern states," said the Batesville, Arkansas, *Eagle,* "is no better than a highway rob-

[68] Governor James K. Polk of Tennessee, *Niles' Register,* 59:56, and Chancellor Harper, *DeBow's Review* X (January, 1851), 62-3.

[69] Quoted by *The National Anti Slavery Standard,* November 8, 1856.

[70] George Fitzhugh, "The Conservative Principle," *DeBow's Review* XXII (April, 1857), 429.

[71] See George Sawyer, *Southern Institutes,* 384; George Fitzhugh, "Southern Thought," *DeBow's Review* XXIII (October, 1857), 343; and Judge Tucker of Virginia, quoted in *The Anti Slavery Bugle,* November 16, 1850. Clement Eaton's "The Resistance of the South to Northern Radicalism," *New England Quarterly* VII (June, 1935), 215-231, is a good treatment of the reactionary attitude encouraged in the South by antiabolitionism.

[72] The Washington, D. C., *National Crisis,* May 15, 1860.

ber." Southern editor J. D. B. DeBow, stung beyond endurance by the abolitionists, replied angrily:

For us there has come to be one sentiment now,—as Southerners, as *Americans,* as MEN, we deny the right of being *called to account* for our institutions, our policy, our laws, and our *government.* For these there is no explanation to be made, no apology; it is sufficient that we, we the people of a State, we the people of half the States in this Union, in our sovereign capacity, in our sovereign right, in our sovereign independence of all other people or peoples on earth, of all mortal men, have decreed our institutions as they are, and so will dare to maintain them![73]

The effect of such "meddling," it was pointed out, was to shift the Southern attitude from apology to defense, to snuff out Southern antislavery opinion, and to reduce the Negro to an even more hopeless state of bondage.

On the matter of racial amalgamation the Southerner was naturally much more sensitive than the Northerner. It was a common belief in the South that abolitionists sanctioned (and possibly practiced) intimate interracial relations, and that they distributed pictures to slaves portraying white women and black men "in unequivocal relations."[74] Stories of this sort had powerful effects on Southern opinion.[75] Since the whole system

[73] Quoted by *The Anti Slavery Bugle,* January 6, 1855; J.D.B. DeBow, "The Negro," *DeBow's Review* III (May, 1847) , 421.

[74] W. G. Simms, in *The Pro-Slavery Argument, op. cit.,* Henry Clay's Richmond, Indiana, speech, in *The Liberator,* October 21, 1842, and correspondence to *The Liberator,* September 14, 1860. The Louisville *Examiner,* reprinted by *The National Anti Slavery Standard,* January 3, 1849, flatly denied this argument.

[75] Nehemiah Adams, *A Southside View of Slavery,* 107-108. On the other hand, sexual relations between white and Negro were well known in the South; Colonel Richard Mentor Johnson, a highly-respected Kentucky politician and Vice President of the United States, installed his slave mistress in his household, openly recognized paternity of his two mulatto daughters, and sent them to school; see Clement Eaton, "Class Differences in the Old South," *Virginia Quarterly Review* XXXIII (Summer, 1957) , 357. The morality of slave-master relationships needs much research; a good introduction to the problem is Kenneth M. Stampp, *The Peculiar Institution* (New York, 1956) , chapter VIII. See also the lively discussion by J. C. Furnas, *Goodbye to Uncle Tom,* 63-4, 80-2, 140-49, *passim.*

of slavery was designed to control the relationship of white and black as well as that of master and slave, the social and racial implications of its abolition would be extremely grave. Negroes were held in bondage, one slaveholder explained, "because we are unwilling to amalgamate with them, and desire to keep our Teutonic blood pure . . .," and an Alabama mass-meeting resolved "that the ascendancy of the white race is in fact the issue now presented . . ., and this ascendancy cannot be maintained by acquiescing in the preliminary assaults and aggressions of the enemies who meditate its overthrow." Slavery, wrote a correspondent to *DeBow's Review,* simply recognized the natural separation of races:

> Our instincts are implanted by nature for wise purposes; they are intended to guard our race from deterioration. It is an abuse of words to call them prejudices. . . . Intermarriage between the white and black races is unnatural, i.e., contrary to the order and design of Providence, and fatal to posterity.[76]

The argument from racial supremacy had tremendous appeal, of course, to the Southern yeoman and poor white, who feared the Negro as an economic competitor and a social equal. To the non-slaveholder, black subordination was a matter of caste, social position, and pride. Henry Clay believed that the freed slave "would enter into competition with the free laborer . . ., reduce his wages, be confounded with him, and affect his moral and social standing." The objective of the abolitionists, Clay warned the Southern worker, was "to unite in marriage (*to him*) the laboring black woman, and to reduce the laboring man to the despised and degraded condition of the black man." The fear of the Negro, as one Southerner summarized

[76] Quoted in *The National Era,* September 7, 1854, and October 31, 1850; *DeBow's Review* X (March, 1851), 349, 351. W. H. Holcombe, *The Alternative: A Separate Nationality or the Africanization of the South* summarized the prevailing Southern view of racial amalgamation and purity. See also the treatment of the race question in U. B. Phillips, "The Central Theme of Southern History," *American Historical Review* XXXIV (October, 1928), 30-44.

it, was a useful device to keep the poor white man content with his lot; "these poor but industrious people" would remain "content to endure life in its most discouraging forms" so long as they were "satisfied that they were above the slave, though faring often worse than he."[77] Thus the threat of social and economic equality of Negro and white, if slavery were abolished, was employed to solidify antiabolitionist sentiment in the South, regardless of class or economic interest.[78]

From the first, the South resented the Northern abolition movement as an attack upon Southern rights and property. Governor McDuffie of South Carolina demonstrated that the production of cotton, the chief source of Southern wealth, depended on slavery as well as on soil and climate; and Chancellor Harper believed it "essential to our property, our character, and the safety of all that is dear to us."[79] Loss of the capital investment in slaves alone, written off as pure loss if they were freed, meant ruin for the South, and as J. H. Hammond put it, "Were ever any people, civilized or savage, persuaded by any arguments, human or divine, to surrender, voluntarily, two thousand millions of dollars?"[80]

The Richmond *Examiner* characterized the institution of slavery as "a thing we cannot do without, that is righteous, profitable, and permanent, and that belongs to Southern society as inherently, intricately, and desirably as the white race itself."[81] If slavery were abolished, prophesied the Charleston *Mercury*, "The owner and the non-owner will fall, side by side, beneath the general ruin. . . . When the foundation crumbles, the superstructure must follow."[82] Identification of slavery with the rights, prosperity, and existence of Southern society

[77] The Washington, D. C., *National Crisis*, May 15, 1860.
[78] *DeBow's Review* VII (January, 1850) , 24. See also DeBow's *The Interest in Slavery of the Non-Slaveholder*, and Clement Eaton, *Freedom of Thought in The Old South*, 248-50.
[79] Message to the Legislature of South Carolina, quoted in the Cincinnati *Philanthropist*, January 1, 1836, and *The Pro-Slavery Argument, op. cit.*, 2.
[80] *DeBow's Review* VIII (January, 1850) , 127.
[81] Quoted in *The Anti Slavery Bugle*, October 21, 1854.
[82] The Charleston *Mercury*, November 7, 1854.

meant that any attack upon the institution was in effect a direct attack upon Southern civilization itself.[83]

The abolition of slavery would mean not only the ruin of the South, it was maintained, but the collapse of true republican government in the United States. Since a vital principle of the proslavery argument was the "conservative feature," the "sheet anchor of the republican system," one of "the best securities of real freedom," therefore abolition would mean that "the fabric of civilization and liberty, which consumed ages in its construction," would be completely destroyed.[84] Abolitionism was, said the Charleston *Patriot*, "an emanation of that spirit that has with giant strides given to numbers an ascendancy over property in the North, and which is never satiated with power."[85] The abolitionists, it was suspected, were motivated by something more than simple humanitarianism. They intended, by unifying Northern opinion through appeals to abolish slavery, to build a great political party which would in time control the Federal government, subvert, and destroy it.[86]

Powerful as these economic, political, and social arguments

[83] For full statements of this idea, consult McDuffie's speech of 1833 at Athens, Georgia, in *Niles' Register*, 45:62-4; "The Address of Southern Delegates in Congress to their Constituents," and the reactions of the Southern press to it, in *The National Anti Slavery Standard*, February 8, March 1, 15, 22, and April 5, 12, 19, 26, 1849; "The Resolutions of the Legislature of South Carolina, Presented to Congress," *The Anti Slavery Bugle*, March 2, 1849; and the editorials from Southern newspapers reprinted by *The National Era*, October 26, 1854.

[84] Robert Barnwell Rhett, *The Anti Slavery Bugle*, July 26, 1851; "A Citizen of Virginia," *The Union Past and Future* (Charleston, 1850), 36; The Richmond *South*, July 8, 1858; and *The Pro-Slavery Argument*, 443.

[85] Quoted in the New York *Emancipator*, April 5, 1838. See also T. R. Dew, "On the Influence of the Republican System of Government upon Literature and the Development of Character," *Southern Literary Messenger* II (March, 1836), 820; and M. Estes, *A Defence of Negro Slavery as it Exists in the United States*, 168-171.

[86] See McDuffie of South Carolina and Shephard of North Carolina, quoted by the Cincinnati *Philanthropist*, January 1, 1836, and March 12, 1839; Edmund Ruffin, "Present Aspects of Abolition," *Southern Literary Messenger* XIII (July, 1847); "Junius" (Calvin Colton), *Political Abolition* (New York, 1843); "Aristides," "Thoughts on the Abolition Question," the Newark, N. J., *Sentinel of Freedom*, February 5, 1839; and S. C. Carpenter, *The Logic of History*.

were in integrating Southern opposition to abolitionism, overshadowing them all was the compelling argument from public and private safety. The South was convinced from first to last that the abolitionists encouraged and planned slave revolts; the specter of Gabriel Vesey, Nat Turner, and Santo Domingo hung always over and beneath every antiabolition argument. Slave insurrections, wrote William Gilmore Simms, "have been singularly infrequent, and perhaps would never have been dreamed of, were their bad passions not appealed to by the abolitionists or their emissaries. They are not a warlike people; are, indeed, a rather timid race. . . ." The juxtaposition of David Walker's *Appeal,* Garrison's *Liberator,* and Nat Turner's Southampton insurrection, from 1829 to 1831, held great significance for the Southern mind.[87] Promoted by the press, the "Black Terror" of slave uprisings filled every slave community and motivated the passage after 1826 of dozens of laws intended to preserve the safety of the white man and his family. If the abolitionists succeeded and the Negro were freed, one Virginian predicted, "The South would be a savage wilderness where the strong would rob and murder the weak without mercy."[88] After 1831, the suspicion that a Nat Turner might

[87] Simms, "Miss Martineau on Slavery," *Southern Literary Messenger* III (November, 1837) , 657. Governor Floyd of Virginia linked Garrisonism and Nat Turner at the time of the revolt, and the connection has been affirmed ever since. Most opinion today denies any direct relationship; see J. C. Robert, *The Road from Monticello,* 5-6.

[88] J. C. Ballagh, "Antislavery Sentiment in Virginia," *South Atlantic Quarterly* I (April, 1902) , 115; J. W. Crowell, "The Aftermath of Nat Turner's Insurrection," *Journal of Negro History* V (April, 1920) , 208-35; Clement Eaton, "A Dangerous Pamphlet in the Old South," *Journal of Southern History* II (Feb.-Nov., 1936) , 322-35; J. C. Robert, *op. cit.,* 3-5; "Reflections on the Census of 1840," *Southern Literary Messenger* IX (June, 1843) , 350-52. In most Southern states slaves were forbidden to leave their homes without a pass after dark, could not assemble outside their own plantations in groups of more than five without a white man present, nor could a free Negro hold religious services for any slaves except in a white man's presence. A slave could own neither a horse nor a firearm, could not work in a print shop or drug store, nor work for pay without the owner's permission. On the other hand, the strictness of enforcement of these laws varied widely from community to community. See Clement Eaton, *The Growth of Southern Civilization 1790-1860,* 77-79.

be in every family was "eating into the very vitals of the South."[89]

After the Southampton insurrection, waves of fear repeatedly swept parts of the South. In 1835 and 1836 incipient slave revolts were reported in Mississippi, Alabama, Virginia, Maryland, and Georgia; *Niles' Register* printed the rumor that "a great simultaneous movement has been made by Tappan and company to produce an insurrection of the blacks."[90] One man was tried and acquitted in Georgia for inciting revolt, and the scare subsided.[91] Scattered reports of planned revolts continued to come throughout the 'forties, until, after 1850, the South became increasingly nervous. The Canton, Mississippi, *Creole* reported in 1849 that danger was growing daily and advised an improved patrol system and tighter supervision over traveling strangers.[92] The Columbus, Georgia, *Times* reported a great revolt of 700 slaves in Lowndes county, Alabama, engineered by abolition agents. Although the report was proved a hoax, it served to illustrate Southern trepidation.[93] In 1855 a conspiracy involving 200 slaves at Garlandsville, Mississippi, was uncovered, though the reports indicated the plot was probably the product of hysteria.[94] In 1856 a great wave of scares swept most of the South. Tennesee, Virginia, South Carolina, Louisiana, Texas, Kentucky, and Mississippi contributed accounts of widespread slave plots, though no actual revolts occurred. At the height of the panic many Negroes were tortured and hanged on the evidence of rumors and frightened

[89] See the remarks of James McDowell and Henry Berry in the Virginia House of Delegates, quoted by Joshua Coffin, *An Account of Some of the Principal Slave Insurrections . . .*, 32-33.

[90] *Niles' Register*, 48:440-41, and 49:118-20.

[91] *Ibid.*, 51:272.

[92] Quoted by *The National Anti Slavery Standard*, September 20, 1849.

[93] *The National Era*, August 28, 1850, and *The Anti Slavery Bugle*, August 31, 1850.

[94] The Negroes, it was claimed, were organizing to "sack the town, murder the inhabitants, and march to a free state." However, confessions were obtained only after whippings, no arms or ammunition were found, and no abolitionist agitators discovered. See the report of the Marion, Mississippi, *Republican*, reprinted in *The National Era*, September 26, 1855, and *The Anti Slavery Bugle*, September 8, 1855.

gossip; as one historian commented, in these times of hysteria, slaves were in far greater danger than their masters.[95] The New Orleans *Picayune* reported a current rumor that a concerted slave effort throughout the entire South was scheduled for the Christmas holidays, but nothing happened.[96]

Gholson of Virginia in 1831 accused the abolitionists of attempting "to conduct the slave to massacre and bloodshed," and the charge was constantly levelled at Northern abolitionist organizations after 1831. The great scare of the mid-fifties brought forth particularly bitter accusations. The *American Organ* of Baltimore believed that abolitionist "preachers prayed and their women longed for a general insurrection of slaves, as that in San Domingo, with the murder and destruction of all around them."[97] The Montgomery, Alabama, *Advertiser* warned that abolition agents, disguised as business men and travelers, were scattered through the South to foment slave discontent, while the Grand Jury of Cass County, Georgia, suspected all travelers, especially Bible agents and missionaries, of spreading insurrectionary doctrines.[98] Edmund Ruffin, speaking of the "plots for simultaneous outbreaks . . . discovered at several remote points," concluded that "all, doubtless, were instigated by abolition agents," while the Jackson, Mississippi, *Daily Mississippian* believed that the "con-

[95] Eaton, *Growth of Southern Civilization*, 75. For reports of the revolt scares, see the reprints of Southern papers in *The Anti Slavery Bugle*, December 20 and 27, 1856 and January 3, 1857; *The National Anti Slavery Standard*, December 27, 1856; and *The National Era*, December 11 and 18, 1856 and January 1 and 8, 1857. Davidson B. McKibben, "Negro Slave Insurrections in Mississippi, 1800-1865," *Journal of Negro History* XXXIV (January, 1949), 73-91, found ninety-one items in New Orleans newspapers between 1850 and 1860 dealing with slave insurrections, thirty-one with unlawful assembly of slaves, and thirty of slave riots—how trustworthy these reports may be is another matter. See also Wendell G. Addington, "Slave Insurrections in Texas," *Journal of Negro History* XXXV (October, 1950), 408-34 for similar statistics.

[96] Reprinted by *The National Anti Slavery Standard*, January 10, 1857. See also Harvey Wish, "The Slave Insurrection Panic of 1856," *Journal of Southern History* V (Feb.-Nov., 1939), 206-91.

[97] Quoted by *The National Era*, August 30, 1855.

[98] Quoted by *The National Anti Slavery Standard*, July 31, 1851, and *Niles' Register*, 49:194.

spiracies" detected among slaves in 1856 showed "that the vile emissaries of abolition, working like moles under the ground, have been secretly breathing the poison of insubordination into their minds."[99]

The abolitionist societies flatly denied any intent of fostering slave revolts, asserting that their only object was "to convince the slaveholders themselves that slavery was wrong, and that justice and their own welfare demanded its abolition."[100] Garrison, the most feared of all abolitionists, was a non-resistant pacifist, and both he and his publisher Knapp always disclaimed incendiary purposes.[101] The Massachusetts Anti Slavery Society told the nation, "Nothing can be further from our wishes than to excite the slave population. . . . We would not sacrifice the life of a single slaveholder to emancipate every slave in the United States."[102] Naturally, intemperate statements, easily interpreted as appeals for insurrection, were made by radical extremists within the abolition ranks, but in general the record of abolitionists remained relatively clear. Slave rebellions were discussed, and methods of assisting slaves to escape were outlined, but little serious evidence exists to support the charge that fomenting revolt was an avowed abolitionist principle.[103] The abolitionist stand on the matter was

[99] DeBow's Review XXIII (December, 1857), 548, and Clement Eaton, Freedom of Thought in the Old South, 100.

[100] Report of the American Anti Slavery Society, The Anti Slavery Bugle, September 27, 1851. See also the reply of John Graham of Ohio to Governor McDuffie, the Cincinnati Philanthropist, April 15, 1836, and "How Can it Be Done?", The Anti Slavery Record II (September, 1836), 97.

[101] "We are far from recommending the publication of anything designed to excite the slaves to insurrection. Pieces with such an object will find no admission in the Abolitionist, and will receive from it nothing but reprobation," The Abolitionist I (January, 1833). See also Garrison's editorial in The Liberator, March 18, 1837.

[102] Niles' Register, 48:456-57.

[103] See W. S. Savage, The Controversy Over the Distribution of Abolition Literature, 11-12, and Herbert Aptheker, "Militant Abolitionism," Journal of Negro History XXVI (October, 1941), 438-45, for analyses of abolition propaganda. The most extreme stand taken by abolitionists is illustrated by "What's Our Duty?", Wideawake Papers, No. 1, 3-4, which states that while abolitionists have no duty to incite insurrections, they should respond to an appeal for assistance from slaves in revolt.

well expressed by the Reverend Edward Barrows in 1836, who thought that "any man that would encourage the slaves to rise up in rebellion against their masters deserves to be hanged." But, he continued, "We cannot consent to stop the discussion of this question at the North for fear the slaves should discover their masters guilty for holding them in bondage."[104]

Some Southerners agreed that the current, almost pathological Southern fear of revolt was largely groundless. A committee of the Tennessee Methodist Conference thought insurrection an improbability, but conceded that abolition propaganda might cause "partial ruin and much misery."[105] The Raleigh, North Carolina, *Register* believed the whole threat of slave rebellion highly overrated, while the *Missouri Democrat* blamed it on Southern politicians who agitated the issue until the populace was over-conscious of it.[106] Yet the fear of slave revolt, increasingly evident in the 'fifties and culminating after the unfortunate raid on Harper's Ferry in 1859, grew until it became perhaps the most important factor in conditioning Southern thought.[107] The New Orleans *Bee* summarized Southern opinion by defining an abolitionist as "a fanatical intermeddler in the institutions of the South, seeking their overthrow by nefarious means"; if he were successful in abolishing slavery, the Southerner was warned, "Your lands will be covered with ruins, and your altar stones with blood and desolation."[108]

While the debates of 1831 and 1832 in the Virginia legislature are generally regarded as marking the last important Southern appearance of antislavery sentiment, some opposition to the institution remained in slave territory up to and through

[104] E. P. Barrows, *A View of the American Slavery Question* (New York, 1836), 106n.

[105] *The Liberator*, April 9, 1836.

[106] *The National Anti Slavery Standard*, August 30, 1849, and the St. Louis *Missouri Democrat*, December 4, 1856.

[107] See the discussion of the effect on the South of the fear of slave revolt, Eaton, *Freedom of Thought in the Old South*, ch. IV; and Stampp, *Peculiar Institution*, chapters IV and V.

[108] Quoted by *The National Anti Slavery Standard*, July 20, 1848, and by the Washington *National Crisis*, May 15, 1860.

the Civil War.[109] A Virginia correspondent of *The National Era* wrote in 1848 that the South was far less unified in support of slavery than its controlled press made it seem, and another Southerner, writing to *The Anti Slavery Bugle,* was of the opinion that a respectable number of men in the slaves states, not daring to voice abolition sentiments, attacked slavery indirectly by supporting universal education, popular elections, and repeal of the law allowing slaveholders to count slaves in political representation.[110] Although such statements may not have represented the general state of affairs, it is true that whereas in the cotton states of the deep South opinion was in almost perfect agreement with the proslavery element, occasional rebels arose to stir up trouble in the border states.[111]

Edward Stanly, speaking in the House of Representatives in 1850, attacked the "double F.F.V.'s" of North Carolina who made the slavery question the main issue of politics and meanwhile neglected the welfare of western counties. Likewise Willie P. Mangum, T. L. Clingman, and Kenneth Rayner of North Carolina never became fully reconciled to the proslavery position.[112] The Wesleyan ministers Adam Crook, Jarvis Bacon, and Jesse McBride, though often involved in lawsuits and frequently threatened, gathered a strong antislavery group about them in North Carolina in the late 'forties.[113] In both North Carolina and Virginia in 1848, a strong but unsuccessful movement developed, backed by Daniel Goodloe, to extend suffrage to all free whites, a move which would have given the western portions of those states power equal to that of the slaveholding eastern counties.[114] As late as 1840, Thomas Marshall was able to call slavery in Virginia "an unmitigated

[109] For an analysis of these debates see J. C. Robert, *The Road from Monticello.*

[110] *The National Era,* June 15, 1848, and *The Anti Slavery Bugle,* June 15, 1849.

[111] See Helper's *The Impending Crisis,* and Goodloe's *Inquiries into the Causes Which have Retarded the Accumulation of Wealth and Increase of Population in the Southern States.*

[112] *The Speech of Edward Stanly of North Carolina, Exposing the Causes of the Slavery Agitation . . .,* March 6, 1850.

[113] *The National Anti Slavery Standard,* August 21, 1851.

[114] *The National Era,* October 12, 1848. The issue of December 23, 1858 reports abolition "colporteurs" still at work in North Carolina.

curse . . . the clog which has stayed the march of her people,"
and the Richmond *Southerner* in 1848 thought two-thirds of
Virginia would favor abandoning the system if a workable
emancipation plan were suggested.[115] Samuel Janney, Edward
Coles, John Botts, and C. F. Mercer were other Virginians
who attacked the system.[116] The lot of the opponent of slavery
in the cotton states remained difficult throughout the pre-war
period, however, and his position in the community precarious.[117]

The most clearly disaffected areas of the South were western
Virginia and Kentucky. During the Virginia debates of 1832
strong opposition to slavery came from the western counties,
which held less than 50,000 slaves in contrast to the half-million in the eastern counties.[118] Antislavery petitions to Congress from Wheeling in 1839 aroused the wrath of the tidewater
Virginians, and as early as 1844 the idea was current in western
Virginia that it might fare better as a separate free state.[119]
Frequent reports of antislavery sentiment came from that area
in the 'forties, and Cassius Clay received one of his greatest
ovations in Wheeling in 1858.[120] Newspapers published in

[115] Quoted by *The Anti Slavery Bugle*, September 19, 1845 and June 23,
1848.

[116] Janney's letter to *The National Era*, September 28, 1848, and the letter of "Vindicator," *ibid.*, June 15, 1848 are examples of antislavery feeling
in Virginia.

[117] For an account of the difficulties encountered by a South Carolina
antislavery sympathizer, see W.H. Brisbane, *Speech . . . Delivered Before
the Ladies Antislavery Society of Cincinnati.*

[118] The speech of George Summers of Kanawha, reported in *The National Anti Slavery Standard*, November 13, 1851, and the Virginia Census
Report, in the Alexandria, Virginia, *Phenix-Gazette*, June 1, 1831.

[119] *The Liberator*, April 19, 1839, and the Cincinnati *Weekly Herald and
Philanthropist*, February 21, 1844.

[120] *The National Anti Slavery Standard*, October 22, 1846, and *The National Era*, December 30, 1847, reported widespread abolition talk in western Virginia. Clay's reception, reported by the Wheeling *Intelligencer*, was
reprinted by *The Anti Slavery Bugle*, October 6, 1858. Representative of
western Virginia feeling in the period are "Address to the People of Western Virginia," and "Outlines of a Scheme for the Removal of Slavery,"
reprinted from the Wellsburg, Va., *Herald*, by *The National Era*, November 25, December 2, and December 16, 1847. See also George Ellis Moore,
"Slavery as a Factor in the Formation of West Virginia," *West Virginia
History* XVIII (October, 1956), 5-9.

Wheeling and the panhandle district of Virginia openly took antislavery stands, and most of their opinions went unquestioned.

The effects of Kentucky antislavery opinion appeared both in that state's 1833 law against the importation of slaves and in its refusal to pass legislation abridging freedom of speech and press.[121] Although the law forbidding the introduction of fresh slave labor provoked an annual struggle for its repeal, it was still on the books through the most violent phases of the antislavery controversy.[122] During the 1830's slavery was discussed pro and con without disturbance, and in 1838 several Kentucky newspapers urged a constitutional convention for the purpose of abandoning the system.[123] Gradual emancipationists, men such as Cassius Clay, Robert J. and William L. Breckenridge, Joseph Speed, and Henry Clay, were numerous. John G. Fee, an outright abolitionist, worked throughout the state in the 'fifties with only minor difficulty.[124] During the constitutional convention of 1849 a sharp discussion of slavery occurred, though no decisive action resulted.[125] Of all the Southern states, Kentucky offered the greatest sympathy to antislavery sentiments, and its subsequent lack of interest in the Confederacy may be at least partially attributed to the fact.[126]

Southern antislavery opinion during the late years of the

[121] See Asa E. Martin, *Antislavery in Kentucky Prior to 1850*, pp. 18-48, and J. W. Coleman, *Slavery Times in Kentucky*, ch. XII, for the history of antislavery in Kentucky.

[122] *The National Era*, March 9, 1848, traces the history of the law.

[123] James Freeman Clarke, *Anti Slavery Days*, p. 27, and extracts in the Cincinnati *Philanthropist*, July 24, 1838.

[124] For typical emancipationist plans, see "Emancipation in Kentucky," reprinted from the Louisville *Examiner* by *The Anti Slavery Bugle*, May 28 and June 4, 1853 and October 14 and 21, 1854. Travellers reported, *ibid.*, February 26, 1847, that while gradual emancipation talk aroused no fears in Kentucky, abolition was greatly disliked.

[125] Reports and summaries of the convention debates, *The Anti Slavery Bugle*, December 8, 1849, and *The National Anti Slavery Standard*, November 22 and 29, and December 20, 1849.

[126] "Abolition in Kentucky," *The Anti Slavery Bugle*, December 20, 1856, summarizes the antislavery history of the state to that date.

controversy was based almost wholly on an appeal to economic interest, an argument made especially cogent by the writing and speeches of Cassius Clay, Daniel Goodloe, and Hinton Rowan Helper. Helper's book, though widely banned and attacked and the central issue of an important case in court, made a deep impression upon Southern non-slaveholders, particularly those of his home state.[127] Clay, however, had been preaching the same doctrine through the South for two decades, and the presence of his name in Helper's dedication is an indication of the debt the author owed the Kentuckian. His oft-repeated thesis, that slavery impoverished the free white worker and bound him over to the political and economic control of the slaveholding aristocrat,[128] found a sympathetic hearing in a good many Kentucky counties. The Louisville *Examiner* believed that if slavery continued to exist, every free white workman "must expect to work for wages but slightly in advance of those received by slaves."[129] The Newport, Kentucky, *Watchman* thought that "wealthy men encourage Slavery more for the purpose of making profits out of the white men, who work hard to become decent livers, than they do for the profit received from the black slave."[130] Reflections of Clay's attitude in western Virginia were common, and insurgents in other Southern states, notably Andrew Johnson of Tennessee, Lumpkin of Georgia, William Gregg and J. H. Taylor of South Carolina, and Francis Blair of Maryland shared his opinion.[131]

[127] Letters to *The National Era*, September 29, 1859.

[128] Speeches in the Kentucky legislature, in the Cincinnati *Philanthropist*, March 10, 1841, his speech in Broadway Tabernacle, in *The Anti Slavery Bugle*, January 30, 1845; his "Letter to the People of Kentucky," the Cincinnati *Weekly Herald and Philanthropist*, February 12, 1845, and his Pittsburgh speech, *The Anti Slavery Bugle*, March 31, 1855.

[129] Quoted by *The Anti Slavery Bugle*, May 4, 1849. Similar articles attacking slavery as a threat to white labor from the Louisville *Journal*, the Louisville *Courier*, and the Newport, Kentucky, *News*, appear *ibid.*, February 19, 1849, December 8, 1849, and December 1, 1855.

[130] *Ibid.*, January 1, 1853.

[131] Cf. the Wellsburg, Va., *Herald*, quoted *ibid.*, January 29, 1859; Andrew Johnson, quoted *ibid.*, August 11, 1855; "Nonslaveholders in the Slave States," December 1, 1849; the letter of Francis Blair, *ibid.*, October

Yet notwithstanding the presence in certain parts of the South of strong antislavery feeling, and despite the appeals of Clay, Helper, and others to the non-slaveholders, the greater portion of the South was united in opposition to abolition and in support of the proslavery element. There was good reason for this unanimity. In the first place, the proslavery faction succeeded in justifying the system economically and scripturally, and in identifying it with the continued existence of Southern civilization. It also succeeded in discrediting the abolitionist as a radical and fanatic, and in enlisting the support of the non-slaveholder by threatening him with slave revolts and Negro equality.[132] It is doubtful if the abolitionists, with all their barrage of arguments, ever really caused any number of Southern proslavery men to change their minds. As a device for maintaining political control of the South and securing unity of public opinion, opportunistic Southern leaders used the threat of abolitionism with great success. Abolition provided them with vast amounts of ammunition and helped to strengthen their attacks on the North by appealing to the South's fear, pride, and self-interest. Southern moderates noted this, and decried the abolitionists' encouragement of proslavery "ultraism." The Louisville *Examiner* editorialized in 1847 that the rabid "pro-slavery Carolina school"

hopes to deepen the pro-slavery excitement, so that they may band all the slave states in one political union, and thus win power and secure it; and for this end, they appeal constantly and ably to the

11, 1856; and "Poor White Folks," *The National Anti Slavery Standard,* January 21, 1847. Robert R. Russell, however, in "The General Effects of Slavery upon Southern Economic Progress," *Journal of Southern History* IV (February, 1938), 34-54, concludes that Helper's thesis was not wholly correct, and that climate, topography, natural resources, trade routes, means of transport, and the character of the white laboring population had much more influence on Southern economic life than slavery or the presence of Negroes.

[132] On this point, see the excellent article by J. H. Steffy of Virginia, "Slavery and the Poor White Man of Virginia," *The National Era,* January 11, 1849. Although many poor whites disliked slavery, said Steffy, they feared the slaveholder's power and especially dreaded Negro social and economic equality.

pride, passion, sectional prejudice, avarice, and fears of these slave States.[133]

The poor white's economic position made his opinion on the question of negligible importance, while the customary South- ern system of uneven representation in state legislatures gave the slaveholding sections disproportionate political power and consequent control of the non-slaveholding areas. Migrations of the yeoman farmer to the West in the 'forties and 'fifties further limited, by depleting its numbers, the effectiveness of the one class from which Southern opposition to slavery might have arisen. Rigid state laws against expression of antislavery opinion, combined with the mob-threat of Vigilance Commit- tees, served to discourage or silence antislavery sentiment all over the South.

It must be conceded that the proslavery argument did its work well, in that it ultimately either eliminated or convinced almost all of its effective opposition in the South in the short span of forty years. In 1818, for example, the General Assembly of the Presbyterian Church, U.S.A., took the official position, with Southern Presbyterian approval, that slavery was a "gross violation of the most precious and sacred rights of human nature . . ., totally irreconcilable with the spirit and principles of the Gospel of Christ." By 1835 the Southern Alabama Pres- bytery was only one of several which condemned antislavery discussion as "distructive (*sic*) to the comfort of the Slave population, the interest of the church, and the stability of established institutions." Gamaliel Bailey achieved an even more dramatic contrast by printing in *The National Era* two quotations from the Richmond *Enquirer* side by side in 1855. In 1832, at the height of the Virginia legislative debates, the *Enquirer* called the slave system "a dark and growing evil." In 1855, it thought slavery "a natural and necessary and hith-

[133] K. M. Stampp, "The Fate of the Southern Antislavery Movement," *Journal of Negro History* XXVIII (January, 1943) , 15. Gamaliel Bailey's "The Slavery Excitement in the South and Party Leaders," *The National Era*, March 14, 1850, is a keen appraisal of Southern politics and anti- slavery agitation.

erto universal hub, element, or institution of society."[134] The difference, representing more than twenty years of agitation, is graphic illustration of the effective work of the proslavery forces in the South.

---

[134] G. C. Whateley, "The Alabama Presbyterian and His Slave," *Alabama Review* XIII (January, 1960), 40, 41; *The National Era*, July 26, 1855.

The "Great Petition Strategy" and the Use of the Mails

II

THE ARGUMENTS IN CONGRESS over the acceptance of abolitionist petitions, and over the right of the antislavery societies to use the mails, were of considerable importance in shaping public opinion during the early phases of the abolition movement. Though these were relatively brief controversies, they assisted the abolitionist materially in his attempt to identify his cause with the larger cause of civil and human rights. To him, the struggle in Congress over petitions and the mails had great implications for the liberties, not just of abolitionists, but of all Americans. Its results might well decide, Harriet Martineau said, whether or not "seven millions of freemen" should "become slaves to a handful of slaveholders."[1]

[1] *The Martyr Age of the United States of America*, 31. The late J. W. Burgess thought "it would not be extravagant to say that the whole course of the internal history of the United States from 1836 to 1861 was more largely determined by the struggle in Congress over the abolition petitions and the use of the mails for abolition literature than by anything else." *The Middle Period*, 274.

Abolitionists demanded absolute freedom to protest against slavery, a "national evil," and considered any infringement upon their right to petition or their right to use the mails as a complete contravention of those rights. Southern slaveholders, on the other hand, who believed that abolitionism represented a threat to their lives and property (both guaranteed protection by the Constitution), disagreed. "The abolitionists," said Calhoun,

are organized throughout every section of the non-slaveholding states; they have the disposition of almost unlimited funds, and are in the possession of a powerful press, which, for the first time, is enlisted in the cause of abolition, and turned against the dominant institution and the peace and security of the South.[2]

The South therefore demanded laws governing the circulation by mail of abolition literature, and restricting the abolitionist use of petitions, as necessary first steps in a legislative program directed at self-preservation.

In both North and South the argument over the mails and petitions helped to crystallize opinion concerning abolitionism and civil rights. In New England, where Garrison and his group were still, in 1836, looked on with suspicion as fanatics, the controversy did much to draw favorable attention to the abolitionist cause. In the West, where the reverberations of abolition sounded only faintly in the 'thirties, the congressional struggle helped to publicize abolitionist aims and to prepare the ground for the later Free Soil movement. For the South, the outcome of the controversy seemed to be one more proof that the slave states could not obtain justice from the Federal government—or protection from the North. Jefferson Davis later listed it among the chief causes of Southern dissatisfaction.[3]

Petitions relating to slavery had been received by Congress

[2] R. K. Crallé, *The Works of John C. Calhoun,* II: 530-31.
[3] T. C. Smith, *The Liberty and Free Soil Parties in the Northwest,* 20, and Jefferson Davis, *The Rise and Fall of the Confederate Government,* II:172.

as early as 1790, when Pennsylvania Quakers and the Pennsylvania Society for the Abolition of Slavery submitted protests concerning the slave trade. Madison insisted at the time upon their discussion and reference, and the special committee established to consider them later reported out several resolutions defining congressional powers over slavery. In subsequent debate the House then deleted from the resolutions all unfavorable criticisms of the institution and declared Congress could neither prevent the slave trade until 1808 nor interfere with slavery in any state. Thus Congress recognized slavery, seemingly, as a local rather than a national institution.[4]

A few petitions came to Congress each session thereafter, asking for action on the slave trade, requesting the abolition of slavery in the District of Columbia, proposing gradual emancipation schemes, and the like. These were usually received without appreciable comment, referred, and buried in committee.[5] However, after 1820 Congress became increasingly sensitive to these petitions and showed some hesitation about discussing them. Petitions asking that Congress abolish slavery in the District of Columbia aroused the suspicion of Southern members, who thought they might be cunning attempts to force Congress to commit itself on abolition. In 1827 such a petition from Baltimore was declared out of order, and in 1828 and 1829 others of the same type were referred and never reported on.[6]

Before 1830 most petitions usually limited themselves to requests for the control of the internal slave trade, for laws governing the treatment of slaves, or at the most for gradual emancipation or colonization. After 1830 the situation changed. Whereas many of the earlier petitions came from Southern colonization or gradual emancipationist groups, those directed to Congress after 1831 came from the North, from the Garrisonian strongholds, and not only increased in number but be-

[4] See "Early Congressional Discussions of Slavery," *DeBow's Review* XXIII (July, 1857), 35-47.
[5] J. W. Burgess, *op. cit.*, 252-254.
[6] Mary Tremain, "Slavery in the District of Columbia," *University of Nebraska Seminar Papers,* No. 2, 61-65.

came much more aggressive in tone. By 1835 a number of alert Southern leaders interpreted these petitions as a definite threat to the system on which, they believed, Southern social and economic security rested. Early that year came the first clear indication of the position the Southern congressional contingent was to take in the years to come—that congressional reception and discussion of antislavery petitions must be stopped.

In February of 1835, Wise of Virginia, speaking in favor of the tabling of a petition for the emancipation of slaves in the District of Columbia, told the House:

Sir, slavery is interwoven with our very political existence, is guaranteed by our Constitution, and its consequences must be borne by our Northern brethren as resulting from our system of government, and they cannot attack the system of slavery, without attacking the institutions of our country, our safety, and our welfare.[7]

In December, Fairfield of Maine presented another petition which, with a subsequent one, was quickly tabled. Boon of Indiana asked that the second petition be read; when this was done, Slade of Vermont moved that it be printed. In the process of debating this motion, Slade began to analyze and discuss the whole question of congressional control of slavery in the District until stopped by a ruling of Speaker Polk.[8] The motion to print was then tabled, but Slade's interrupted speech crystallized the Southern belief that something should be done to curb discussion of slavery in Congress. "I cannot see the rights of the Southern people," declared Hammond of South Carolina, "assaulted day after day, by the ignorant fanatics from whom these memorials proceed."[9] Slade, one of the few abolitionists in Congress, quickly reminded Hammond that the signers of petitions were not necessarily fanatics. They included, he said, people interested in free speech and the

[7] A. B. Hart, *Slavery and Abolition,* and T. H. Benton, *Abridgement of the Debates of Congress . . .* XI:1399.

[8] Burgess, *op. cit.,* 254-258.

[9] *Register of Debates, 24th Congress, 1st Session,* 1867.

right of petition as well as abolitionists.[10] So agreed John Quincy Adams, who said as Hammond's motion to table was discussed:

In a large portion of the country every individual member who votes with you will be left home at the next election, and someone will be sent who is not prepared to lay these petitions on the table. You will have discussion. A discussion on the merits of slavery. On such a discussion every speech made by a member north of Mason and Dixon's line will be an incendiary pamphlet.[11]

The first decisive move to arrest the flood of abolitionist petitions came in the opening months of 1836. On January 4, Glascock of Virginia presented to the House a resolution which reflected the strategy of the Southern bloc. Simply tabling petitions, he pointed out, would not satisfy the South. Instead, the House ought to go on record "that any attempt to agitate the question of slavery in the House is calculated to disturb the compromises of the Constitution, to endanger the union, and, if persisted in, to destroy, by a servile war, the peace and prosperity of the country."[12] On February 8, Pinckney of South Carolina proposed a more diplomatic method of disposing of the petitions by reference to a special committee, and after some debate, Pinckney's suggestion was adopted.[13]

On May 18, this committee made its report. The first section denied Congress the power to abolish slavery in any state; the second affirmed that slavery must not be interfered with in the District of Columbia; and the third provided that "all petitions, memorials, resolutions, propositions, or papers relating in any way or to any extent whatever to the subject of slavery or the abolition of slavery shall, without being printed or referred, be laid upon the table and that no further action whatever be taken thereon."[14] The second resolution met

[10] *Congressional Globe, 24th Congress, 1st Session,* 48.
[11] Benton, *op. cit.,* XIII: 9.
[12] *Niles' Register,* 49: 317.
[13] *Ibid.,* 49: 406-408.
[14] *Ibid.,* 50: 241.

some opposition from Southern representatives who thought it implied that Congress possessed power over slavery in the District, though it ought not to use it. However, the report was passed, with minor changes, on May 26, and the first so-called "gag-rule" went into effect. John Quincy Adams rose from his seat to denounce it as "a direct violation of the Constitution of the United States, of the rules of the House, and the rights of my constituents."[15]

The Pinckney "gag" spurred the abolitionists to greater effort, and they resolved to embarrass Congress by a flood of petitions. "Every name signed to a petition," said Henry B. Stanton in 1836, "is a nail driven into the coffin of slavery."[16] Abolitionists hoped through their campaign to accomplish three aims: to unify abolition interests upon a common issue; to force a discussion of slavery in Congress (which provided a public sounding board as well as franking privileges) ; and to involve the Southern congressmen in a public controversy that could do slavery little good and perhaps much harm. They hoped, they admitted later, "to take possession of Congress and turn it into a vast Anti Slavery Debating Society, with the whole country as an audience."[17] And, incidentally, they thought they might gain a token victory by inducing Congress to abolish slavery in the District of Columbia.

In 1837 the American Anti Slavery Society, under the direction of Stanton, Weld, and Whittier, evolved an efficient organization for the circulation of petitions through the mobilization of more than a thousand antislavery societies. Printed petitions, or directions for drawing them up, went from the Society's presses to the local and state groups, which in turn distributed them, solicited signatures, and returned them to the societies for transmission to state legislatures and Congress.[18] The results were almost immediately evident. The

---

[15] For a complete account of the discussions, see *ibid.*, 50: 204, 224-225, 241-249, and 256.

[16] The Cincinnati *Philanthropist*, December 2, 1836.

[17] The Salem, Ohio, *Anti Slavery Bugle*, June 15, 1850.

[18] An account of the petition strategy is found in G. H. Barnes, *The Antislavery Impulse*, 132-137, 140-149. D. L. Dumond, *Antislavery*, 242-48,

number of petitions submitted to Congress during the first eighteen months of the campaign increased from 23 to 300,-000.[19] The American Anti Slavery Society reported that during the year 1837-1838, 412,000 petitions reached the House, and about two-thirds of that number the Senate.

The tenor of these petitions is indicated by the Society's breakdown of the total sent to the House: 130,200 for the abolition of slavery in the District of Columbia; 182,400 against the annexation of Texas; 32,000 for the repeal of the "gag-rule"; 21,200 for legislation forbidding slavery in the territories; 22,160 against the admission of any new slave state; and 23,160 for the abolition of the interstate slave trade.[20] Birney stated that the number of signers of petitions for abolition in the District totalled more than a half-million by 1838. Stanton calculated that two million signatures in all had been gathered by the national society in 1838 and 1839.[21] Since the total number of abolition society members was no more than 100,000, it was clear that the signers included many who were not abolitionists, but who, as defenders of the right of petition, probably were persuaded to join the abolitionists in their campaign.[22]

Opposition to the Pinckney resolutions developed in the House almost at once. Their chief opponent was John Quincy

---

is an excellent brief treatment of the controversy. See *The Philanthropist,* October 8, 1839, for an example of the organization of the campaign. With detailed instructions for preparing, circulating, signing, and sending, six sample petitions were reprinted—for abolition of slavery in the District, against Florida's admission as a slave state, against interstate slave trade, against the annexation of Texas, for recognition of Haiti, and for repeal of state "black laws." Similar forms and instructions, for presentation to state legislatures only, are given in the Utica, New York, *Friend of Man,* November 20, 1839.

[19] A. C. McLaughlin, *A History of the American Nation,* 319.

[20] Austin Willey, *History of the Antislavery Cause in State and Nation,* 83.

[21] *Correspondence Between F. H. Elmore and James G. Birney,* 46, and Henry Wilson, *The History of the Rise and Fall of the Slave Power in the United States,* 1:273.

[22] Barnes, *op. cit.,* 134, and the analysis of petition signatures by Henry Clay, Calvin Colton, ed., *Works,* VIII:139-160. See also the excellent discussion of petitions by W. G. Fowler, *The Sectional Controversy,* 129-131.

Adams, who said at the time that he was less concerned about abolition than about protecting the constitutional right of petition. Adams, after his defeat for re-election to the Presidency, came to the House in 1830 on the Antimasonic ticket; though he had presented antislavery petitions as early as 1831, he had at the same time deprecated them as leading "to ill-will, to heartburning, to mutual hatred . . ., without accomplishing anything else."[23] Even in 1836, after expressing his opinion of abolition to a friend, he admitted that he probably fell short of "the standard which you believe to be the true faith."[24] However, Adams's opposition to the Pinckney resolutions stemmed from his belief that the right of petition involved not only reception but consideration (or at least referral to the proper committee for disposal) as the practice had been since 1829.[25] The adoption of the Pinckney "gag" seemed to him a direct threat to civil liberties; thus he dedicated himself "to sustain the right of petition in the citizen, and the freedom of speech in this House, and the freedom of the press, and of thought, out of it."[26] Before the organization of the abolitionist bloc in the House five years later, Adams carried the campaign against the "gag" very nearly alone.

When the Pinckney rules expired at the end of the 1836 session, Hawes introduced a similar set early in the 1837 session, which were passed on January 18, 1837. The abolitionists'

[23] C. F. Adams, ed., *The Memoirs of John Quincy Adams*, VIII:434, 454.

[24] *Proceedings of the Massachusetts Historical Society* (1902) , 457. Garrison recognized this, saying that Adams was "zealous in protesting an effect and yet was resolved not to strike at the cause;" W. P. and F. J. Garrison, *William Lloyd Garrison*, II, 325.

[25] *Register of Debates, 24th Congress, 1st Session*, 1867. See also Tremain, *op. cit.*, 70-76, for discussion of petition disposal to 1836.

[26] Quoted by H. B. Stanton, *Remarks in Representatives Hall . . . Before the Committee of the House of Representatives of Massachusetts*, 43. Adams frequently reiterated his stand. In 1837 he pointed out, "It is for the sacred right of petition I have adopted this course," and in 1840, "My struggle has been for the right of petition—freedom of speech—freedom of debate—freedom of Press;" quoted by W. H. Seward, *The Life and Public Services of John Quincy Adams*, 289, and the Cincinnati *Philanthropist*, April 21, 1840. See also Adams's *Letters from John Quincy Adams to his Constituents*, and his *Speech upon the Right of the People, Men and Women, to Petition . . ., Delivered in Fragments of the Morning Hour*, June 16-July 7, 1838.

recognition of the advantages that might accrue from "gags" came slowly, but as the petition campaign organized by the American Anti Slavery Society grew, the publicity generated by the abolitionists attracted attention to the apparent attempt of Congress to withdraw the right of petition. The harrying attacks of Adams were of great value to the abolitionists and were always fully reported in the press.[27]

Less than a month after the passage of Hawes' resolutions, the ex-president embroiled the House in a fight over a petition from twenty slaves which he asked permission to present on February 6. The chair left it to the House, and in the acrimonious debate that followed, Adams, a master of parliamentary maneuver, drew the Southern members into denying slaves even the right of petitioning God, or free Negroes and anyone of "poor moral character" the right of petitioning Congress on any matter whatever. "The next step," said Adams, driving his point home, "will be to inquire into the *political* beliefs of the petitioners."[28] When it appeared that the petition actually was a request for the *retention* of slavery, a resolution to censure Adams (for creating a false impression and injuring the dignity of the House) was introduced by Drumgoole of Virginia. The motion failed when it could not be proved Adams's act was a parliamentary offense.[29] Shortly afterwards the Massachusetts legislature formally condemned Hawes' resolutions, resolving:

That the resolution above named is an assumption of power and authority, at variance with the spirit and intent of the Constitution

[27] The press kept close track of Adams's maneuvers in the House, usually reprinting those portions of debates in which he participated. See for example Adams's activity in 1837—the petition of one hundred and fifty women, *Niles' Register*, 51:316-318, the petition of nine "ladies" of Fredericksburg, *ibid.*, 51:96-97, and his brush with Wise of Virginia, *ibid.*, 52:254.

[28] J. F. Clarke, *Antislavery Days*, 55, and *Niles' Register*, 51:385-390.

[29] *Congressional Globe*, 24th Session, 2nd Session, 164-176, and W. H. Seward, *op. cit.*, 286-290. One of Adams's most withering speeches, directed at Waddy Thompson of South Carolina, was occasioned by this debate, and reprinted in Adams's *Letters . . . to his Constituents*, 50. Another interesting speech is that of Lincoln of Massachusetts on the right of petition, in *The Liberator*, March 4, 1837.

of the United States, and injurious to the cause of freedom and free institutions; that it does violence to the inherent, absolute, and inalienable rights of man; and that it tends essentially to impair those fundamental principles of natural justice and natural law which are antecedent to any written constitutions of government. . . .[30]

Another flareup came in December, 1837, when Congressman Slade of Vermont presented resolutions from the Vermont legislature, requesting representatives and senators to use their influence to abolish slavery in the District of Columbia. Legislative resolutions naturally had a slightly different standing from those which came from individuals or societies, and, after some angry debate, a caucus of Southern representatives arranged for a committee headed by Congressman Patton to introduce more stringent rules governing petitions the next day. These resolutions were therefore presented and passed "in the spirit of peace and harmony, not to exasperate or excite agitation and angry feeling. The desire of those with whom concurrence was offered, was, to extinguish and not to kindle the flame of discord and excitement in the country."[31]

In less than a month, on January 12, 1838, Atherton of New Hampshire introduced a similar set of resolutions at the opening of the 1838 session to take the place of Patton's, which expired at the end of the 1837 session.[32] From this time on the petition controversy became a game of wits, the abolitionists' representatives seeking ways to elude the House rules, and the Southern members, with their Northern party allies, attempting to silence them. Adams, Slade of Vermont, and Joshua R. Giddings were the chief offenders, Giddings having arrived in the House in 1838 from the Western Reserve of Ohio with instructions to bring abolition into national focus in every

[30] *Massachusetts Assembly, 1837, Senate Document 84, April 12, 1837,* and *Niles' Register,* 52:150.

[31] *Niles' Register,* 53:262.

[32] The breakdown of the vote, in the Cincinnati *Philanthropist,* January 8, 1839, illustrates the party-line strength. Yea: Northern Democrats 53, Southern Democrats 33, Southern Whigs 40, Northern Whigs 0. Nay: Northern Democrats 12, Northern Whigs 60, Southern Democrats 1, Southern Whigs 5.

way possible.[33] Petitions were presented against the Atherton rule, against the annexation of Texas, for the repeal of all laws in the District "inconsistent with the principles of the Declaration of Independence," for new naturalization and citizenship laws irrespective of color, for the protection of abolitionists in the South, and so on—all topics which, though related to slavery, did not come under the specific ban of the House rules, and which could thus be used as points from which to launch an attack on slavery.[34]

To do away with the bothersome preliminary of introducing and passing new rules governing slavery petitions at every new session, the House eventually adopted on January 28, 1840, after some acrimonious debate, Johnson's resolutions as Standing Rule 21.[35] This rule, operative until 1844, was more stringent than its predecessors. Previous practice had been to receive but automatically table abolition petitions, whereas the new rule stated that they "shall not be received by this House, nor entertained in any way whatever."[36] At the opening of each session until 1844 an attempt was made to repeal it and the attempt always failed; however, the guerilla tactics of Adams, Slade, and Giddings, who made each debate on the 21st rule a running debate, each time publicized the abolitionist cause.

By the opening of the 1842 session, the abolitionists in the

[33] Letter of Uri Suly, Painesville, Ohio, to Giddings, November 27, 1838, Giddings papers, Ohio State Archaeological and Historical Society, Columbus. A good brief account of Giddings' career is that of Byron Long, "Joshua Reed Giddings, A Champion of Political Freedom," *The Ohio Archaeological and Historical Quarterly* XXVIII (Jan., 1919), 1-47.

[34] Such petitions were usually tabled by separate motion. See the accounts of these subterfuges in Joshua Giddings' correspondence for 1838-1839, Giddings papers.

[35] For summaries of the debate over Johnson's resolutions, see *Niles' Register*, 57:366-367. The remarks of Cooper of Georgia, Stanly of North Carolina, Biddle of Pennsylvania, Garland of Virginia, Alford of Georgia, and others, and a general discussion of the debates, are to be found in the Cincinnati *Philanthropist*, February 10, 17, and 24, 1840. The best contemporary accounts of the abolitionist points of view may be found in Adams's "Letters to the Citizens of the United States," *ibid.*, May 21 and June 18, 1839, *The Speech of Mr. Slade of Vermont . . ., Delivered in the House of Representatives, January 18 and 20, 1840* (Washington, D. C., 1840), and "The Right of Petition," *The National Era*, January 18, 1849.

[36] D. L. Dumond, *Antislavery Origins of the Civil War*, 66.

House were organized for a concerted attack on the "gag-rule."
With the astute help of Theodore Weld and Joshua Leavitt,
Giddings formed a "select committee" of antislavery men, including Slade, Adams, Mattocks of Vermont, Andrews of Ohio,
Borden of Massachusetts, James of Pennsylvania, and a few
more, to press a discussion of slavery upon the House despite
the rules.[37] Early in the session John Quincy Adams presented
a petition from Haverhill, Massachusetts, asking Congress to
adopt measures breaking up the Union of free and slave states
—an ironic answer to Southern threats of secession.[38] It was
Adams's belief that this petition, properly presented in respectful language, should be referred to a committee for a report
showing cause why it should not be granted; in other words,
Adams wished to establish the distinction between the right
to present a petition and have it considered, and the substance
of the petition itself, a distinction he always maintained.[39]

To silence Adams permanently, a group of Southerners introduced a resolution of censure, accusing him of high breach
of privilege, contempt, a proposition to commit perjury, and
treason. The ensuing debate, which lasted nearly eleven days,
gave Adams and the abolitionists a magnificent opportunity to
bring the petition struggle to nationwide attention.[40] Finally,
unable to muster enough strength, Southern leaders agreed to
drop the matter if the offending resolutions were tabled.[41]

[37] Barnes, *op. cit.*, 178-182. See also G. H. Barnes and D. L. Dumond,
The Letters of Theodore Weld, Angelina Grimké Weld and Sarah Grimké,
175-176, 403-405.

[38] There is a good reason to believe this petition was the work of John
Greenleaf Whittier; see Whitman Bennett, *Whittier, Bard of Freedom*,
179-180.

[39] "I contend that the main reason for which anyone can rightly reject a
petition is the impropriety of granting the prayer it contains;" remarks
in the House, December 17, 1838, quoted by the Cincinnati *Philanthropist,*
January 8, 1839.

[40] Adams and Giddings were generally viewed as the champions of freedom by the Northern press; see the clippings reprinted in *The Liberator*,
February 25 and April 22, *et seq.*

[41] Giddings' eye-witness report appeared in the Rochester, New York,
Democrat, November 19, 1854, and the New York *Daily Tribune*, December 7, 1854.

Two months later the rules were seriously breached once more by Giddings, whose introduction of the *Creole* resolutions (a slave-ship case) brought another motion of censure which was lost in parliamentary procedure. A second resolution of censure, however, was adopted 175 to 69, and Giddings resigned from the House, only to return from a special election in Ohio with a substantial vote of support.[42] From such blows the "gag-rules" never recovered. At the opening of the 1843-1844 session they were nearly repealed, and the next year, when the attention of the nation was focused on Texas and Mexico, they were swiftly rescinded by a 108-80 vote.[43] Their repeal, read a resolution of the unbowed South Carolina legislature, was a "flagrant outrage upon our rights, and a decided step towards the subversion of our institutions."[44]

In the Senate the petition controversy was of less importance, for that body received less than half the number of petitions sent to the House. Since it possessed no well-organized antislavery bloc, the Senate drew less attention from the abolition societies. One group of Southern senators, including Henry Clay, favored treating all petitions respectfully, feeling that a battle over them might play directly into abolitionist hands. "I have always been disinclined to give a chance to any portion of the country to reproach Congress for the non-reception of petitions," said Clay later. "I have believed that it

[42] *Congressional Globe, 27th Congress, 2nd Session*, 342-346; R. P. Ludlum, "Joshua Giddings, Radical," *Mississippi Valley Historical Review* XXIII (1937), 49-60; and the complete account in Giddings' *History of the Rebellion; Its Authors and Causes* (New York, 1864).

[43] A breakdown of the vote, from the Cincinnati *Weekly Herald and Philanthropist*, December 18, 1844, shows that it followed sectional rather than party lines. Yeas (to repeal): Northern Democrats, 55, Northern Whigs, 48, Southern Whigs, 5. Nays: Southern Whigs, 16, Southern Democrats, 48, Northern Democrats, 16. The Northern votes against repeal came primarily from Illinois and New Hampshire. For a graphic illustration of the growth of slavery as a sectional issue, compare the vote on the 1838 resolutions, note 32. Though still unsympathetic to abolitionism, many Northern congressmen believed the 21st rule an unwise method of silencing it; see *The Remarks of Alexander Duncan of Ohio, Delivered in the House . . ., January 6, 1844*, and "The Speech of Mr. Beardsley of New York . . .," in *The National Anti Slavery Standard*, January 25, 1844.

[44] The Cincinnati *Weekly Herald and Philanthropist*, December 31, 1844.

would have been wisest to receive and refer them, without opposition, and report against their object in a calm, and dispassionate, and argumentative appeal to the good sense of the whole community."[45] Another group of men, among them Brown of North Carolina, Grundy of Tennessee, King of Georgia, and Preston of South Carolina, believed that the best method of handling petitions was to ignore them, or to dispose of them with the least possible hubbub. A struggle over the right of petition, they warned, was exactly what the abolitionists wanted, and open debate on the question would do more benefit than harm to the abolitionist cause.[46]

John C. Calhoun, however, refused to ignore the issue, and believed strongly that this particular challenge to Congress must be met immediately. "We can never be more united or better prepared for the struggle," he said, "and I, for one, would much rather meet the danger now, than turn it over to those who are to come after us."[47] Therefore, when on January 7 and 11, 1836, petitions for the abolition of slavery in the District of Columbia were presented to the Senate by Morris of Ohio and Buchanan of Pennsylvania, Calhoun moved at once to table them as "a foul slander on nearly one-half the states of the Union," and asked that action be taken to put a stop to "that agitation which had prevailed in so large a section of the country."

The ensuing debate, which lasted until March, found Calhoun and Leigh of Virginia leading a discussion of whether or not Congress had the power to legislate on slavery at all. Daniel Webster believed the subject "must be discussed calmly, dispassionately, and fully"; all petitions should be received, referred, and considered, for "to reject the prayer of a petition at once, without reference or consideration, was not respectful . . ."[48] Congress, replied Calhoun, held no power over slavery wherever it existed. Thus abolitionists had no right to discuss

[45] Calvin Colton, *Speeches of Henry Clay*, II:420, and *Works*, VIII:41.
[46] Summaries of speeches in Richard Crallé, ed., *The Works of John C. Calhoun*, III:140-202.
[47] *Ibid.*, II:486.
[48] *Niles' Register*, 50:57-58.

the system at all, and Congress had the right to pass laws protecting slavery from attacks.[49]

Eventually, Calhoun's motion to table was lost, and the Senate accepted a compromise resolution, offered by James Buchanan of Pennsylvania, which provided for the reception of a petition but the rejection of its contents. Buchanan's compromise became standard Senate practice, for it avoided the stigma of refusing to receive petitions, but at the same time provided a way to refuse their requests. In April Henry Clay presented some petitions from Kentucky against admitting Arkansas as a slave state, but asked that they be tabled, saying, "In presenting them I only performed a duty—a duty in reference to petitions, of a constitutional, almost a sacred character," while Buchanan presented a Quaker petition of the same type a few weeks later with a similar request.[50]

But Calhoun refused to compromise the matter. In December, 1837, in reply to a memorial presented by Swift of Vermont from his state legislature, he introduced resolutions defending slavery, reaffirming his belief in the state as the sole arbiter of the slave system, and denying Congress the right to receive petitions concerning it or the right to legislate against it. Abolition in the free states, or attempts to influence Congress against slavery, were in his opinion unconstitutional, "a manifest breach of faith and a violation of the most solemn obligations, moral and religious. . . ."

Calhoun's resolutions were, he explained, a test measure; their passage or rejection would force the Senate to declare itself for the abolitionists, or for the South. In substance they held that the states were sovereign, that they had complete control over their internal institutions, that the Federal government must protect the domestic institutions of the states, and that since no state nor Congress had the power to abolish slavery in the District, any attempt to influence Congress by petition to that end was dangerous to the South's institutions.[51]

[49] Crallé, *op. cit.,* II:465-90.
[50] *Niles' Register,* 50:117. See also his letter of August 13, 1836, on the duty of presenting petitions, *ibid.,* 51:151.
[51] Crallé, *op. cit.,* III:140-142.

His resolutions caused some stir in the Senate; Thomas Morris of Ohio considered them a serious threat not only to the right of petition but to the right of free expression:

The object is to prevent the discussion of slavery in any of the States; but the Resolutions strike at all discussion. I regard these Resolutions as the most damning attempt against American liberty, that has yet been brought forward in Congress, since the foundation of the Republic, and as such I oppose them.[52]

Morris' view received some support from Henry Clay, who attempted to clarify the Senate's position by putting it on record with a set of generally-agreed principles about petitions. Clay proposed that the Senate agree that slavery was purely a matter of state control, that all petitions touching slavery in any state be rejected without debate, and that petitions touching abolition in the District be received and referred to committee.[53] While the Senate passed a combined version of Clay's and Calhoun's proposals, it refused to adopt those portions of Calhoun's denying the abolitionists' right to submit petitions or Congress' right to receive them. Calhoun and others brought up the matter again, but the Senate continued to follow the principle adopted in 1836—that abolition petitions would be received but either tabled or rejected—until the petition flood receded and the matter no longer was controversial.[54]

The eight-year controversy revolved primarily about two questions, the second of which proved to be the more important to the abolitionists: did the people have a right to petition Congress for the abolition of slavery, and did the disposal of the petitions by Congress constitute a threat to civil liberties? To the first, the abolitionists answered affirmatively; Theodore Weld's pamphlet, *The Power of Congress over the District of Columbia,* summarized their arguments admirably.

[52] B. F. Morris, *The Life of Thomas Morris,* 105-106.

[53] *Congressional Globe, 25th Congress, 2nd Session,* 55; *Niles' Register,* 54:257-8, and Crallé, *op. cit.,* III:168-169, report the December debates.

[54] See, for example, the handling of petitions from Ohio and Massachusetts in 1840, *Niles' Register,* 58:10, 57-58, and 59:316.

Slavery, he argued, existed only by the force of positive law which supported it. If the institution could be legislated into existence, it could therefore be legislated out of existence by repeal of the laws which established it. Since Congress made the laws for the District, it could therefore abolish slavery within the District by so legislating, and petitions requesting such action were perfectly in order. "The law," said Weld, "by *creating* slavery, not only affirmed its existence to be within the sphere and under the control of legislation, but also the *conditions* and *terms* of its existence, and the *question* whether or not it should exist."[55]

Giddings, agreeing with Weld's so-called "municipal" theory of slavery, amplified it by explaining that since slavery was a matter which concerned free as well as slave states, and that since the free states did not wish to be involved in the support of it, citizens of free states had the right to petition the Federal government to refuse to assist it.[56] John Quincy Adams next cited the acts prohibiting the importation of slaves after 1808 as a precedent for Federal interference with slavery in the states, inferring from that the right of individuals to petition the Federal government for abolition.[57] James G. Birney contended that abolition petitions were justified since "slavery in the District and territories, and the domestic slave trade are under the control of political action . . .," and his argument was often repeated in the House.[58]

On the other hand, the Southern contingent, led by Calhoun, denied that any citizen possessed the right to petition Congress for the abolition of slavery in the District, states, or territories. Slavery, said Calhoun, was purely a matter for state control; Congress had no power over it, and petitions asking

---

[55] *The Power of Congress over the District of Columbia*, 6. The legislatures of Pennsylvania in 1828, New York in 1829, Massachusetts and Vermont in 1837, and Connecticut in 1838 passed resolutions recognizing Congressional power to abolish slavery in the District.

[56] *Speeches in Congress* (Boston and Cleveland, 1853) , 52-72.

[57] Speech of May 25, 1836, *Niles' Register*, 50:277.

[58] The Cincinnati *Philanthropist*, December 30, 1836, and *Appendix to the Congressional Globe, 26th Congress, 1st Session*, 654-55, and *24th Congress, 1st Session*, 83-84.

Congress to legislate against it were out of order. "The subject," said Calhoun,

is beyond the jurisdiction of Congress: they have no right to touch it in any shape or form, or to make it the subject of deliberation or discussion. In opposition to this view, it is urged that Congress is bound by the Constitution to receive petitions in every case and on every subject, whether it is within its Constitutional competency or not. I hold this doctrine to be absurd . . ."[59]

Furthermore, since petitions for the abolition of slavery were construed as a threat to Southern property, they were actually unconstitutional.[60] In addition, Calhoun and others claimed that the original creation of the District of Columbia involved an agreement to protect the property rights of those Virginia and Maryland citizens whose land was ceded to the Federal government to form it. Congress, therefore, had no constitutional right to destroy those property rights by abolishing slavery, and petitions to that effect were useless.[61] By such arguments, the debate over the powers of Congress in regard to slavery proceeded undiminished, as did the disagreement over the constitutionality of petitions requesting its abolition. In the end both questions remained substantially unsettled.[62]

Within the House, and to a lesser degree within the Senate, the members divided into four loosely defined groups on the petition issue. The abolitionist group was small, and naturally opposed to any attempt to suppress petitions dealing with slavery. Another faction, drawn mainly from the North but

[59] Crallé, op. cit., II:627. Register of Debates, 24th Congress, 1st Session, 1109, shows that the legislature of Maine voted agreement with this view in a memorial submitted to Congress in 1836.

[60] Ibid., III:443. William Jay made the point, however, that it is not within the province of the House to decide the constitutionality of the acts, but that of the Supreme Court; Miscellaneous Writings, 402.

[61] Speech of Pickens of South Carolina, January 21, 1836, reprinted in The Philanthropist, February 19, 1836. See also Appendix to the Congressional Globe, 24th Congress, 1st Session, 18, 289; 26th Congress, 1st Session, 744; 24th Congress, 2nd Session, 315; and the opinion of James Buchanan, Niles' Register, 55:91.

[62] See Register of Debates, 24th Congress, 1st Session, 2020-2070, for the gist of these arguments, and the summary in Ludlum, op. cit., 243-251.

with a sprinkling of members from the upper South, followed the lead of the abolitionists, not because of any deep antislavery beliefs but because of concern for the preservation of civil liberties. Against these two groups were arrayed the extremist Southerners, who believed the right of petition less important than the protection of slavery, and a body of Northern and Southern middle-of-the-roaders, who favored the "gag" because of their dislike of agitation.

For example, both the Baltimore *Sun* and the Wheeling *Tri-Weekly Gazette* felt the House resolutions a threat to the right of petition, "among the most valuable of a freeman's privileges," and believed the course of the Southern members a mistaken one.[63] Tallmadge of New York objected sharply to Calhoun's view, and believed that "the citizen has a right to petition even for that which Congress is prohibited by the Constitution from granting," while Henry Clay was always sensitive to infringements of the right.[64] Charles Hammond of the Cincinnati *Gazette,* though not an abolition sympathizer, warmly supported Adams as "a defender of one of the great fundamental rights of freemen."[65]

On the other hand, the fact that Pinckney's resolution in 1836 received 82 of its 117 yeas from free-state representatives was evidence of a Northern desire to keep antislavery agitation out of Congress. It was generally suspected that the abolitionists were less mindful of the sanctity of the right of petition than of the political advantages that might accrue from a controversy over it. Elisha Whittlesey of Ohio wrote: "1 thought Mr. Adams was inconsistent. He was a stickler for the right of petition, but he would receive only abolition petitions. I did not see how the right of petition was secured, when it was determined not to act on the petitions."[66] Atherton of New Hampshire, in presenting his "gag" of 1838, called the aboli-

<hr />

[63] The Baltimore *Sun*, December 23, 1837, and the Wheeling *Tri-Weekly Gazette,* January 1, 1836.

[64] Crallé, *op. cit.,* III:441, and Colton, *op. cit.,* VIII:141.

[65] F. Weisenburger, *The Passing of the Frontier 1825-1860*, 377; Vol. III of Carl Wittke, ed., *The History of the State of Ohio.*

[66] Letter to J. W. Edwards, September 14, 1844, Whittlesey correspondence, Western Reserve Historical Society, Cleveland, Ohio.

tion petitions ". . . dangerous, not only to the rights of the citizens of the slaveholding states, but also, to the highest degree, to the integrity of the Union."[67] The general assembly of the Presbyterian Church, meeting in Pittsburgh, voted them "useless and dangerous to peace and order," while a meeting in Troy, New York, thought them "unwise, inexpedient, and incendiary."[68] Accounts of the discussions in Congress indicate that most members, aware of the explosive nature of the question, treated it gingerly, agreeing that the right of petition was involved, but uncertain as to what extent. Must petitions be received; and, if received, acted upon and considered; and if considered, also openly debated?[69]

A conclusive answer was never found. The abolitionists staunchly maintained that the right of petition included the right to have petitions received and considered; if it did not, they countered, of what use was the privilege? Thus Adams attacked the Pinckney "gag":

I assume it as a principle that it is the duty of this House to receive the petitions of all the citizens of the United States, if couched in respectful language; and I further assert it as a principle, that it is our duty not only to receive, but to consider them; and I say that if we receive and refuse to consider, we shelter ourselves under a distinction unworthy of this House. . . .[70]

[67] *Congressional Globe, 25th Congress, 3rd Session*, 24.

[68] *Niles' Register,* 49:73, and 50:155.

[69] Henry Wilson, *op. cit.,* I:309-312.

[70] *Speech Upon the Right of the People* . . ., *op. cit.,* 24. On December 18, 1837, he presented an anti-abolition petition from his district favoring the retention of slavery in the District, but the House tabled it, refusing his bait; *Niles' Register,* 53:259. For further abolitionist opinion on the right of petition, see J. G. Birney, "The Right to Petition Congress," *The Philanthropist,* January 22, 1836; W. E. Channing, *Remarks on the Slavery Question in a Letter to Jonathan Phillips, Esq.,* Appendix, note A, 89-100; speeches of Winthrop of Massachusetts and Giddings of Ohio in the House, *The National Anti Slavery Standard,* February 29 and March 14, 1844; and the editorial by David Lee Child, *ibid.,* March 14; Alvan Stewart, "Speech Delivered at Pennsylvania Hall, Philadelphia, May 15, 1838," in *Writings and Speeches on Slavery,* 118-128; and William Jay, "Address to the Friends of Constitutional Liberty . . ." *Miscellaneous Writings,* 396-408.

This Congressional method of disposing of abolition petitions, said the abolitionists, might well be applied to any petitions, whatever their subject. Whittier pointed out in the *Essex Gazette,* that

... the fatal precedent is now established that Congress may trample in the dust any future petition of the people on *any* subject whatsoever. . . . Are the people prepared for such a resolution? It is a declaration of independence on the part of their representatives, —independence of the people![71]

The Pinckney resolutions which denied the right of petition, the abolitionists warned, were but the first of a series of attempts designed to destroy other civil liberties. "Let it be remembered," said Slade,

... that the course which may now be adopted, as an expedient to suppress the utterance of hostility to slavery, may hereafter be drawn into a precedent to suppress the popular voice on other subjects, and that thus, gathering strength, encroachment may go on from conquering to conquer, until at last it shall sweep away . . . all the guarantees of popular rights.[72]

Adams believed that "all discussion, all freedom of speech, and all freedom of the press" might soon be "violently assailed in every form in which the liberties of the people should be attacked."[73]

Calhoun and other Southerners denied that the Congres-

---

[71] Quoted by *The Philanthropist,* July 1, 1836.

[72] *Speech on the Right of Petition, Delivered in the House . . .,* 5. Cf. the Natchitoches, La., *Herald,* January 12, 1838: "Many, both at the North and the South, would deprive abolitionists of the right of petition. However *expedient* it may be in the present instance, *we are opposed* to the adoption of any resolution to that effect; it would be establishing a precedent dangerous alike to the liberties of the South and the North." For the definitive treatment of this argument, see "To the People of the United States, or to Such Americans as Value Their Rights . . .," *A Collection of Valuable Documents,* 54-75.

[73] Josiah Quincy, *A Memoir of John Quincy Adams,* 250; see also H. B. Stanton, *Remarks . . ., op. cit.,* 71, and Horace Greeley, ed., *The Writings of Cassius M. Clay,* 35-36.

sional method of handling abolition petitions violated any principles of civil liberty, and discounted the abolitionist warnings as nothing more than scareheads. In the first place, Calhoun thought the right of petition one of the least important of rights, an anachronism unnecessary in an era of representative government. It possessed a function in colonial days, he admitted, but under a republic which considered the government the agent of the people, it served no useful purpose —how, he asked, could the people, the master, petition the government, its servant?[74]

Nor did the right to submit a petition necessarily imply a right to reception, consideration, or discussion. "To extend the right of petition," he explained, "beyond presentation is clearly to extend it beyond that point where the action of the Senate commences, and, as such, is a manifest violation of its constitutional rights."[75] Another view held that the right extended only to questions arising under the scope of the Constitution; since slavery was a state and not a constitutional question, petitions for its abolition were simply not to be received at all.[76] Similarly, it was argued that when the right of petition conflicted with House rules, it extended only to the acceptance of the petition, and to no further consideration.[77]

The Southern group also argued that the right of petition might be abridged if its exercise or misuse constituted a threat to property, peace, and order. "Any right," said William Johnson of Maryland, "reserved to the people, carries restrictions upon its exercise . . .," and he cited restrictions upon suffrage,

[74] Crallé, op. cit., III:440.

[75] Ibid., II:476. This speech, given March 9, 1836, is the most complete exposition of the extreme Southern view. For a similar view, see Calvin Colton, "A Northern Man," Abolition a Sedition, 41.

[76] Beardsley of New York, in the House, January 5, 1844, quoted by The National Anti Slavery Standard, January 25, 1844, and Hammond of South Carolina, Remarks . . . On the Question of Receiving Petitions . . ., 1-3. See also the resolution of the Georgia legislature, December 19, 1836, that "Congress has no right to receive any petitions whatever . . . upon any matter whatsoever not within the constitutional sphere of its action." Niles' Register, 51:210.

[77] Summary in J. K. Paulding, Slavery in the United States, 104-105.

speech, press, and other civil liberties, placed there for the national welfare.[78] That the unlimited use of the right of petition by abolitionists was a threat was generally agreed by all congressmen from the lower South. Governor McDuffie of South Carolina, in his legislative message of 1836, warned that "as long as the halls of Congress shall be open to discussion of this question, we can have neither peace nor security."[79] Calhoun believed the right of petition, in abolitionist hands, had degenerated into an instrument for attacking the South and was no longer a guarantee of civil liberty, while Henry Clay, though respectful of "the full force of the privilege," did not like "the political uses which have been made of it."[80] Another Southerner thought the whole affair "a pitiful pretence" to shield "a faithless violation of the (*Southern*) rights guaranteed by the Constitution."[81]

It is quite clear that from the abolitionist point of view the controversy concerned the defense of a specific civil liberty, and that from the Southern viewpoint it involved the safety of the slavery system. Though the abolitionists claimed to be defenders of the right of petition, the South was convinced that they actually intended by a misuse of that right to force Congress to establish Federal control of slavery. The petition strategy was simply the first move, thought Calhoun, in a campaign to abolish slavery by national action:

In the present contest, the question on receiving constitutes our frontier, it is the first, the exterior question, that covers and protects all the others. Let it be penetrated by receiving this petition, and not a point of resistance can be found within, as far as this

[78] William Johnson, *Speech Delivered in the House of Representatives, January 25, 27, 28, 1840,* 30-32. This is one of the best discussions, from the moderate Southern viewpoint, of the whole controversy. Worth reading as well is the speech of Garland of Louisiana in the House, December 30, 1839, arguing that while the right of petition is sacred, it cannot be used to deprive citizens of other states of privileges and property; *Niles' Register,* 57:301.

[79] *The Liberator,* December 17, 1836.

[80] Crallé, *op. cit.,* III:441-445, and W. G. Fowler, *op. cit.,* 115.

[81] Wayne Gridley, "Slavery in the South . . ." reprinted from *The Southern Quarterly* (October 1845), 2.

Government is concerned. If we cannot maintain ourselves there, we cannot on any interior position.[82]

Thus, from the first, the question of allowing petitions for abolition to be received by Congress was one of the utmost importance to the South. "The South has taken a stand on this subject," said one writer, "from which she will not depart. She will not permit the discussion, for one moment, of such petitions. She will consider the abolition of slavery in the District of Columbia as forbidden ground."[83] Most Southerners recognized the danger of admitting that Congress could legislate upon slavery in the District, and the part that petitions might play in forcing such an admission. Governor McDuffie warned the South Carolina legislature that

When this crisis shall arrive, those who now claim for Congress the constitutional power to emancipate the slaves in the District of Columbia, will as boldly claim the same power in regard to the states—their whole course demonstrates that this is the consummation at which they are aiming.[84]

Likewise, in discussing the Pinckney resolutions, Pickens of South Carolina told the House that "if the power be asserted in Congress to interfere here, or any approach made toward that end, it will give a shock to our institutions and the country, the consequences of which no man can foretell."[85] Calhoun concurred that acceptance of abolition petitions would "throw open to the abolitionists the halls of legislation, and enable them to establish a permanent position within these walls, from which to carry on their operations against the institutions of the slaveholding states"; they would establish in time "permanent jurisdiction over the subject of slavery,

[82] Crallé, *op. cit.*, II:484. *The Charleston Mercury*, December 27, 1837, agreed: "Until, by some decisive action, we compel silence, or alter the Constitution, agitation and insult is our eternal fate in the confederacy."

[83] Quoted by Tremain, *op. cit.*, 82, from *The South Vindicated*.

[84] *The Philanthropist*, December 23, 1836. The same view is expressed a year earlier by "A Citizen of Georgia," *Remarks on Slavery*, 17.

[85] *Ibid.*, February 19, 1836.

not only in the District, but in the States themselves."[86] The South, then, in attempting to prevent the reception and discussion of abolition petitions in Congress, was not fighting primarily against the right of petition, but for the preservation of its chief economic and social system.

Nevertheless, whatever the South's justification for its stand in the petition controversy, the "gags" passed by the House and the compromise measures adopted by the Senate were unwise, for they allowed the abolitionists to link their cause with the popular issue of civil liberty.[87] In the years that elapsed between the Pinckney resolutions and the removal of House Rule 21, and partly because of the controversy, the abolition movement gained hundreds of adherents in the North. A few Southerners perceived the danger. One, during the attacks on John Quincy Adams, cried, "Beware how you make a martyr to the right of petition!" and John Botts of Virginia firmly believed that the argument over petitions "made more abolitionists in one year, by identifying the right of petition with the question of slavery, than the abolitionists would have made for themselves in twenty-five years."[88] Rives of Virginia declared in the House, during debates on the Atherton "gag," that the "Southern fanatics . . . are likely to do more injury to our cause than five hundred men such as Garrison, Tappan, Thompson, Adams, and Slade."[89] Once public opinion accepted the abolitionists as the champions of civil rights, their cause prospered. The petition controversy gave abolitionism its first opening wedge into national politics, and projected its political representatives, men such as Giddings, Slade, and Adams, into national prominence.[90]

[86] Crallé, *op. cit.*, II:482.

[87] See the discussion by A. C. McLaughlin, *A Constitutional History of the United States*, 481.

[88] Ludlum, *op. cit.*, p. 76 and *The National Anti Slavery Standard*, October 11, 1856.

[89] *Niles' Register*, 55:312.

[90] The political significance of the controversy is seen in the shift of free-state votes in the House on the successive "gag-rules." Pinckney's resolutions of 1836 received 82 of their 117 yeas from free-state representatives, Atherton's of 1839 received 49 of 126, while Johnson's of 1840, which

Whether the right of petition was actually endangered during the controversy is not easily determined. It is true that the campaign was deliberately conceived and executed as a means of agitation, and that the abolitionist method of drawing up petitions—printed on the societies' presses by thousands, with lists of signatures, some questionable, pasted on—were clearly open to question. Certainly the Houses of Congress possessed the right to make and interpret their own rules and to facilitate the disposal of their business.[91] Yet, on the other hand, the stubborn fact remained that while Congress continued to admit and act upon thousands of other petitions of sometimes doubtful constitutionality, it did not willingly accept a single one against slavery. When it was evident that the principle of suppression, underlying five successive "gags" in the House and incorporated into a standing rule, might be applied to petitions concerning any other subject unpleasant to a majority in Congress, the argument took on a different complexion. The Executive Committee of the American Anti Slavery Society pointed out to the uncommitted bystander:

Can the Constitution at the same time secure liberty to you, and expose us to oppression—give you freedom of speech, and lock our lips—respect your right of petition, and treat ours with contempt? No, fellow-citizens, we must all be free, or all slaves together.[92]

The fact that the Southern bloc in Congress, aided by Northern sympathizers, seemed willing to compromise a basic civil right in order to maintain slavery, lent credibility to one of the abolitionists' greatest propaganda weapons—the charge that an aggressive slave-power cabal was conspiring to destroy all traditional liberties—and brought many hitherto neutral or suspicious men into the ranks. As Charles Sumner wrote in 1836, during the debates over the first "gag-rule":

---

passed by a margin of but 114 to 108, received 28 from the North, of which 19 came from the three states of New York, Ohio, and Pennsylvania.

[91] Cf. the discussion of this point by Avery Craven, *The Coming of the Civil War*, 177.

[92] *The Philanthropist*, July 8, 1836.

We are becoming abolitionists at the North fast; riots, the attempts to abridge freedom of discussion, and the conduct of the South generally, have caused many to think favorably of immediate emancipation who have never before been inclined to it.[93]

The dispute over the abolitionists' use of the mails, though more brief than the controversy over petitions, developed at about the same time and was concerned in the same fashion with the interpretation of a civil right as well as a legal one. Early antislavery publications, such as Lundy's *Genius of Universal Emancipation*, Embree's *Emancipator*, the early Ohio *Philanthropist*, and various other papers circulated in the Southern mails without encountering appreciable opposition. However, the Vesey revolt of 1822 and the Turner revolt of 1831 made the South conscious of the possible effects on slaves of antislavery propaganda. Although it is certain that neither revolt was inspired by antislavery literature, popular opinion tended to connect them. Georgia, for example, shortly after the Turner insurrection, offered a $5000 reward for the trial and conviction "under the laws of this state, (of) the editor or publisher of a certain paper called the *Liberator*."[94]

After the formation in 1833 of the national abolitionist group, the American Anti Slavery Society, it was some time before the conflict over the distribution of antislavery literature in the mails became an issue. In 1835 the Society embarked upon a pamphlet campaign intended "to awaken the conscience of the nation, North and South," to the evils of slavery. A fund of $30,000 was appropriated to provide for agents, periodicals, and free distribution of abolition publications. It was planned to publish a different periodical each week of the month—in the first week a folio paper, *Human*

---

[93] E. L. Pierce, *Memoir and Letters of Charles Sumner*, I:173. See also the remarks of Rogers of New York in the House, February 23, 1844, reprinted in the Cincinnati *Weekly Herald and Philanthropist*, March 6, 1844, on the role of the petition struggle in the growth of abolition's political power.

[94] W. L. Savage, *The Controversy over the Distribution of Abolition Literature*, 3-41; J. J. Chapman, *William Lloyd Garrison*, 51; and W. P. and F. J. Garrison, *op. cit.*, I:247.

Rights; in the second a magazine, *The Anti Slavery Record;* in the third *The Emancipator,* an enlarged sheet; and in the last *The Slave's Friend,* a juvenile tract. In addition the Society planned to issue pamphlets, tracts, bound volumes, circulars, and prints; until it changed its policy in 1840, it flooded the nation with such publications.[95]

In the fiscal year ending May, 1836, the Society printed and circulated more than a million pieces of antislavery literature.[96] During the next year, publications fell off to 161,000; from May, 1837 to May, 1838, they totalled 646,000; and for the period ending in May, 1839, the total reached 724,000.[97] Until a traveling agent system was developed in 1837, distribution was primarily by mail, to names on file in the New York offices drawn from the subsidiary societies, newspapers, and public records. Congressmen, ministers, theological students, state officials and legislators, newspaper editors, justices of the peace, and prominent citizens in all states received copies of the Society's publications *gratis.* A subscription list was slowly built up, containing some Southern subscribers, but none of the publications ever operated at a profit.[98]

[95] W. P. and F. J. Garrison, *op. cit.,* I:493. *Human Rights* cost twenty-five cents a year, *The Anti Slavery Record* $1.50 a thousand, *The Emancipator* fifty cents a year, and *The Slave's Friend* one cent a copy. From 1835 to 1837 the Society also published *The Quarterly Anti Slavery Magazine,* a semi-literary journal for "reading and thinking men." See *The Emancipator* for August, 1835, and Janet Wilson, "Early Antislavery Propaganda," *More Books: Bulletin of the Boston Public Library* XIX (November, 1944), 352-355.

[96] *Third Annual Report of the American Anti Slavery Society . . .,* May 10, 1836, 3, 35. Totals were *Human Rights,* 240,000; *Anti Slavery Record,* 385,000; *Emancipator,* 210,000; *Slave's Friend,* 205,000; miscellaneous, 36,000. Totals do not include publications of state or local societies.

[97] *Correspondence Between F. H. Elmore and James G. Birney,* 18-19, Henry Wilson, *The History of the Rise and Fall of the Slave Power in America,* I:272,273, and the Cincinnati *Philanthropist,* May 14, 1839. The 1837 totals included 7877 bound volumes, 47,250 tracts or pamphlets, 4100 circulars, 10,490 prints, 9000 copies of the *Quarterly Anti Slavery Magazine,* 131,500 copies of *The Slave's Friend,* 189,400 copies of *Human Rights,* and 217,000 of *The Emancipator.*

[98] *Fourth Annual Report of the Massachusetts Anti Slavery Society* (Boston, 1836), 17-18; *Second Annual Report of the American Anti Slavery Society* (New York, 1835), 48-53; *The Emancipator,* October 12, 1837;

In July of 1835 the mail steamer to Charleston, South Carolina, carried a number of packages of these publications. Stirred by rumors of "incendiary" materials, a group of citizens entered the United States post office at Charleston, removed the packages, and burned them publicly on July 30.[99] In August a city-wide mass meeting viewed "with *abhorrence* and *detestation* the attempt to deluge our State with Incendiary publications," and appointed a committee of twenty-one, headed by ex-governor Robert Y. Hayne, to inspect the mails in cooperation with the postmaster and to burn any objectionable matter. In addition, the city council offered a reward of $1000 for the apprehension of any person bringing an incendiary publication into the city or distributing it; any person who voluntarily received, harmonized in feeling with, or held communication with abolition societies, agents or publications was, the council decided, "an enemy of the state."[100]

Postmaster Huger of Charleston immediately wrote to Amos Kendall, President Jackson's Postmaster General, asking for instructions for the disposal of future shipments of antislavery publications. At the same time he wrote Postmaster Gouverneur of New York City, the point of origin of the offending literature, requesting him to hold all abolitionist papers addressed to Charleston until Kendall's ruling clarified the matter. Kendall's reply, dated August 4, was indefinite. He had no authority, he concluded, to exclude abolition literature from the mails or to prohibit its transportation or delivery; yet, he continued, he would not direct Huger to deliver it.

---

and the report of R. G. Williams, the American Anti Slavery Society's publishing agent, in the Cincinnati *Philanthropist, December 12, 1836.* After 1836 circulation was obtained by mail subscriptions, travelling agents, a new library system, and the "colporteur," or travelling distributor; see Janet Wilson, *op. cit.,* 354-355, and *The National Era,* January 5, 1854.

[99] For accounts see W. L. Savage, *op. cit.,* 16-17; Dumond, *Antislavery,* 206-10; Clement Eaton, "Censorship of the Southern Mails," *American Historical Review* XLII (January, 1943) , 267; and *Niles' Register,* 48: 403. Charleston citizens had burned Angelina Grimké's *Appeal to the Christian Women of the South* in 1830.

[100] *Niles' Register,* 48:441, 446-447.

"I cannot sanction, and will not condemn, the steps you have taken . . .," he wrote. "We owe an obligation to the laws, but a higher one to the communities in which we live." The postmaster who stopped distribution of such "inflammatory papers" would, he believed, "stand justified before country and all mankind." A few weeks later Kendall, replying to a request from a committee in Petersburg, Virginia, reiterated his stand; though abolitionist publications were within the letter of the postal laws, they violated the spirit of the regulations, a fact that justified "any measure necessary to effect their exclusion."[101]

Kendall's position met favor in both North and South, temporarily. A meeting at Richmond, Virginia, recommended the appointment of a "committee of vigilance" to keep watch over post offices, ships, and hotels. A meeting in Louisa County, Virginia, passed resolutions to "sustain all postmasters in detaining and publicly destroying all abolition papers." Similar meetings and resolutions were reported before December of 1835 in "many other towns in Virginia," "many places in Mississippi," in "Mobile, Montgomery, Greensboro, Tuscaloosa, and in different parts of the Southern states."[102] As far west as Missouri reports of the Charleston incident caused editorial comment. Elijah Lovejoy, publishing the St. Louis *Observer,* was denounced and threatened with violence, and two men were ejected from the Marion County Colonization Society as "avowed advocates and missionaries of abolition who came among us to instruct our slaves to rebellion by the use of incendiary pamphlets."[103] In Clinton, Mississippi (a town especially sensitive to threats of revolt because of the

[101] *Niles' Register,* 48:448, and 49:8, and the Richmond *Enquirer,* August 25, 1835. Editorials from Southern papers, warning that if the Postmaster General could find no authority to intercept objectionable material, "those states whose peculiar institutions are involved must take the law into their own hands," were reprinted in *Niles' Register,* 48:402-404.

[102] *Niles' Register,* 48:400, 439, and 49:90; letter of J. W. Womack of Greenville, Alabama, in Hilary Herbert, *The Abolition Crusade and its Consequences,* 79-80.

[103] N. D. Harris, *The History of Negro Servitude in Illinois,* 70, and H. A. Trexler, *Slavery in Missouri, 1804-1865,* 120-121.

contemporary depredations of the Murrel gang), a meeting, under "the discretionary powers conceded by the Postmaster General," ordered censorship of all mails, including private letters; any persons who received or wrote "incendiary" materials would be fined $10 and refused aid by civil authorities "from any assault or violence that may be inflicted upon them by a justly incensed populace"—an invitation to a lynching.[104]

However, the majority of the Southern public meetings suggested that control of the mails ought to be established by some sort of law, rather than mob action. Governor Gayle of Alabama expressed the hope in 1835 that the distribution of abolition literature would soon be legally controlled, and the legislature of Georgia in the same year requested a Federal law regulating such publications.[105] But in the absence of legislation, cases of spontaneous local censorship of the mails became increasingly frequent.[106] "The United States Mail shall not be permitted to shield your incendiary publications from the flames," one Southerner wrote in defiance, "and if you continue to be equally regardless of my rights and my life, there is no law and no country that shall protect yours."[107]

The Southern point of view found considerable sympathy in parts of the North. A meeting at Faneuil Hall in Boston, August 22, 1835, condemned the abolitionists' use of the mails as "incendiary"; a meeting at Portland, Maine, on August 15, 1835 declared the transmission of abolitionist literature by mail to be "an alarming perversion and abuse of this invaluable medium of communication"; and a meeting in Philadelphia during the same month reached the same conclusion. Meetings in New York City; Utica, New York; Bangor, Maine;

---

[104] *Niles' Register*, 48:403; the Cincinnati *Philanthropist*, April 8 and June 10, 1836; and H. B. Stowe, *Key to Uncle Tom's Cabin*, 397. The penalty was shortly made "immediate death."

[105] T. M. Owen, "An Alabama Protest Against Abolitionism in 1835," *Gulf States Historical Magazine* II (July, 1903), 30-31, and *Niles' Register*, 49:245.

[106] The Cincinnati *Philanthropist*, June 10, 1836, drew up a list of one hundred cases in Virginia, Kentucky, and Mississippi only.

[107] R. W. Bailey, *The Issue Presented in a Series of Letters on Slavery*, 35.

Portsmouth, New Hampshire; and Newark, New Jersey, reflected the temper of Northern opinion.[108] The New York *Evening Star* thought that these "vile pamphlets should be seized as common nuisances against the morality and peace of the community, as will (*sic*) effectually secure the public from being contaminated or exasperated by their inflammatory doctrines, either through the press or the postoffice, or any other medium. . . ." The Oneida County, New York, grand jury ruled that antislavery publications in the mails were inflammatory documents and as such should be destroyed.[109]

Though the Northern press was fairly unanimous in condemning the abolitionists' use of the mails to disseminate their propaganda, a few editors (mostly political opponents of the Jackson administration) interpreted Kendall's ruling as a threat to freedom of opinion. The Boston *Atlas* pointed out that the Postmaster General was actually expressing sanction of lawbreaking, and condoning an illegal act. The New York *Commercial Advertiser* thought it "the assumption of a dangerous authority that may be pleaded in *other* instances; it will be easy to make a pretext, a *precedent* being established," while the Schenectady *Cabinet* and the Boston *New England Advocate* believed Kendall's letter amounted to nullification.[110] The *New York Evening Post,* viewing Kendall's letter with "surprise and regret," said:

If, according to his ideas of patriotism, every postmaster may suspend the operations of the laws in his supreme discretion, we trust that Mr. Kendall may be permitted to retire from a post where such opinions have extensive influence. . . . Who gives a right to judge of what is incendiary and inflammatory? Was there any reservation of that sort in his oath of office?[111]

[108] *Niles' Register,* 48:454-456, and 49:9-12, 40; the New York *American,* September 12, 1835; and the Boston *Advertiser,* September 9, 1835.

[109] The Cincinnati *Philanthropist,* January 1, 1836, and *Niles' Register,* 49:78.

[110] All reprinted in *Niles' Register,* 48:448, and 49:45-46.

[111] Quoted by W. H. Smith, *The Political History of Slavery,* I:46. The editorial was probably written by William Leggett. As punishment for the protest, *The Evening Post* lost the patronage of publishing the list of uncalled-for letters at the New York post office; *Niles' Register,* 49:45.

As the controversy wore on, it became clear that it involved a highly important principle—that of the right of an unpopular minority to use the mails, without censorship, to plead its case to the public. As Elizur Wright, in the New York office of the American Anti Slavery Society, wrote to James Birney in 1835, "Let them press laws abridging our freedom of speech —so much the better."[112] The grand jury of Tuscaloosa County, Alabama, indicted R. G. Williams, publishing agent of the American Anti Slavery Society, for publishing and circulating *The Emancipator*. When Governor Gayle of Alabama requested his surrender from Governor Marcy of New York, he raised the interesting legal question of whether or not a person in one state could commit a crime in another state without leaving his own. Marcy refused to allow Williams' extradition, on the obvious ground that he had never been in Alabama.[113]

Neither did the disposition of abolitionist literature in the New York City post office tend to strengthen public confidence in the safety of the mails. Postmaster Gouverneur, after holding abolitionist papers from the mail, some weeks later requested from Kendall an order to resume transmission, hoping to settle the matter. When Kendall refused to give the order, Gouverneur asked the Society to desist voluntarily from mailing its literature through his office. This the Society refused to do, since it was willing to pay postage, standing on "the rights and privileges we possess in common with our fellow citizens." Lacking Kendall's authority, Gouverneur decided to hold the publications anyhow. Though the American Anti Slavery Society wished to test his decision in the courts, it decided to wait until public opinion was more favorable. Eventually, in a vaguely worded letter, Kendall agreed that the abolitionists had a right to distribute their literature in any state where their action was not specifically prohibited by law, but, he

[112] D. L. Dumond, ed., *The Letters of James G. Birney*, I:256.

[113] A. B. Hart, *Slavery and Abolition*, 289. Oliver Johnson, *William Lloyd Garrison and His Times*, 219, said the indictment was made on the basis of two sentences in one copy of *The Emancipator*.

told Gouverneur, "Were I situated as you are, I would do as you have done." There the matter rested.[114]

Two factors contributed to the shift of Northern sentiment to the abolitionist side in the mails controversy: the aggressive attitude of the Southern states, and the extremely good case put up by the American Anti Slavery Society. Hezekiah Niles, judging from the hundreds of newspapers he clipped for his *Register,* believed that Southern demands for severe and punitive antiabolitionist laws (some of which declared it "a duty of the Northern States to prohibit discussions," and asked for "a most fearful surveillance of the postoffice") concluded:

These things on the part of the South have caused a great reaction in the north, and thousands and thousands of those who felt entirely disposed, and really were so, to cooperate in putting down the abolitionists, through the force of public opinion . . . are halting in their action.[115]

When President Andrew Jackson approved Kendall's ruling and in his message to Congress in December of 1835 called attention to the advisability of a Federal law prohibiting the circulation of "incendiary publications intended to instigate the slaves to insurrection,"[116] the abolitionists were able to put their complete case before the public. The reply of the Executive Committee of the American Anti Slavery Society, addressed to Jackson, was a masterful piece of propaganda. The abolitionist case, they reminded Jackson, had not yet been heard; the Society had been condemned on charges that were vague, indefinite, and untrue. The accusation that the Society

[114] Correspondence between the American Anti Slavery Society and Gouverneur, and between Kendall and Gouverneur, *Niles' Register,* 48:447-448, and 49:8-9. Accounts of the dispute are given in Henry Wilson, *op. cit.,* I:267-269, and Bayard Tuckerman, *William Jay and the Constitutional Movement for the Abolition of Slavery,* 65-67. The abolitionists held Kendall's view a direct violation of Article VII of the Constitution.

[115] *Niles' Register,* 49:64-65.

[116] For Jackson's message, see J. D. Richardson, *Messages and Papers of the Presidents,* III:175 *et seq.* Earlier Jackson had advised Kendall that exposing subscribers to and receivers of abolition literature to public disapproval would curb its circulation; see his letter to Kendall, August 9, 1835, in J. S. Bassett, *The Correspondence of Andrew Jackson,* V:360-361.

intended to foment revolt was, they said, absurd in the light of the facts. In the first place, the Society had long been on record as opposing violence in abolishing slavery. Second, abolitionists mailed nothing to slaves, who ordinarily received no mail and who usually could not read. Last, the Society threw all its publications open to inspection, suggesting that a special congressional committee try to discover a single inflammatory passage in any of them. "We never intend," concluded the reply, "to surrender the liberty of speech, or of press, or of conscience—blessings we have inherited from our fathers, and which we mean, so far as we are able, to transmit unimpaired to our children."[117]

In reality, the charge of incendiarism levelled against the abolitionists was more imaginary than real. The aim of abolitionist societies, they constantly reiterated, was to convince the South and the nation of the sin of slaveholding by appeals to the national conscience. Examination of antislavery literature tends to bear out abolitionist claims of innocence. The publications seized at Charleston and burned were *The Emancipator* for August, 1835, number seven of *The Anti Slavery Record*, number three of *The Slave's Friend*, and *Human Rights* for July, 1835. Analysis of these issues fails to disclose "incendiary" material and indicates that they were probably planned for Northern consumption.[118] There is little evidence to show that

[117] Tappan, Jay, Cox, Rankin, and Wright, "The Protest of the American Anti Slavery Society," *A Collection of Valuable Documents*, 41-53, and Henry Wilson, *op. cit.*, I:268.

[118] The editor of *Human Rights* specifically denied any intent to circularize slaves, writing that the publications "sent to the slave states have been directed to professional and distinguished citizens, and in no instance, to our knowledge, to any slave or even free colored man." Robert Williams, the publishing agent of the American Anti Slavery Society, wrote a similar disclaimer, saying that all of the Society's publications "address not the slave but his master." See Joseph A. Del Porto's account of the affair, *A Study of American Antislavery Journals*, unpublished dissertation, Michigan State University, 1953, 210-13. *The Emancipator* contained: "Human Rights—The Necessity for their Discussion"; "Dr. Hopkins on Slavery: A Proposal to Republish"; "We Shall be Overrun with Them," an answer to fears of a flood of Negroes to the North; "The General Association of Massachusetts"; "Report of the Rhode Island Society"; a discussion of Lane Seminary and gradualism; an article on George Thompson; notes on antislavery society publications; "The General Treatment

the abolitionist societies at any time distributed in the South publications intended for slave consumption or to incite revolts.[119]

Yet it was widely believed in the South during the controversy over the mails that such was the abolitionists' intent, a view given official sanction by Jackson's message. Said one paper, "The Press with its herculean power is rolling off sheet after sheet of vile and incendiary matter which is scattered like firebrands over the land." An Alabama lawyer wrote in August, 1835, "The antislavery societies in the Northern and Middle States are doing all they can to destroy our domestic harmony by sending among us pamphlets, tracts, and newspapers—for the purpose of exciting dissatisfaction and insurrection among our slaves." The rival American Colonization Society did its share in propagating the legend, stating that the design of the American Anti Slavery Society was, "beyond a doubt, to foment a servile war in the South—they have been heard to say, blood must be shed, and the sooner the better. . . ."[120] Once established, the belief was difficult to erase, and no doubt remains widely accepted to this day.[121]

---

of Slaves in the Southwest"; two poems titled "The Sorrows of Yambo" and "A Negro Woman's Lamentation"; an account of a slave kidnapping. *The Anti Slavery Record* contained: the story of Stephen Downing, a fugitive slave; the story of a New York free Negro whose wife was taken back to slavery; "Slavery a Sin," an extract from the Declaration of the Ohio Anti Slavery Society; a report on free Negroes in Ohio; a slave kidnapping case; a criticism of the colonization plan; and an account of abolition meetings in Pittsburgh. *The Slave's Friend,* a juvenile, contained: the story of two Negro children and their capture in Africa; a poem, "The Poor Mother"; a story, "The Little Blind Boy"; the story of Henry Scott, the son of a fugitive slave; a Biblical dialogue on slavery; "What Can We Do?" an appeal for funds; three stories of Negro children; a prayer; a poem, "The Little Bird's Complaint"; and an article, "A Common Excuse," proving that abolition is possible.

[119] See also W. S. Savage, *op. cit.,* 11-12, for a similar conclusion.

[120] The Columbus, Georgia, *Republican Herald,* quoted by the Cincinnati *Philanthropist,* February 17, 1837; Hilary Herbert, *op. cit.,* 79; and William Jay, *Tendencies of the American Colonization Society and the American Anti Slavery Society,* 144.

[121] For examples, see *Niles' Register,* 48:439, 441, and 52:387; Nehemiah Adams, *A Southside View of Slavery,* 8-10; and the accusation of Governor Randolph of Virginia, quoted by the Salem, Ohio, *Anti Slavery Bugle,* September 27, 1851. Adams, 107-108, repeated the common Southern story

Changes of public opinion, as well as a disagreement over the proper method to employ, were largely responsible for the failure of Congress in 1836 to pass legislation controlling the abolitionist press and its use of the mails. Shortly after the delivery of Jackson's message, Beardsley of New York advised preparation of a bill referring the matter to the House Committee on the Post Office and Post Roads. This was done, but the Committee's report never appeared before the House. The question was really settled in the Senate, where Calhoun suggested referring the issue to a special committee of himself, two Northerners, and two Southerners, since the Senate Committee on the Post Office and Post Roads had but one Southern member.[122] This was agreed, and on February 4, 1836, the committee reported, though only Calhoun and Mangum of North Carolina, of the five-man committee, had assented to the report.

The point of disagreement lay in whether or not control of the mails in this matter should be in Federal hands, as Jackson had suggested, or within the power of the states. Calhoun argued that a Federal law would infringe upon the states' reserved powers in violation of the first amended article of the Constitution, and that it might imply that Congress could legislate on slavery in the states. "If Congress may this year decide what incendiary publications are, they may decide next year what they are not, and thus laden the mails with real or corrupt abolitionism," said Calhoun. "It belongs to the States, and not to Congress, to determine what is or what is not calculated to disturb their security."[123] Instead, Calhoun intro-

that abolitionists distributed pictures of white women and Negro men "in unequivocal relations." Another prevalent rumor, that handkerchiefs printed with "incendiary pictures" were sent South, was officially denied by Mayor Otis of Boston, *Niles' Register,* 45:43. In reply to the charge that it had printed "incendiary pictures," *The Anti Slavery Record* retaliated by printing pictures from stereotype casts made in New York for Southern newspaper advertisements for runaway slaves; see the end page of the issue of July, 1836.

[122] For a complete account of the Congressional debates, see W. S. Savage, "Abolitionist Literature in the Mails, 1835-1836," *Journal of Negro History* XII, 170-74; and *Register of Debates, 24th Congress, 1st Session,* I:383 *et seq.*

[123] Alexander Harris, *A Review of the Political Conflict in America,* 77.

duced a bill designed to place regulatory power over the mails within the states, providing that no deputy postmaster should receive nor transmit "any pamphlet, newspaper, handbill, or any other paper, printed or written, or pictorial representation, touching the subject of slavery, addressed to a person or postoffice in a state territory, or district whose laws forbade such material or to deliver such to anyone except those entitled by state law to receive it."[124]

The ensuing debate in the Senate was inconclusive. Davis of Massachusetts pointed out that if state law could define "incendiary," the Declaration of Independence could already be legally barred from the mails of several Southern States. King of Georgia agreed with Calhoun that state law was supreme in this instance, and that the Federal power should be enlisted only insofar as it might assist in its enforcement. Daniel Webster believed the proposal violated the right of property, since mail was the property of the addressee; Buchanan of Pennsylvania favored Calhoun's suggestion, but only on grounds of necessity and not principle.[125]

Calhoun's major speech in defense of the bill came on April 12. Basing his argument on state sovereignty over slavery, he explained that while the power over the mails was delegated to Congress, the power over slavery was reserved to the states. In a conflict between reserved and delegated powers, the lower yielded to the higher; therefore the states' power of regulation of the mails in regard to slavery was paramount. In answer to objections, he denied that the principle of such postal regulation might ever be applied to matters of morals and religion; that no rights of speech or press were violated by his bill; that few postmasters would abuse their new authority by prying into personal mail; and he pointed out that his proposal applied not to all abolition literature, but only to those kinds prohibited by the laws of certain states.[126]

[124] The full text of the committee report is in *Niles' Register*, 49:391, 408-410.

[125] Various points of view are summarized by Savage, *op. cit.*, 175-180.

[126] Richard Crallé, *The Works of John C. Calhoun*, I:509-533.

The debates over Calhoun's proposal elicited unfavorable comment from North and South. It was noticeable, said a number of editors, that his bill gave the deputy postmaster the power to interpret the term "incendiarism" and the right to bar offending materials from the mails. Such a law might well be two-edged, wrote the editor of the Natchez, Louisiana, *Courier,* who believed a man would much rather "receive a bushel of abolition literature, which could easily be burned, than have his own private affairs pried into by every rascally deputy postmaster or clerk, who might choose to say he suspected they contained incendiary matter."[127] Noticeably, the bill's wording might be interpreted to include the inspection of private correspondence, a clear violation of the citizen's right to privacy.

The difficulties of distinguishing what was "incendiary," a term never clearly defined in the South, were immediately apparent.[128] James G. Birney, in a lucid analysis of Calhoun's argument, pointed out that there was a great likelihood of misuse of the terms "inflammatory" and "incendiary," and that until they were fully and clearly defined, all liberty of thought was endangered.[129] The Philadelphia *Evening Star* believed that such regulatory mail laws constituted the first and most important step in an attack upon civil liberty, and characterized Calhoun's bill as "a conspiracy against the rights of freemen." The Boston *Daily Advocate* termed it "an absurdity . . . , as abhorrent to our free notions as a censorship of the press," while the Dayton, Ohio, *Republican* went further:

The next step will be to stop the circulation of all antimasonic papers, then those that are opposed to the administration. This done,

[127] Quoted by *The Anti Slavery Record* II (December, 1836), 164.
[128] See the Lexington, Kentucky, *Intelligencer,* quoted by the New Richmond, Ohio, *Philanthropist,* January 29, 1836.
[129] The New Richmond, Ohio, *Philanthropist,* January 8, 1836. As an example Birney cited the postmaster at Augusta, Kentucky, who threw out copies of *The Philanthropist* addressed to subscribers in Pittsburgh when the mail passed through the Augusta office on its way up the Ohio river— a case of a postal employee censoring mail not addressed to his office; *ibid.,* February 26, 1836.

and their censorship fairly established, we will become the *white* slaves of the masters of the black slaves of the South. Lynch law will become the exclusive law of the land, and will be enforced against any who dare to utter sentiments not in accordance with those of their masters.[130]

The state legislature of Vermont protested the bill, and the abolitionists warned that the principle of censorship that Calhoun's proposal contained could be extended to include the opinions of any group.[131]

While debate recurred sporadically in the Senate, the House Committee on the Post Office and Post Roads in May brought in a bill which reversed the position taken by the Senate committee. It prohibited, under penalty, any postmaster from detaining "any letter, package, pamphlet, or newspaper with intent to prevent the delivery of same." In June this passed the House. In the Senate the Calhoun bill, revised to make the receiving rather than the sending office responsible for transmitting suspicious matter, lost 25 to 19, the vote splitting on sectional lines. Admitting defeat, the Senate, with a few minor changes, accepted the House bill the same month, and the two were brought into agreement in July. The post office now had a definite policy based upon the principle of non-interference, and though the law was frequently circumvented in subsequent years, the principle remained.[132] "It can be seen," conceded the Richmond *Compiler,* "that no law can ever be constitutionally passed for the purpose of restraining the fanatics of the North in their crusade against our rights."[133]

Failure to control the distribution of abolitionist literature by Federal legislation did not mean, however, that the mails were thrown open at once to the antislavery presses. Southern states which did not already have laws governing the circula-

[130] *Ibid.,* January 15, July 1, 1836, and *The Liberator,* April 2, 1836.

[131] *Niles' Register,* 51:210, Garrison's editorial in *The Liberator,* April 16, 1836, and William Jay in the Utica, N. Y., *Friend of Man,* July 22, 1840.

[132] Savage, *op. cit.,* 175-189, and Lindsay Rogers, *The Postal Power of Congress; A Study in Constitutional Expansion,* 139-144.

[133] *Niles' Register,* 49:236.

tion of "incendiary" matter quickly passed them, and other states strengthened existing legislation. South Carolina depended upon its law of 1820, and Kentucky on laws passed in 1799 and 1831. North Carolina had already passed similar legislation in 1830, Louisiana and Mississippi in 1831, and Alabama in 1832 and 1835. Maryland's law of 1835 sufficed for a time; Missouri enacted legislation of the usual type in 1837; and Georgia relied upon local statutes. Virginia, in 1836, passed a law requiring postmasters to notify justices of the peace whenever they saw "incendiary" publications; that officer would then judge their offensiveness, burn them publicly if they violated the law, and arrest the addressee if he subscribed to them. Throughout the years the Southern states reaffirmed and strengthened these laws, adding new interpretations and closing loopholes.[134]

The Federal mails law of 1836 was largely a dead letter in the South, where it was generally interpreted to mean that the Federal power over the mails ceased at the reception point. Cases of violation of both the spirit and the letter of the law were frequent, particularly in Virginia, where the state law of 1836 gave postal officials clear authority to censorship of the mails. *The Liberator* had no Southern subscribers, but other antislavery publications reported numerous cases of interference with subscribers' copies. Birney's *Philanthropist*, which had a fairly large subscription list in the upper South, reported a growing number of complaints after 1836. The Salem, Ohio, *Anti Slavery Bugle*, the Washington *National Era*, the New York *National Anti Slavery Standard*, *The Emancipator*, and the New Hampshire *Herald of Freedom* all suffered difficulties with Southern postmasters and vigilance committees.[135]

Newspapers other than those published by antislavery soci-

---

[134] Summaries of Southern legislation 1820-1861 may be found in Eaton, *op. cit.*, 268-269, and Savage, *op. cit.*, 5-6.

[135] The Cincinnati *Philanthropist*, January 1, 1845, and February 2, 1836; the Salem *Anti Slavery Bugle*, August 21, 1844 and October 30, 1846; *The National Era*, October 17 and 24, 1850, November 13, 1851, January 15, 1857, and January 6, 1859; *The National Anti Slavery Standard*, October 20, 1855. See also Eaton, *op. cit.*, 208.

eties were also destroyed or detained if they contained objectionable matter. In 1838 copies of the Baltimore *Religious Magazine* containing an article called "Bible Slavery" were taken from the post office at Petersburg, Virginia, and burned. The Circleville, Ohio, *Religious Telescope,* published by the United Brethren, was burned at Glenville, Virginia, in 1853. The Pittsburgh *Dispatch* was burned at Wirt Courthouse, Virginia; the Pittsburgh *Saturday Visitor* could not be delivered to subscribers in Charlestown, Virginia; and the postmaster at Parkersburg, Virginia, refused to give subscribers copies of the *Western Christian Advocate* of Cincinnati.[136] *Harper's Magazine* was proscribed in Virginia and North Carolina. Other Northern publications banned from the mails in Southern localities were the New York *Herald,* the New York *Eagle,* the Philadelphia *Saturday Evening Post,* the Greenfield, Massachusetts, *Gazette,* the New Bedford, Massachusetts, *Mercury,* the Philadelphia *Daily Republic,* the Boston *Courier,* the Springfield, Massachusetts, *Republican,* and the Boston *Atlas,* while Greeley's New York *Tribune* in particular was singled out for attack.[137]

Probably the single Southern incident of importance involving the mails was the rather complex case of John M. Barrett, who was arrested in 1849 in Spartanburg, South Carolina, under an 1820 law which provided a year in jail and a thousand-dollar fine for a white man who brought into the state "any paper with intent to disturb the peace and security of the state, in relation to the slaves thereof." Barrett, an Indiana freesoiler, was travelling through the South to gather statistics for a gazetteer to be published by Harwood and Company of New York. He was accused of placing in the post office several bundles of printed letters signed "Brutus," ad-

---

[136] C. D. Cleveland, *Anti Slavery Addresses of 1844 and 1845,* 33; *The Anti Slavery Bugle,* April 10, 1846, September 10, 1853, and July 25, 1857; and *The National Era,* October 17, 1850.

[137] "The New Reign of Terror," *Anti Slavery Tract Number 4* (New York, 1860), 10-12, cited forty such cases of destruction or refusal to deliver. See also *The Anti Slavery Bugle,* December 1, 1848, October 7, 1854, October 4 and 18, 1856; *The National Anti Slavery Standard,* February 6, 1845, January 17, 1857, and June 29, 1848; and the Charleston, S. C., *Standard,* September 18, 1856.

dressed to local citizens. These were seized from the mails by the Spartanburg vigilance committee. Barrett, however, claimed that he did not know what the letters contained, and that they had been given to him by a friend for mailing.

In addition, a letter addressed to one John Thompson at the Spartanburg post office was, it was believed, really meant for Barrett. Local authorities claimed that it must contain instructions for fomenting trouble among slaves. But Barrett would not accept the letter; when Postmaster Legg was subpoenaed as a witness and asked to produce and open the Thompson letter, he refused on the ground that he was forbidden by postal regulations to do so. Though Postmaster General Collamer upheld Legg's action, Legg was jailed briefly in contempt of court. Barrett was placed under $2000 bond, which was promptly raised for him in the North, and the case was eventually discharged a few months later when it began to take on the proportions of a *cause célèbre*.[138]

The charges against Barrett were vague and difficult to prove. The "Brutus" letters in question were hardly incendiary, since they were composed wholly of attacks on the domination of South Carolina by slaveholders, and appealed to non-slaveholders and poor whites to unite in opposition to aristocratic rule.[139] Barrett, in fact, received substantial encouragement from local yeomanry after his arrest, and Southern newspaper opinion was to some extent divided on whether or not the letters were really inflammatory. The Raleigh, North Carolina, *Register* thought that in arresting Barrett, South Carolina had done great injustice to the Southern cause. The South, it believed, had "infinitely more to fear from the adoption of interference with the mails than she has to hope from it."[140]

[138] A complete running account appeared in *The Anti Slavery Bugle*, August 18 and November 10, 1849, and *The National Anti Slavery Standard*, July 25, August 2, 9, 16, 30, and October 25, 1849.

[139] The "Brutus" letters are reprinted in full in *The National Era*, August 16, 1849. Some Southern papers claimed the letters actually contained a complicated secret code message for organizing a revolt.

[140] Reprinted by *The National Anti Slavery Standard*, August 30, 1849. Similar editorials from the Nashville *True Whig*, the New Orleans *Courier*, and the Edgefield, South Carolina, *Advertiser* were reprinted in the issue of September 13, 1849.

In general the Southern interpretation of the Federal mails law of 1836 held that state laws, governing the reception and distribution of "incendiary" matter through the post office, were supreme. Virginia's Attorney General Tucker summarized the Southern view by stating that Federal power over the mails ceased when they reached their destination; "At that point, the power of the State becomes exclusive. Whether the citizens shall receive the mail matter, is a question exclusively for her determination."[141] Since most Southern states had statutes allowing inspection of the mails by the postmaster or other local authorities, the Federal law was effectively nullified.[142] In 1857 United States Attorney General Cushing gave this interpretation additional sanction when he ruled that a Mississippi statute forbidding delivery of "incendiary" matter was not in conflict with the Federal law of 1836, and that no postmaster was required to deliver materials "the design and tendency of which are to promote insurrections."[143] Similarly, Postmaster General Holt in 1859 ruled that the Virginia statute of 1836 did not conflict with Federal law. To the postmaster at Falls Church, Virginia, he wrote that any postmaster might, after inspection of the mails, withhold delivery of any matter of "incendiary character." "The people of Virginia," he said, "may not only forbid the introduction and dissemination of such documents within their borders, but, if brought there in the mails, they may, by appropriate legal proceedings, have them destroyed."[144]

In effect, then, the argument had returned by the late 'fifties to very nearly the same state it was in 1835, with the exception of the fact that removal from the mails and destruction of

[141] "The New Reign of Terror," *op. cit.,* 7.

[142] However, Second Assistant Postmaster General Warren ruled in 1851 that the postmaster at Eufala, Alabama, must deliver copies of *The National Era* to local subscribers, though the postmaster protested that the paper was "incendiary" and its delivery forbidden by Alabama law; *The National Era,* October 24, 1850, and November 13, 1857.

[143] *Official Opinions of the Attorneys General,* VIII:501.

[144] "The New Reign of Terror," *op. cit.,* 9. For a discussion of the implications of the Cushing and Holt decisions, see this and *The National Era,* December 15, 1859.

abolitionist literature by 1859 had legal sanction, and that the laws applied to all types of mail. Since the abolitionists had given up their mail campaign by the early 'forties, the result of the controversy did not significantly affect them. Coming as it did, however, during the opening years of the petition controversy and the struggle over the freedom of the press, the dispute over the mails strengthened the abolition cause by merging it with the larger and more important cause of civil liberty. The nationalization of the question, the extremity of the Southern position, and the intemperance of Southern opinion, coupled with the inability of either side to agree on what was incendiary and what was not, made the question of the mails, brief though its period of discussion was, a factor of some importance in building favor in the North for the abolitionist movement.

Abolitionism and Academic Freedom

III

BEFORE THE CIVIL WAR the intellectual life of the South was controlled by a relatively small group of wealthy landowners. Their ownership of the Negro (the South's chief source of labor) and of the best Southern land gave the larger slaveholders an influence on Southern life highly disproportionate to their numbers, and control as well over the middle class and poor white segments of society. Fully aware that it was slavery that made their position possible, the slaveholders were particularly sensitive to anything which might threaten or weaken that institution. They were convinced, therefore, that education in the South, white and Negro alike, must be governed by interests friendly to slavery.

There was, of course, general agreement at the South that the Negro should receive no schooling at all. First of all, the ominous fact that both Denmark Vesey and Nat Turner could read (or so it was supposed) was not lost on Southern minds.

Second, the theory that slavery was a "positive good" for Negro and white man was based on the supposition that the Negro was, by reason of his innate inferiority, incapable of being educated; Negro education was thus a contradiction in terms. By the early 'thirties most Southern states had laws on their statute books forbidding the teaching of Negroes, though they were often disregarded. One planter boasted of twenty slaves who could read, and Frederick Douglass, the most famous fugitive slave of them all, had been taught to read by his own mistress. The instruction at home of one or two trusted slaves was usually not regarded as a serious infringement of the law, but the establishment of Negro schools was quite a different matter. Despite the obvious pressures involved, there were nevertheless about a dozen Negro schools in various parts of the South, taught by dedicated Southern white men and women. As the temperature of the proslavery argument rose, the majority of these schools disappeared.[1] Missouri passed a law against Negro education in 1847, while Tennessee, Kentucky, and Maryland passed no specific legislation, depending rather upon the force of public opinion. To most Southerners, a slave who could read was potentially dangerous; therefore

. . . the laws in question are imperiously demanded by a regard for public safety, not because 'slavery is most compatible with profound ignorance,' but because . . . slaves would have placed in their hands those 'other documents, books, and papers,' inculcating insubordination and rebellion.[2]

[1] John Hope Franklin, *From Slavery to Freedom: A History of the American Negro*, 200-1. Joseph Turner, editor of the Georgia *Countryman*, declared in 1862 that so little attention was paid to these laws in his community that they "have never prevented a negro who desired it from learning to read. I have never known a case of punishment for its violation"; Eaton, *Growth of Southern Civilization*, 80. There was also some feeling in the South that education of the poorer white class was perhaps unnecessary; see Eaton, *Freedom of Thought in the Old South*, 144-53, and "The Modern Abomination of Free Schools," Richmond *Examiner*, December 28, 1856. Edgar W. Knight, *A Documentary History of Education in the South* provides a wealth of information on Southern education prior to 1860.

[2] "Ought Our Slaves Be Taught to Read?" *DeBow's Review* XVIII (January, 1855), 52-3. A complete list of the laws governing Negro literacy

And though the laws were often overlooked by lenient masters, only a small percentage of slaves possessed the barest rudiments of an education.[3]

The educated free Negro was accounted even more dangerous than the educated slave, and in many parts of the South the teaching of freed slaves was specifically prohibited by law.[4] Typical was Missouri's act of 1847, which provided a $500 fine and six months' imprisonment for operating a free Negro school. A Georgia act levied a $500 fine and imprisonment on a white man who taught a free Negro to read, and the same fine plus a whipping on one free Negro who taught another.[5] The Southern attitude toward Negro education was perhaps most clearly expressed in the Virginia House of Delegates in 1832:

> We have, as far as possible, closed every avenue by which light can enter . . . [their] minds. If we could extinguish the capacity to see the light, our work would be completed; they would then be on a level with the beasts of the field, and we should be safe.[6]

Nevertheless, a surprisingly large number of free Negroes

in the South is cited in H. K. Beale, *A History of the Freedom of Teaching in American Schools*, 120-26. A useful brief exposition of Southern educational principles and attitudes is Clement Eaton, *Growth of Southern Civilization*, 114-19, 311-12.

[3] C. G. Woodson, *The Education of the Negro Before 1861*, estimated that ten percent could read, a figure most authorities agree is too high. Amos Dresser once calculated that about one out of every fifty slaves could read and write; a Georgian guessed that about 5000 slaves in his state were literate. There is no trustworthy method of determination. See John Hope Franklin, *op. cit.*, 201. However, it seemed to be a fairly common practice for masters to leave orders and funds in their wills for the education of manumitted slaves until the tightening of Southern law stopped the practice; Helen T. Catterall, *Judicial Cases Concerning Slavery*, Index, "Education, Manumitted Slaves." Catholic schools seem to have admitted some Negroes, according to Madeleine H. Rice, *American Catholic Opinion in the Antislavery Controversy*, 57.

[4] E. B. Reuter, *The American Race Problem*, 261-62.

[5] H. A. Trexler, *Slavery in Missouri 1804-1865*, 83, and Catterall, *op. cit.*, III:33.

[6] William Goodell, *The American Slave Code in Theory and Practice*, 323.

seem to have learned the fundamentals of literacy, especially in the upper South. In 1820 there were two hundred adult Negroes studying in the Baltimore schools; free Negroes in Virginia and North Carolina seem to have received instruction from other free Negroes and occasionally white teachers, and there is evidence that elsewhere Negroes studied privately without much hindrance. Texas, Tennessee, Kentucky, Florida, and Maryland did not legally ban the teaching of free Negroes, though after the 'thirties the pressure of community opinion undoubtedly kept their instruction at a minimum. Some of the best Negro schools were found in Washington, where a Negro teacher named John Adams established the first school in the District of Columbia for members of his race.[7]

Early in the antislavery controversy, the slaveholding interests in the South recognized the dangers of allowing free and open discussion of slavery in the schools and colleges. Sentiment against the institution, it was feared, might eventually become strong enough to lead some future generation of conscience-stricken slaveholders to destroy their own means of dominance just as the abolitionists predicted. Therefore the slaveowners hoped to make certain, when slavery became an important issue after 1831, that the schools refrained from discussions of the system and that educators in the schools neither encouraged nor tolerated any open expression of ideas about it. The rapid unification of Southern opinion behind slavery made it possible to justify, to a greater extent than before, more rigid supervision of the Southern educational system. As a correspondent for *DeBow's Review* explained:

When the public mind of our section was divided as to the justice and propriety of the institution, when probably a large majority of even our own people regarded the existence of slavery among us as a blot on our fair name . . ., it was not then to be wondered at that we should remain indifferent as to the views presented to our youth on this subject, and that we should carelessly allow them to peruse, even in their tender years, works in which slavery was denounced as

[7] Franklin, *op. cit.*, 226-27.

an unmitigated evil. . . . Such a course may have been defensible at that period, but tell me, what show of propriety is there in its continuance at the present day? We have become awake to the rightfulness and justice of our stand.[8]

Not only were Southern leaders anxious to clear the schools of any antislavery sentiment, but they were equally convinced that teachers ought to foster in Southern youth the idea that slavery was a positive good, the belief that upon it the South's wellbeing and future rested. "Young men," said one Southerner, ". . . ought to be prepared by education to make useful citizens in the society where their property is, and where they are destined to live."[9] This meant, the Richmond *Enquirer* explained, that.

Every school and college in the South should teach that Slave Society is the common, natural, rightful, and normal state of society. . . . They should also teach that no other form of society is, in general, right or expedient.[10]

Keeping antislavery opinion out of the common schools of the South was a relatively simple matter, since these schools were closely controlled by the communities which they served. For that matter, common schools usually found little reason to introduce the topic at all. Institutions of higher learning, less closely allied to local interests and possessing a wider range of interests, were more likely to touch upon slavery. Control of ideas in these institutions was hardly more difficult. State universities depended upon state funds and reflected rather accurately the demands of state legislatures. Private colleges, governed by boards of trustees drawn from the upper brackets of Southern society, were equally sensitive to prevailing opinion. Dependent as they were upon public support, Southern colleges and universities had nothing to gain by an unsympathetic discussion of slavery. Neither did the majority of

[8] "Our Schoolbooks," *DeBow's Review* XXVIII (1860), 435-36.
[9] Quoted by Eaton, *op. cit.*, 211.
[10] The Richmond, Va., *Enquirer*, August 29, 1856.

teachers in the South usually have much reason to discuss, much less criticize, the slave system. Teachers reflected and agreed with public opinion, and for the most part had no great interest in opening what was assumed to be a closed question.[11]

By 1840, slavery as a topic of discussion had been virtually banned in educational institutions throughout the South. By 1850 the control of Southern education by slaveholding interests was virtually complete. The few disturbances that rippled the surface of educational calm in the South occurred, with one notable exception, in the border states. In general after 1840 there existed in Southern colleges and universities a rigorous regimentation of opinion concerning slavery and topics related to it. Student liberty of expression on the subject did not exist in any practical sense; and in the words of a North Carolina editor, faculties had been "thoroughly sifted and weeded of those who might covertly circulate opinions not in sympathy with our social institutions."[12]

The trend of Southern opinion may be illustrated by the rapid disappearance of antislavery sentiment in Southern colleges. In 1832 Judge William Gaston, in a commencement address at the University of North Carolina, criticized slavery on both economic and moral grounds without significant opposition. Five years later George Tucker of the University of Virginia, in his *Laws of Wages, Profits and Rents*, freely predicted the death of the institution on economic grounds.[13] However, these were exceptions and not the rule. The Reverend David Nelson, a Presbyterian minister and also an agent of the American Anti Slavery Society, helped to establish

[11] A reason may be indicated by the Richmond *Examiner's* statement that it was "an unwritten law" of the South "to shoot an abolition schoolmaster." In 1857 one Kentucky schoolmaster was beaten for possessing a volume of Wesley's sermons that included one against slavery. See Beale, *op. cit.*, 148, 150.

[12] Virginius Dabney, *Liberalism in the South*, 53, and Eaton, *op. cit.*, 204.

[13] Gaston's speech went through five printed editions; Tucker, however, in his *History of the United States*, became the apologist of slavery. See Eaton, *op. cit.*, 200-201.

Marion College at Palmyra, Missouri, in 1832, and became its first president. The antislavery character of his staff immediately caused trouble; his professors were publicly heckled and some of the school's pamphlets and books were burned by a mob. Marion students who attempted to establish a Negro Sunday School were threatened, and a slave girl whipped for attending it. In 1836 Nelson read a communication at a religious meeting from a Colonel Muldrow, offering $10,000 to begin a fund to indemnify masters for loss of slaves when and if emancipated. This eventually forced Nelson to resign his post and leave the state. After his departure, the Marion faculty forbade the students to converse with slaves, to circulate antislavery literature, or to hold public or private meetings to discuss slavery.[14] By 1859 the strength of public opinion was so great that President Barnard of the University of Mississippi was very nearly dismissed because he, with two faculty members, voted to expel a student who had severely beaten Barnard's Negro servant.[15]

The sensitivity of Southern feeling was nowhere made clearer than in the celebrated case of Professor Benjamin S. Hedrick of the University of North Carolina. Hedrick was a native North Carolinian, educated at the University and at Harvard. Brought up in one of North Carolina's antislavery communities, he came into contact with abolition groups in the North during his stay there in the 'fifties, though there is no evidence that he expressed himself publicly on the subject after he began teaching at North Carolina in 1854.[16] Suspecting the University of harboring Northern sympathizers, William Holden,

[14] "Fourth Annual Report of the American Anti Slavery Society," *Quarterly Anti Slavery Magazine* II (July, 1837), 395-97; Trexler, *op. cit.*, 119; and D. L. Dumond, ed., *The Letters of James G. Birney*, I:332n.; Benjamin G. Merkel, "The Abolition Aspects of Missouri's Antislavery Controversy," *Missouri Historical Review* XLIV (April, 1950), 232-54.

[15] For a complete account, see John Fulton, ed., *The Memoirs of Frederick A. P. Barnard*, 246-53. Barnard later became president of Columbia University.

[16] J. G. deR. Hamilton, *Benjamin Sherwood Hedrick*, and *The National Anti Slavery Standard*, October 5, 1856, give accounts of the Hedrick case; also Dabney, *op. cit.*, 211, and Eaton, *op. cit.*, 203-204.

editor of the North Carolina *Standard,* wrote during the campaign of 1856, "If there be Frémont men among us, let them be silenced or required to leave. . . . Let our schools and seminaries of learning be scrutinized; and if black Republicans be found in them, let them be driven out."[17]

A week after Holden's editorial appeared, a recent graduate accused Hedrick of stating that if North Carolina had a Frémont ticket (which it had not) he would support it. The professor replied through the columns of the *Standard* that he was not an abolitionist, but thought that the South for its own good should critically re-examine the slavery system—the interests of North Carolina were wholly at his heart, and he believed the state would find greater prosperity in freedom. As for Frémont, he simply believed him to be "on the right side of the great question."[18]

Aroused opinion led the Secretary of the Board of Trustees to write to President Swain, asking for Hedrick's dismissal, but the faculty voted only to censure Hedrick for expressing political opinions in violation of college tradition. "While we feel bound to declare our sentiments frankly on this occasion, we entertain none other than feelings of personal respect and kindliness for the subject of them," read the resolution, which passed by a 12-1 vote. Public sentiment remained unsatisfied by the faculty's gesture, however, and urged on by Holden and other editors, the Board of Trustees finally requested Hedrick's resignation. President Swain replied that Hedrick, who had "the courage of a lion and the obstinacy of a mule," refused to resign. If Hedrick were to be dismissed, said Swain, the dismissal had best be deferred and made on non-political grounds; by charter the University could not dismiss a professor for his political or religious opinions, and though Hedrick might have violated college tradition, he could not legally be fired. The Executive Committee of the Board de-

[17] Hamilton, *op. cit.,* 8.

[18] See Hedrick's defense, *The National Anti Slavery Standard,* October 25, 1856; the Salem, Ohio, *Anti Slavery Bugle,* October 25, 1856; and the editorial of the New York *Times,* October 14, 1856.

cided to censure Hedrick once more, but public pressure became so powerful that it was soon forced to remove him officially on the ground that his continued presence was injurious to the University.[19]

Hedrick's dismissal graphically illustrated the inability of the South to tolerate the most moderate and reasonable criticism of slavery from within its own boundaries and within its own educational institutions. The great Francis Lieber of South Carolina College nearly lost his position in 1855 when the Columbia, South Carolina, *Times* discovered in the *Encyclopaedia Americana* (of which Lieber had been an editor in 1828) an article derogatory to slavery.[20] As President Barnard of the University of Mississippi pointed out, a Southern university was at the mercy of the Southern public, which, through the legislatures or the trustees, could ruin the institution at a moment's notice on charges that might be false, or partly false, or inspired by hysteria or bigotry.[21]

The case of Dr. Francis Lieber of South Carolina College, one of the more liberal institutions in the South, furnished another example of how the prevailing atmosphere of intellectual repression prevented one of the South's best political thinkers from contributing to a consideration of the region's most important problem. Lieber, nationally-known as a political philosopher, entertained strong antislavery opinions which he kept to himself for twenty years; in fact, his silence itself was construed by some to indicate antislavery sentiments, so that by saying nothing Lieber apparently incriminated himself even more. He once prepared an excellent series of letters on the slavery issue intended for John C. Calhoun, but felt

[19] Hamilton, *op. cit.*, 35-41. See also Hugh T. Lefler, *The History of North Carolina*, II:479-80. Hedrick moved to the North and joined the government service, but returned to North Carolina after the Civil War and played an important part in North Carolina's reconstruction. Henry Harrisse, an instructor, who dissented because he believed Hedrick's case was badly handled, left the University and bitterly attacked the Southern policy of academic repression in the French *Revue de L'Ouest* of New Orleans. See Eaton, *op. cit.*, 205.

[20] *The Anti Slavery Bugle*, May 31, 1856.

[21] John Fulton, *op. cit.*, 53.

constrained by the pressure of opinion to leave them unpublished. Lieber and Hedrick were no doubt only two of many Southerners who kept quiet, indicating how much the South lost by suppressing academic freedom, and how its ability to discuss its own problems suffered from its fear of open debate.[22]

In the border states of the upper South there was much wider latitude of academic expression. Dr. Tomlinson of Augusta College, Kentucky, held antislavery views and expressed them in public for more than a decade.[23] Two members of the faculty of Kentucky's Centre College served as officers of the state antislavery society organized at the college in 1835, and J. G. Birney held a teaching position there in 1834.[24] Kentucky too was the scene of the only important experiment in biracial education held in slave territory. Berea College, founded in 1858 by John G. Fee, admitted both Negro and white students; but an unfortunate misinterpretation of a remark made by Fee concerning John Brown led to trouble. In December of 1859 an armed group of sixty-two citizens visited the college and ordered the faculty to leave the state within ten days; Governor Magoffin refused Fee's appeal for police protection and the faculty moved to Cincinnati. Yet Berea existed for a year in a slave state without serious opposition, and had not the current excitement over Harper's Ferry precipitated a popular fear of Negro insurrection, it might have lasted much longer. There was, even after the withdrawal of the school to Ohio, some protest in Kentucky against the action of the mob.[25]

[22] Richard Hofstadter and Walter Metzger, *The Development of Academic Freedom in the United States*, 256-7. Hofstadter's and Metzger's discussion pp. 253-61, "Slavery and Abolition," is a good brief summary of the issue. See also Frank Friedel, *Francis Lieber: Nineteenth Century Liberal*.

[23] *The Liberator*, August 11, 1848.

[24] William Birney, *James G. Birney and His Times*, 154-55. Birney, however, was later refused a permanent appointment because of his views; Dumond, *op. cit.*, I:277-80.

[25] *The Autobiography of John G. Fee*, 124-128, and Fee's letter to *The National Anti Slavery Standard*, September 12, 1857. The land upon which Berea was built was a gift of Cassius Clay, the Kentucky emancipationist.

At Cumberland University in Lebanon, Tennessee, Judge Nathan Green, a slaveowner himself, did not hesitate to express his antislavery views in his law classes. Though he was attacked in the newspapers as "a dangerous man to the South, not fit to instruct Southern youth," he still was not dismissed.[26] Probably the clearest example of suppression of opinion in the upper South occurred in 1855 at Bethany, the Reverend Alexander Campbell's college in northwest Virginia. Of the 130 theological students being trained there for the ministry of the Disciples of Christ, thirty were from the North, and of these some ten or more held antislavery opinions. After he referred to the "sin of slaveholding" in a sermon, a student from Canada named Burns was saved from a local mob only by the intervention of law officers. A student petition that Burns and his friends restrict themselves solely to expounding the Gospel, approved by President Campbell and the faculty, resulted in the departure of twenty Northern students rather than "surrender the right of speech and submit to the rule of a mob."[27]

The strong sectionalist movement and the rapid growth of the "positive good" theory of slavery led to an attempt to insulate the South's educational system even more completely against antislavery discussion and opinion. That Northern textbooks were standard in the Southern schools was a fact long deprecated by Southern leaders. George Fitzhugh felt that:

All books in the whole range of moral science, if not written by Southern authors, within the last twenty or thirty years, inculcate abolition either directly or indirectly. If written before that time, even by Southern authors, they are likely to be as absurd and as dangerous as the Declaration of Independence, or the Virginia Bill of Rights. It is all important that we should write our own books. It matters little who makes our shoes.[28]

[26] W. P. Bone, *A History of Cumberland University, 1842-1935,* 79-83, and the Savannah, Ga., *News,* July 10, 1858.

[27] *The Anti Slavery Bugle,* January 19, 1855. The Reverend Campbell's proslavery views were well known; see *The Liberator,* April 30, 1836.

[28] George Fitzhugh, "Southern Thought," *DeBow's Review* XXIII (1857), 341.

As early as 1835 *The Georgia Telegraph* asked for a censorship of Northern school texts, and a year later Duff Green, a relative of John C. Calhoun, obtained a charter in South Carolina for a textbook publishing firm. *The Southern Educational Journal* announced a series of textbooks "carefully revised and freed from all objectionable pieces," and one Edwin Herriot advertised in the *Southern Home Journal of Education and Domestic Industry* for a series of texts which would "discourage Northern agents and their schoolbooks" and exclude "the pernicious doctrines of abolitionism." "It surely becomes us," resolved the Trustees of Jefferson College in Mississippi, "to preserve our children from any influence that might mislead their judgment or weaken their patriotism."[29]

By 1850 the nativist movement in Southern education had gained wide support. Censorship of Northern-printed texts became fairly common in the South,[30] and nearly all of the Southern commercial conventions which met yearly from 1853 to 1860 went on record in favor of Southern-written and Southern-printed textbooks. The Memphis Convention of 1853, for example, recommended to the Southern states "the education of their youth at home as far as practicable; the employment of native teachers in their schools and colleges; the encouragement of a home press; the publication of books adapted to the educational wants and the social conditions of these States. . . ."[31]

Though its feelings were sometimes too easily offended by Northern texts, the South's position can be better understood by noting that one text printed in the North explained "the time is rapidly approaching" when slaves "shall wrest their

[29] R. B. Flanders, *Plantation Slavery in Georgia*, 286; Bessie L. Pierce, *Public Opinion and the Teaching of History in the United States*, 137-8; John S. Ezell, "A Southern Education for Southrons," *Journal of Southern History* XVII (August, 1951), 305, 306.

[30] For cases see *The National Era*, September 29, October 20, and December 8, 1853.

[31] "The Memphis Convention," *DeBow's Review* XV (September, 1853), 268; also "The Great Southern Convention in Charleston," *ibid.*, XVI (June, 1854), 638; and other convention reports, *ibid.*, XVII (1854), 508, XXI (1856), 553, and XXII (1859), 504.

independence from their masters, upon the very same principle and with the same justice that the Americans wrested their independence from Great Britain." Another taught that the colonial manners of New England were "better and more agreeable" than those of the South, and that the Mexican War was "a compromise of human rights for the interests of slavery." Yet thirty years earlier, probably few slaveholders would have objected, as one did in 1860, to this statement found in a Northern-edited text:

The Negro thrives best in a warm climate; it is, therefore, in the South alone that slavery, which originally existed in all the colonies, has taken such a hold, and continued so long, that the removal of the evil, though much to be desired, has become, year by year, a question of greater difficulty.[32]

A number of attempts were made to provide textbooks for the Southern market, without much success. One of the books most frequently criticized by Southerners was Francis Wayland's *Elements of Moral Science,* perhaps the most widely-used of all texts for standard courses in "Moral Philosophy." Wayland, president of Brown University and a strong anti-slavery man, included in his book chapters on "The Nature of Personal Liberty" and "Modes in which Personal Liberty May be Violated," which were in fact powerful antislavery lectures. William A. Smith, president of Randolph-Macon College in Georgia, wrote a competing text to correct "the fatal direction both as regards the principles of the institution and the institution itself" implanted "in the minds of young men" by Wayland. One of the more interesting attempts to counteract such offending textbooks was D. H. Hill's famous

[32] *Appleton's Complete Guide of the World,* quoted in *DeBow's Review* VIII (1855), 661, and *Willson's United States, ibid.,* XII (1857), 557; and J. D. B. DeBow, "Our Schoolbooks," *ibid.,* XXVIII (1860), 437. DeBow's essay, "Southern Schoolbooks," *ibid.,* XIII (1852), 258-66, is an interesting and judicious discussion of the problem. For further information on De-Bow as Southern propagandist, consult Robert F. Durden, "J. D. B. DeBow: Convolutions of a Slavery Expansionist," *Journal of Southern History* XVII (November, 1951), 441-62.

Algebra, written when the future Confederate officer was professor of Mathematics and Civil Engineering at Davidson College in South Carolina. Hill inserted anti-Northern and pro-Southern propaganda into his algebra problems with great skill. Some of them involved Yankees who sold watered milk and wooden nutmegs, others the Massachusetts witchcraft trials, the "treason" of New England in the War of 1812, and the "cowardice" of the Indiana troops in the Mexican War; the Southern gentlemen in his book came off much better.[33] But very few of the Southern publishing companies planned by Green and others materialized, and at the outbreak of the war, despite a decade of complaint, the Southern schoolbook trade still remained largely in the hands of Northern publishers.

At the same time that Northern texts were undergoing scrutiny and censorship, a movement developed to rid Southern schools of Northern or Northern-trained teachers. "We tell you," wrote a North Carolina editor, "that in nine cases out of ten, when you employ Northern teachers, you press a viper to your bosom, that will sting you by infusing into the minds of his pupils thoughts, feelings, and tastes opposed to Southern interests and Southern institutions. . . ." It might even be better, suggested one writer, that young Southerners "remained in honest ignorance and at the plough handle, than that their plastic minds be imbued with doctrines . . . at war with the very fundamental principles upon which the whole superstructure of their society . . . at home . . . is based."[34] A great many Southern leaders received their education in Northern colleges, a fact which not only galled native pride but seemed inherently dangerous to slavery. The South depended upon young Northerners for its supply of teachers and tutors, and after 1850 protests began to be lodged against the practice

[33] Hal Bridges, "D. H. Hill's Anti-Yankee Algebra," *Journal of Southern History* XXII (May, 1956), 220-22. Francis Wayland, *The Elements of Moral Science,* 1837 ed., 200-6, 207-16.

[34] *The Anti Slavery Bugle,* March 28, 1857; and Craven, *Growth of Southern Nationalism,* 254.

of hiring teachers from free territory.[35] The commercial conventions, as they inveighed against Northern books, also warned against Northern teachers. The Savannah convention of 1856 declared that "the South must teach its own sons from its own books," and agreed to appoint a committee to make plans for teacher-training.[36] A proposal for a great Southern university, in which Southern youth would be taught Southern doctrine by Southern teachers, resulted in the establishment by Bishop Leonidas Polk of the University of the South at Sewanee, and represented the culmination of the sectional movement in Southern education.[37]

In the end, the refusal of the South to allow freedom of discussion in its institutions of higher learning proved disastrous. It led ultimately to a complete misunderstanding of the plantation system, and fostered intolerance of frank discussion of other problems connected with slavery. The intelligent Southerner who might have been a constructive critic of his region's economic and political structure was forced, by 1850, to maintain a sterile silence. As a consequence, during the decade when the South most needed discussion of its problems, the universities and colleges, which should have been fruitful sources of progressive thought, found themselves unable to speak. The trend toward sectionalism and insularity in the South found no corrective. The "positive good" argument for slavery developed absurdities which no Southerner of intellectual prestige dared deny; the faults of slavery, of which an earlier South had been well aware, were glossed over by indiscriminate, enthusiastic praise of its virtues. By 1855 the South had lost all sense of proportion in regard to slavery, making claims for the system that few intelligent slaveholders thirty

[35] See, for example, "Home Education at the South," *DeBow's Review* XVIII (May, 1855), 656; "Wants of the South," *ibid.*, XXIX (August, 1860), 219; "Southern Education for Southern Youth," *ibid.*, XIX (October, 1855), and the article by H. R. Garnett, *ibid.*, X (April, 1851), 476-78. President Swain of North Carolina was severely attacked in 1858 for hiring a Northerner; see Eaton, *op. cit.*, 213.

[36] *The National Anti Slavery Standard*, February 7, 1857.

[37] "A Central Southern University," *DeBow's Review* XXIII (November, 1857), 499-503, and W. M. Polk, *Leonidas Polk, Bishop and General*.

years earlier would have accepted as reasonable.[38] Because Southern teachers and scholars had been denied their function for thirty years, the South could neither understand nor tolerate self-criticism.[39]

The growing importance of the slavery issue was reflected in the tendency in the Northern non-slaveholding states to suppress discussion of it. This was especially apparent before 1840, for by that time the abolitionists had gained enough support in the North to render the schools relatively free from anti-abolitionist pressure.[40] But before 1840 the force of public opinion was powerful enough to constitute a real threat to academic freedom in the free states. Influential Northerners were aware that one result of open criticism of slavery might be a Southern boycott of Northern goods. Southern markets, it was assumed, would be closed to those states sympathetic to abolition; schools which actively offended Southern feelings therefore were a distinct liability. Northern business interests wished to make it clear that they were either neutral or anti-abolitionist, and one method of reassuring the South was to suppress in educational institutions any discussions of slavery to which the South might object. There were many in the North who could see no reason to create disorder, disunion, and disturbance. Thus, for a time, as one historian concluded, "Through its own power in the South, and its allies in the North, this great slavery interest controlled the schools of both sections."[41]

[38] For example, *DeBow's Review* XXI (November, 1857), 454, said: "Slavery is necessary as an educational institution, and is worth ten times all the common schools of the North. . . . Slavery educates, refines, and moralizes the masses by separating them each from the other, and bringing them into continual intercourse with masters of superior minds, information, and morality."

[39] W. E. Dodd, the Chicago *Tribune*, July 15, 1932; John Lofton, "The Enslavement of the Southern Mind, 1775-1825," *Journal of Negro History* XLIII (April, 1958), 132-39.

[40] The shift of Northern opinion is graphically illustrated by the experience of Frederick Gunn of Washington, Connecticut. In 1837 he was forced from his school and the town for his abolitionist views; in 1847 he returned and set up another school without opposition; B. C. Steiner, *The History of Education in Connecticut*, 59-60.

[41] H. K. Beale, *op. cit.*, 112.

In the South, fears of slave revolt and racial amalgamation served to prevent the education of the Negro. Though slave revolt was not an issue in the North, the prospect of racial equality in education proved nearly as effective as a means of denying schooling to the Negro. In general, Northern legislatures were of the opinion that public funds for educational purposes could be granted only to segregated Negro schools. Before 1848 Ohio made no provision for any public funds to educate Negro children, and even forbade, under an 1829 law, their admission to public schools.[42] Finally in 1849 a tax on Negroes was levied to provide for those children with more than one-half Negro blood.[43] Indiana made no provision whatever for Negro schooling, and in 1853 the legislature specifically objected to it.[44] Pennsylvania, New Jersey, New York, Rhode Island, Connecticut, Massachusetts, New Hampshire, Vermont, and Illinois provided tax funds for separate Negro schools during the 'thirties and 'forties, whereas Michigan, Wisconsin, and Iowa allowed Negroes to attend the regular public schools.[45] However, the greater burden of Negro education in the North fell on the private schools maintained by abolition and colonization societies. Before 1830 New Haven, Connecticut, had two such schools; Boston, three; Portland, Maine, one; Philadelphia, three; New York, two; and probably a few more existed in other cities.[46] After 1830 the impetus given to Negro education by the new abolition societies is shown in the fact that in Ohio alone, in 1837, the Ohio Anti Slavery Society maintained twenty Negro schools.[47]

Despite the efforts of the abolitionists to support Negro schools and the establishment of separate Negro schools by most Northern legislatures, public opinion in the North was undecided on the issue of Negro education. Fearing offense

[42] *Ohio Session Laws* (1828-1829), 72-3.

[43] G. T. Stephenson, *Race Distinction in American Law*, 165, and H. T. Catterall, *op. cit.*, V:9, case of Lane *vs.* Baker, et al.

[44] C. G. Woodson, *op. cit.*, 332.

[45] *Ibid.*, 309-315.

[46] Alice Adams, *The Neglected Period of Antislavery*, 73-4.

[47] Report of Augustus Wattles, the Cincinnati *Philanthropist*, September 15, 1837.

to the South, or an influx of Negroes if colored institutions were allowed to exist in their localities, some communities attempted to keep them out by legal and extra-legal means. A plan for a Negro manual-training school in New Haven, Connecticut, was dropped in 1831 when a public meeting voted 70 to 4 that the idea was "an unwarrantable and dangerous interference with the internal commerce of other states, and ought to be discouraged," a resolution that met with general approval in the press.[48] Attacks upon teachers of colored schools or upon their buildings were not unusual, and such teachers were often treated as pariahs by the communities in which they worked.[49] Citizens at Zanesville, Ohio, tore down a Negro school in 1836. The teacher of another near Chillicothe was mobbed a few years later, while the teacher of a Negro school at Steubenville, Ohio, was shunned by local citizens as a suspected radical.[50]

However, many Negro schools were allowed to operate without serious opposition. The schools figuring in the greatest disturbances in the North were those which, in defiance of local prejudice, accepted both white and Negro pupils. Noyes Academy in Canaan, New Hampshire, admitted fourteen Negroes in 1834; in 1835 its building was dragged from its foundations into a swamp by 300 men and 100 yoke of oxen after a town meeting had decided that "the Abolitionists must be checked and restrained within Constitutional limits, or American liberty will find a speedy grave."[51] Eleutherian Institute at Lancaster, Indiana, which admitted white and Negro students, was frequently the target of attacks and finally was burned in 1850.[52]

[48] Oliver Johnson, *William Lloyd Garrison and His Times*, 123; see also E. P. Southall, "Arthur Tappan," *Journal of Negro History* XV (April, 1930), 172-76, and Henry Wilson, *The History of the Rise and Fall of the Slave Power in America*, I, chapter XVII, and M. H. Rice, *op. cit.*, 72.

[49] H. K. Beale, *op. cit.*, 132.

[50] Letter to Emily Robinson, November, 1837, in the Robinson mss., Western Reserve Historical Society, Cleveland, Ohio.

[51] Leon Whipple, *The Story of Civil Liberty in the United States*, 118, and the Boston *Morning Post*, August 18, 1835.

[52] W. G. Thompson, "Eleutherian Institute," *Indiana Magazine of History* XIX (June, 1923), 110-111.

There were a number of such cases, but the most celebrated example of the temper of Northern resistance to integrated education was the case of Prudence Crandall, who established a school for girls in Canterbury, Connecticut, in 1831. Her Quaker background and Garrison's *Liberator* converted her to abolition shortly thereafter, and after searching for a way to serve the cause, she concluded that she could best make her contribution by offering education to Negro girls. In early 1833 she announced that her school in April would be "opened for the reception of young ladies and little Misses of color."[53] A town meeting in March passed resolutions opposing the idea, and resolved that "the government of the United States, the nation with all its institutions, of right belong to the white men, who now possess them. . . ."[54]

A committee was appointed to remonstrate with Miss Crandall and to offer to reimburse her for her investment in the school if she would desist.[55] As opposition developed, Miss Crandall decided that she would restrict her school to Negro girls only. Garrison came to her assistance, and the New England Anti Slavery Society and the Rhode Island Anti Slavery Society determined to push her case to the limit. The school opened on April 1 with about twenty Negro girls. Immediately it faced a town boycott. The shops refused to sell her food, civic services were cut off, and town officials attempted to prosecute her students under an old pauper and vagrancy law, but dropped the case when Samuel May, a Unitarian minister of nearby Brooklyn, Connecticut, raised $10,000 to cover fines and expenses.[56]

In May of 1833 Andrew T. Judson, a Canterbury lawyer and

---

[53] *The Liberator*, February 25, 1833, and subsequent issues.

[54] R. H. Weld, *Slavery in Connecticut*, 23.

[55] *The Liberator*, April 6, 1833; see also "A Canterbury Tale," *The Abolitionist* I (April, 1833), 60-63, for accounts.

[56] Edwin and Miriam Small, "Prudence Crandall, Champion of Negro Education," *The New England Quarterly* XVII (December, 1941), 506-39, gives a detailed story of the school. John C. Kimball, *Connecticut's Canterbury Tale* (Hartford, Conn., 1888) is an account by one of the Connecticut antislavery sympathizers. D. L. Dumond's chapter on the Crandall case, *Antislavery*, 211-17, is a good summary of its implications.

an official of the American Colonization Society, obtained the passage of a state law forbidding instruction of Negroes from outside the state in any but free public schools, except by permission of the town—a law aimed directly at the Crandall school.[57] Determined to follow the test case through, Miss Crandall was arrested in August under the law and detained in county jail for one night.[58] She was tried in Brooklyn, Connecticut, with Andrew Judson as chief prosecutor and three good lawyers, hired by Arthur Tappan (of the American Anti Slavery Society), to defend her. The argument dealt chiefly with the constitutionality of the Connecticut law, Judson contending that Negroes were not citizens and thus not entitled to educational privileges beyond those the community wished to bestow. Lawyers Ellsworth and Strong argued for the defense that the Negro girls were citizens of other states and constitutionally entitled to reciprocal privileges and immunities. The jury failed to agree (rumor had it that the vote was 7 to 5 for conviction) and the case remained unsettled.[59] In the next term's court, however, Miss Crandall was convicted, but the decision was appealed and quashed in July of 1834.[60] Though Miss Crandall and her supporters won the case, the school was soon forced to close. She and her students were threatened, the school well was filled with manure, the druggist refused to sell her medical supplies, food stores refused to sell her food, and attempts were made to burn the building. In the face of constant hostility she eventually conceded defeat.[61]

[57] *The Liberator*, June 15, 1833, and *The Abolitionist* I (July, 1833), 97-98.

[58] E. and M. Small, *op. cit.*, 527. She was placed in a cell recently vacated by a murderer, a fact the abolitionist press publicized widely.

[59] *The Abolitionist* I (September, 1833), 140-41, and *The Liberator*, August 31, 1833, provide accounts of the trial.

[60] *The Abolitionist* I (November, 1833), 162-70, and Anna T. McCarron, "The Trial of Prudence Crandall for the Crime of Educating Negroes in Connecticut," *The Connecticut Magazine* XII (Summer, 1908), 225-32.

[61] E. and M. Small, *op. cit.*, 529. Prudence Crandall soon married and moved to Illinois. In 1886 the Connecticut legislature voted her an annuity.

Since both abolitionists and antiabolitionists considered the Canterbury affair as a test case, it furnished the clearest example of the issues involved in the question of Negro education in the North. Samuel J. May, who was projected into national prominence by his part in the proceedings, believed that the importance of Prudence Crandall's right to maintain her school transcended Connecticut, that it was a question of "whether the people in any part of our land will recognize and generously protect the inalienable rights of man without distinction of color."[62] The abolitionist lawyers based their defense on the principle that the Negro possessed an inalienable right, as well as a constitutional one, to education.[63] Judson's prosecution rested on the thesis that Negroes were not citizens and as such had no rights at all, that the Declaration and the Constitution had never meant them to be citizens or to have rights, and that Prudence Crandall's actions were in defiance of public policy.[64] Quite clearly defined in the case was the popular fear of racial equality and racial amalgamation; though the school was originally intended to be biracial and was then changed to a Negro school, neither policy was acceptable to Canterbury citizens. The committee appointed by the meeting of March, 1833, protested, "Once open this door and New England will become the Liberia of America!"[65] Judson informed the jury during the course of the first trial that "the *professed* object is to educate the blacks, but the real object is, to make the people yield their assent by degrees, to this amalgamation of the two races, and have the African race placed on the footing of perfect equality with Americans." Out of court, he spread the story that Miss Crandall's aim really was to train Negro girls as brides for New England bachelors.[66] In addition,

[62] Letter to Andrew Judson, *The Abolitionist* I (April, 1833), 79. See also the discussion of May's part in the affair in T. J. Munford, *A Memoir of Samuel J. May*, 148-52.

[63] Arguments of the defense, McCarron, *op. cit.,* 228-32.

[64] Andrew T. Judson, *Remarks to the Jury, on the Trial of the Case, State vs. Prudence Crandall.*

[65] *The Liberator,* April 6, 1833.

[66] A. T. Judson, *op. cit.,* 22, and E. and M. Small, *op. cit.,* 516.

the antagonism of the American Colonization Society to the school served to define the divergent educational aims of the abolitionists and the colonizationists, the latter desiring to educate the Negro for life in a far-removed colony of his own race, the former wishing to prepare him for a place in American society.[67]

Another attempt, less successful, was made during the years 1830-1845 to prevent discussion and promulgation of abolition doctrines in Northern colleges. Legislatures and boards of trustees wished to avoid embroilment in any agitation over slavery likely to mean adverse publicity for their institutions. Faculties and administrative officers, aware that Southerners made up a significant percentage of the student bodies of many Northern schools, and quite conscious of the wishes of their boards, wished to avoid offense.[68] In the majority of colleges, of course, abolition did not become an important issue. In the eastern colleges, difficulties caused by abolitionist activity were relatively minor and confined to the period before 1840, by which time the antislavery forces had won enough Northern support to make slavery a reluctantly acceptable topic for academic discussion. Andover Theological Seminary reported dissension in 1833 between colonizationists and abolitionists in the student body, and its administrative officers solved the problem by suppressing both groups—a student abolitionist society was dissolved, and students forbidden to sign antislavery petitions to Congress.[69] At Oneida Institute, an abolition hotbed, the students organized an antislavery

[67] See the statement of the aims of both in William Jay, *An Inquiry into the Character and Tendency of the American Colonization and American Antislavery Societies*, 30-47.

[68] For example, the famous law school at Litchfield, Connecticut, graduated 200 Southerners (among them John C. Calhoun) or one-fifth of all its graduates. Pennsylvania in 1846 drew nearly half its students from the South, while Harvard, Yale, and Princeton had between sixty and one hundred students a year from the South until 1860; Eaton, *op. cit.*, 209-10. Amherst had an especially large number of Southern students from 1830-1840, according to W. S. Tyler, *A History of Amherst College*, 190.

[69] *The Liberator*, September 28, August 24, and August 31, 1833, and April 10, 1840.

society in 1833, and under the direction of Beriah Green from Ohio increased their activities until they drew denunciations from the Utica city council and the state legislature, and threats from the community.[70]

At Amherst an abolition society was formed in July of 1833, and grew by 1834 to include one-third of the student body.[71] Clashes between it and the student colonization society led President Humphreys in October, 1834, to declare that the society was "alienating Christian brethren, retarding and otherwise injuring the cause of religion in the College, and threatening in many ways the prosperity of the institution," and to request its voluntary dissolution. The society refused to dissolve, whereupon the faculty decided that it might continue if it met no oftener than once a month, solicited no new members, discontinued public and private discussions, corresponded with no newspapers, and limited itself to prayers for the liberation of the slave. The society refused to accept these conditions, and finally in February of 1835 it was officially suppressed by faculty action. "Indeed," said the faculty report, "we are not aware that any society such as yours exists in any respectable College but our own in the land."[72]

Three years later it was reported that Amherst students were not allowed to discuss slavery on public occasions, but might presumably do so in private groups. By 1839 opinion had changed to the extent that a student petition that a visiting minister be refused permission to preach, because he was a slaveholder, seems to have been favorably acted upon by the administration.[73] Abolitionist students at Hamilton College in New York endangered their annual state appropriation by

[70] *The Abolitionist* I (August, 1833), 125, and R. S. Fletcher, *A History of Oberlin College*, I:146-47.

[71] Announcements in *The Liberator*, August 3, 1833, and *The Abolitionist* I (August, 1833), 124-25. The society grew out of a debate held July 10, 1833, by the Athenian Society and presided over by Henry Ward Beecher; it later planned to establish a school for Negroes in Amherst.

[72] W. S. Tyler, *op. cit.*, 247-51.

[73] The New York *Emancipator*, January 4, 1838, and *The Massachusetts Abolitionist*, August 15, 1839.

signing an antislavery petition to the legislature. Both president and faculty disclaimed knowledge of the petition; after promising to discourage abolitionists in the college, they finally received the grant with a legislative warning.[74] But student abolition societies were formed at Auburn, Dartmouth, Williams, and Union, and other eastern colleges experienced little trouble.[75]

In the colleges and seminaries of the western states the controversy over slavery was more violent. Western Reserve College in Ohio, already a stronghold of the American Colonization Society, was badly split by the abolitionist-colonizationist argument. President Storrs, a strong colonizationist, was converted to immediatism by *The Liberator* in 1831, the first college president to declare himself an abolitionist. He was soon supported by two influential young faculty members, Beriah Green and Elizur Wright, Jr. Through their speeches and writings, some of which were published in *The Liberator,* these three men became nationally known abolitionists by 1833. When a student society, organized in the fall of 1832 under faculty auspices, sent out speakers through northern Ohio, opposition from local colonizationists forced the college trustees to request that such agitation cease. Storrs left in ill health in 1833, and Wright and Green finally resigned under pressure. Though Western Reserve had never been proslavery in sympathy and had admitted Negro students during the heat of the controversy, it soon lost its reputation as the center of Western abolitionism and received, unjustly, the label of conservative.[76]

[74] *The Liberator,* April 21, 1837, and *Niles' Register,* 52:98-99.

[75] *The Liberator,* April 23, July 2 and 23, 1836; G. H. Barnes, *The Antislavery Impulse,* 228; and Fletcher, *op. cit.,* I:185. However, a Negro minister was beaten at Princeton in 1836, Carl Follen dropped from the staff and Horace Mann hooted at Harvard in 1834, and Seward rejected as Phi Beta Kappa speaker at Yale in 1850; see the Cincinnati *Philanthropist,* November 25, 1836, and *The Anti Slavery Bugle,* September 14, 1850 and June 7, 1851. *The First Annual Report of the Union College Antislavery Society* lists fifty-one student members.

[76] G. W. Knight and John R. Commons, *History of Higher Education in Ohio,* and F. C. Waite, *Western Reserve University, The Hudson Era.*

Less than a year later, in 1834, Lane Seminary in Cincinnati became the scene of the most dramatic case of the period involving academic freedom. Control of the Seminary had been taken over by Arthur Tappan in 1831 in order to provide a western theological school for the training of young men in the evangelistic faith of the famous Charles Grandison Finney. When the school opened under the new administration of President Lyman Beecher, one of the students was Theodore Weld, who had been earlier converted to abolition while at Oneida.[77] Weld and others, anxious to settle the dispute over abolition versus colonization, planned a series of discussions to resolve the issue.[78] In February of 1834 the students held a series of nine meetings, attended by the entire student body and all but a few of the faculty, which resulted in an overwhelming vote in favor of immediate emancipation. Nine more evenings were devoted to an analysis of the colonization plan, which was almost unanimously voted down. Shortly afterwards the Lane students began to spend time working with the Negroes of Cincinnati, organizing clubs and schools and preaching immediate abolition.

The Board of Trustees of Lane, composed primarily of local businessmen, remembered the race disturbances in the city in 1830 and were acutely aware of Cincinnati's trade connections with the South. The students' activities led the Board to con-

[77] G. H. Barnes, *op. cit.*, 12-41, gives an account of Weld's earlier years and the establishment of Lane. Professor Calvin Stowe of Lane's faculty was the husband of Beecher's daughter Harriet, later to become famous in her own right. Benjamin P. Thomas, *Theodore Weld, Crusader for Freedom,* is an excellent biography. See also Frank G. Beardsley, *A Mighty Winner of Souls: Charles G. Finney.*

[78] The account of the Lane Controversy is adapted from Fletcher, *op. cit.*, I:150-165, and Harriet Martineau, *The Martyr Age of the United States of America,* 9-13; Sydney Strong, "The Exodus of Students from Lane Seminary to Oberlin in 1834," *Papers of the Ohio Church History Society,* IV (1893), 1-16; Charles Beecher, ed., *The Autobiography and Correspondence of Lyman Beecher;* and D. L. Dumond *Antislavery,* 158-65. A partial account of the debates themselves may be found in Henry B. Stanton, *The Debate at Lane Seminary . . . ,* and Weld's account, *A Statement of the Reasons Which Induced the Students of Lane Seminary to Dissolve their Connection with that Institution.*

sult with President Beecher, who considered such agitation unwise, and who, with some of his faculty, had earlier frowned upon the debates.[79] By the summer of 1834 the local press began to take notice of the Lane students' work. Charles Hammond of the Cincinnati *Gazette* warned that "Ohio will give no countenance to the followers of Garrison and Tappan,"[80] while the *Journal* editorialized, "There may be room enough in the wide world for *abolitionism* and *perfectionism,* and many other *isms,* but a school, to prepare pious youth for preaching the gospel, has no legitimate place for any of these."[81]

President Beecher left for a tour of the East, and in his absence the situation became increasingly tense. A visit by several Negroes to the school excited such comment that the Executive Committee of the Board of Trustees suggested a set of resolutions recommending the dissolution of all antislavery societies at the institution. They also outlawed "discussion and conduct among the students calculated to . . . excite party animosities, stir up evil passions amongst themselves or in the community, or involve themselves with the political concerns of the country."[82] In October the Board confirmed these resolutions, forbidding meetings for any purpose other than study or devotion, outlawing all public addresses, dissolving both abolition and colonization societies as "tending to enlist the students in controversies foreign to their studies," and delegating power to the Executive Committee to dismiss any student who stirred up controversy.[83]

Though Beecher pointed out that he did not intend to enforce these rules rigidly, forty students applied for dismissal, issuing a manifesto to the Trustees:

Free discussion, being a duty, is consequently a *right,* and as such is inherent and inalienable. It is *our* right. It was before we entered

[79] Strong, *op. cit.,* 9.
[80] The Cincinnati *Gazette,* July 17, 1834.
[81] Reprinted by *The Liberator,* October 25, 1834.
[82] Fletcher, *op. cit.,* I:158.
[83] The Cincinnati *Gazette,* October 22, 1834.

Lane Seminary: privileges we might and did relinquish: advantages we might and did receive. But this right the institution 'could neither give nor take away. . . .' Proscription of free discussion is a sacrilege! It is boring out the eyes of the soul. It is the robbery of mind. It is the burial of truth. If institutions cannot stand upon this broad footing, let them fall.[84]

The manifesto was widely copied in the press, and the abolitionists seized the opportunity it gave to advance their case. Said *The Emancipator:*

> Better that the brick and mortar of Lane Seminary should be scattered to the winds . . . than that the principle should be recognized that the truth is not to be told, nor sin rebuked, nor the rights of bleeding humanity plead for, for fear of a mob.[85]

Despite the attempts of Beecher (who was himself sympathetic to antislavery) to resolve the dispute amicably, the students (with two professors, Mahan and Morgan) withdrew to nearby Cumminsville to establish a seminar and continue their work. After four months they were approached by President Shipherd of Oberlin.[86] Demanding and receiving assurances that entire freedom of speech would be granted, that Negro students would be admitted on an equal footing with whites, and that faculty rather than trustee rule be instituted, many of the "Lane Rebels" enrolled at Oberlin. From their ranks there came an infusion of energy into the movement that furnished the impetus for abolitionizing the West. Theo-

[84] Fletcher, *op. cit.*, 162-63. Weld, older than most of the students and a natural leader, was perhaps most responsible for the failure to compromise, according to Strong, *op. cit.*, 10. The Lane faculty declared that "the difficulties originated and continued by the instrumentality of an influential member of the abolition society," probably meaning Weld. Beecher pleaded with Weld to remain at the school, working quietly for abolition, saying, "The whole valley of the Mississippi is in our hands if we will not play the fool"; see an interview with Weld by the New York *Sunday Herald,* September 15, 1889.

[85] *The Emancipator*, November 11, 1834. See also the Columbus *Ohio Observer,* and the Pittsburgh *Friend,* quoted by *The Liberator,* January 10, 1835, for similar sentiments.

[86] Strong, *op. cit.*, 9.

dore Weld, however, embarked upon a career as an abolition agent, refusing a post on Oberlin's faculty.[87]

The Lane Seminary dispute illustrated the fundamental issues at stake in the clash in Northern educational institutions between abolitionists and the conservative element. Fear of economic reprisal clearly lay beneath the resolutions of the Lane trustees, and equally implicit in the action taken by both trustees and faculty was a desire to keep order, to avoid the agitation of an unpopular question.[88] The fact that the Lane students established Negro schools in Cincinnati and met Negroes socially on an equal plane emphasized another facet of the problem. Though from the students' point of view freedom of discussion was the major issue, it is clear that their acceptance of the Negro as an equal played a large part in arousing popular indignation against them.[89]

Oberlin's swift rise to prominence as an "abolition school" after the Lane episode made it the target of frequent attacks. *The Western Monthly Magazine* pointed out in 1836 that it was the only school in the country that taught the "foul abomination" of abolition, and in 1837 the first of several attempts to check its growth was made by the Ohio legislature, which allowed the college's trustees to incorporate a branch only if it excluded colored students. One legislator declared that he "did not want the statute book disgraced with the

[87] Barnes, *op. cit.*, 72-77, 103-104 discusses the significance of Weld and the Lane Rebels in the abolition movement.

[88] See Beecher's plea for calmness and sobriety in academic discussion, in his *Address at Miami University, September 29, 1835,* especially pp. 38-41.

[89] Weld's pamphlet, *A Statement of the Reasons . . . , op. cit.* Strong, *op. cit.,* 10, believed racial equality to have been the most important principle involved, though the insistence of the Lane group upon faculty control and complete freedom of discussion at Oberlin indicates how much it was concerned with these. Later Fee's Berea College was partially staffed by Oberlin students, and Eleutherian Institute in Indiana was deeply influenced by Oberlin. Numerous manual-labor schools of the next decade owed much to Oberlin's example. It was not, however, the first college to admit Negroes, for Western Reserve, Princeton, Middlebury, Bowdoin, Dartmouth, and Lane preceded it in this policy; see Fletcher, *op. cit.,* I:177-8, and Waite, *op. cit.,* 167.

name of Oberlin. . . ."[90] In 1840 an attempt to repeal the school's charter failed in the legislature, and another in 1841. In 1842 a petition signed by four hundred citizens asked that its charter be repealed on the ground that the college was "dangerous to liberty and morality, and an excrescence upon the body politic," but the bill was lost by postponement.[91] In late 1842 another attempt very nearly succeeded. The bill passed the required three readings in the House, was tabled by a single vote on December 8, and recommitted to the Judiciary Committee on December 19. Four days later the Committee returned it with recommendation for its passage and it was ordered engrossed. On January 23, 1843, the bill was killed by but seven votes—the last serious legislative attack upon the school.[92]

The Lane controversy was followed by other less dramatic disturbances in other western colleges. Twenty students at Marietta College in Ohio, under the inspiration of Theodore Weld (then an agent for the American Anti Slavery Society), formed an abolition society in 1835. Their first meetings were broken up by a mob of townspeople, but they kept their society alive by meeting in private homes. In 1836 they announced a public meeting, and were saved from a mob only by the intervention of college and town officials.[93] At Hanover College in Indiana a student abolition group met in 1836 against the wishes of the Board of Trustees, who quickly informed the public that "no such society is authorized . . ., nor will it be encouraged," and suppressed it.[94] A year later

[90] Fletcher, *op. cit.*, I:442. James Hall, editor of the *Western Monthly Magazine*, warned the West of the abolitionists' "bold step of seizing upon several institutions of learning, for the purpose of perverting the young mind, and rearing up conspirators for the war of fanaticism . . .," V (January, 1836), 3.

[91] *Ibid.*, I:441-9, gives an account of legislative attempts to dissolve the college.

[92] *Journal of the House of Representatives of the State of Ohio, 41st Assembly, 1st Session, 1842*, 19, 26, 30, 35, 110, 136, 147, 227.

[93] The Cincinnati *Philanthropist*, December 23, 1836.

[94] *Ibid.*, April 1 and 8, 1836, and *The Liberator*, April 23, 1836. Nearly a third of Hanover's student body came from the South.

Franklin College at New Athens, Ohio, whose faculty and trustees were both abolitionist, encountered strong local opposition. The community refused to support the college, and when Franklin was forced to sell its building for debt, a group of New Athens businessmen purchased it and founded a rival school, Providence College, on strictly antiabolitionist principles. Providence, however, soon failed, and Franklin continued.[95]

From the impetus of the Lane debates, the students of Miami University in Ohio organized an abolition society in 1834, including among its members James G. Birney, Jr. President Bishop of Miami, a colonizationist, was criticized for allowing the society to exist and his refusal to suppress it was a factor in his dismissal in 1841. The society had by that time, however, strong influence both in the college and the community, and was indirectly responsible for the abolitionist stand later taken by the Presbyterian church in Ohio.[96] Other disputes were reported before 1840 in Ohio—at Kenyon, Muskingum, and Granville—and at Illinois College and Knox in Illinois.[97] Later, in 1843, David Nelson's Mission Institute at Quincy was partially burned by a mysterious fire, while the Galesburg Manual Labor Institute, modelled on a plan similar to Oberlin's, was wholly destroyed.[98] Professor McClintock of Dickinson College, Carlisle, Pennsylvania, was nearly dismissed for

[95] Knight and Commons, *op. cit.*, 204.

[96] J. H. Rodabaugh, "Miami University, Calvinism, and the Antislavery Movement," *Ohio Archaeological and Historical Quarterly* 48 (January, 1939), 66-73.

[97] Barnes, *op. cit.*, 228; Beale, *op. cit.*, 153; G. H. Rammelkamp, "Illinois College and the Antislavery Movement," *Illinois Historical Society Transactions* (1908), 190-209; Fletcher, *op. cit.*, I; 185; and Knight and Commons, *op. cit.*, 32. Knox College was an important center of Illinois antislavery activity; for a complete study consult Herman R. Muelder, *Fighters for Freedom: The History of the Antislavery Activities of Men and Women Associated with Knox College.* Mission College at Jacksonville and Knox at Galesburg were all openly antislavery institutions, settled from New England and strongly Presbyterian. Knox, under President Blanchard, became abolitionism's strongest western academic outpost, and Galesburg itself a center of abolitionist activity in the fugitive slave years.

[98] N. D. Harris, *The History of Negro Servitude in Illinois.*

protecting a fugitive Negro during a riot in 1847; later he was brought to trial but acquitted.[99] Though abolitionists claimed that the Reverend D. D. Whedon was forced from the faculty of the University of Michigan for advocating the "higher law" doctrine, the claim is doubtful in view of a faculty reorganization at the same time.[100]

The suppression of abolitionist discussions was never a problem of overwhelming importance on Northern campuses. There were a number of cases reported by the abolitionist societies which involved students and faculty antislavery sympathizers, but there were no more than a dozen which could be considered of major importance. In these, and others which drew attention from the press, suppression of abolitionist talk was justified usually on three main grounds: first, that it might cause loss of public support for the institution; second, that it lay beyond the scope of the school's academic program; and third, that it might cause unrest in the college and community. Since in many cases the college authorities allowed or encouraged colonization societies, it is likely that fear of abolitionist methods, more than anything else, motivated the boards and faculty committees. Legislative interference with institutions of higher learning materialized less frequently than the colleges themselves expected, though it is no doubt true that the threat of legislative reprisal occurred to more than a few college administrators and conditioned their course of action. With the penetration of abolitionism in the influential levels of Northern communities, and its entrance into politics, opposition to discussions of slavery in the colleges lessened, until by 1850 it had virtually disappeared as an important issue.

[99] M. D. Conway, *Autobiography*, I:50-53, and *The Anti Slavery Bugle*, September 24, 1847.

[100] *The National Era*, February 5, 1852; *The National Anti Slavery Standard*, February 26, 1852; and the Detroit *Advertiser*, February 3, 1852.

Abolitionism and Freedom
of the Press

IV

THE ABOLITIONIST PRESS was one of the most influential
factors in the consolidation of antislavery opinion in the
North after 1830. Abolitionist newspapers, edited by shrewd
and able men, circulating in hundreds of Northern hamlets,
provided a means of tying together the numerous small and
scattered local societies, and of forming a medium of communication between them and the state and national antislavery
organizations. Through the press, information could be quickly
and accurately disseminated to the officers and members of
local societies. Instructions on voting, on making up petitions,
on obtaining new members, on refuting common antiabolitionist arguments, and similar useful material appeared in their
columns, giving each reader the benefit of methods and ideas
worked out and tested by the state and national societies. Reports of debates in state legislatures and in Congress, analyses
of votes on important legislation, and the records of senators

and representatives, furnished each member with a weekly check on the legislative progress of the movement. After the collapse of the national societies in 1840, and with the emergence of the state and local societies as the units of power, these newspapers played a major part in shaping and unifying abolitionist thought and policy.

There were three characteristics of the American journalistic tradition, all fully developed by the early nineteenth century, which did much to shape the nature of the abolitionist press. First, American journalism possessed a powerful tradition of freedom of expression, guaranteed by the Constitution and recently tested by the Alien and Sedition Acts. Editors were extremely jealous of their prerogatives, and reacted swiftly to real or imagined attempts to infringe upon them. Second, there was a well-established reform press. Under the stimulus of the great humanitarian impulse of the early nineteenth century, dozens of magazines, newspapers, and periodical publications (many, of course, ephemeral) espoused almost every imaginable philanthropic cause. Antislavery papers fitted quickly and easily into this already-existing format. Third, contemporary journalism was vehemently aggressive and partisan, partly in imitation of British journalistic style, and partially in reflection of the bitter political battles of the Federalist and Jacksonian decades. American editors called names, dealt in scurrilities, challenged each other to duels, and engaged in fist-fights, horsewhippings, and canings.

William Lloyd Garrison's *Liberator,* which during the first decade of the abolitionist movement set the tone for its press, was not unique among newspapers in its aggressiveness. In an age of violent journalism, Garrison's paper was simply more violent than most, though his rhetoric could have been matched by a number of non-abolitionist editors. His entrance into the antislavery field, hitherto more or less monopolized by amenable Quaker editors such as Benjamin Lundy, was spectacular, and most of his Southern counterparts immediately identified him with typical Northern abolitionist journalism. His gift, as John Jay Chapman called it, for "debauchery of language," led him to characterize certain of his opponents (to cite one of a hundred extremes) as "the human hyenas and jackals of America, who delight to listen to negro groans, to revel in negro blood, and batten upon human flesh," or to assail some of his brother editors to the South as "rum-drinkers, lechers, pimps, and knaves."

"If you would reform the Southern man," one Southerner advised the abolitionists in a plea for temperance,

say, if you please, that his explanations do not entirely satisfy you; but say something of them; give them some regard, some weight. For he knows, and so do you, that his views and feelings are such as an intelligent and honest man may well entertain.[1]

It was Garrison's reply to this kind of appeal, that since slavery was a crime against God and man, "I should use just such language as is most descriptive of the crime." "The tendency of your remarks is to prejudice their minds against a cool discussion of the subject," President Francis Wayland of Brown, himself an antislavery man, told Garrison. "There shall be no neutrals," said Garrison. "Men shall either like me or dislike me."[2] It is not surprising that the Southern press developed a high degree of sensitivity to *The Liberator,* or that the South was convinced that no crime against it was too black for Garrison and his friends to contemplate.

Excluding pamphlet, magazine, and other periodical publications, the abolitionists published between thirty and forty newspapers during the period 1830-61. These were largely supported by national and state and, in a few cases, by local societies.[3] The greatest expansion of the abolitionist press came

[1] Joseph Stiles, quoted in Stanley Elkins, *Slavery,* 93.

[2] Nye, *Garrison,* 50-51. Avery Craven, *The Growth of Southern Nationalism,* 189-92, has collected some excellent examples of Northern editorial violence.

[3] New York State possessed eight abolitionist newspapers, New England nine, Philadelphia four, Illinois two, Michigan two, Indiana one of brief life, and Ohio two. See the lists given by Samuel J. May, *A Catalogue of Antislavery Publications in America; The Legion of Liberty and the Force of Truth,* Appendix; William Birney, *James G. Birney and His Times,*

in the late 'thirties and 'forties, and by 1845 a highly skilled group of editors had developed, men such as Birney, Marius Robinson, and Gamaliel Bailey in the West, and Garrison, William Goodell, Joshua Leavitt, N. P. Rogers, J. G. Whittier, Oliver Johnson, David Lee Child, James Russell Lowell, and others in the East.

Prior to the appearance of journals supported by the various abolitionist societies, a few antislavery papers had existed, edited mostly by Quaker reformers. Charles Osborn, a North Carolina Quaker, published *The Philanthropist* in Ohio in 1817 and 1818, selling out to Elisha Bates, who continued it until 1822. Elihu Embree, another Quaker, began *The Manumission Intelligencer* in Tennessee, changing its title to *The Emancipator* in 1820, but ceasing publication that same year. Benjamin Lundy, also a Quaker, edited *The Genius of Emancipation* in Ohio in 1821, moving it successfully to Tennessee, Baltimore (where he employed young William Lloyd Garrison as editorial assistant), Washington, Philadelphia, and finally Lowell, Illinois, where it ceased with his death in 1839. Meanwhile, Lundy also published *The National Enquirer* briefly in Philadelphia, which later became *The Pennsylvania Freeman* under the editorship of John Greenleaf Whittier. These early journals, however, unlike those published by the abolitionist societies, were usually mild in tone and were concerned with other reforms in addition to antislavery. Few of them, with the exception of Lundy's *Genius* during its Baltimore years, experienced any serious hostility.[4]

Of the antislavery society newspapers, five were probably

404; and T. C. Smith, *The Liberty and Free Soil Parties in the Northwest*, Appendix. The best discussion of antislavery journalism is that of Joseph A. Del Porto, *A Study of American Antislavery Journals*, unpublished doctoral dissertation, Michigan State University, 1953. See especially his chapters on Garrison and *The Liberator*, 71-191, and on the major antislavery editors Lundy, Goodell, Leavitt, Bailey, and others, 231-85.

[4] George W. Julian, "The Rank of Charles Osborn as an Antislavery Pioneer," *Indiana Historical Society Publications* II (1891), 231-67; Annetta C. Walsh, "Three Antislavery Newspapers in Ohio Prior to 1823," *Ohio Archaeological and Historical Quarterly* XXXI (1922), 172-212; *The Life, Travels and Opinions of Benjamin Lundy* (Philadelphia, 1847); Del Porto, *op. cit.*, 38-71.

the most influential. Garrison's Boston *Liberator* served from 1831 to 1865 as the semi-official organ of the Massachusetts Society and the voice of antislavery New England. *The National Anti Slavery Standard* of New York City, published by the American Anti Slavery Society from 1842 to 1862, was edited at various times by Rogers, David Lee Child and his wife Lydia Maria, Sydney Gay, Edmund Quincy, James Russell Lowell, Maria Weston Chapman, and Oliver Johnson. The Washington, D. C., *National Era,* organ of the American and Foreign Anti Slavery Society from 1847 to 1860, was edited through most of its career by Gamaliel Bailey. The Philadelphia *Pennsylvania Freeman,* published from 1838 to 1854 and absorbed by *The National Anti Slavery Standard,* served the Eastern Pennsylvania Anti Slavery Society, edited by Whittier, McKim, and others. In the West, the Ohio Anti Slavery Society sponsored the Cincinnati *Philanthropist* from 1836 to 1846, edited by Birney and later by Bailey. The Western Anti Slavery Society, beginning in 1845, published *The Anti Slavery Bugle* of New Lisbon and Salem, Ohio, edited in turn by Benjamin and Elizabeth Jones, Oliver Johnson, and Marius Robinson. The state and local societies often published newspapers, some of them ephemeral, and many non-abolitionist papers sympathetic to the cause were willing to publish abolitionist items.

The pattern of the abolitionist newspapers soon became standardized. Even the South recognized the adeptness of abolition journalism, complimenting it backhandedly as "zealous, able, and efficient."[5] The papers, which usually ran to four pages, carried verbatim reports of speeches in Congress or at conventions, sermons, and passages from selected antislavery books or pamphlets. Included as a general practice were edi-

[5] A Charleston, S.C., circular, reprinted in the Salem, Ohio, *Anti Slavery Bugle,* September 24, 1847. It is impossible to ascertain precisely the extent of abolitionist or antislavery sympathy in contemporary newspapers, since the identifications depended wholly upon the particular editor's definition of the terms. William Birney, *op. cit.,* 413, listed 33 newspapers as favorable to antislavery in 1835; the *Annual Report* of the New England Antislavery Society for 1834 listed 28; Benjamin Lundy's *Genius of Universal Emancipation* for February, 1833, listed 17.

torial selections from the Southern press, speeches by proslavery men, or extracts from proslavery books, either allowed to condemn themselves without editorial comment or debated in parentheses or footnotes by the editor. A huge exchange system, built up from hundreds of newspapers, enabled the abolition editor to keep in touch with the status of the controversy everywhere—despite the increasing sensitivity of Southern feelings, exchanges between abolitionist and Southern newspapers continued until late in the 'fifties.[6] Those societies which supported agents in the field carried weekly reports of their activities, and these, with correspondence from other societies, enabled the reader to survey at a glance the progress of the movement in most of the states. Editorials on national and local questions took up a large portion of each issue, and a column or two of poetry, a serialized novel or sketch, book reviews, or literary criticism, filled out the paper.[7]

The interests of the editors were reflected in each paper— Garrison's *Liberator* in its aggressive tone and preoccupation with pacifism, women's rights, and humanitarianism, perhaps bore most strongly the imprint of its editor's personality, whereas *The National Anti Slavery Standard,* which frequently changed editors, displayed the least. *The Pennsylvania Freeman* showed a strong Quaker slant, while *The Philanthropist,* under Birney and Bailey, leaned toward an emphasis on politics. Bailey's *National Era,* perhaps the best edited and most professional of the group, was especially competent in its treatment of political and economic questions, while its literary department, reflecting the hand of Whittier, was probably the best of any newspaper of the decade.[8]

[6] See the varying replies to *The National Anti Slavery Standard*'s request for exchanges, April 19 and 26, 1849. Except for South Carolina, most Southern editors agreed to exchange.

[7] *The National Era,* for example, published *Uncle Tom's Cabin,* Whittier's *Leaves from Margaret Smith's Journal,* and novels by the popular Grace Greenwood and Mrs. E. D. N. Southworth.

[8] A short-lived proslavery paper, *The Southern Press,* edited by Ellwood Fisher and E. deLeon, was founded in 1850 expressly to combat *The National Era,* a grudging compliment to Bailey's editorship. See *The National Era,* June 20, 1850, *et seq.*

Southern objections to the existence of a Northern abolition-ist press rested for the most part upon a single charge—that the circulation of such newspapers encouraged slave revolts. The abolition editor, said the Charleston, South Carolina, *Mercury,* was ". . . a foreign enemy, creeping about under disguises, and demanding for malice and treachery the protec-tion due to honesty and good faith. He will go just as far as the patience of the community will admit of."[9] Whether or not the popular Southern fear of Negro insurrection was justi-fied is beside the point. The facts are that it was strong, and that it was a major factor in the shaping of Southern opinion concerning freedom of speech and of the press.[10] The memory of the Santo Domingo and Vesey conspiracies of an earlier time was still fresh in 1830. Immediate tightening of legal restrictions upon press, speech, and opinion followed Nat Turner's tragic attempt of 1831, and all abolitionist publica-tions were henceforth suspect.[11] From that time on it was a common Southern belief that the abolitionist press was to be one of the primary tools in fomenting slave revolt.[12]

Nor did the growth of the abolitionist press find favor with many Northerners. Abolitionist editors received anonymous threats and were harassed by constant libel suits; abolitionist reporters might be evicted from meetings or roughed up; bricks and stones smashed abolitionist office windows; stage-coach drivers now and then simply threw abolitionist journals

[9] Quoted by *The National Era,* May 11, 1848.

[10] Clement Eaton, *Freedom of Thought in the Old South,* Chapter IV, has an excellent discussion of the part played by the "black terror" in the formation of Southern opinion. Herbert Aptheker, *American Negro Slave Revolts,* 150-162, 386-395, points out that the fear of revolt had been used since Federalist days as a device to secure political unity among Southern whites and to secure support for the slave system.

[11] See J. W. Cromwell, "The Aftermath of Nat Turner's Insurrection," *Journal of Negro History* V (April, 1920), 208-235.

[12] For examples, see the speech of Gholson in the Virginia legislature in 1831, in G. M. Weston, *The Progress of Slavery,* 183; *The Speech of Wil-liam Cost Johnson of Maryland . . . , Delivered in the House of Repre-sentatives,* January 25, 27, 28, 1840, 48-50; and the speech of George Randolph of Virginia, quoted by *The Anti Slavery Bugle,* September 27, 1851.

out of the mail. A substantial number of the mobs in the North were directed against abolition editors, the most obvious examples being the Boston mob of 1835 against Garrison, the Utica riots of 1835, the Cincinnati riots of 1836 against Birney, and the fatal Alton mob of 1837 over Lovejoy's Illinois *Observer*. A good many citizens in the North favored some legal control of the abolitionist press, and the attempt in 1836 to impose restrictions upon it had surprisingly powerful backing. The Doylestown, Pennsylvania, *Democrat* believed abolitionist papers deliberately instigated slaves to "murderous designs against the laws," and *Graham's Magazine* declared in 1846 that no legitimate Philadelphia periodical should permit the word "slavery" to appear in its pages.[13] In general, nonabolitionist Northern editors (with a few exceptions such as Horace Greeley) either refused to allow abolition material in their columns or actively opposed the cause. Gamaliel Bailey calculated in 1845 that nine-tenths of the Northern press was either neutral or directly inimical to the abolitionists.[14] As late as 1860 Northern editors were still defending slavery or decrying attacks upon it, with Stinson, Van Evrie, and Bennett of the three powerful New York papers being probably the most influential of the group.[15]

Yet, despite widespread opposition, abolitionist journalism expanded and flourished, and after 1840 it encountered little significant difficulty in the North. The reasons for the cessation of active opposition were two-fold. First, it was obvious that abolition newspapers neither intended nor tended to incite slave revolts. The cool, intelligent journalism of men such as Birney and Bailey belied any such accusation, and even the aggressive Garrison's columns could rarely be suspect. The

[13] *Niles' Register*, 52: 887, and Virginius Dabney, *Liberalism in the South*, 134. According to the preface of the anonymous *Remarks on the Constitution, By a Friend of Humanity*, The Philadelphia *Evening Star*, however, printed antislavery material prior to that date.

[14] The Cincinnati *Weekly Herald and Philanthropist*, May 28, 1845. See also his editorials on the Northern press, *ibid.*, April 22, October 14, 1846.

[15] See H. C. Perkins, "The Defense of Slavery in the Northern Press on the Eve of the Civil War," *Journal of Southern History* IX (Feb.-Nov., 1943), 501-32.

abolitionist societies and their editors denied again and again that their publications were intended for the slave (who received no mail and who usually could not read) and the content of their newspapers proved their point. Garrison always explicitly denied charges of incendiarism, while the American Anti Slavery Society, which controlled the most powerful publications, from the beginning disclaimed any intent of inciting revolts. Garrison, in the first number of *The Liberator,* warned the Negro poetically that

> Not by the sword shall your deliverance be;
> Not by the shedding of your masters' blood.

A non-resistant pacifist who did not believe in any form of violence, he wrote, "It is not the avowed object of the *Liberator* to stir up insurrectionism, but the contrary. Nothing can be more fatal to our hopes . . . than such silly, phrenzied, anti-Christian proceedings."[16] Furthermore, the Southern tendency to apply the term "incendiary" to almost any antislavery argument soon robbed the accusations of any real conviction.[17]

A second, and much more important reason for the removal of the threat to the abolitionist press in the North was the fact that the controversy by 1840 began to take on dangerous implications; remarked one author,

The tendency of this system (*slavery*) to suppress the freedom of speech and press is most alarming. Let this freedom, guaranteed to every citizen of the United States by the constitution, be once destroyed on this point, and it will be an easy work to destroy it on every other point.[18]

[16] Garrison's editorial, *The Liberator,* March 18, 1837, the statement of the American Anti Slavery Society, *The Anti Slavery Bugle,* September 27, 1851; and Russel B. Nye, *William Lloyd Garrison and the Humanitarian Reformers,* 53-4.

[17] See a discussion of the Southern definition of "incendiary," from the Baltimore *Visiter,* reprinted in *The National Anti Slavery Standard,* January 21, 1847.

[18] E. P. Barrows, *A View of the American Slavery Question* (New York, 1836), 38.

For their part, abolition editors regarded themselves as defenders of the freedom of the press, and depended upon the American belief in the sanctity of that right to protect them and to secure a hearing. "Modern despots," thought a *Liberator* correspondent in 1833, would not openly infringe upon it; "An *imprimatur* on the press would arouse the people to rebellion—this they well know."[19]

Not all Northern editors agreed with the abolitionists' definition of editorial freedom. The editor of the Ohio *Western Reserve Chronicle* no doubt reflected a sizeable segment of journalistic opinion when he wrote that while he was adamant in favoring the right of free discussion, "There may be times and places, when and where the exercise of this high prerogative, on particular subjects, may be obnoxious to the community; and in such cases the will of the people should undoubtedly be obeyed." Nevertheless, standing upon their traditional and constitutional rights, abolition editors from the outset determined to take full advantage of them and constantly reiterated their privilege to do so. Garrison, Birney, Bailey, and Goodell believed that establishing freedom of the press for minorities was one of the more important aspects of the controversy over slavery, and that their struggles to obtain it were of vital importance to the American tradition.[20] The American Anti Slavery Society, in its *Declaration of Sentiments and Constitution* of 1835, carefully reprinted all Federal and state constitutional guarantees of free speech and press, and in its official list of principles, drawn up by William Jay, stated:

We believe that American citizens have the right to express and publish their opinions of the constitutions, laws, and institutions

[19] T. Fisk, *The Liberator*, February 23, 1833.

[20] *The Western Reserve Chronicle,* quoted in *The Emancipator* (New York) August 30, 1837. Also see Garrison, "The Rights of God—Free Discussion—Freedom of the Press," and "Free Speech and Free Inquiry," *The Liberator,* January 30, 1846, and April 2, 1847; Birney's letter to Gerrit Smith, D. L. Dumond, ed., *The Letters of James G. Birney,* I:243; Goodell, *Slavery and Antislavery,* 583; and Bailey, "The Duty of an Antislavery Editor," "The Responsibilities of the Press," "The Duty of the Press," and "Journalism and Liberty," *The Philanthropist,* April 28, 1840, August 13, 1839, April 8, 1846, and September 2, 1846.

of any and every State and nation under heaven; and we mean never to surrender the liberty of speech, of the press, and of conscience,—blessings we have inherited from our fathers, and which we intend, so far as we are able, to transmit unimpaired to our children.[21]

The abolitionists, therefore, took the ground that they intended to avail themselves of their right to freedom of the press guaranteed to them by law and tradition, never retreated from that stand, or allowed the North to forget that they had taken it.[22] Lending strength to their position was the fact, as their editors often pointed out, that one of the greatest evils of slavery was the denial in the South of freedom of speech and opinion in regard to it. "Liberty of opinion, liberty of speech, and liberty of the press do not exist in the Southern states of the Union," said Richard Hildreth, "any more than under any other despotism," and William Goodell, concluding his exhaustive analysis of the effect of slavery upon liberty, termed the Southerner a virtual slave. The same thing could happen, Garrison warned, in the North.[23]

If the existence of slavery meant the denial of freedom of the press in South or North, the editor who attacked slavery was therefore, by plain logic, the defender of a free press.[24] Placed upon this ground, the position of the abolitionist editor was well-nigh impregnable. By it his demands for the fullest journalistic liberty, within reason, were made clearly intelligible to the Northern public. The vital factors in bringing about this shift in Northern opinion were the Birney case of

[21] Bayard Tuckerman, *William Jay and the Constitutional Movement for the Abolition of Slavery*, 70.

[22] See C. W. Julian in the House, May 14, 1850, in L. M. Child, *George W. Julian, Speeches on Political Questions* (New York, 1872), 10. "Acting within the Constitution, and resolving not to go beyond its granted powers, we mean to avail ourselves of a free press to disseminate our views far and wide. If truth is incendiary, we shall still proclaim it; if our constitutional acts are firebrands, we shall nevertheless do our duty."

[23] Richard Hildreth, *Despotism in America*, 93, and William Goodell, *The American Slave Code in Theory and Practice*.

[24] For a complete exposition of this view, see Henry Ward Beecher, "Silence Must be Nationalized," *The National Anti Slavery Record*, June 21, 1856, and W. E. Channing, *Works*, II: 61.

1836, the attempts to secure legislative control of the abolitionist press in 1836, and the death of Lovejoy in 1837.

James G. Birney, an Alabama slaveholder, was converted to the antislavery cause in the 'twenties, partially through the efforts of Theodore Weld. After disposing of his slaves, he embarked upon a career as an abolitionist editor, choosing the border state of Kentucky (his native state) for his first venture.[25] In 1835, when he announced a plan to establish a paper, the *Philanthropist*, in Danville, Kentucky, the news was received with some misgiving in that state. A committee of Danville citizens, none of them particularly antiabolitionist, asked him to avoid trouble by postponing publication until the state legislature completed discussions of legislation governing such journalistic ventures. This Birney refused to do, calling their request "a withdrawal of the freedom of the press." "I am fully convinced," he continued, "that the general Assembly of the State has no authority to restrain the right secured by the Constitution to every citizen 'to speak, write, and print on any subject.' "[26]

A mass meeting of Danville citizens, after some discussion, decided that although Birney had a right to publish a paper, he had no right to publish "incendiary" material. Another group of thirty-three citizens, however, disagreed, writing Birney that they were "jealous of the right secured every citizen freely to write, speak, or print . . ." and requesting his presence at another mass meeting in order to explain his principles. But when feelings began to run high, Birney's job printer hurriedly sold his shop and his successor refused to continue the printing contract. Deciding that "a newspaper professedly

[25] William Birney, *op. cit.*, chapters I-IV, and Birney's account, *The Philanthropist*, October 14, 1836, of his early career. The best modern biography is Betty Fladeland, *James Gillespie Birney: Slaveholder to Abolitionist*.

[26] D. L. Dumond, *op. cit.*, I: 199-210. An earlier *Philanthropist* had been published by the Quakers Osborn and Bates at Mount Pleasant, Ohio, from 1818 to 1822, followed by Lundy's *Genius of Universal Emancipation*, published for a year at the same place. See Annetta C. Walsh, "Three Anti Slavery Newspapers Published in Ohio Prior to 1823" *The Ohio Archaeological and Historical Quarterly* XXXI (Sept., 1922), 172-211.

of the abolition character cannot be published in this state," Birney made plans to move the *Philanthropist* to Cincinnati under the auspices of the Ohio Anti Slavery Society.[27]

On the eve of his removal to Ohio, Birney believed that his project was as vital to the maintenance of the freedom of the press as it was to spreading of abolition sentiments. He wrote the editor of the Cincinnati *Journal*, in November, 1835:

> The subject of slavery will be discussed. . . . *(The people)* will discuss it, and ask its discussion from others, whom they may consider qualified to undertake it;—and though they may, in times of public safety, be 'still as the breeze'—yet, attempt to wrest from them the freedom of speech, the liberty of the Press, and thus to tear down the barriers erected by Patriotism against the assaults of Despotism, and they will be found, as ever, 'dreadful as the storm.'[28]

The *Philanthropist* was established in Cincinnati in January of 1836, though for the first four months the printing was done at New Richmond, twenty miles north of the city.[29] The city's reaction was for the most part unfavorable. Of the existing local newspapers, only Hammond's *Gazette* defended Birney's right to publish, though Ohio's constitution plainly guaranteed him that privilege.[30] The *Post*, the *Whig* and the *Republican* believed the *Philanthropist* definitely dangerous.[31] A Kentucky editor wrote, "We have no doubt that his office will

---

[27] *Ibid.*, I: 213-215, 230-231, 250.

[28] *Ibid.*, I:270.

[29] William Birney, *op. cit.*, 204-219, gives an account of Birney's first few months in Cincinnati.

[30] Charles Hammond was an able defender of free speech and press, the right of petition, and the rights of free states. Though he approved Ohio's "black laws," the fugitive slave laws, and opposed "organized abolition," he consistently defended the abolitionist's right to speak and publish, and gained the wholehearted respect of Ohio's antislavery men. For an account of this brilliant editor, see F. P. Weisenburger, "Charles Hammond, The First Great Journalist of the Old North-West," *Ohio Archaeological and Historical Quarterly* XLIII (October 1934), 340-427. Hammond's attitude toward abolition is given in the *Philanthropist*, April 16, 1839, and in his obituary, by Gamaliel Bailey, *ibid.*, April 7 and May 5, 1840.

[31] F. P. Weisenburger, *The Passing of the Frontier, 1825-1850*, 373-374, Vol. IV of Carl Wittke, ed., *The History of the State of Ohio*.

be torn down, but we trust Mr. Birney will receive no personal harm," while a meeting in Clinton, Mississippi, resolved that his paper was "A direct attempt to peril the lives and fortunes of the whole population," and informed Cincinnati that it was "the duty of every good citizen to break up by any means . . . any such nefarious design."[32]

Not long after the first issues of the *Philanthropist* came from the press, the *Republican* declared that "the interference of individuals not residing in those states where slavery is recognized, and who are not ameanable (*sic*) to their laws . . ., is unjust, unpatriotic, unchristian, and revolutionary in its tendency," and the *Whig* called for a mass-meeting of citizens to discuss the advisability of allowing Birney's paper to continue. On January 22 this meeting was held and attended by Birney, who explained his stand. As a Southerner and former slaveholder, he argued, he knew the South well, and he felt that the abolition of slavery would prove of immense advantage to it. As for encouraging revolts, the abolition of slavery now, he reasoned, would prevent revolts later, when the Negro population had increased to the point where a successful insurrection was possible. He did not intend, he explained, to attack the Union, nor to violate the privileges guaranteed to him by the constitutions; he simply intended to exercise his rights, within reason, to discuss and propagate a legitimate constitutional reform.[33] The meeting nevertheless passed resolutions of censure, despite his eloquence.[34]

Birney's defense failed to allay the fear in the minds of the city's prominent men that Cincinnati, which enjoyed a highly profitable trade with the slave states of the Ohio and Mississippi valleys, might suffer a Southern boycott if abolitionism were allowed to flourish in Ohio.[35] The *Republican* of January 22 pointed out that "Southern feeling is strong in this city,

[32] Beriah Green, *Sketches of the Life and Writings of James G. Birney*, 46, and William Birney, *op. cit.*, 197.
[33] Birney's account, the *Philanthropist*, January 29, 1836.
[34] Birney discussed these in detail, *ibid.*, February 26, 1836.
[35] See W. A. Mabry, "Antebellum Cincinnati and Its Southern Trade," *American Studies in Honor of William Kenneth Boyd*, 60-86.

and the interests of her *merchants,* her *capitalists,* and her *tradesmen,* are too deeply interwoven with the interests of the slave states . . . to admit of the *uninterrupted* operation of a society tending to separate the ties which connect the city to those states." On January 30 the same paper called for the citizens to "put down abolition and abolitionists, *peaceably if we can, and forcibly if we must.*"[36] Hammond of the *Gazette,* however, wrote, "We are opposed to abolition, to antislavery efforts. But we are not afraid to hear the advocates of these measures speak."[37]

Despite the efforts of the *Republican* to precipitate an incident, nothing occurred until July 12, when a small group broke into the *Philanthropist* offices and destroyed some printer's equipment, leaving the press untouched. Handbills were afterwards distributed through the city, explaining the attack and asking for public support "to eradicate an evil which every citizen feels is undermining his business and property." Placards, bearing the legend "Abolitionists Beware," appeared in various public places.[38] Though the *Gazette* deplored the acts, Editor Hammond reminded Birney that slavery was the business of the slave states, "in which the people of the free States have *nothing* to do," and the *Whig* and the *Journal and Luminary* followed much the same line of reasoning.[39] Antimob editorials, however, appeared in several Western papers, such as the Lexington, Kentucky, *Intelligencer,* the Greensburgh, Iowa, *Repository,* and the Piqua, Ohio, *Western Courier,* which remarked, "We care nothing for the abolitionist because he is such, but we would protect him in his full exercise of the freedom wherewith the Constitution and all the civil institutions of our country has made him free. . . . The people

[36] The Steubenville, Ohio, *Herald,* March 25, 1836, warned Cincinnati that its press was encouraging a mob.

[37] The *Philanthropist,* January 22, 1836.

[38] *Ibid.,* July 15, 1836, and the Cincinnati *Republican and Commercial Register,* July 22, 1836.

[39] The Cincinnati *Gazette,* July 18, 1836, and the *Philanthropist,* July 15, 1836.

are beginning to open their eyes upon this subject in the different non-slaveholding states of the Union."[40]

The reaction of the *Western Courier* showed that the main issue involved in the *Philanthropist*'s difficulties was no longer abolition but the right of a minority to speak and print. Recognizing the broader implications of this issue, the Ohio Anti Slavery Society quickly cried havoc. When, after the mob of July 12, a citizens' committee asked the Society if it intended to continue the *Philanthropist,* the Society replied that it did —compliance with a request to desist meant the end of a free press in Ohio. Said the Society:

We have now, to some degree, from the force of circumstances, committed to our custody the rights of every free man in Ohio, of their offspring, of our own. . . . We have embraced with a full determination by the help of God to maintain unimpaired the freedom of speech and the liberty of the press, *the palladium of our rights.*[41]

"There is no longer any doubt," said Birney, "that there exists . . . a secret confederacy, whose bond of union is a covenant to put down the liberty of the press and free speech."[42] Thus the battle was joined—to the abolitionists one over constitutional liberties, to the antiabolitionists one over civic and national welfare.

The resolutions adopted by a city-wide meeting held July 21 made clear the stand taken by Birney's opposition. While recognizing "the constitutional right of liberty of speech and of the press," the meeting, "anxious to preserve the peace and tranquillity of our city," wished to "continue those amicable relations which have hitherto existed between the States." Therefore it was necessary "to utter a warning voice to those concerned in the promulgation of abolition doctrines, through the aforesaid press, because we believe their course calculated to inflame the passions of one portion of our yet happy country

[40] Reprinted in the *Philanthropist,* July 29, 1836.
[41] William Birney, *op. cit.,* 243.
[42] The Cincinnati *Gazette,* July 20, 1836.

against the other, and to lessen that moral influence upon which the perpetuity of our Union mainly depends."[43]

The gathering of July 21 was followed by a larger and better-organized meeting held at the Lower Market House on July 23, presided over by Postmaster William Burke and attended by nearly every prominent member of Cincinnati's commercial interests. After discussion of Birney's refusal the meeting adopted several resolutions introduced by Wilson N. Brown, to the effect that slavery was an evil, but one for which the present generation was not responsible; that its existence was constitutional; that an abolitionist press in Cincinnati threatened the city's prosperity; and that abolitionists in the city were abusing the liberty of the press.

Brown specifically warned against mob action, saying, "We may and should use all lawful means to suppress abolition publications, but I trust we shall go no further." However, his resolutions contained the clause that "if abolition publications persist, we cannot hold ourselves responsible for the consequences." A committee which included Senator Jacob Burnet (also an ex-judge of the supreme court), bank presidents Josiah Lawrence and Robert Buchanan, Nicholas Longworth (the city's richest man), and D. T. Disney, ex-speaker of the Ohio House, was appointed to inform Birney of the meeting and to warn him of the danger of continuing to publish his paper.[44]

The committee requested a conference with Birney for July 25. He replied that the request should properly be addressed to the Executive Committee of the Ohio Anti Slavery Society, which published the paper. On the 27th, the Market House Committee asked both Birney and the Executive Committee

[43] The *Philanthropist*, July 29, 1836. The Cincinnati *Republican and Commercial Register*, July 23, 1836, said: "We believe also that their *(the abolitionists')* influence has operated injuriously to the interests and character of our city. Cincinnati is intimately connected with the slave states in business and social intercourse."

[44] See the accounts in the Cincinnati *Republican and Commercial Register*, July 26, 1836; of Walker, secretary of the meeting, the Cincinnati *Gazette*, August 15, 1836; and Birney's in *The Narrative of the Late Riotous Proceedings Against the Liberty of the Press in Cincinnati. . . .*

to meet with them, but Birney's absence from the city necessitated the substitution of Augustus Wattles, corresponding secretary of the Society. The two groups met on the 28th, with the result that the Society's executive board flatly refused to suspend its newspaper or to curb any of its activities. Unable to find any basis for agreement, both sides retired, but Editor Charles Ramsay of the *Republican and Commercial Register* reminded Birney, "There are points beyond which public sentiment, even in a free government, may not be trifled with with impunity."[45]

In two days the storm broke. On July 30 a crowd attacked Pugh's print shop, where the *Philanthropist* was printed, destroyed the press, and scattered the type. Marius Robinson, Birney's young assistant, had the forms set up for the next issue, and by pretending to be a member of the mob, escaped with them. Failing to find Birney or Robinson, the crowd went to Birney's home, where young William Birney, in an artful "little boy" speech, dissuaded them from burning the house. From Birney's home the group went to Church Alley in the Negro section of the city, broke into several Negro homes, and wrecked a saloon. At the request of the Mayor, lest it "disturb the respectable parts of the city," the mob shortly dissolved. Birney, returning to the city the next day, went into hiding, while the forms of the paper were spirited to Wilmington, Ohio, for printing on schedule.[46]

The news of the Cincinnati riots, the first major attack upon the abolitionist press in the North, evoked varying comments in the nation's newspapers. With the exception of Charles Hammond, who had attacked the Market House meeting as inflammatory and who bitterly berated the mob,[47]

[45] July 26 and 30, 1836.
[46] For accounts see Birney's letter to Lewis Tappan, Dumond, *op. cit.*, I:349; William Birney, *op. cit.*, 240-55; *Niles' Register*, 50:397-99; the Cincinnati *Republican*, August 1, 1836; Birney's *Narrative . . ., op. cit.*; and the biographical sketch of Marius Robinson by his wife, Robinson papers, Western Reserve Historical Society.
[47] The Cincinnati *Gazette*, August 15, 1836. Ramsay of the *Republican*, August 5, 1836, claimed that the Market House meeting was really intended to prevent a mob.

Cincinnati editors generally condoned the whole thing. The *Republican* of August 1, thought it "the most systematic, orderly, and wellbehaved mob we have ever witnessed," and the *Whig* of August 2 said that "few seem to be dissatisfied with the result, or *(have)* the slightest sympathy with the sufferers." In the same vein a citizens' meeting on August 3 held Birney and the Ohio Anti Slavery Society wholly responsible for the disturbance, affirmed its confidence in the city's civil authorities, and designated the local colonization society as the only approved antislavery organization.[48] The Ohio Society was quick to put its case before the public, however, and published Birney's account of the affair, *The Narrative of the Late Riotous Proceedings Against the Liberty of the Press in Cincinnati,* almost at once. Thus Birney became, in the space of a few weeks, a nationally-known figure in abolitionist circles and "a key witness," as the Massachusetts Anti Slavery Society called him, "in the great trial now pending between Liberty and Despotism."[49] Birney himself kept up a constant crusade against "the commercial and slaveholding aristocracy of the South, and of the kindred commercial aristocracy in Cincinnati," gaining converts for the cause, among them lawyer Salmon P. Chase.[50]

Most Northern editors refused to deal lightly with the Cincinnati case, and, like the abolitionists, regarded it a definite threat to liberty of the press. Hezekiah Niles wrote in his

[48] The Cincinnati *Republican,* August 1, 1836. Similar statements from the Wheeling *Gazette* and the New York *Courier and Enquirer* were reprinted in the issue of August 8, 1836.

[49] *Proceedings of the Massachusetts Anti Slavery Society, Fifth Annual Report* (Boston, January 25, 1837), 6.

[50] "The Reign of Terror," *The Philanthropist,* September 23, 1836. Chase was rumored to have offered $10,000 to buy Birney a new press, which he denied, writing in the Cincinnati *Gazette,* August 4, 1836, "Much as I have deprecated the course of the Abolitionists, I regard all the consequences of the publications, as evils comparatively light, when contrasted to the evils produced by the prevalence of the mob spirit. Freedom of the press and constitutional Liberty must live or perish together." The Birney incident brought Chase to the abolitionist side, and he defended the editor in court during a fugitive slave case a few months later; see F. P. Weisenburger, *The Passing of the Frontier, op. cit.,* 373-75.

Register that the riots "evince a settled determination on the part of the people not to tolerate incendiary attempts to excite the fears of the sister states, but they have taken a direction hardly less censurable than the course pursued by the abolitionists themselves."[51] William Cullen Bryant of the New York *Evening Post,* in a long editorial, concluded, "We hold that this combination of the few to govern the many by terror of illegal violence is as wicked and indefensible as a conspiracy to rob on the highway."[52] The Salem, Ohio, *Landmark,* of August 10, 1836, thought the mob had "struck a heavier blow at the liberty of speech, the freedom of the press, and the right of free discussion, than any outrages of a similar character that have preceded it." The New York *Sun* believed the mob established a thoroughly dangerous precedent, "that a real or pretended opinion of the majority of the people should be the governing principle, even though it be in opposition to existing law."[53] The Dayton, Ohio, *Republican* was of the opinion that the mob accomplished nothing except to gain support for the abolitionists.[54] Birney himself reprinted editorials from twenty-three Northern papers expressing disapproval of the mob and pointing out the inherent danger to an editor's freedom to speak out.[55]

The entrance into the abolitionist movement of the respected and influential New England divine, William Ellery Channing, was perhaps one of the more important results of the Cincinnati incident. Deprecating the abolitionist influence as "almost wholly evil," Channing had once written that "it

[51] *Niles' Register,* 50:391.
[52] August 8, 1836.
[53] Reprinted in the *Philanthropist,* October 21, 1836.
[54] Reprinted in *The Liberator,* November 19, 1836.
[55] October 21, 1836. Listed were editorials from the Pittsburgh *Gazette,* the Troy *Times,* the Columbus, Ohio, *Ohio Argus,* the Indianapolis *Indiana Palladium,* the Sandusky, Ohio, *Clarion,* the Springfield, Mass., *Pioneer,* the Pittsburgh *Times,* the Cleveland *Advertiser,* the Lynn, Mass., *Record,* the Dayton, Ohio, *Journal and Herald,* the Lowell *Messenger,* the Columbus *Ohio Atlas,* the Carlisle, Pa., *Herald* and *Expositor,* the Boston *Times,* the New York *Journal of Commerce,* the New York *Evening Post,* the Greensburgh, Iowa, *Repository,* the Cincinnati *Western Christian Advocate, The Western Banner,* and *The Pennsylvania Sentinel.*

has stirred up bitter passions, and a fierce fanaticism, which have shut every ear and every heart against its arguments and persuasions."[56] But the news of the attack on Birney stirred Channing deeply. In December of 1836, in a widely-reprinted open letter to Birney (whom he had never met), he praised the editor for his resistance to this, "the first systematic effort to strip the citizen of freedom of speech." Although in the methods employed by the abolitionists he still found "much to censure," he now looked on them "with unmixed respect." "In their persons," he continued, "the most sacred rights of the white man and the free man have been assailed. They are sufferers for liberty of thought, speech, and the press; and, in maintaining this liberty amidst insult and violence, they deserve a place among its most honored defenders."[57] Channing's letter expressed fairly accurately the impression made upon Northern conservatives by the events of 1836. The relationship thus established between abolition and civil liberty lent much-needed prestige to the movement.[58]

Within a few weeks of the Cincinnati riots, the efforts of antiabolitionists, North and South, to impose some sort of legal control upon the antislavery press continued, lending further credence to the abolitionists' claim that the incidents in Ohio simply marked the prelude to a great and concerted attack upon Northern liberties. In 1831 a Virginia group requested Mayor Otis of Boston, one of the chief antislavery publishing centers, to explore the possibilities of legal action against abolitionist presses operating in Massachusetts, particularly *The Liberator*. While Otis agreed that some kind of action might

[50] *Works*, II:131 132.

[57] See *ibid.*, II: 155-177 for the complete letter. It appeared in the *Philanthropist* in installments, December 9, 1836 to January 27, 1837. Birney's reply in defense of abolitionist methods of agitation, "Remarks on Dr. Channing's Letter," appeared in the issue of December 23, 1836.

[58] The *Philanthropist* subsequently flourished under the editorship of Birney and of Gamaliel Bailey, who joined its staff shortly after the mob of 1836 and took over the editorial chair in 1837. In 1841, however, a mob destroyed the press again; see the *Liberator*, September 24, 1841, and Henry Wilson, *op. cit.*, I:557.

eventually be necessary, he judged it unwise to attempt it.[59] Later, in requesting the extradition of publisher R. G. Williams from Governor Marcy of New York, Governor Gayle of Alabama held the opinion that "no remedy short of severe penal statutes, passed by the states where slavery does not exist, will be effectual for our relief."[60] The success of Southern attempts to control the mails in 1835 also encouraged the South to begin a more vigorous campaign to convince Northern legislatures to control or suppress the abolitionist press at the source. The South's chief complaint was that such publications might incite slave revolts; at the same time, it was also clear that some Southern leaders feared that continued campaigning by the abolitionist press might strengthen the abolitionist case to the point that antislavery forces might eventually become powerful enough to control state legislatures and dictate national policy.[61]

Beginning in late 1835, Southern legislatures drafted resolutions, transmitted to the legislatures of those Northern states in which abolition publishers were especially active, requesting that official action be taken against them. Governor McDuffie of South Carolina, in his annual message of 1835, thought that the South should "demand of our sovereign associates the condign punishment of those enemies of our peace, who avail themselves of the sanctuaries of their respective jurisdictions to carry on schemes of incendiary hostility against the institutions, the safety, and the existence of our state."[62] The joint committee on federal relations of the South Carolina legisla-

[59] *Niles' Register*, 45:43, and J. J. Chapman, *William Lloyd Garrison* (Boston, 1921), 53-54. The grand jury of Frederick County, Virginia, in finding a true bill against Tappan and the New York City Anti Slavery Society, also asked New York to pass regulatory legislation; *Niles' Register*, 49:194.

[60] *Niles' Register*, 49:290.

[61] Cf. the statement of Duff Green, the editor of *The United States Telegraph*, September 4, 1834, and reprinted in the *Philanthropist*, January 29, 1836: "We do not believe that the abolitionists intend, nor could if they would, to excite the slaves to insurrection. The danger of this is remote. We believe that we have most to fear from the organized action upon the consciences and fears of the slaveholders themselves."

[62] The New Richmond, Ohio, *Philanthropist*, January 1, 1836.

ture responded with a petition to the Northern states to "make it highly penal to print, publish, and distribute newspapers, pamphlets, tracts, and pictorial representations, calculated and having an obvious tendency to excite the slaves of the slave States to insurrection and revolt."[63] Governor Swain of North Carolina, in his 1835 message, also attacked abolitionist publications, and his legislature passed a similar memorial for transmission to the North, which Georgia duplicated within a few weeks.[64] Alabama and Virginia passed resolutions of the same type, and by February of 1836 all had been submitted to Northern legislatures.[65]

The proposed legislation, in Southern opinion, had nothing to do with the tradition of a free press. The South Carolina legislative committee, noting the objection that such laws might violate the "great principle of liberty of the press," considered that "the objection rests upon no just foundation." "There is certainly some difference," it stated, "between freedom of discussion and the liberty to deluge a friendly and coterminous state with seditious and incendiary tracts."[66] To James Hammond of South Carolina, a free press meant "well-regulated, legal freedom, and not unrestrained licentiousness."[67] True, "freedom of the press and speech were sacred and inviolable rights," but they "had been abused by those who would prostitute them for their own purposes." Joseph Lumpkin, one-time governor of Georgia, thought Northerners were only "entitled to discuss in their newspapers, periodically, and in any other mode except politically, the abstract question of

[63] *Ibid.,* January 22, 1836.

[64] *Niles' Register,* 49: 187, 218, 245, and A. B. Hart, *Slavery and Abolition* (New York, 1906), 237.

[65] South Carolina and North Carolina in December, 1835, Alabama in January, 1836, and Virginia and Georgia in February, 1836; see Goodell, *Slavery and Antislavery, op. cit.,* 414-415. Kentucky and Mississippi later transmitted similar memorials.

[66] *Niles' Register,* 49: 319.

[67] J. H. Hammond, *Remarks . . . on the question of Receiving Petitions* (Washington, n.d.), 16. Hammond believed the laws of libel and slander furnished necessary legal precedent.

slavery . . ., provided it be done with a view to assist, and not to injure, to convince and not to irritate."[68]

The Richmond *Enquirer* and the Charleston *Patriot* thought the Southern memorials in no way violated editorial freedom of speech, but the Richmond *Compiler,* after reviewing all the state and constitutional guarantees of journalistic freedom, concluded dispiritedly that "no law can constitutionally be passed for the purpose of restraining the fanatics of the North."[69] In the upper South there was disagreement over the memorials. The Wheeling *Tri-Weekly Gazette* warned that the "popular cry against any abridgement of the press" would strengthen abolition rather than crush it, and its editor, S. H. Davis, thought the South's reasons for its action wholly inadequate.[70]

The Southern memorials met both approval and disapproval in the North.[71] Four years earlier, Judge Peter Thatcher of Boston's Municipal Court had ruled that it was "an undoubted misdemeanor, and indictable as such in common law," to publish in one state with the intent to send it to another, a publication "designed to incite slaves to revolt." At least one editor, J. T. Buckingham of the Boston *Courier,* advocated legislation specifically to suppress the *Liberator.*[72] At about the same time that South Carolina was drafting its request, a pamphlet by William Sullivan circulated in Boston, recommending that Massachusetts enact laws forbidding the publication of antislavery material, and even meetings to discuss abolition. Simi-

[68] Ruth Scarborough, *Opposition to Slavery in Georgia Prior to 1861* (Nashville, 1933) , 190, and *Niles' Register,* 45:86.

[69] The *Philanthropist,* January 8, 1836, and *Niles' Register,* 49:236-237. Ritchie of the *Enquirer* earlier stated, in the issue of February 4, 1832, that a ban on colonization society publications would violate editorial freedom.

[70] Wheeling, Virginia, *Tri-Weekly Gazette,* August 21 and 28, 1835.

[71] The most concise statement of the antiabolitionist point of view on press regulation is that of Calvin Colton, *Abolition a Sedition,* 20-35, while the abolitionist case is summarily presented in William Goodell's review of T. R. Sullivan's *Letters Against the Immediate Abolitionists* and William Sullivan's *Political Class Book* in *The Quarterly Anti Slavery Magazine* I (January, 1836) , 171-178.

[72] Oliver Johnson, *William Lloyd Garrison and His Times,* 212-213.

larly Editor Noah of the New York *Evening Star* framed a bill for presentation to the state legislature, defining as a misdemeanor the printing of any material tending to incite insurrection.[73] Silas Wright of New York, speaking in the Senate, assured the South that soon, either by legal or extra-legal means, abolitionist publications would be suppressed.[74]

Such statements were of great help in enlisting support for the abolitionist press and in consolidating Northern opposition to the Southern memorials. Freestate editors, jealous of their journalistic prerogatives, were united against the Southern petitions, though many of them censured the abolitionist press for its intemperance. William Leggett of the New York *Evening Post* believed secession preferable to a gag-law on the press.[75] The New York *Sun* editorialized, "Although we are decidedly opposed to the fanatical course of the immediate abolitionists . . ., we shall nevertheless raise our arm in fearless independence against the insolent invasion of the dearest and most sacred rights of our free states," and the Boston *Courier* thought that "the mere suggestion of legal interference with the press" would be "a signal for revolution."[76] The New York *Plain Dealer* warned that the North would "never surrender the right of free discussion, on the subject of slavery, nor on any other subject."[77] The ensuing argument gave the abolitionists an excellent opportunity to blend their cause with the larger cause of civil rights, and to build conservative support in the North on the foundations already laid by the Birney case.[78]

[73] William Goodell, *Slavery and Antislavery*, op. cit., 409-410, and *Niles' Register*, 49:80.

[74] Henry Wilson, *The History of the Rise and Fall of the Slave Power in America*, I:319.

[75] W. H. Smith, *The Political History of Slavery*, I:45.

[76] The *Philanthropist*, February 12, 1836, and *Niles' Register*, 49:80.

[77] The *Philanthropist*, February 3, 1837.

[78] The abolitionists intended, in the event of successful passage of restrictive legislation, to print and circulate in the South copies of the Declaration of Independence and the Virginia Constitution, both of which contained "incendiary" sentiments, to test the laws; *The Anti Slavery Record* II (December, 1836), 159.

The memorials of the Southern legislatures were transmitted to New Hampshire, Maine, New York, Massachusetts, Connecticut, Vermont, Rhode Island, Pennsylvania, and Ohio in early 1836. All of the Northern legislatures, with the exception of Vermont, at first seemed to favor the Southern point of view, though most agreed that the passage of the requested legislation would certainly encounter constitutional difficulties. Vermont refused to introduce any bill of any kind affecting the press, on the ground that no state legislature, nor even Congress, possessed the right to abridge freedom of speech or press. The Ohio legislature, though it promised its moral assistance to the South, could see no constitutional means of suppressing abolitionist publications.[79] In New Hampshire, Maine, and Connecticut, attempts were made to introduce bills to control antislavery journals, but all eventually failed. In Rhode Island, a bill introduced in 1836 to curb abolition agitation, although it passed through committee, was defeated by the energetic efforts of George Curtis and Thomas W. Dorr.[80]

The Pennsylvania legislature referred the Southern petitions to the House Committee on the Judiciary, of which Thad Stevens was chairman. Although former governor Wolf thought that the abolitionist press ought to be checked, if a constitutional means of doing so could be found, his successor, Joseph Ritner, sharply denounced the Southern demands.[81] Stevens' committee submitted an unfavorable report, declaring that "every citizen of the non-slave states has a right to think and freely to publish his thoughts on any subject of national and

[79] W. S. Savage, *The Controversy over the Distribution of Abolition Literature*, 43-61, gives a complete account of Northern legislative reactions.

[80] See Garrison's report of the progress of the "gag-laws," the *Liberator*, July 2, 1836; A. Harris, *A Review of the Political Conflict in America* (New York, 1876), 78; and Oliver Johnson, *op. cit.*, 216. The Connecticut legislature decided that the abolitionists were not yet strong enough in the state to warrant repressive action; see *The Report of the Committee of the Connecticut Legislature* . . ., July 11, 1836, Mason papers, Burton Collection, Detroit Public Library.

[81] Harris, *supra cit.*, 75, and the *Philanthropist*, January 29, 1836. Ritner's message is given in full in *The Legion of Liberty and The Force of Truth*; see also Whittier's poem, "Ritner," *Works* (Boston and New York, 1888), VIII:47.

State policy."[82] New York's Governor Marcy agreed that regulatory laws might be passed, but doubted that public opinion would sustain them; at his suggestion a legislative report promised some kind of possible future action. A bill was finally proposed, making a misdemeanor "all writings and pictures, made, printed, or published within this State, with a design or intent, or the manifest tendency thereof, to excite to, or cause insurrection . . ., or to cause on the part of slaves an abandonment of the service, or a violation of the service the master has a legal right to claim." Since New York City was the center of the powerful American Anti Slavery Society and the New York Anti Slavery Society, the abolitionists were deeply conscious of the bill's significance, and after a long campaign, saw its defeat.[83]

The bitterest fight came in Massachusetts, where the incumbent Whig party favored antiabolitionist legislation and was capable of passing it. Governor Edward Everett, in his message of 1836, pointed out that anything "calculated to excite an insurrection among the slaves, has been held, by competent legal authority, an offense against the peace of this Commonwealth, which may be prosecuted as a misdemeanor at common law," and asked all citizens to abstain from a discussion which might prove to be "the rock on which the Union will split."[84] The abolitionists replied, "We can neither permit the gag to be thrust into our mouths by others, nor deem it the part of 'patriotism' to place it there ourselves. The more fiercely our rights are assailed, the closer we will hold them to our hearts."[85]

---

[82] Wilson, *op. cit.*, I:237. The complete report of the committee, however, conceded the right of the Southern states to control criticism of their insitutions and denied the Congressional right of interference; *Niles' Register*, 50:324-25.

[83] Leon Whipple, *The Story of Civil Liberty in the United States*, 114; W. H. Smith, *op. cit.*, I: 42-3; William Goodell, *Slavery and Antislavery*, 415. See also Alvan Stewart, "Response to the Message of Governor Marcy, February, 1836," *Writings and Speeches on the Slavery Question*, 58-86.

[84] Goodell, *Slavery and Antislavery*, 415, and *The National Anti Slavery Standard*, July 21, 1855.

[85] John G. Whittier, *The Philanthropist*, March 8, 1836.

The Southern memorials to Massachusetts Governor Everett referred to a five-man legislative committee headed by George Lunt. Recognizing the very real threat to the influential abolitionist press of Boston, Samuel J. May, corresponding secretary of the Massachusetts Anti Slavery Society, asked the Lunt committee for a hearing in February, 1836—not to defend abolitionism, he wrote, but "to avert any action of the Legislature that might infringe the liberty of speech, or of the press." On March 4, May, Loring, Sewall, Garrison, Southwick, Follen, Jackson, and Goodell appeared before the committee. After hearing speeches by May and Loring, who defended abolitionist publications and denied their intent to incite revolt, chairman Lunt refused to allow Professor Follen, a well-known Harvard scholar, to speak, claiming that the abolitionist attitude was truculent and disrespectful; thereupon he dissolved the hearing.

The Society protested to the Legislature, and on the 8th the Lunt committee again met representatives of the Society before a large audience in the House of Representatives. May repeated his remarks of the 4th, followed by Sewall, who argued the constitutional right of the abolitionists to free speech and press. Follen also spoke, and then William Goodell threw the hearing into an uproar by turning from a defense of the press to a heated attack upon the Southern "slavepower" which, he charged, was deliberately conspiring to rob the free states of "those liberties brought to Massachusetts by the Pilgrims and cherished by their descendants." The real question, he cried, was "one of *liberty and rights—not black,* but *white and black!*" Lunt, after warning Goodell to moderate his remarks, ended the session. The wide publicity given the hearing, however, removed the immediate threat of legislative action. Though the Lunt committee's final report criticized the abolitionists as disunionists, agitators, visionaries, as well as enemies of peace and the Constitution, it recommended no legislation.[86]

[86] The best account of the hearings is the report of the Massachusetts Anti Slavery Society, *An Account of the Interviews Which Took Place, on the 4th and 8th of March, Between a Committee of the Massachusetts Anti*

The most important case involving the freedom of the press, and the one which did more than any other to enlist support for abolitionists in the North, was that of Elijah Lovejoy, who was killed by a mob while defending his *Observer* press in Alton, Illinois, in November of 1837. Lovejoy, a native of Maine and a graduate of Princeton Theological Seminary, settled in Missouri in the early 'thirties to edit the St. Louis *Observer*, a religious newspaper. Though not an abolitionist at the time, and unaffiliated with any abolitionist society, he frequently discussed the slavery question in his columns.

Some of his remarks offended proslavery men in St. Louis, and in November, 1835, a meeting of citizens warned him to desist. "Freedom of speech and press," their resolution read, "does not imply a moral right . . . to freely discuss the subject of slavery . . ., a question too nearly allied to the vital interests of the slaveholding States to admit of public disputation." Lovejoy replied by standing squarely upon his constitutional rights, which, he stated, gave him "a warrant for using, as Paul did, all freedom of speech. If I abuse that right, I freely acknowledge myself amenable to the laws."[87] In addition, he pointed out that the citizens of St. Louis were establishing a dangerous precedent. "Today a public meeting declares that you shall not discuss slavery," he wrote:

Tomorrow another meeting decides it is against the peace of society that the principle of popery be discussed. . . . The next day a decree is issued against speaking against distilleries, dram shops,

---

Slavery Society and the Committee of the Legislature (Boston, 1836). The copy in the Oberlin College Library bears corrections and additions in Goodell's hand. Goodell's *A Full Statement of the Reasons Which Were In Part Offered to the Committee of the Legislature . . ., Showing Why There Should Be No Penal Laws . . . Respecting Abolitionists,* gives his speech in full and adds some material, and his version in *Slavery and Antislavery,* 419-20, gives a summary account. The *Liberator,* March 19 and 26, 1836, also reported the hearings.

[87] Horace Greeley, *The American Conflict,* I:132-33. It is interesting to note that the St. Louis meeting, while conceding Lovejoy's civil right to discuss slavery, denied him the moral right to do so. Lovejoy preferred to make his stand solely upon constitutional grounds, believing his moral right not to be at issue in the case.

and drunkenness. And so on to the end of the chapter. The truth is, my fellow citizens, if you give ground a single inch, there is no stopping place.[88]

Lovejoy's spirited defense won him some backing in St. Louis and a great deal among abolitionists generally. Newspapers in Cincinnati, Boston, New York, and Philadelphia commented favorably on his reply, which was reprinted by newspapers throughout the country. Soon, however, Lovejoy was forced to leave St. Louis under threat of personal injury because of his editorial attacks upon a lynching mob that burned a Negro in early 1836.[89] He set up his *Observer* offices in Alton, Illinois, not far away. Before bringing his press to Alton, he defined his position: he did not intend to publish an abolition paper; however, he was opposed to slavery, and would speak against it when the occasion arose; most of all, he was concerned with the maintenance in Illinois and the West of the liberty to speak, write, and publish. Prophetically he wrote, "For one we distinctly avow it as our settled purpose, never, while life lasts, to yield to this new system of attempting to destroy, by means of mob-violence, the right of conscience, the freedom of opinion, and of the press."[90] However, the *Observer's* press was wrecked by a mob almost immediately upon its arrival. Lovejoy published his paper from a new one for some time without serious difficulties.[91]

[88] The St. Louis *Observer*, November 5, 1835.

[89] N. D. Harris, *The History of Negro Servitude in Illinois*, 74-5. A free mulatto named Francis McIntosh, who had killed an officer while resisting arrest, was taken from jail and slowly burned to death. Judge Lawless of St. Louis, during the investigation, directed a grand jury verdict to "act not at all upon the matter," since responsibility could not be fixed and the case was "beyond the reach of human laws." H. A. Trexler, *Slavery in Missouri 1804-1865*, 119, believes Lovejoy's expulsion from St. Louis was occasioned more by his vitriolic attacks on Judge Lawless than by his views on slavery.

[90] The Alton *Telegraph*, July 27, 1836, and the *Philanthropist*, December 2, 1836.

[91] The following summary of Lovejoy's career is taken from J. and O. Lovejoy, *Memoir of the Reverend Elijah P. Lovejoy*, Henry Tanner, *The Martyrdom of Lovejoy*, and E. Beecher, *Narrative of the Riots at Alton.* . . . The New York *Emancipator* also published an excellent brief sketch

The editor's increasing aggressiveness on the slavery question began to arouse considerable local comment. Whatever his previous professions, he had gone over to a militantly abolitionist stand by the spring of 1837, and the *Observer* was clearly on the way to becoming an abolitionist paper. A mass meeting of Alton citizens in July appointed a committee to warn him, to whom Lovejoy replied, once more placing his case on the issue of a free press, that no public meeting "could dictate what sentiments should not be discussed in a duly authorized newspaper."[92] Twice during August he was threatened, and on August 23 his offices were sacked and his press destroyed.[93] His appeal to the general public to donate funds for a new press was quickly answered, for it took less than a month to collect the necessary $1500. Significantly, his request for assistance made no mention of slavery, but solicited contribution for the purpose of maintaining the freedom of the press in Illinois.[94]

On September 21, Lovejoy's newly arrived third press was destroyed by a mob, and an appeal went out for funds to purchase a fourth. Twice more he received threats, and in early October, while visiting his wife, who was ill in Missouri, he was pursued by a mob and barely escaped injury. Later in October the Illinois Anti Slavery Convention, meeting in Al-

of Lovejoy and his career as a journalist in an undated extra, which appeared between the issues of February 8 and 15, 1838. Recent studies of Lovejoy are John Gill, *Tide Without Turning: Elijah P. Lovejoy and The Freedom of the Press*, 1959; and Merton L. Dillon, *Elijah P. Lovejoy, Abolitionist Editor*, 1961.

[92] N. D. Harris, *op. cit.*, 84.

[93] According to the Alton correspondent of the *Philanthropist*, September 8 and 22, 1837, this mob was composed of "gentlemen of property and standing," including the postmaster and the Methodist minister.

[94] "The question of the supremacy of the law of our State is one of deep interest to us all, and we do not feel at liberty to yield to the violence of a mob. We are therefore determined to sustain the laws and guard the freedom of the press without reference to the fact whether we agree or differ with the doctrines of it," a statement prepared by Lovejoy to be published over the signatures of the contributors, reprinted by A. L. Bowen, "The Antislavery Convention Held in Alton, Illinois, October 26-28, 1837," *Journal of the Illinois Historical Society* (October, 1927), 349-50.

ton, resolved that "the cause of human rights, the liberty of speech and of the press imperitively (sic) demands that the press of the Alton *Observer* be reestablished at Alton with its present editor."[95]

The growing asperity of the argument in Alton prompted the Attorney General of Illinois to lead two public meetings, sponsored by influential local citizens on November 2 and 3, which attempted to find some means of silencing the *Observer*. The main charge was that the paper endangered the peace and order of the community. Though Lovejoy himself attended the second meeting and spoke movingly in his own defense,[96] the meeting concluded by resolving that "no discussion of slavery, by any paper or editor, would be permitted in Alton." Further, it was "deemed indispensable to the peace and harmony of this community that the labors and influence of the late editor of the *Observer* no longer be identified with any newspaper enterprise in this city."[97] Lovejoy at once voiced his intention of disregarding the warning.

His fourth press arrived on November 5, and at the Mayor's request was placed in a warehouse for safekeeping, pending removal to the *Observer* offices.[98] Lovejoy, aware that there

[95] *Ibid.*, 342. This convention prepared for the formation of a state antislavery society, and "many of the delegates present, though opposed to the abolition of slavery, were advocates of free discussion," noted *Niles' Register*, 53: 165.

[96] Oliver Johnson, *op. cit.*, 226-27, gives excerpts from Lovejoy's speech, which concluded prophetically, "Sir, I dare not flee away from Alton. Should I attempt it, I should feel that the angel of the Lord, with drawn sword, was pursuing me wherever I went. It is because I fear God that I am not afraid of all those who oppose me in this city. No sir, the contest has come here, and here it must be finished. Before God and you all, I here pledge myself to continue it, until death; and if I fall, my grave shall be made in Alton."

[97] N.D. Harris, *op. cit.*, 90.

[98] Accounts of the mob are bitterly partisan. See the various accounts of J. and O. Lovejoy, Tanner, and Beecher, *op. cit.*; F. A. Flower, *History of the Republican Party*, 47-59; N. D. Harris, *op. cit.*, 68-99; the official report of Mayor John Krum of Alton, in the *Philanthropist*, December 12, 1837, and *Niles' Register*, 53: 165; an eyewitness account by a correspondent of the Cincinnati *Journal*, November 16 and 23, 1837; and William S. Lincoln's *The Alton Trials*, a stenographic report of the testimony offered in the riot trials.

were plans to destroy it, gathered a group of armed supporters who barricaded themselves in the warehouse to protect the press.[99] At nine o'clock of the evening of November 7, a mob formed, numbering between twenty and thirty, intending to march on the warehouse. Although Mayor Krum spoke to the group, hoping to break it up, the mayor later admitted that "the civil authorities could do little towards dispersing the mob except by persuasion." The mob moved on the warehouse and threw stones, breaking several windows. Responsibility for the first shot was never determined, but one bullet from a gun within the building killed Lyman Bishop, one of the attackers, and the mob withdrew, stunned by the sudden tragedy.[100]

Mayor Krum, seizing the opportunity, approached the warehouse and asked the defenders to surrender the press in order to avoid further bloodshed, but his request was refused as the mob returned with ladders, from which they attempted to set fire to the roof of the building. Four or five defenders rushed from the warehouse, fired a few shots, and set up ladders to mount the roof and extinguish the blaze. Lovejoy, standing in the open doorway, made a perfect target, and fell with five bullets in his body. Within a few minutes his supporters surrendered and were allowed to escape, but the mob finished burning the warehouse, battered the press with hammers, and threw it in the river. Lovejoy was buried the next day, and abolition had its first martyr.[101]

The Alton tragedy rocked the North to its foundations. With it abolitionism and freedom of the press merged into a

[99] About fifty men guarded the press during the day, but at the time of the attack fewer than twenty remained within the building.

[100] Mayor Krum, *op. cit.*, stated that the first shot fired was that which killed Bishop; the Cincinnati *Journal*'s eyewitness account, *op. cit.*, in common with Beecher's, Tanner's, and the Lovejoys', claimed that the mob fired first.

[101] Twelve of Lovejoy's men were tried in January, 1838, on the curious legal charge of resisting attack and unlawful defense of property, and were acquitted. On January 19 several members of the mob were tried for riot, and judged not guilty. See the accounts of Lincoln, *op. cit.*, the Alton *Telegraph*, January 24, 1838, the Cincinnati *Philanthropist*, February 13, 1838, and *Niles' Register*, 54:6-7.

single cause. Presses had been wrecked before, and editors mobbed, but the death of an abolitionist editor at the hands of an armed mob, defending his property in a free state, was a different matter. Lovejoy's death, said John Quincy Adams, gave "a shock as of an earthquake throughout this continent, which will be felt in the most distant region of the earth."[102] Ralph Waldo Emerson "sternly rejoiced that one was found to die for humanity and the rights of free speech and opinion." The "martyr of Alton" became the topic of countless sermons through the North, and few indeed were those who did not read or hear stories praising the editor as a martyr to liberty.[103]

The argument of the abolitionists that slavery would either engulf liberty, or freedom snuff out slavery, never had better proof than Lovejoy gave it. To many who condemned the abolitionists as radical, they were now not merely agitators for black freedom, but defenders of traditional American rights; as one abolitionist phrased it, "large accessions were made to the ranks of pronounced and avowed abolitionists" after the news from Alton spread.[104]

Northern newspapermen joined in condemning the mob. Though many decried the excesses of abolition journalism, few expressed anything but the conviction that, as the St. Louis *Commercial Bulletin* said, "One wrong is no justification for another." The editor of the small-town Homer, New York, *Republican and Eagle* echoed his city brother: "In any way in

[102] J. and O. Lovejoy, *op. cit.*, Introduction.

[103] Quoted by J. J. Chapman, *op. cit.*, 281. See, for examples, the sermons of Thomas Stone, *The Martyr of Freedom, A Discourse Delivered at East Machias, Maine*, and Beriah Green, *A Discourse in Commemoration of the Martyrdom of the Reverend Elijah P. Lovejoy, Delivered at Broadway Tabernacle. . . .*

[104] Henry Wilson, *op. cit.*, I:387. The statement recalls Channing's prophetic warning in *Slavery* (Boston, 1836) : "One kidnapped, murdered abolitionist would do more for the violent destruction of slavery than a thousand societies." The reaction of the Ohio Western Reserve was typical. Dozens of meetings, protesting Lovejoy's death, were held, and that area, heretofore hesitantly abolitionist, became one of the most thoroughly abolitionized areas in the nation; see E. C. Reilley, *The Early Slavery Controversy in the Western Reserve*, ms. dissertation, Western Reserve University Library, 174-78.

which this matter can be viewed, Mr. Lovejoy was a martyr to the cause of American liberty, the cause of the Constitution, the rights of man, and the laws of Heaven. . . ." William Cullen Bryant wrote:

> The right to discuss freely and openly, by speech, by the press, by the pen, all political questions, and to examine and animadvert upon all political institutions, is a right as clear and certain, so interwoven with our other liberties, so necessary, in fact, to their existence, that without it we must fall at once into despotism and anarchy. . . . We regard not this as a question connected with the abolition of slavery in the South, but as a question vital to the liberties of the entire Union.[105]

Horace Greeley, writing in *The New Yorker*, summarized the opinion of editors everywhere:

> Mr. Lovejoy's errors, or those of the abolitionists generally, have nothing to do in any shape with the turpitude of this outrage. But for the act of inflexibly maintaining the common rights of every citizen in defiance of the audacious tyranny of the multitude, he may well be deemed a martyr to public liberty.[106]

As if to emphasize that Lovejoy's death was a blow to civil liberties everywhere, a request by one hundred Bostonians for the use of Faneuil Hall for a memorial meeting was refused by the city authorities, lest it stir up too much excitement. The denial caused a greater stir than the meeting would have. Garrison fulminated in the *Liberator,* and Channing's biting letter to the Mayor was reprinted in dozens of newspapers:

[105] The *Philanthropist*, December 12, 1837; Del Porto, *op. cit.*, 119; and the New York *Evening Post*, November 18, 1837. This issue of the *Philanthropist* and that of November 21 reprint thirty-one editorials from various newspapers, while Harris, *op. cit.*, 96, lists forty-three, all condemning the Alton mob. The *Emancipator*, November 23, 1837, to February 8, 1838, reprinted one hundred and sixty-one editorials while the *Liberator,* November 24 to December 22, 1837, reprinted more than fifty. Of these, fewer than a dozen, reprinted in the *Emancipator*, January 18, 1838, expressed the opinion that Lovejoy's fate was deserved.

[106] Don C. Seitz, *Horace Greeley,* 137.

Has it come to this? Has Boston fallen so low? Are our fellow citizens to be murdered in the act of defending their property and of assuming the right of free discussion? And is it unsafe in this metropolis to express abhorrence of the deed? If such is our degradation, we ought to know the awful truth. . . .[107]

Permission was hastily granted and Faneuil Hall was crowded with a group not wholly abolitionist, but interested in protesting against what seemed a danger to freedom.[108] The Faneuil Hall meeting (marked by the appearance of Wendell Phillips as the great orator of the abolition movement) spread the news of the Lovejoy case through New England to a degree that the abolitionist press alone would never have been able to accomplish.[109]

The threat to freedom of the press, beginning with the suppression of Birney's newspaper in Kentucky and culminating in the Alton mob of 1837, was relatively brief in duration, but long-lasting in its influence on Northern opinion.[110] It gained a great deal of support for the abolition movement in the North by convincing large numbers of people that abolitionism and civil liberty were related, and that attacks on one

[107] See Garrison, Channing, and others, the *Liberator,* December 8, 1837. Channing, it should be noted, disapproved of the abolitionists' agressiveness, and as a non-resistant pacifist censured Lovejoy for his use of arms. See *A Letter to the Abolitionists* . . . also published in the *Liberator,* December 22, 1837.

[108] J. J. Chapman, *op. cit.,* 129. Harriet Martineau, *The Martyr Age of the United States of America,* pp. 39-40, quoted an eyewitness who calculated that only about one-third of the audience were abolitionists.

[109] For an account of the meeting, see the *Liberator,* December 15, 1837, and *The Proceedings of the Massachusetts Anti Slavery Society, Sixth Annual Report,* and its appendix, (Boston, 1838). Phillips' impassioned reply to Attorney General Austin may be found here and in his *Speeches, Lectures, and Letters,* 240 ff.

[110] A few minor disturbances occurred after 1837. Samuel Davis of the Peoria, Illinois, *Register,* though not an abolitionist, refused to publish his paper after a warning from a mass meeting in 1843, and left town; see *The National Anti Slavery Standard,* February 18, 1843. M. R. Hall, editor of the Cambridge, Ohio, *Clarion of Freedom,* had his offices wrecked in 1847 and moved his paper to New Concord, Ohio; see *The National Era,* September 23, October 14, and December 2, 1847. *The National Era* offices were stoned in 1848; *ibid.,* April 27 and May 4, 1848.

endangered the full enjoyment of the other. It removed the last restrictions from the abolitionist press, allowing abolitionist propaganda free publication and circulation in the non-slave states. It gave abolitionists the opportunity of reaching a wider audience than before, plus the added protection of the right to cry "martyr" if expression or circulation of abolitionist arguments were stopped or hindered. Possibly more important, the disturbances over the abolitionist press lent credence to the claim that the fight for Negro freedom involved a struggle for white freedom, that the two were parts of the same whole. A decade later, when the abolitionists put forward in earnest the charge that a gigantic "Slave Power conspiracy" had long plotted to subvert American liberties, the attacks on the press of 1835 to 1837 formed part of a pattern of proof that seemed highly plausible.

In the South, freedom of the press was not a major issue until the appearance of David Walker's *Appeal to the Colored Citizens of the World* in 1829, the beginning of Garrison's attacks on slaveholders in the *Liberator* in 1831, and the Southampton revolt of 1831 changed public attitudes. The temper of the earlier South was mildly antislavery; emancipation and colonization societies had been fairly numerous in the South, and their work met little real opposition.[111] In the lower South and the seaboard states, the pressure of public opinion kept newspaper discussion of the question to a satisfactory minimum.[112] Antislavery men in the states of the upper South, bordering on free soil and with a smaller Negro population, found public opinion much more tolerant. Seven newspapers, antislavery in aim, were founded in the border states before 1830—*The Emancipator* (Tennessee, 1819), *The Manu-*

[111] Alice Adams, *The Neglected Period of Antislavery*, ch. II. Garrison, working for Benjamin Lundy in Baltimore in 1829, publicly censured Walker's pamphlet and decried such efforts to stir up slave unrest; Nye, *Garrison, op. cit.*, 53.

[112] Clement Eaton, *op. cit.*, 163, 173. Joseph Gales, for example, editor of the Raleigh, N. C., *Register*, in 1816 could not publish an antislavery article in the face of this widespread taboo; see Clement Eaton, "Freedom of the Press in the Upper South," *Mississippi Valley Historical Review* XVIII (March 1932), 484-5.

mission Intelligencer (Tennessee, 1819), *The Abolition Intelligencer* (Kentucky, 1822), *The Genius of Universal Emancipation* (Maryland and Tennessee, 1821), *The Western Luminary* (Kentucky, 1823), and *The Liberalist* (Louisiana, 1828).[113] In addition, other newspapers often carried items of antislavery flavor.[114]

The reaction in the South to Nat Turner, Walker, and Garrison, was to call for an immediate re-examination of the slavery question as it concerned freedom of speech and expression. The result was that movements for the repression of material "tending to incite insurrection" appeared in all of the states of the lower South by 1836. In Virginia, hope was held for the eventual solution of the slavery problem by some means of emancipation, but the proslavery victory in the debates of 1832 soon shackled the press by law as well as by public opinion.[115] In South and North Carolina the revolt scare brought almost immediate passage of retaliatory laws, and in Kentucky, though no legal restrictions were placed upon the press, there was general distrust of editors who favored emancipation.[116] The prevailing attitude toward abolitionist publishers was well represented by Governor McDuffie of South Carolina, who told the legislature in 1835 that such men

[113] Virginius Dabney, *op. cit.*, 91-2; William Birney, *op. cit.*, 85-6; and E. C. Coleman, *op. cit.*, 294. A. E. Martin, *Antislavery in Kentucky Prior to 1850* (Louisville, 1918), 65, names the Russelville *Messenger* and *The Kentucky Reporter* as papers with abolitionist leanings. Birney, p. 404, lists but eight emancipationist papers in the North during the same period.

[114] Lundy's *Genius of Universal Emancipation* often copied these. In one year, 1828, of forty-four such items, ten were from non-abolitionist border-state papers; see Birney, *op. cit.*, 405. All had disappeared by 1832; Milo Mower, in fact, the publisher of the New Orleans *Liberalist*, was imprisoned in 1830 on charges of circulating "a seditious and inflammatory handbill among the colored people." Del Porto, *op. cit.*, 214.

[115] Thomas Ritchie of the Richmond *Enquirer* and John Hampden Pleasants of the Richmond *Whig* both fought for freedom of the press for antislavery opinion, but the debates of 1832 marked the last appearance of the liberal Virginia tradition. See Eaton, *Freedom of Thought in the Old South*, 172-74.

[116] Clement Eaton, "A Dangerous Pamphlet in the Old South," *Journal of Southern History* II (Feb.-Nov., 1936), 323-35; and A. E. Martin, *op. cit.*, 76-77.

should be put to death without benefit of clergy. A Charleston meeting in the same year stated that abolition editors were "no more entitled to the protection of the laws than the ferocious monster or venomous reptile," and a Williamsburg, Virginia, meeting decided that they should be punished immediately by death without resort to law.[117]

The pressure of aroused Southern opinion was reflected in the swift passage of legislation governing antislavery publications. The case of Georgia was typical. The Georgia Constitution guaranteed freedom of speech in much the same language as the Federal Constitution's Bill of Rights. Restrictions on the press were negligible. Georgia still retained its colonial law which made "any attempt by writing, speaking, or otherwise" to incite a slave revolt punishable by death, but there were no prosecutions recorded under it. In 1823, as tension heightened, the legislature began to tighten slave codes, passing a law which forbade any gathering of more than ten slaves without the presence of an overseer "capable of bearing arms." Slaves were prohibited from assembling for "questionable reasons," while justices of the peace were empowered to break up such meetings and sentence the participants "without trial" to 25 lashes on the bare back. 1829 and 1830 brought a barrage of additional legislation. Free Negroes were forbidden from "communicating with the colored people of this state," and from working in print shops or newspapers. The Code of 1835 reaffirmed the older statute by exacting the death penalty for printing or circulating anything tending to incite slave insurrections.[118]

Similar laws governing the press appeared first in the eastern and lower South, while the western South, strongly influenced by the legislatures of the slave states, followed their lead in the 'forties and 'fifties. The Maryland law of 1840 provided ten to

[117] Herman Von Holst, *Constitutional and Political History*, II:118; Edward Channing, *History of the United States*, V:161; and F. G. de Fontaine, *A History of American Abolitionism*, 30.

[118] Ida M. Martin, "Civil Liberties in Georgia Legislation 1800-1830," *Georgia Historical Quarterly* XVL (December, 1961), 329-44; Ruth Scarborough, *op. cit.*, 187-88.

twenty years' imprisonment for circulation of incendiary matter, or for "making, printing, or engraving it, or assisting in such."[119] The Virginia code of 1836 forbade any member or agent of an abolition society to come into Virginia, express his views, or print or circulate any material tending to incite revolt. Postmasters and justices of the peace in Virginia could censor the mails, and any free white person possessed the power of arrest. The amended Virginia law of 1849 made it a crime punishable by a year in jail and a fine not exceeding $500 merely to deny the right to own slaves. For circulating incendiary publications, Virginia exacted thirty-nine lashes for the first offense and death for a second.[120]

North Carolina ruled that such printing or circulating of inflammatory opinions was punishable by lashing and a year's imprisonment for the first, and death for a second violation, while Mississippi provided jail sentences and fines for expressing "sentiments likely to produce discontent among the colored class."[121] South Carolina placed a penalty of $1000 and one year in jail on the white man who published or possessed abolition literature, and death for the third offense by a free Negro; in 1859 the state put the finishing touches to its law by making it a crime to subscribe to or even to receive an abolition paper.[122] Louisiana laws of 1830 provided penalties for publishing, speaking, or writing, "in court, bench, stage, or pulpit," anything tending to excite slaves, and the revised code went further by making it a high misdemeanor to write, publish, or speak anything which tended "to destroy that line of distinction which the law has established between the several classes of this community," adding a fine of $300 to $1000 and imprisonment of six months to three years.[123] Tennessee and

---

[119] *Niles' Register*, 58:230.

[120] Eaton, *Freedom of Thought in the Old South,* 127, and "A Dangerous Pamphlet . . .," 481-2; and William Goodell, *The American Slave Code in Theory and Practice*, 385.

[121] Goodell, *The American Slave Code . . .*, 385.

[122] W. S. Savage, "Abolitionist Literature in the Mails, 1835-1836," *Journal of Negro History* XII (April, 1928), 156-7, and Eaton, *Freedom of Thought . . .*, 129-30.

[123] Eaton, *Freedom of Thought . . .,* 130, and Stroud, *A Sketch of the Laws Relating to Slavery in the Several States . . .*, 104-5.

Alabama laws followed the Maryland and Virginia laws of 1836, while Kentucky passed no legislation affecting the anti-slavery press until 1860, after the John Brown raid.[124]

These laws reflected the dominance of the slaveholding class in Southern society. They were justified not upon what they really represented—the need for protection of vested interests in cotton and slaves—but instead upon the need for protecting the white population from slave insurrections.[125] The fear of a Negro revolt, actuated by Walker, Garrison, and Nat Turner, proved to be an effective device for controlling the press in the South from 1831 until the Civil War.

Legalized abridgments of free press and thought were justified in the South on several grounds. For one thing, it was widely believed that criticism of the institutions of some states by residents of others was unconstitutional; suppression of abolitionist opinion therefore was not a violation of civil rights.[126] Again, it was argued that suppression of abolitionist literature was best for slaves, to say nothing of the white man. If slaves could read (as most could not), they might read anti-slavery publications, which would "tend to make them restless and discontented, and would probably seduce them to a course that would ensure their ruin. . . ."[127] There was the appeal to safety—if the Negro were freed through the dissemination of antislavery opinion North or South, "the fabric of Southern civilization and liberty, which consumed ages in its construction," was doomed.[128]

Freedom of the press, as it came to be defined in the South, meant merely the right to publish certain specific things without previous permission. It did not include the right to publish licentious material or material tending to disturb the peace, nor did it mean freedom from responsibility after publication,

---

[124] Missouri did not call for legislation governing "freesoil and abolitionist publications" until 1855, but its 1804 law imposed death for conspiring to foment slave revolts; see H. A. Trexler, *op. cit.*, 202n.

[125] Cf. J. S. Bassett, *Slavery in the State of North Carolina*, 98-101.

[126] See the opinion of General Harrison, in the Utica, N. Y., *Friend of Man*, July 22, and October 7, 1840.

[127] "A Citizen of Georgia," *Remarks on Slavery, Occasioned by Attempts to Circulate Improper Publications in the Southern States*, 24.

[128] E. N. Elliot, *Cotton is King and The Pro-Slavery Argument*, 442.

or freedom to discuss the domestic institutions of other states.[129] "Men cannot speak, write, nor act in such a manner as to endanger the moral well-being of society," said one Southerner. "Let us pay no regard to the claim which may be asserted for the independence of the press," said another. "If in the exercise of their independence they choose to print, we in the exercise of our independence may choose to suppress, to the uttermost of our power, what we deem inflammatory, dangerous, mischievous."[130] In the face of the "Black Terror" of slave revolt, which dominated Southern thought for thirty years, few noticed (or if they did, dared mention) that the laws against antislavery publications infringed directly upon the right of the free white man in the South to speak and print. Nor was it explained that these laws provided penalties for offenses not clearly defined, and ones which an editor could not be sure of avoiding until after he had committed them.[131]

Despite the frightening language of the statutes, it was the pressure of public opinion, rather than any legal threat, that kept the Southern press free of antislavery matter. The courts' interpretations of the laws were uniformly lenient and prosecutions of Southern editors relatively few. Southern editors, for the most part, accepted and applauded restrictions on the press, and instead of protesting, ferreted out suspected antislavery men and whipped up feeling against them. *The Georgia Telegraph* in 1835 advised banning all Northern newspapers of any kind from the state; the Columbia, South Carolina, *South Carolinian* warned in 1849 that *The National Anti Slavery Standard* and *The Pennsylvania Freeman* were circulating in the state and advised mob action; and the Macon

---

[129] W. S. Jenkins, *Proslavery Thought in the Old South*, 443.

[130] Anonymous, *The South Vindicated from the Treason and Fanaticism of the Northern Abolitionists*, 31, and "Appomatox," the Richmond, Va., *Enquirer*, February 4, 1832.

[131] For critical views of the Southern laws abridging freedom of the press, and their threat to civil liberty, see Gamaliel Bailey, the *Philanthropist*, March 31, 1840; Stroud, *op. cit.*, 104-8; and H. R. Helper, *The Impending Crisis* (New York 1860), 408-10. Bailey points out the salient fact that Southern laws specifically defined their own terms.

Citizen in 1853 threatened the editor of *The Saturday Evening Post* of Philadelphia because he printed a letter from Frederica Bremer praising *Uncle Tom's Cabin.*[132]

The Southern editor with abolitionist ideas was discouraged by public pressure long before his utterances reached the prosecution stage, as in the case of Samuel Ludwig of Savannah, who was simply run out of town on suspicion rather than for anything he published.[133] In Louisiana, for example, the first arrest for public expression of abolition opinion was not reported until February of 1860.[134] In North Carolina the Quaker editor, William Swaim, undoubtedly would have tested the law severely had he not died in 1834. Swaim kept up an aggressive antislavery crusade in his Greensboro *Patriot* from 1829 until his death, challenging the law in no uncertain terms: "Before we will relinquish our right to think, speak, print, and publish our own deliberate opinions in relation to *public* men and *public* measures, we will renounce existence itself."[135] The earliest widely publicized case involving a violation of the laws governing the circulation of abolition propaganda was that of Dr. Reuben Crandall of New York, who was arrested in Washington, D. C., in 1835 on charges of inciting slaves to revolt. He was accused of lending copies of *The Emancipator* and other papers to a friend, who left them in a neighboring store. Crandall (a brother of Prudence Crandall) was held in jail for eight months before he was tried and found not guilty. The flimsiness of the charge and the length of his incarceration gave the abolitionists an excellent opportunity to hail Crandall as a martyr to freedom of speech

[132] R. B. Flanders, *Plantation Slavery in Georgia*, 286, and *The Anti Slavery Bugle*, May 18, 1849, and March 19, 1853. Editor Andrews of the *Citizen*, however, refused to divulge in 1850 the name of a correspondent who sent in allegedly offensive matter, and took a firm stand on freedom of the press; see the Augusta, Ga., *Chronicle and Standard*, August 27, 1850, and *The National Anti Slavery Standard*, October 24, 1850.

[133] *The National Anti Slavery Standard*, March 8, 1857.

[134] T. E. Dabney, *One Hundred Great Years*, 116.

[135] Eaton, "Freedom of the Press in the Upper South," *op. cit.*, 487.

and press, and to warn of the threat to civil liberty implicit in such regulatory laws.[136]

The only important cases prosecuted in Virginia were those of Lysander Barrett in 1839 and Samuel Janney in 1850. Barrett and ten others were charged with the circulation of petitions asking Congress to abolish slavery in the District of Columbia. The verdict was not guilty, the court holding that "to sustain a prosecution . . . , the person accused must be a member or an agent of an abolition or antislavery society."[137] Janney, a Quaker, published in the Leesburgh *Washingtonian* a refutation of a speech declaring that slavery possessed Biblical sanction. He was indicted on charges of publishing an incendiary article. The charge was thrown out as incorrect, and a second indictment charged him with denying the right of ownership in slaves. Janney, appearing before a jury of slaveholders, put up a brilliant defense and won acquittal.[138]

Not only newspapers, but books and magazines were carefully watched in the South.[139] Northern publishing houses often put out separate editions of books for Southern trade, excising or softening antislavery passages.[140] Several of Miss Sedgwick's novels, Renwick's *Life of John Jay*, *The Memoirs of Freeborn Garretson*, J. K. Paulding's *Letters from the South*, various Sabbath school books, and Peter Parley's *First Book of*

[136] A. B. Hart, *op. cit.*, 235; Henry Wilson, *op. cit.*, I:306-7; Oliver Johnson, *op. cit.*, 483; and for an account of the trial, see *The Trial of Reuben Crandall, M. D., Charged with Publishing Seditious Libels*, and *The Trial of Reuben Crandall, M. D., . . . Carefully Reported and Compiled from the Written Statements of Court and Counsel. . . .*

[137] Helen T. Catterall, *Judicial Cases Concerning American Slavery*, I:196. In 1848 this loophole was plugged by broadening the term "abolition agents" to "any free white person."

[138] *The National Era*, July 11, 1850, and *The National Anti Slavery Standard*, July 25, 1850, reprint the details of the case and Janney's defense. He had previously contributed to *The National Era* under the name "Virginia"; see the issue of January 31, 1850.

[139] See the survey made of current novels by the Columbia *South Carolinian* and the Richmond *Examiner*, reprinted in *The National Era*, September 1 and 29, 1853.

[140] Letter of Harper and Brothers to a Charleston bookseller, the New York *Emancipator*, August 11, 1836.

History were among those expurgated for Southern sale.[141] Two booksellers were given five days to leave Mobile, Alabama, after the local Committee of Vigilance had inspected their stock. In Parkersburg, Virginia, three men convicted of possession of an unnamed antislavery poem were put under bond to keep the peace for three years. In Charleston, South Carolina, the agent of *The New World,* which was serializing Dickens' *American Notes,* submitted it to the South Carolina Association for a ruling. The committee of the Association believed it should be suppressed, but deciding that since any attempt to suppress Dickens would obviously fail, let the paper circulate.[142]

Possession of *Uncle Tom's Cabin* or of Helper's *The Impending Crisis* placed the owner in real jeopardy; however, judging from the number of replies to and attacks on the books in Southern papers, both must have found plenty of readers in the South. Samuel Green of Dorchester County, Maryland, reportedly received a prison sentence for possession of Mrs. Stowe's work, and a Maryland free Negro was later sentenced for the same offense.[143] Helper's book was judged to be an even greater danger to the South than *Uncle Tom's Cabin* and its ownership was denounced in most Southern states as treason.[144] In 1859 Daniel Worth was indicted in North Carolina for selling and circulating the book, and tried under the law of 1830. The defense maintained that the statute did not prevent the distribution of abolition material to whites, but was intended to bar distribution to slaves and free

[141] *The Anti Slavery Bugle,* January 26, 1850 (misprinted 1849), and February 9, 1850.

[142] The Mobile, Alabama, *Register,* August 17, 1856; *The Anti Slavery Bugle,* May 3, 1846; and *The National Anti Slavery Standard,* December 22, 1843. One of the books in the Mobile case, according to *The National Era,* August 28, 1856, was Frederick Douglass' autobiography; however, the vigilance committee, true to form in such cases, refused to divulge the offending books lest people be encouraged to read them.

[143] Hart, *op. cit.,* 217, 234, and *The National Era,* October 28, 1858.

[144] *The National Era,* September 28, 1859. For a study of Helper and his book, see Hugh T. Lefler, *Hinton Rowan Helper: Advocate of A White America.*

Negroes. Convicted and given a light sentence, Worth appealed, but the Supreme Court upheld the lower court on the ground that in a mixed population "it was not necessary . . . that the sale should be to a slave or a free negro . . . nor read in the presence of either," to warrant conviction.[145]

The struggle for freedom of the press in the South lasted longest and was most nearly successful in the upper South, where the Quaker-natural rights-frontier tradition was strongest and the Negro population small. Tennessee, in the 'twenties, supported a manumission society and two antislavery newspapers. Elihu Embree, probably the first emancipationist editor in the West, established the Jonesboro, Tennessee, *Manumission Intelligencer* in 1819 (later called *The Emancipator*) as the organ of the Tennessee Manumission Society.[146] After Embree's death in 1820, Benjamin Lundy's *Genius of Universal Emancipation* followed for three years. But the passage of legislation in the 'thirties removed Tennessee from the list of Southern states which permitted open antislavery opinions, and the battle for a free press was transferred to Kentucky and western Virginia.

In western Virginia, proximity to the free states of Pennsylvania and Ohio, a large foreign-born and a small slave population made the antislavery press a minor issue. That section held a long-standing grudge against the slaveholders of eastern Virginia who controlled the state,[147] and Virginia law govern-

---

[145] Catterall, *op. cit.*, II:237-38, and Eaton, *Freedom of Thought in the Old South*, 141-42. The Court decided, however, that circulation of the book to satisfy curiosity, rather than to propagate its principles, was legal. Worth put up bond and moved to Indiana after his Supreme Court plea failed. See Noble J. Tolbert, "Daniel Worth: Tarheel Abolitionist," *North Carolina Historical Review* XXXIX (July, 1962), 284-305.

[146] For an account of Embree's career, see Elijah Embree Hoss, *Elihu Embree, Abolitionist.*

[147] In 1860 western Virginia had only 149 slaves in a population of more than 45,000, according to J. G. McGregor, *The Disruption of Virginia*, 12. The Wheeling *Tri-Weekly Gazette*, February 8, 1836, judged Channing's *Slavery* to be a respectable and competent discussion of the question, and took Hammond of South Carolina to task for attacking it. Examples of western Virginia antislavery thought are: the Reverend Henry Ruffner, "A Slaveholder of West Virginia," *Address to the People of West Virginia, Showing that Slavery is Injurious to the Public Welfare* . . .; and an edi-

ing the press simply became a dead letter in the western counties. The Ceredo *Crescent,* the Kanawha *Republican,* the *Kanawha Valley Star,* though lukewarm to abolitionism, felt free to espouse the cause if they wished, and during the 'fifties numerous avowedly antislavery papers flourished in the area. The Wellsburg *Herald* consistently published antislavery items, and the Wheeling *Daily Enterprise* was founded in the 'forties as an antislavery publication. In 1848 Anson Berkshire established the antislavery Moundsville *Crisis,* while the Wheeling *Gazette* in 1855 favored repeal of the fugitive slave laws, of the Kansas-Nebraska bill, and the total abolition of slavery in the District of Columbia.[148]

The Wheeling *Intelligencer,* one of the most influential papers in the upper South, favored freedom of speech and press on the slavery question, and the Wheeling *Times and Gazette* came out openly for abolition. In 1854 the latter paper published a series of articles about the possibility of abolishing slavery in the state which aroused some proslavery opposition. A mass meeting was called at Wheeling Courthouse to discuss suppression of the paper, but the meeting instead voted to uphold editor Wharton, resolving that Wheeling "would have and sustain one independent newspaper, which did not fear to boldly speak the truth."[149]

After Lovejoy's troubles in 1835, Missouri reported no noteworthy cases involving the antislavery press, nor did Maryland,[150] but Kentucky, which passed no laws governing the

torial in the Wheeling *Intelligencer,* April 13, 1857, declaring slavery "an unmitigated curse." The Wheeling *Times and Gazette* engaged in a sharp debate, reprinted in *The Anti Slavery Bugle,* April 29, 1854, with the Richmond *Whig,* over the slavery question. It is to be noted that Helper's *The Impending Crisis,* 368-69, quotes the Wellsburg *Herald,* the Wheeling *Gazette,* and the Wheeling *Intelligencer* as antislavery evidence, and that Charles Hammond of the Cincinnati *Gazette,* Birney's supporter, was a product of the Virginia panhandle.

148 Eaton, *Freedom of Thought in the Old South,* 181-83; *The Anti Slavery Bugle,* February 9, 1846, June 9, 1848, and August 25, 1855.

149 The Wheeling *Intelligencer,* November 5, 1853, February 7 and 18, 1859, and the account of the meeting in *The National Era,* April 27, 1854.

150 The Baltimore *Sun,* December 23, 1837, stated that it would pursue a calm and neutral policy on the slavery question, and most of the state's papers followed a similar course throughout the period. In 1846 Dr. Snodgrass' Baltimore *Saturday Visiter,* a mild reform paper, was investigated by

publication of "incendiary" material until 1860, became a battleground. The influence of men such as Henry Clay, the small number of slaves in the state, and its proximity to the Western abolition center of Ohio, combined to give the state a tolerant attitude toward discussion of the issue that was unique among the slave states. Emancipation and manumission newspapers, such as *The Abolition Intelligencer* and *The Western Luminary*, circulated in the state before 1830, and in 1833, while the furor over Garrisonian abolition boiled in the eastern South, the Louisville *Herald* announced that in Kentucky "a candid discussion of slavery" was "not only permitted but invited by the public sentiment." James Freeman Clarke's *Western Messenger* printed extracts from Channing's antislavery writings, and its editor was proud to say in 1836 that "we are not afraid of discussing this or any other question here." Clarke participated in a three-day symposium on slavery, and later engaged in a debate which was fully reprinted in the Louisville *Journal*.[151] The temper of the Kentucky press during the 'thirties, while other states in the South were passing strict regulatory laws, was admirably reflected by the *Western Presbyterian Herald* in 1838:

The liberty of the press should be sustained; mob violence should be discountenanced, not for the sake of abolitionism, nor in fact for the sake of any other cause good or bad, but for the sake of truth and righteousness, and for the great principle of civil liberty.[152]

Within a few years, however, this attitude was put to the test by Cassius Marcellus Clay.

---

the state legislature after it had printed a speech by Cassius Clay of Kentucky, but nothing resulted; see the Cincinnati *Weekly Herald and Philanthropist*, January 28 and February 11, 1846, for the legislative discussions. In Missouri, a mob dumped the press of the free-soil Parkville *Luminary* in the river, but St. Louis papers protested the act; see *The Anti Slavery Bugle*, May 5 and 12, 1855.

[151] A. E. Martin, *op. cit.*, 65; *The Western Messenger* IV (August, 1836), 58; and James Freeman Clarke, *Antislavery Days* (New York, 1884), 25-6.

[152] Quoted by Martin, *op. cit.*, 78. See also similar quotations, *loc. cit.*, from the Louisville *Journal* and the Maysville *Eagle*.

Clay represented a native Kentucky antislavery tradition that stemmed mostly from the non-slaveholding yeomen and the poor white class of Kentucky, from men who believed that slavery was a liability to the state's social, economic, and political future. Thomas Speed of Bardstown thought in 1834 that because of slavery Kentucky had "fallen in the rear of her younger sister (*Ohio*)," and hoped that Kentucky might soon "unite her wisdom in a conventional council to relieve posterity from this blighting curse." The Louisville *Journal* in 1837 believed slavery "operates prejudicially on the middle and working classes . . .," and "has effectually prevented our State from developing its resources," while Robert Wickliffe of Lexington expressed the fear that slavery was developing a landed aristocracy in Kentucky.[153] Clay, who by the 'forties had come to represent this faction in Kentucky politics, based his opposition to slavery not on grounds of any concern for the Negro, but on the welfare of the 600,000 free white non-slaveholders of the state.

Slavery, in his opinion, drove out white labor, disadvantaged the middle- and lower-class white, and vested the ruling power of the state in a small group of rich, aristocratic slaveholders. It was not so much slavery itself, but the "white tyrant" who through slavery ruled the white worker, that was his target, and whose dominance he wished to destroy by abolishing slavery.[154] Clay was no abolitionist; he favored gradual emancipation, the payment of compensation to slave owners from state funds, the exile of free Negroes, and the withholding of votes from freed slaves. He wished to prove, he said, "to the

[153] The Cincinnati *Gazette*, July 18, 1834, and the *Philanthropist*, January 20 and October 6, 1897.

[154] For Clay's views, see Horace Greeley, ed., *The Writings of Cassius Marcellus Clay*, "Speech at Tremont Temple," "Letters on the Slave Trade," "Address to the People of Kentucky," "Speech in New York," and excerpts from *The True American*, 256-57, 316-17, 346-7, 404-6, 417-18, *et passim*. See also David L. Smiley, "Cassius M. Clay and Southern Abolitionism," *Register of the Kentucky Historical Society* (October, 1951); and David Smiley, "Cassius M. Clay and John G. Fee: A Study in Southern Antislavery Thought," *Journal of Negro History* XLII (July, 1957), 201-13.

people of the South, that he warred not upon *them,* but upon *Slavery,* that a man might denounce tyrants without being the enemy of his country."[155]

Clay's plans matured in the founding of a newspaper, *The True American,* at Lexington, Kentucky, and he felt it an important part of his mission "to determine whether liberty of speech is longer possible in a slave state." Civil liberties, he wrote, were among the first casualties of a despotism; one of the strongest of his objections to slavery arose from the fact that it always caused "the practical loss of liberty of speech and of the press." The majority of Southern newspapers were "mouthpieces of the slaveholders," and *The True American,* he averred, would speak out against them, with the protection of his pistol and Bowie knife if the laws of God and society offered none.[156]

His declaration of intent in 1845 to found a newspaper drew varying reactions. The Lexington *Inquirer* thought that "agitation of the subject can do no good, but will doubtless do much harm," whereas the Richmond *Farmer's Chronicle* believed the time was ripe "to look the question *(of slavery)* full in the face." The Lexington *Journal* thought that Clay had the support of "a large class of respectable citizens," but the Lexington *Observer,* leaving unquestioned his right to publish such a paper, thought that even a moderate discussion of the question might unsettle the Negro population, and that safety

[155] *Ibid.,* 478, and *The Anti Slavery Bugle,* October 31, 1845. Clay proposed first to free all female slaves at twenty-one, to provide for the purchase of existing male slaves after thirty years, and to eject the present free Negro population to colonies or to the free states. Racial amalgamation he did not believe to be a problem. A Kentucky correspondent of the *Bugle,* October 3, 1845, thought Clay represented "the views of three-quarters of the people of his native state." The Northern abolitionists did not regard Clay as "occupying the true position," but respected him for his championship of a free press. See Benjamin Jones' opinion of Clay in *The Anti Slavery Bugle,* August 29, 1845, Gamaliel Bailey's in the Cincinnati *Weekly Herald and Philanthropist,* February 4, 1846, and Eliza Lee Follen's poem, "To Cassius Clay," *The Liberty Bell.* For a recent and authoritative study, see David L. Smiley, *Lion of Whitehall: The Life of Cassius M. Clay,* Madison, 1962.

[156] *Writings,* 36, 37, 76, 213-14, 257-274, and his letter to the Cincinnati *Gazette,* reprinted in *The National Anti Slavery Standard,* August 4, 1855, and his prospectus of *The True American, ibid.,* March 6, 1845.

was of more importance than freedom of the press. The Frankfort *Commonwealth* could see no reason why Clay should not publish his paper, so long as the tone of the discussion was maintained at a high level.[157]

The True American was launched in June, 1845, from offices which Clay had prepared for any eventuality. He backed the doors with sheet iron, put two four-pounder brass cannon loaded with nails at the head of the stairs, stored Mexican lances and shotguns in his office, cut a trap door for escape to the roof, and stored kegs of powder, fired by remote control fuses, next to his press. Thus equipped, resting his case on his constitutional right to a free press, Cassius Clay set out to publish his paper.[158]

However, *The True American* lasted only three months. Current rumors of a revolt among Lexington free Negroes, supposedly encouraged by Clay, and the aggressive tone of his paper, touched off immediate opposition.[159] A mass meeting, held August 14, decided that Clay's publication was "dangerous to the peace of the community, and to the safety of our homes and families." Thomas F. Marshall, a political rival of Clay, accused the paper of "bringing fire into a magazine. . . . As such, the peace and safety of this community demand its instant and entire suppression."[160] Clay replied the next day in a special issue, that "the idea of insurrection in Kentucky, where there are about six whites to one black, is ridiculous, and only used by the slaveholders as a Bugaboo, to maintain the ascendancy of their power in the state. . . ." A committee

[157] *The National Anti Slavery Standard,* March 6 and 20, 1845, and the Cincinnati *Weekly Herald and Philanthropist,* February 24 and September 10, 1845.

[158] Coleman, *op. cit.,* 307, and *The True American,* June 3, 1845.

[159] *The Weekly Herald and Philanthropist,* August 27, 1845. Clay believed that an article insulting to slaveholders, sent in anonymously and published during his illness, aroused most of the opposition; see his explanation in *The Anti Slavery Bugle,* July 14, 1849.

[160] For accounts of the meeting, see *The National Anti Slavery Standard,* August 28 and September 4, 1845, and *The Anti Slavery Bugle,* September 19, 1845. Marshall's speech, found here and in W. L. Barre, *The Speeches and Writings of Thomas F. Marshall,* 200-208, is perhaps the best example of Southern logic in support of suppressing journalistic freedom on the grounds of public safety.

of citizens, however, obtained an injunction against his paper, and while Clay lay ill on August 18, they entered his offices, dismantled and packed his equipment, and shipped it to Cincinnati.[161]

The action of the Lexington committee aroused a great deal of adverse comment. The New York *Herald* and the Cincinnati *Herald* thought *The True American* received exactly the treatment it deserved, complimenting Lexington on its orderly procedure, but the Northern press in general upheld Clay and condemned the committee. Protest meetings in Cincinnati and Pittsburgh passed resolutions of support to Clay, and in Syracuse, a large meeting sponsored by abolitionists resolved that "any attempt by mob violence, or otherwise, to trammel the press, is to be regarded as virtual treason. . . ."[162] Kentucky opinion tended to sympathize with Clay. A meeting in Mason County, while admitting that "the laws should be held sacred," thought that "the interposition of popular force" was justified in this instance, but the Frankfort *Yeoman* laid the mob's action directly at the door of the slaveholders, who were "too jealous of their rights to permit discussion . . ., mildly or vituperatively." The Georgetown *Christian Intelligencer,* noting "that there is an immense portion of the population of this state that regards slavery as a very great political evil," spoke up for "the right of Mr. Clay and every other freeman to discuss the subject of slavery."[163]

[161] Accounts are found in *Niles' Register,* 68:408; *The Anti Slavery Bugle,* September 5, 1845; *The National Anti Slavery Standard,* August 28 and October 23, 1845; the Hallowell, Maine, *Liberty Standard,* September 11, 1845. Clay's version appears in *The True American,* October 7, 1845, and *Writings,* 301-36. Henry Clay left Kentucky on a sudden trip between August 15 and 18, but his son, J. B. Clay, served as secretary of the citizens' committee. After returning from the Mexican War Cassius Clay sued and collected $2500 damages for the committee's action.

[162] *The Weekly Herald and Philanthropist,* October 1, 1845, and *The National Anti Slavery Standard,* September 4 and 25, October 2, 1845.

[163] *The Weekly Herald and Philanthropist,* September 3 and November 19, 1845, and January 28, 1846; and *The National Anti Slavery Standard,* September 11, 1845.

Abolitionism and Freedom of the Press

The True American found its most eminent defender in George Prentice, editor of the influential Louisville *Journal*. Though not an emancipationist, Prentice was a strong believer in the freedom of the press. Clay, he believed, though hot-tempered, was an honest editor and the accusations made against him were obviously false. The issue, as Prentice saw it, was neither slavery nor slave revolts, but freedom:

> The law which secures to every slaveholder his property in his slaves is regarded by him as sacred, but it is not more sacred than the law which gives every man the right to utter and publish any opinions he pleases in regard to slavery.[104]

Though the rival Louisville *Times* attempted to stir up feeling against Prentice, he stubbornly refused to retract, declaring that while he would not himself agitate the question of emancipation, he reserved the right to do so when and if he found it necessary.[165]

The incident of August 18 did not mark the disappearance of the antislavery press in Kentucky. Clay continued to publish *The True American* from Lexington, though it was printed in Cincinnati, until he left for the Mexican War in June of 1846.[166] The Louisville *Examiner*, founded in June of 1847 by J. C. Vaughan "to show the people of Kentucky the grievous losses they are obliged to bear in consequence of slavery," ran without opposition until December, 1849, when

[164] The Louisville *Journal*, August 21, 1845, and *The Weekly Herald and Philanthropist*, August 27, 1845.

[165] *The Anti Slavery Bugle*, December 12, 1845, and *The Weekly Herald and Philanthropist*, November 19, 1846. For a tribute to Prentice by another great Southern journalist, see Henry Watterson, *George Dennison Prentice: A Memorial Address*.

[166] *Writings*, Introd., vii, and *The Weekly Herald and Philanthropist*, March 25, 1846. Under the direction of Clay's assistant, the paper lost money and expired in October, 1846. At the time of its expiration it listed 2200 subscribers in Kentucky, with additional circulation in Tennessee, Virginia, and North Carolina; see *The Weekly Herald and Philanthropist*, October 28, 1846.

it died for lack of support.[167] The Lexington and Louisville *Progress of the Age*, another temperate antislavery paper, met the same fate in the 'fifties. The Lexington *Atlas* took a strong antislavery position in the late 'forties, and during the constitutional convention of 1849 the question of emancipation was freely discussed, pro and con, by newspapers throughout the state. Kentucky's two avowedly abolitionist papers did, however, encounter stronger opposition than that faced by the temperate emancipationist or mildly antislavery journals. John Brady, the editor of a self-confessed abolitionist paper, was driven out of Lexington in 1855, while William S. Bailey's Newport *News* ran into trouble from the date of its founding. Destroyed by a mob in 1851, and reestablished as *The Free South*, with Cassius Clay's blessing, it lasted until 1859, when another mob wrecked it during the John Brown scare.[168]

While the difficulties of Brady and Bailey reflected the feelings of Kentucky toward immediate abolition, the case of *The True American* revealed the basic objections of the South's proslavery element to a free press. Clay was an emancipationist, not an "immediatist," who belonged to no abolitionist societies, and his attack upon slavery was not based upon those social, moral, and religious opinions to which Southern feelings were most sensitive. He was no friend of the Negro, and by no stretch of the imagination could he be accused of favoring racial equality or amalgamation. He clearly had no intention of inciting slave revolt, and he wrote for white readers only. His aim was simply the destruction of the dominance of the

[167] Vaughan, a South Carolinian and a temperance advocate, had previously served on the staff of *The True American* and founded his paper to replace it; see his prospectus in *The National Era*, July 1, 1847, and *The National Anti Slavery Standard*, November 2, 1848. See also "Shall the Discussion Go On?" in *The Anti Slavery Bugle*, November 10, 1849, for an estimate of Vaughan.

[168] Martin, *op. cit.*, 122-23, and Coleman, *op. cit.*, 319-20. See the attacks on Bailey, reprinted in *The Anti Slavery Bugle*, October 23, 1852. Bailey published the paper from his home after 1851, with the assistance of his wife and children; see *The National Anti Slavery Standard*, March 22 and August 15, 1856; and Will Frank Sheeley, "William Shreve Bailey, Kentucky Abolitionist," *Filson Club Historical Quarterly* (July, 1957).

white slaveholding group by the destruction of the economic system which gave it power. Yet, despite the large amount of agreement with his views in Kentucky, and despite all the constitutional guarantees of his right to publish, his paper was suppressed. The case of *The True American* showed how effectively a small but powerful faction, whose interests were threatened by antislavery discussion, could excite a Southern community into acts that were perhaps against its best interests and which did not represent the majority point of view. The mass meeting, the committee of respectable citizens, the flavor of legality imparted by orderly procedure, the justification of the act by a quasi-legal appeal to public safety—all indicate organized leadership and well-developed techniques. Though the Clay incident engendered much discussion of curbing the press by law, attempts to do so failed. In 1846 a bill introduced into the legislature for the control of antislavery papers passed the Senate, but lost in the House.[169] The principle it embodied was not successfully revived in Kentucky until the eve of the Civil War.

The controversy over the freedom of the press was extremely important in shaping public attitudes toward abolitionism in both North and South after 1830. In the North it was a major factor in convincing a hitherto neutral public that the institution of slavery carried an inherent danger to the freedom to speak and write. Prominent conservatives in the North showed, particularly in their reactions to the events of 1836 and 1837, that they considered freedom of the press a vastly more vital issue than the immediate abolition of slavery. Suppression by legal (or extra-legal) means of an abolitionist paper presented a potential threat to any newspaper, whatever its editorial complexion. In the South, the controversy materially assisted the slaveholding group in solidifying popular opinion against any kind of open antislavery discussion in the press. The threat of a slave revolt, supposedly encouraged by the press, unified Southern thought on the slavery question

[169] Martin, *op. cit.*, 117, and *The Weekly Herald and Philanthropist*, January 28, February 4, 11, and 25, 1846.

in a fashion impossible in any other way, and convinced many doubters and dissenters that a neutral position on slavery was untenable.

The controversy, too, marked a turning-point in the history of journalism. Abolition was, except for the alien and sedition laws, the first really important issue in the struggle for freedom of the press that the nation had encountered since the founding of the republic. The restrictive laws of the South, and the almost universal failure of Southern newspapers to continue publication if they were critical of domestic institutions, showed that a powerful minority of vested interests could, by controlling legislatures and molding public opinion, effectively nullify Federal and state constitutional guarantees of free speech and press. Through all the state laws and public resolutions passed in the South ran then a single theme—the duty of the press to respect the interests of the community. Despite constitutional guarantees, legislators and public alike justified the suppression of editorial opinion on the principle *salus populi suprema lex;* an editor might have a legal right to publish as he wished, but in the interests of society he did not have a moral right to do so.

On the other hand, the refusal of Northern legislatures to abridge freedom of publication, and the gradual perception by the free states of the relation between abolition and the tradition of civil liberty, showed how the North saw the issue in another fashion. By 1840, Northern public opinion had accepted a definition of freedom of the press which allowed the editor to espouse unpopular minority causes, to criticize popular institutions, or to attack, with the intention of changing, the *status quo.* The place of the antislavery press in developing and determining that view should not be underestimated; Clay, Birney, Goodell, Lovejoy, Garrison, Bailey, and the rest, during the critical period 1830-1850, gave direction to the road American journalism has since followed. Edmund Quincy, another editor, summed up the abolitionist contribution to the civil liberties tradition in a speech to the American Anti Slavery Society on its twenty-fifth anniversary by saying, "If it were possible that the antislavery movement could fail of final success . . ., still this nation and the world would owe a lasting debt to it, for the vindication of the free press and free speech which they have achieved . . ., the great incidental victory of the antislavery movement."[170]

The Day of the Mob

V

BEFORE 1830, though sensitive to antislavery talk, the South nevertheless allowed a limited amount of free discussion. Yet at the same time signs of displeasure indicated a growing public uneasiness about the slavery question. One "Hieronymous" in 1825 complained of newspaper comments on slavery; a meeting in Smithfield, Virginia, was broken up by local magistrates in 1827; and the Manumission Society of North Carolina in 1826 deplored the increasing tendency in the South to stifle criticism of its domestic institutions. The most rigid control of antislavery discussion before 1830 existed in South Carolina, but after that date fears of Garrisonian abolition and slave revolt spread suspicion of antislavery opinion throughout the South in general.[1]

It was imperative, after the beginnings of the aggressive phase of abolition, for the dominant slaveholding group to

[1] See the discussions in Alice Adams, *The Neglected Period of Anti-Slavery 1808-1831*, 111-114; Ruth Scarborough, *Opposition to Slavery in Georgia, Prior to 1860*, 171-185; William Birney, *James G. Birney and His Times*, 71-72; and D. L. Dumond, *Antislavery*, 218-23.

prevent the dissemination of antislavery doctrines. The South could be self-critical; a decade of reports from Southern commercial conventions reprinted in *DeBow's Review* shows that slaveholders themselves recognized that slavery had its faults, yet it is significant that none of the resolutions passed by these conventions ever had really practical results. To retain political and economic control of the South, the slaveholders believed that no deep-seated criticism of slavery could safely be tolerated. This group, with its chief institution at stake, could not allow frank discussion of it, and, for obvious reasons, hoped to identify its private interests with the public welfare of the South at large.[2]

In the deep South the suppression of antislavery criticism after 1830 was relatively simple, for there, as one historian phrased it, "existed the most perfect agreement known in Anglo-Saxon history."[3] In the upper South, where cotton and Negroes were less of an issue, repression was more difficult, and though independent thinkers were discouraged, recalcitrants continued to appear in the border states until the Civil War. But throughout the South it was possible by the passage of state and local legislation to control and minimize, and, if need be, to prohibit entirely antislavery opinion and discussion among Southerners, and to prevent the spread of such doctrines in the region by Northerners.

With the exception of Kentucky, every Southern state eventually passed laws controlling and limiting speech, press, and discussion. The decision of an Alabama court in 1837, for example, made any person "who shall proclaim to our slaves the doctrine of universal emancipation . . . a subject for criminal justice." The Virginia Code of 1849 punished by imprisonment up to a year, and a fine up to $500, any person who "by speaking or writing maintains that owners have no right of property in slaves," while Louisiana's penalty for conversation "having a tendency to promote discontent among free colored people, or insubordination among slaves" ranged from twenty-one

[2] Lewis Tappan, *Address to the Non-Slaveholders of the South.*
[3] W. E. Dodd, *The Cotton Kingdom* (New Haven, 1919), 70.

years at hard labor to death.[4] The passage of such laws was justified as a means of preventing slave revolts, presumably stirred up by abolitionists.[5] Not all Southerners agreed that these measures were necessary. The Richmond *Whig* thought the Virginia law of 1836 "far worse than lynching or lynch law," while the Louisville *Gazette,* applauding Kentucky's refusal to pass restrictive legislation, thought the preservation of free speech more important than the suppression of antislavery opinion.[6] Such objections were unusual, however, and the laws remained on the statute books, reaffirmed and strengthened in subsequent years.[7]

Though these statutes served to hamper free expression of antislavery opinion in the South, they did not fully suppress it. Most of the laws dealt out punishment for "incendiary" talk, or "opinions tending to incite insurrection,"—terms vaguely defined and charges difficult to establish—a fact recognized by Southern courts, whose verdicts were usually lenient. Legal processes were often slow, loopholes could be found, and there were strong feelings in the South that better ways of controlling antislavery opinions ought to be found. To remedy these defects and to provide swifter and more effective punishment, the South turned to the citizen-mob, long known on the frontier as "lynch law."[8] Though isolated cases of mob

[4] Helen T. Catterall, *Judicial Cases Concerning Slavery,* II:141; and William Goodell, *The American Slave Code,* 384.

[5] Catherine E. Beecher, *Essay on Slavery and Abolition,* 89; and R. W. Bailey, *The Issue, Presented in a Series of Letters on Slavery,* 54-55.

[6] Clement Eaton, *Freedom of Thought in the Old South,* 127; and the Cincinnati *Philanthropist,* December 18, 1838.

[7] Cf. the resolution of the Georgia Presbytery, quoted in the *Philanthropist,* January 18, 1836, that it will "countenance no minister, or merchant, or mechanic, come from where he may, who holds the sentiments of Northern abolitionists."

[8] James E. Cutter, *Lynch Law,* 91 ff. The Savannah *Republican,* reprinted in *The National Anti Slavery Standard,* June 28, 1849, believed that while Southern laws were satisfactory, they were often too unwieldy and their punishments too light for abolitionist incendiaries. Excellent discussions of why the South was especially prone to the use of extra-legal methods are Clement Eaton, "Mob Violence in the South," *Mississippi Valley Historical Review* XXIX (Dec., 1942), 351-71, and C. S. Sydnor, "The Southerner and the Laws," *Journal of Southern History* VI (Feb., 1940), 3-24.

action occurred before 1833, the development of the mob as a means of suppressing abolitionism reached its climax during the period 1833-1840, receding in the North after 1845 and continuing with undiminished force in the South until the Civil War.[9]

There were in the South two threats to the security of slavery: the Southerner who entertained unsound opinions, and the Northerner (whether abolition agent or casual traveller) who might spread antislavery doctrine. To silence the one and eject the other, if legal means were too slow or not justified by the case, the citizen-mob, in the opinion of the pro-slavery element, was by far the most effective instrument. By appealing to the popular dread of racial amalgamation and Negro equality, and most of all by raising the specter of slave revolt, mobs were not difficult to organize in the South. Governor Hammond of South Carolina advised his legislature that abolitionism could be "silenced in but one way—*Terror—Death*," and a group of citizens who cooperated to suppress abolitionism, he believed, was "no more a mob than a rally of shepherds to chase a wolf out of their pastures."[10] As Southern proslavery opinion became more unified, the mob came to be known, in most Southern states, as a "vigilance committee," or "committee of safety," and to be granted quasi-legal status in many Southern communities.

The mob usually began as a city or county-wide mass meeting at which prominent local citizens pointed out how Northern abolitionists and their Southern sympathizers threatened the security of the community. The meeting then appointed a central committee, varying from six to sixty members, composed of judges, militia officers, lawyers, merchants, and planters. This central committee, which might or might not split

[9] Hezekia Niles, from his reading and clipping of hundreds of newspapers, thought 1835 the worst mob year. In one week he clipped five hundred items of mob violence, many of them over the slave question; *Niles' Register*, 49:1, 49. Notable too were the Irish riots in New York and New Orleans, anti-Catholic and labor riots in Massachusetts, and election riots in New York.

[10] Elizabeth Merritt, *James H. Hammond, 1807-1864*, 32-33, and *DeBow's Review* VII (December, 1849), 491.

up into sub-committees with separate duties, held the right in some communities to levy funds, act as a duly-constituted legal body, and to punish offenders, reporting to a later mass meeting for approval of its acts.[11]

At Athens, Alabama, for example, in 1835, a public gathering appointed a central committee of twenty members, divided into separate sub-committees responsible for each section of the county. The committees were ordered to use "all energetic means in ferreting out, and detecting any person or persons that may attempt to circulate among the community, any pamphlet, tract, or other seditious publication of any kind whatever, or tampering with slaves, with a view to excite insurrection. . . ."[12] Richmond, Virginia, formed a similar committee in August, 1835, and Jefferson, Tuscaloosa, Madison, and Mobile counties in Alabama in September, 1835. A "committee of safety" of thirteen members, with county sub-committees headed by militia officers, was appointed by a meeting at Barnesville Courthouse, South Carolina, on September 15, 1835, and Barnwell District of South Carolina formed one a week earlier.[13] The pattern was repeated again and again over the next few years in the states of the deep South.[14]

The existence of the committees of vigilance was always justified on the grounds of public safety. "It has always been the case," reported the committee of Spartansburg, South Carolina,

among civilized nations, when any radical change of their institutions or form of government is attempted, to organize Committees such as this (no matter by what name they are called) whose power rose

[11] See the analysis of "Defensor" (William Thomas), *The Enemies of the Constitution Discovered . . .*, 48-53.

[12] The Athens, Alabama, *Watchman*, August 22, 1835.

[13] *Niles' Register*, 48:445-446; the Cincinnati *Philanthropist*, January 15 and June 17, 1836; and *The Liberator*, April 2, 1836.

[14] See the lecture given in Cincinnati by J. M. Barrett on these committees, October 29, 1849, reprinted in *The National Anti Slavery Standard*, November 22, 1849. "The New Reign of Terror in the South," *Anti Slavery Tract Number 4*, lists fifty such committees, which it believes a conservative figure.

superior to the law, and whose duty it was to protect peaceable citizens in their rights and property, and their persons from violence in any form and from any quarter.[15]

Punishment of offenders under the law was highly desirable, but, concluded the committee of South Carolina's Barnwell District, "where the laws of the land are insufficient to meet the emergency, the laws of natural justice and self-preservation shall supply the deficiency—*we are deliberately and advisedly determined* that the guilty *shall not escape!*"[16]

The duties of the committees involved conferring with the local postmaster; seizing and burning all antislavery mails; enforcing local and state laws concerning slaves, free Negroes, and communications with them; preventing "the spread of abolition writings and opinions among our people"; questioning and inspecting the effects of all suspicious travellers; and, in general, "taking care of the rights and interests of the district against incendiaries." Some committees made regular inspection of all hotel, inn, and tavern registers, questioned suspicious travellers, and inspected their baggage.[17] Frequently the committees were empowered by the community to offer rewards for the apprehension of offenders. Barnesville, South Carolina, offered $1000 for the delivery to the sheriff or the committee of safety of "anyone interfering with our peculiar rights." The committee of Savannah, Georgia, offered $10,000

[15] The Spartansburg, South Carolina, *Spartan*, reprinted in *The National Era*, November 1, 1849.

[16] The Cincinnati *Philanthropist*, January 15, 1836. The Spartansburg committee decided, "We may in some instances have to rise above the law; but where the law will apply the remedy, we will resort to legal proceedings." For an example of this, see the Louisville *Courier*, quoted by *The Anti Slavery Bugle*, January 17, 1852; a man found selling forged passes to Negroes, to enable them to escape patrols, could not be convicted under Kentucky law since only Negro testimony could be obtained. He was, however, lashed by a mob and shipped away on a steamer.

[17] The report of the committee of Barnwell District, South Carolina, the *Philanthropist*, January 15, 1836; of the Barnesville, South Carolina, committee, *The Liberator*, April 2, 1836; of the Spartansburg, South Carolina, committee, *The National Era*, November 1, 1849; and the *Philanthropist*, June 10, 1837.

for Amos A. Phelps; East Feliciana, Louisiana, $50,000 for Arthur Tappan; Mount Meigs, Alabama, $50,000 for Arthur Tappan or any other prominent abolitionist; New Orleans $100,000 for Tappan and LaRoy Sunderland, the editor of *Zion's Watchman;* and another Louisiana group had a standing offer of $500 for "any abolitionist whatsoever."[18] The punishments meted out by the committee to those suspected of abolitionist opinions ranged from shaving the head, blacking the face, selling at public auction, and other indignities, to manhandling and transportation out of the community by various means. Serious physical punishments, such as lashing, beating, or stoning were comparatively rare.

The vigilance committee was a tribute to the techniques of group control worked out by the dominant Southern class. It had the support of the overwhelming majority of the community, based on the principle of self-protection, which appealed to all classes of whites. Its orderly procedures, its use of the democratic process of mass meeting and election of officers, its leadership drawn from the upper echelons of the community, its quasi-legal flavor—all these combined to reduce any lingering doubts of its legality and to raise it above the level of ordinary mob law in the eyes of respectable people.[19] Its authority, however, was always vested in a small executive group whose acts, so long as they did not run counter to the opinions of the majority, were relatively uncontrolled. Essentially the committee possessed independent financial, legislative, executive, and judiciary powers; the committee, either as a whole or part, could make its own law, define it, enforce it, and judge and punish offenders against it. The inherent dangers of the vigilance committee were perfectly clear, yet so unified was Southern opinion that no important opposition to the system ever developed. In fact, its power increased rather than diminished over the years preceding the Civil War.

[18] *The Liberator,* April 2, 1836, and the *Philanthropist,* May 5, 1837.

[19] The actions of a committee of vigilance were perfectly legal, said the anonymous *The South Vindicated from the Treason and Fanaticism of the Northern Abolitionists* (Philadelphia, 1836), 109, for they were "sanctioned by the highest legal authority known to the State—the *entire* mass of citizens . . ., and dictated by dire necessity."

Though its activities were obviously violations of Federal and state laws guaranteeing free speech and expression, the vigilance committee was, in Southern opinion, a necessary community organization. Free speech, as it was defined in the slave states, did not allow criticism of slavery—a perfectly logical attitude from the proslavery point of view. If it was right to have slavery, it was right to have its defenses; if speech against slavery was wrong, there was no other alternative than to suppress it, by law or without law.[20]

Definitions of free speech in the South provide some interesting insight into the proslavery mind. The Frankfort, Kentucky, *Commonwealth* believed no one was entitled to speak on the subject of slavery "unless he speak in terms acceptable to those who alone have any responsibilities and powers in regard to the question." The Norfolk, Virginia, *Herald* said that "free speech" meant only "implicit obedience to our laws. . . . The thing is very simple, and cannot be possibly misunderstood, we should think . . ." Richard Yeadon of the Charleston *Courier* defined it as "freedom to discuss slavery with the whites, but not with Negroes"; a Southerner, he pointed out with some logic, might not be allowed to preach "agrarianism and sedition" to the Irish laborers of New York.[21] A "Lady of Georgia" could not understand the objections to the whole issue—"We have made up our minds about it, and because our decision does not suit abolitionists, they clamor that we wish to restrain the discussion." *The Western Presbyterian Herald* gave the definition most generally accepted in the South: "Freedom of speech is to be distinguished from licentiousness. No man has a moral right to use the power of speech in defiance of reason and revelation."[22] Based on such grounds, the vigilance com-

[20] See the analysis of the Southern position by Henry Ward Beecher, "On Which Side is Peace?" J. R. Howard, ed., *Patriotic Addresses*, 197-98.

[21] The Cincinnati *Weekly Herald and Philanthropist*, September 17, 1845; "The New Reign of Terror," *op. cit.*, 60-61; and Yeadon's debate with Parker and Garrison in New York, *The National Anti Slavery Standard*, October 18, 1856, an intelligent and fairminded discussion of the Southern position.

[22] "Southern Slavery and Its Assailants," *DeBow's Review* XVI (January, 1854), 46-62, and *The Western Presbyterian Herald*, September 28, 1837.

mittee claimed that it possessed moral, if not legal, reasons for existence, and from a Southern viewpoint what it did was not a violation of freedom of speech.

The extent of Southern vigilance committee activity during the years 1835 to 1860 is almost impossible to determine. Judging from the newspaper accounts carefully kept by the abolitionist newspapers, and making allowances for cases which received no notice in the press, Garrison's figure of three hundred "lynchings," as they were usually termed, seems not too high.[23] Though the years after 1850 were those of greatest violence, the beginning of vigilance committee activity dated roughly from 1835. In that year the Charleston post office was raided and abolitionist literature burned by such a committee, and four Ohioans, suspected of slave-tampering, were whipped at Kanawha Salines, Virginia, by a "committee of safety."[24] In May of 1836 a committee of fifty, incensed at Dr. Nelson's Palmyra College in Missouri, cleared the county of suspected abolitionists. In June the Reverend Aaron Kitchell of New Jersey, an itinerant preacher, was tarred and feathered by a committee of twelve in Hillsborough, Georgia.[25] In January of 1837 John Hopper (son of the Quaker abolitionist Isaac Hopper), barely escaped a dangerous mob in Savannah, Georgia, after a local committee found a colonizationist pamphlet in his baggage. Later in the year a British sea-captain was beaten by a mob in Jacksonville, Florida, for antislavery views.[26]

The experience of George Rye of Woodstock, Virginia, was perhaps typical of how some committees operated. Rye ex-

[23] *The Liberator*, December 19, 1856. Cutter, *op. cit.*, 86, cites Garrison's figure with misgivings. "The New Reign of Terror," *op. cit.*, documents one hundred and fifty cases, while David Lee Child, *The National Anti Slavery Standard*, August 17, 1843, counted one hundred up to that time. Abolition publications were likely to use the term loosely and are hence unreliable, but no other records exist.

[24] *Niles' Register*, 49:76-77.

[25] *The Liberator*, June 18, and August 13, 1836, and the Cincinnati *Daily Gazette*, July 4, 1836.

[26] *The Liberator*, April 21, 1837, and the New York *Emancipator*, November 9, 1837. Hopper escaped to a ship with help of the mayor of Savannah.

pressed himself against slavery so well in talking with friends in 1836 that one of them asked him to write out his arguments for private perusal. The next year, after Rye had defended a local minister for preaching a sermon on colonization, his false friend showed Rye's paper to the local committee of vigilance, who summarized and published it in a local newspaper as an example of "incendiary talk." On the basis of these opinions, which the committee itself had published, Rye was tried, convicted, and fined for attempting to foment slave insurrections.[27]

The most famous case of the 'thirties was that of Amos Dresser. Dresser, a Lane Seminary student selling Bibles in the South, was apprehended by the Nashville, Tennessee, committee in July of 1835, after a search of his hotel room. He was judged guilty by the committee of belonging to an abolition society, of having antislavery papers in his baggage and antislavery opinions in his diary, and of having circulated such. Though Dresser claimed to have used only a copy of *The Emancipator* for wrappings for his stock of Bibles, and to have broken no Tennessee law, he was given twenty lashes in the marketplace, his belongings were confiscated, and he was allowed twenty-four hours to leave town.[28]

During the 'forties, vigilance activity showed no signs of decreasing. The Reverend T. S. Kendall of the Presbyterian Church was sent by the Baltimore Association Synod in 1839 into Virginia and South Carolina. At Smyrna, South Carolina, he was taken into custody by the local committee for reading a copy of the Synod's official letter on slavery in church. Though the letter was judged by a local lawyer to contain nothing contrary to South Carolina law, the minister was tarred and manhandled by the committee.[29] A committee of safety was formed in each township of Marion County to examine travellers and to eject suspects with a threat of five hundred lashes if they re-

[27] Correspondence of George Rye to *The National Era*, October 5, 1848.

[28] *The Emancipator*, October, 1835, and December, 1836; *The Anti Slavery Record* I (November, 1835), 121-123; and Dresser's own account, *The Narrative of Amos Dresser, with Stone's Letters from Natchez.*

[29] Kendall's account, *The Philanthropist*, November 4, 1840.

turned.[30] In 1836 the committee of safety at Yorkville, South Carolina, seized the New York salesman for Brandeth's Pills after discovering a plan for a slave uprising in his baggage. After he had been transported bodily (and with some roughness) out of the county, the "conspiracy," it turned out, was actually a plan for a sales campaign to sell pills through the South.[31]

On the other hand, H. P. Byram of Brandenburg, Kentucky, successfully withstood the local committee on its own ground. Convicted of subscribing to the Cincinnati *Weekly Herald and Philanthropist*, of casting a vote for an emancipationist candidate, and of entertaining antislavery opinions, Byram petitioned the governor of Kentucky for protection of his rights under the state constitution and frightened the committee away.[32] Less fortunate was W. H. Brisbane, M. D., of St. Peter's Parish, South Carolina. After Dr. Brisbane returned from a Northern visit to give out certain opinions against slavery, he was forced to leave town in forty-eight hours by orders of a subcommittee of the St. Peter's committee of vigilance.[33] In the famous Barrett case in Spartansburg, South Carolina, it was the committee of vigilance which figured prominently in the arrest and prosecution of the suspect, and after Barrett's release, a mass meeting voted full confidence in the committee and urged that its activities continue.[34] And it was the vigilance committee of Lexington, Kentucky, that dismantled the press of the *True American* in the famous Cassius Clay incident of 1845.[35]

The greatest activity on the part of Southern vigilance committees came in the 'fifties. By that time the organization of Southern opinion had reached its final stage, the technique of the citizen-mob had been perfected, and increased tension in South-North relations had excited Southern feelings to the

[30] H. A. Trexler, *Slavery in Missouri, 1804-1865*, 131.
[31] *The Anti Slavery Bugle*, August 25, 1846.
[32] The Cincinnati *Weekly Herald and Philanthropist*, December 9, 1846.
[33] The Charleston *Mercury*, August 29, 1840, and *The National Era*, October 4, 1849.
[34] *The National Anti Slavery Standard*, September 20, 1849.
[35] Horace Greeley, ed., *The Writings of Cassius Marcellus Clay*, 301-326.

breaking point. A wave of slave revolt scares during the 'fifties caused suspicion to fall on Southerner and travelling Northerner alike, and the merest indication of antislavery sentiment was likely to attract the attention of a local committee. The system spread during the decade until some states, such as South Carolina, were networks of interlocking committees, and at least one serious case of organized mob action occurred every year after 1850.

In January, 1850, Elijah Harris, an itinerant schoolteacher from Dunbarton, New Hampshire, was arrested on a writ issued by the justice of the peace of Clinton, Barnwell District, South Carolina. He was arraigned not before the court, but before the local committee of safety, which convicted him of carrying in his trunk an antislavery sermon by a New Hampshire minister. The committee shaved his head, tarred and feathered him, and gave him twelve hours to leave town.[36] During the same month a Scotsman, Robert Edmond, a native of Charleston, South Carolina, was tarred and feathered on suspicion of teaching Negroes to read, and later in the year Jackson Evans of Ebenezer, South Carolina, received similar treatment for "expressing abolition opinions."[37] In October, 1850, the Georgetown, South Carolina, committee, suspecting a Maine sea-captain and his first officer of abolitionism, whipped them and put them on their ship with twenty-four hours to leave the harbor.[38] Captain Elisha Betts of Eufaula, Alabama, an aged veteran of the Indian wars, was discovered by the local committee to be a subscriber to *The National Era*. Though Betts protested that neither his ideas nor those of the *Era* were incendiary, he was exiled from the community and advised to leave the state.[39]

Northern travelling agents and merchants had an especially difficult time in the South after 1850. Dr. L. B. Coles of Boston, a book salesman and lecturer on physiology, was jailed in Co-

---

[36] *The National Anti Slavery Standard*, January 28, 1850.

[37] *The Anti Slavery Bugle*, January 12, 1850, and *The National Era*, October 31, 1850.

[38] *The Anti Slavery Bugle*, November 16, 1850.

[39] Captain Betts' account and the discussion by Gamaliel Bailey, *The National Era*, October 3 and 17, 1850.

lumbia, South Carolina, in January, 1851, under an old local law forbidding the sale of books printed outside the state. No lawyer would take his case, but after his baggage had been searched and his letters examined by the local committee, he was fined and released.[40] At Cheraw, South Carolina, John Malone, a New York window-shade salesman, was heard to say that he did not believe "a poor white man stood as good a chance in a slave state as in a free one." For this statement, judged to be incendiary, he was arraigned with his employer, James Colwell, before the local vigilance committee and convicted. A delegation of five men took the two culprits to Wilmington, North Carolina, where a guard took them to Norfolk, Virginia. Norfolk authorities jailed them for two days and put them on a New York steamer.[41] At Troy, Alabama, a one-legged clockmender from New York State was ducked and ridden out of town on a rail as "a thoroughly dangerous man" for "speaking freely about free soil" in July of 1851.[42] The Reverend Edward Matthews, an agent of the American Free Mission Society and a friend of Cassius Clay's, was arrested near Richmond, Kentucky; his clothes were ripped off, he was thrown eleven times into a pond, and driven out of town by the local committee.[43]

Native Southerners fared little better. Nathan Bird Watson of Warrenton, Georgia, was convicted by the local committee of safety of "promulgating abolition opinions, and visiting Negro houses . . . , as we suppose, for the purpose of inciting our free and slave population to insurrection and insubordination." The committee blacked his face, put him on the next train for Atlanta, and notified the committees of surrounding communities of his offense.[44] The Reverend McBride and the Reverend

[40] Coles' account, *The National Era*, February 13, 1851.

[41] Colwell's account, The New York *Herald*, reprinted in *The Anti Slavery Bugle*, October 4, 1856.

[42] *The National Anti Slavery Standard*, July 31, 1851.

[43] *The Anti Slavery Bugle*, March 15 and April 12, 1851, and *The National Era*, April 3, 1851.

[44] *The National Era*, July 31, 1851, and *The National Anti Slavery Standard*, July 24 and September 1, 1851. For a similar case in North Carolina, see *The National Era*, September 15, 1853.

Crooks of the Wesleyan Methodist Church were driven from their circuits in Guilford County, North Carolina, during 1851, by a committee (which included a minister, a member of the state legislature, and several Methodist elders) for expressing antislavery opinions.[45]

The case which most graphically illustrated the power that committees of vigilance came to possess in the South was that of John Cornutt, a slaveholder of Grayson County, Virginia. When a local Wesleyan minister was accused of inciting slaves to revolt because he preached a sermon against slavery to his white congregation, Cornutt, a man of some community standing, protested the charge as absurd. As a result, he was tarred and feathered and lashed by the local committee of safety. However, Cornutt recognized some of his assailants and swore out warrants for their arrest. The committee met and passed resolutions warning all lawyers against taking the case on pain of additional tar and feathers, and warned the judge and court that the case was not to be tried. But the court did meet, only to be broken up by a mob led by the committee. Immediately afterward a mass meeting voted to form a new vigilance committee of two hundred members, to be divided into sub-committees. Further, it voted that the names of all presumed antislavery men in the county and of those holding suspicious opinions were to be reported to the central committee; that no clerks of county or circuit courts were to be permitted to issue writs against citizens for acts committed while expelling or punishing abolitionists; that no sheriff was to be permitted to serve such writs; that all candidates for county office must subscribe to these doctrines; and that all election officials must pledge to cast out the votes of known abolitionists in all elec-

[45] *The Anti Slavery Bugle,* July 26, 1851. Both men had been tried previously for giving antislavery religious books to a child. Crooks was acquitted, but McBride drew a year in prison and twenty lashes; *The National Anti Slavery Standard,* November 21, 1850. The Wesleyan Methodists of Guilford County, an avowed antislavery group, had organized a church of forty members and applied for admission to the Alleghany Conference in 1849. By 1851 the church counted more than five hundred members; *The Anti Slavery Bugle,* September 20, 1851.

tions. Cornutt and the judge who convened the court, it was added, must give the committee "positive assurance" of their soundness on the slavery question or leave the county immediately. Neighboring Wythe County endorsed the resolutions and promised to follow suit.[46]

Not all cases were so spectacular as Cornutt's. The committee of Mineral Spring, Kentucky, forced Janus West to sell his property and move from Kentucky in late 1854.[47] For possession of three copies of the New York *Tribune*, a man was blacked and shipped out by train by a mob led by the sheriff of Greensboro, Georgia, in March of 1855.[48] William Phillips, a Kansas abolitionist, was tarred and feathered, his head shaved, and he was sold at auction by a Negro in Weston, Missouri, in May of 1855.[49] John Jollife of Cincinnati, a Virginia-born lawyer, was threatened in Barnwell District, South Carolina, for executing of the will of Elijah Willis of Cincinnati, which provided for the freeing of the slaves he had left behind in South Carolina.[50] Editor Ludvigh of the Baltimore *Torch*, a German paper, was hustled out of Savannah, Georgia, in 1857 because his paper supported Frémont.[51] John G. Fee, the Kentucky abolitionist, was mobbed in Rockcastle County in 1857, in Madison County in early 1858, and at Lewis Chapel a few days later.[52]

The National Anti Slavery Standard of January 10, 1857, listed eight cases in two months of Southern vigilance committee activity. Among them was that of a Massachusetts man, charged with teaching Negroes to read, who was given eighty

---

[46] *The Anti Slavery Bugle*, May 15, 1852; *The National Era*, May 13, 1852; the Wytheville, Va., *Republican* and the Richmond *Times*, reprinted by *The National Era*, October 16, 1851.

[47] Correspondence of *The Anti Slavery Bugle*, January 27, 1855.

[48] *Ibid.*, April 14, 1855.

[49] H. A. Trexler, *op. cit.*, 199.

[50] *The National Era*, July 5 and 19, 1855.

[51] Letter to *The Anti Slavery Bugle*, March 28, 1857. Frémont men were closely watched in the South; see the letter of Timothy Stannard of Fairhaven, Virginia, *ibid.*, November 29, 1856.

[52] *Ibid.*, August 15, 1857, March 4 and 13, 1858. Fee was mobbed twenty-two times.

lashes in Jacksonville, Florida, and shipped under guard to Savannah for transportation to New York. The committee of Fairfield, North Carolina, drove out one Rowland Chapman in February, 1857, as a suspected abolitionist, and a New Yorker was arrested in Lynchburg, Virginia, in May of 1857 when the Lynchburg committee found, by searching his baggage at his hotel in his absence, that antislavery opinions appeared in letters addressed to him from friends.[53] J. L. Bowers, a Quaker of Charlestown, Maryland, was tarred and feathered for suspected complicity in slave escapes. He sued members of the local committee, but when he appeared in court a mob seized him and put him on the next train out of town.[54] In Oxford, Mississippi, after a man was tried and acquitted of fomenting insurrection, a meeting of townspeople appointed a committee of five to remedy the court's mercy; he was publicly whipped and driven out of town.[55]

Often threats alone were sufficient. "The least suspicion of disloyalty to slavery," wrote a Tennessean, "the least hint of antislavery sentiment on the part of anyone, brought upon such person infamy and the curse of social outlawry." The Georgia correspondent of the New York *Tribune* complained, "We are under greater surveillance here than are the Emperor Jo's subjects in Hungary."[56] Lorenzo Sherwood, a member of the Texas legislature, expressed the opinion in the Texas House in 1856 that Congress had a right to legislate upon slavery in the territories. A Galveston meeting resolved that he should never speak of slavery again on pain of "consequences to which we need not allude."[57] *DeBow's Review* was of the opinion that Sherwood's remarks were close to "incendiary," an interesting commentary

[53] *The National Anti Slavery Standard*, February 14, 1857, and *The Anti Slavery Bugle*, May 9, 1857.

[54] The Charlestown, Maryland, *News*, June 26, 1858, and *The Anti Slavery Bugle*, November 6, 1858.

[55] The Memphis, Tennessee, *Appeal*, quoted by *The Anti Slavery Bugle*, October 11, 1857.

[56] Clement Eaton, *op. cit.*, 285-86, and *The Anti Slavery Bugle*, October 4, 1856.

[57] *The Anti Slavery Bugle*, August 2, 1856, and *The National Anti Slavery Standard*, August 2, 1856.

on the Southern definition of the term as it had developed by 1856.[58] Another politician, John Botts of Virginia, who did publicly oppose slavery, was held "an enemy to the interests and institutions of Virginia," threatened with prosecution under state law, and with personal harm if the law did not suffice.[59] The Reverend Charles Malcolm was discharged from his church in Virginia, in 1856, for "certain remarks . . . leading to the belief that you tend to teach abolition sentiments."[60] Cassius Clay and John G. Fee encountered some mobs while lecturing through Kentucky, but successfully maintained the right of free speech with local support.[61]

Cases carried to law usually received clemency. When a citizen of Louisiana was sentenced to five years at hard labor for saying that "this is a free country and negroes . . . are as free as white men," judgment was arrested on the ground that criminal intent was not proved.[62] An influx of Northerners into Virginia coincided with several prosecutions, the most important case being that of the Reverend Jarvis Bacon of Grayson County, who was convicted and fined for maintaining in a sermon that slavery did not have Biblical sanction. The judgment was reversed on the ground that he had not, as provided by the law of 1847-1848, specifically denied the right of ownership in slaves.[63] The temper of the South of the 'fifties, however, was short. The Charleston *Telescope* thought that if a man spoke against slavery, "in the same moment his tongue shall be cut out and cast upon the dunghill," whereas Parson Brownlow of Tennessee thought mobs should "whip, black, and ride on a

[58] *DeBow's Review* XXI (September, 1856) , 276.

[59] The Richmond *Enquirer* and the Richmond *Whig*, quoted by *The Anti Slavery Bugle*, September 27, 1856.

[60] *The National Anti Slavery Standard*, October 18, 1856. The elder Malcolm, once president of Georgetown University, had previously been exiled from Kentucky for the same offense.

[61] *The National Era*, August 9, 16, and 23, 1855, and *The Anti Slavery Bugle*, January 23, August 1, 4, and 25, 1855.

[62] H. T. Catterall, *op. cit.*, III:163.

[63] *Ibid.*, I:222, and *The Anti Slavery Bugle*, July 6 and November 10, 1849.

rail" any person "who dares to utter one word in opposition to slavery."[64]

It was evident to the people of the Northern states that vigilance committee justice in the South threatened the whole American tradition of civil liberties. The abolitionists pointed out that where slavery existed, the rights of man were always subverted; depriving the Southern white man of his right to free speech was simply the first step toward depriving the Northern citizen of his. "What liberty," asked William Goodell, after making an analysis of Southern laws governing discussion of slavery, "is there for *white* people in the South? They share deeply in the bondage of the blacks."[65] And after reprinting a letter from a Southern subscriber, recounting a brush with a vigilance committee, James G. Birney remarked, "Such is the liberty of the white man where slavery reigns."[66] The widespread opposition in the South to the circulation of Helper's *The Impending Crisis,* a book addressed not to Negroes but to Southern whites, impressed the North with the truth of the abolitionist claim. When Owen Lovejoy, during a particularly bitter passage at arms over Helper's book in the House, asked if he could repeat his remarks in Richmond, Martin of Virginia replied with deadly seriousness, "We would hang you higher than Haman."[67]

The full implication of these things was not lost on Northerners. William Thomas, though he refused "to utter one syllable in favor of the peculiar sentiments of the abolitionists," expressed the fear that the acts of Southern committees of vigilance foreshadowed a determined attempt to destroy American rights; after the civil rights of the white citizen were erased, would there not be substituted for them the laws of the mob

[64] *The National Anti Slavery Standard,* June 16, 1855, and July 12, 1856. Summaries of a number of Southern cases involving free speech are found in the anonymous *Southern Notes for National Circulation,* 11-31, and *The National Era,* January 12, 1860.

[65] William Goodell, *op. cit.,* 386.

[66] The Cincinnati *Philanthropist,* June 10, 1837.

[67] *The Speech of the Honorable Owen Lovejoy of Illinois, Delivered in The House of Representatives, April 5, 1860,* 16.

and those who controlled it?[68] The Columbus *Ohio Observer* thought that "When it once becomes general to substitute mobs for law, our liberties are gone, and we are a ruined nation," and the Boston *Observer* editorialized, "Let it once be established that a mob may, under any pretense, usurp the functions of the courts of justice, and Liberty will have fallen upon her own sword."[69] Warning the South against the consequences of tolerating vigilance committees, another Northerner remarked:

The man, then, who presumes to intimate that because a particular community may be opposed awhile to certain opinions, that that community have a right, therefore, by mob law, or any other law . . . to forcibly suppress the discussion and constitutional promulgation of those opinions . . . is encouraging the prevalence of a doctrine fraught with imminent danger to the constitution itself.[70]

There can be little doubt that such committees exercised a more powerful control over the life of the white man than any other agency in the South. That this control was increasing rather than diminishing is illustrated by the organizational pattern of one of the last committees to be formed, that of Bibb County, Alabama. All citizens, according to its constitution, became members of the General Committee upon signature in the "book." Any twenty such signers constituted a quorum, empowered to "denounce any man as a bad man, and unworthy to reside amongst honest men . . . , to be expelled from the neighborhood." The chairman of the General Committee selected a "secret committee" of five to fifteen members, whose identities were to remain secret, and who, "in appropriate disguises," were assigned to carry out the expulsion orders of a meeting of any twenty members.[71] Beginning with the forma-

[68] "Defensor" (William Thomas), *op. cit.*, 121. See also *The Speech of the Honorable Sidney Edgerton of Ohio, Delivered in the House of Representatives, February 29, 1860*, 3.

[69] Quoted by *The Liberator*, November 22, 1834, and September 13, 1834.

[70] S. B. Treadwell, *American Liberties and American Slavery Morally and Politically Illustrated*, xxv.

[71] *The National Era*, April 14, 1859. The resemblances to the later Ku Klux Klan are obvious.

tion of the first citizens' groups in the early eighteen-thirties, the development of the vigilance committee system tended inevitably in this direction. Had it not been for the intervention of war, there is ample reason to believe that such enormous grants of power to these committees would have become general practice throughout the South.

The concurrent development of a move to suppress free speech on the slavery question in the North, though less violent and of shorter duration, did much to convince a large segment of previously neutral or hostile opinion that, in sanctioning mob action against the abolitionist groups, the North was seriously endangering its own liberties. In seizing upon the issue of free speech versus mob law, antislavery men turned the controversy to their advantage. In defending a fundamental right of democracy they saw that they might also convince Northerners that the institution of slavery was in itself a danger to democratic principles.[72] The period of mob violence in the free states ranged from 1833 to 1845; after the latter date cases of mob action were relatively infrequent, though by no means non-existent. The reasons which lay behind the formation of Southern vigilance committees were obvious—fear of slave revolt, racial equality, and racial amalgamation—but in the North the most powerful of these clearly did not apply.

Yet it is undeniably true that for nearly fifteen years the citizenry and officialdom of several Northern states either condoned or actively assisted in suppressing an unpopular minority. What, then, led citizens of free states to promote and sanction antiabolitionist mobs? Although the constitutions of all the states, slave and free, contained guarantees of free speech, press, and assembly, apparently a sizable number of communities were willing to resort to extra-legal means to suppress abolition opinion. As an Ohioan wrote in 1836:

When a body of men with such feelings and principles begins to distract the nation with their mad schemes, it is high time for a

[72] See, for example, "Slavery—The Right of Northern Interference," *The Anti Slavery Record* II (December, 1837), 1-13.

community to notice them. I am no advocate of Lynch law, but I must say that if Lynch law is to be practised, I know of no fitter subjects for its operation than such fanatics.[73]

Northern mobs, like Southern ones, were organized and led by prominent, respected members of the community. The abolitionists, in fact, coined a term to describe them—"respectable mobs." Oliver Johnson, Phillips, Garrison, Birney, and Goodell, all of whom made a study of mobs, agreed, in Goodell's words, that they were

. . . either countenanced, instigated, or palliated by that description of citizens who complacently consider themselves and are commonly denominated the *higher classes of society*—the men of wealth, of office, of literature, of elegant leisure, including politicians, and that portion of the clergy who naturally associate with that class just described, or are dependent on them.[74]

Garrison's analysis of Northern mobs is probably the most authoritative. They were, he believed, supported by several groups: first, by those who believed abolitionism a threat to peace and order, men who simply disliked agitation; second, by those who, for business reasons, believed abolitionism a threat to Southern trade connections; third, by those who believed abolitionists to be infidels, anti-Biblical, religiously unorthodox; fourth, by those who feared racial equality and amalgamation; and fifth, by those who believed the slavery controversy, if unchecked, might break up the Union.[75] *The National Anti Slavery Standard* agreed on the whole with Garrison's analysis, believing that mob leadership was ordinarily drawn from the

[73] Correspondent of the Medina, Ohio, *Free Press,* quoted in *The Liberator,* April 16, 1836.

[74] William Goodell, *Slavery and Antislavery,* 407. See also Birney, quoted by Leon Whipple, *The Story of Civil Liberty in the United States,* 94 ff.; Wendell Phillips, "Mobs and Education," *Speeches, Writings, and Letters,* 319-20; Oliver Johnson, *Garrison and His Times,* 211-12; and Garrison, *Proceedings of the Anti Slavery Meeting Held in Stacy Hall . . . ,* 17-19. Goodell once planned a book on mobs; *op. cit.,* 407n.

[75] *Proceedings of the Anti Slavery Meeting Held in Stacy Hall . . . ,* 17-19.

ranks of "first, the aristocracy of wealth," who saw in the movement a threat to economic interest; second, those who ". . . are unwilling that the negroes should be turned loose to remain among us, in the full enjoyment of equal rights, in civil and religious society," and third, from the hoodlum element, "drunken and deceived mobocrats whose arguments consist of vulgar blackguardism, brickbats, and rotten eggs."[76]

The resolutions of the mass meetings called to protest abolition activity bear out these explanations. Before breaking up an abolition gathering at nearby Putnam, a mob in Zanesville, Ohio, placarded the town with exhortations to "rid ourselves of the disgrace of amalgamation." Another mob in Martinsville, Ohio, attacked an abolition meeting for the reason that abolitionists were "for equalizing with the Black and trying to reduce all the White laboring men to the same condition."[77] A meeting in Utica, New York, in 1836, labelled the coming abolitionist convention in that city as dangerous to peace, to the constitution, to the stability of the Union, and an insult to New York's Southern friends.[78] The Clermont County, Ohio, Anti Slavery Society was accused by a public protest meeting of "designing to divide the Union . . . , to excite slaves to insurrection and murder, attempting a union of Church and State," and of "scheming . . . to gain honor and distinction."[79]

Politics, too, played a part in arousing antiabolitionist sentiment. James Birney thought it "remarkable that no mob had ever attacked the abolitionists except after special training by politicians who had something to hope from the favor of the South. . . . It is the editors of a venal press, to-be expectants of office, congressmen, judges, postmasters, etc., that we are to look

[76] "Anti Slavery and Its Opposers," *The National Anti Slavery Standard*, September 8, 1842.

[77] The Cincinnati *Philanthropist*, July 15, 1836, and March 10, 1840.

[78] The Utica *Observer*, reprinted in the New Richmond, Ohio, *Philanthropist*, January 8, 1836. This convention was later driven from Utica by the threats of a mob. Gerrit Smith of Peterboro offered it haven at his home, and the abolitionist cause gained the support of that wealthy philanthropist.

[79] The Cincinnati *Philanthropist*, May 12, 1837.

for for the cause of these frequent and shameful outrages."[80] But according to contemporary accounts, the chief motives for attacks on abolitionists in the North apparently were economic, social, religious, and political, in approximately that order of importance.[81]

The method of organizing Northern antiabolitionist mobs resembled the pattern established in the South, though Northern groups were much less united and much less permanent. It began with a mass meeting of citizens, addressed by prominent members of the community, which passed resolutions condemning abolitionist activity in general or the acts of a particular abolitionist or society. A group of executive officers was elected by the meeting, with a subcommittee to warn the offenders, and in some cases to take action against them. The committee usually dissolved after doing its work, leaving no permanent organization.

Northern mobs usually were little more than an annoyance to the abolitionists. William Birney thought them "as a general thing, not dangerous either to life or limb, or beyond the power of the police to control," and Weed, an Ohio lecturer, wrote, "These mobocrats are all great cowards and seldom do anything but make swelling threats . . . I have been in a great many mobs but have never apprehended a great deal of danger."[82] In breaking up abolition meetings, the mobs rarely resorted to physical violence, but instead were usually no more than rude and rowdy. Throwing eggs, ink, or paint; shaving the tails of

[80] *Ibid.*, published from New Richmond, Ohio, January 8, 1836. See also "Hints on Abolition Mobs," *The Anti Slavery Record* II (July, 1836) , 9.

[81] Samuel J. May, *Recollections of Our Anti Slavery Conflict* (Boston, 1869) , 127-28, reported a conversation with a New York merchant who said, "We cannot afford, sir, to let you and your associates endeavor to overthrow slavery. It is not a matter of principles with us. It is a matter of business. . . . We mean, sir, to put you abolitionists down, by fair means if we can, by foul means if we must." Also, Garrison's religious unorthodoxy was notorious, and the joining of the abolitionist ranks by Weld and other of the Finney revivalists did not tend to gain the confidence of orthodox religious circles.

[82] William Birney, *James G. Birney and His Times*, 251-52, and E. Weed to Elizabeth Robinson, February 16, 1837, Marius Robinson papers, Western Reserve Historical Society Collections, Cleveland.

horses or driving them off; placing red pepper or asafoetida in the meetinghouse stove; drowning out the speaker with drums, horns, or shouts; blockading the building in which the meeting was to be held or in a few cases setting it on fire—these were common methods of dispersing abolitionist meetings.

Abolitionist newspapers were ordinarily handled more drastically—throwing away type, pounding the press with hammers, dumping it in a river or pond, or burning the building.[83] More dangerous was an occasional stoning or clubbing. Mount Eaton, Ohio, reported a man killed in 1846 by a brick, and Fred Douglass' hand was crippled by an Indiana mob.[84] Most annoying to abolition agents was the damage done to clothes, which, on an agent's meager salary, constituted a large item of expense. Some agents wore "storm suits" of old clothes when a mob threatened.[85]

Abolitionist agents, during their training period, were taught how to conduct themselves in the presence of a mob. They were warned at the beginning of the trials they faced, and what their choice entailed. "Let every abolitionist," Theodore Weld told prospective antislavery agents, "debate the matter once and for all, and settle it with himself whether he is an abolitionist from *impulse* or *principle*—whether he can lie upon the rack—and clasp the faggot and tread with steady step the scaffold. . . ." They were told not to be discouraged, that mob action really an indication that abolitionism was gaining in a community. "Every abolition lecture they break up is a ruinous victory to the cause of slavery," reminded *The Anti Slavery Record.* Don't provoke mobs, it continued, but do everything to avoid them. Proceed as if a mob could not occur, and act surprised if one does. If a mob breaks into a meeting, keep on as

---

[83] J. F. Hume, *The Abolitionists*, chapter XIV, gives many accounts, drawn from experience, of typical mobs in Ohio.

[84] Letter of A. Baer to *The Anti Slavery Bugle*, July 3, 1846, and J. F. Hume, *op. cit.*, 42. The career of Douglass, an escaped slave who later purchased his freedom, may be studied in Benjamin Quarles, *Frederick Douglass*, and Shirley Graham, *There Was Once A Slave: The Heroic Story of Frederick Douglass.*

[85] Hume, *op. cit.*, 42-3.

long as possible, hoping that the intruders will eventually tire. Do not resist violence—"Be persecuted if you must"—and after the mob has retired, find out and publish the names of its instigators and leaders.[86] Although a good many in the North believed that the abolitionists deliberately drew attacks in order to gain sympathy, evidence to support the accusation is difficult to establish.[87]

The responsibility of newspapers in encouraging mobs in the North was great; nearly every disturbance, said the abolitionists, was either assisted or condoned by the press. The Lynn, Massachusetts, *Record* thought that the New York papers bore a large share of the blame for that city's mobs of 1834 and 1835, and the Lowell, Massachusetts, *American* blamed the New York *Herald*, the New York *Globe*, and the Springfield, Massachusetts, *Republican* for encouraging the mob of 1850. Garrison pointed out that before the famous Boston mob of 1835, only one newspaper in the city did not attempt to incite mob action, that paper being Hallett's *Daily Advocate*.[88] Examination of

[86] "Hints on Abolition Mobs," *The Anti Slavery Record* II (July, 1836), 1-10. Theodore Weld and Henry B. Stanton were probably the most expert handlers of mobs in the abolitionist ranks. Some of Weld's achievements were especially amazing; see D. L. Dumond and G. H. Barnes, eds., *The Letters of Theodore Dwight Weld, Angelina Grimké Weld, and Sarah Grimké;* G. H. Barnes, *The Anti Slavery Impulse;* Henry B. Carrington, *Theodore Weld and A Famous Quartette;* and Barnes and Dumond, *op. cit.,* I:310.

[87] In the careers of Weld and Stanton, the two most mobbed men in the movement, there is little to indicate the justice of the accusation. However, the unorthodox methods of Garrison, Stephen S. Foster, Parker Pillsbury, C. C. Burleigh, and a few others, if not calculated to stir up opposition, certainly succeeded in doing so. Abby Kelly was given to statements such as "Washington and Jefferson were slaveholding thieves, living by the unpaid labor of robbed women and children!" Naturally, she was the center of numerous disturbances. For a study of the more spectacular antislavery speakers, see Hazel C. Wolf, *On Freedom's Altar: The Martyr Complex in the Abolition Movement,* "Lambs Among Wolves," 68-79, an account of Foster, Pillsbury, Henry B. Stanton, Amos Phelps, James Thome, John Alvord, Sereno Streeter, and others. See also Louis Filler, "Parker Pillsbury: An American Antislavery Apostle," *New England Quarterly* XIX (September, 1946), 315-37.

[88] *The Liberator,* December 20, 1834; *The Anti Slavery Bugle,* March 15, 1851; and *Proceedings of the Anti Slavery Meeting Held in Stacy Hall . . ., op. cit.,* 21.

the contemporary press lends some credit to their claim. The Boston *Courier and Enquirer,* for example, in 1834, believed that if abolitionists "openly and publicly promulgate doctrines which outrage public feeling, they have no right to demand protection from the people they insult."[89] Charles Ramsey, editor of the Cincinnati *Republican and Commercial Register* (which had much to do with the Birney mob of 1836) advocated *"action . . . upon the subject (of abolition)* by our citizens."* The Oswego, New York, *Gazette,* before an abolition mob in 1840, believed that "Men have no right . . . to talk *anything* which will necessarily produce a breach in the peace," and as late as 1856 *The Day Book,* New York's most violently antiabolitionist paper, hoped for the day "when, in short, an Abolitionist will be lynched as readily in New York and Boston as in Charleston or New Orleans."[90]

The abolitionist agents and speakers, as the incidence of mobs increased, found new and effective ways to place their case before the public. By 1840 the movement was divided into two fairly well-defined groups, one based on the moralistic-religious position of Weld, Garrison, and the Lane "rebels," the other on the political-legal position of Birney and his circle. While the Liberty party and its supporters carried the battle against slavery into Congress and the courts, the other group seized on popular contemporary evangelistic techniques of conviction and conversion as a means of convincing North and South alike of the necessity for abolising slavery by moral suasion. "If we express our opinions firmly and frankly," wrote David Lee Child in simple religious faith, "they will give up their slaves. . . . The thing may be done with the stroke of a pen." To gain popular support for their cause, the "moral abolitionists" identified themselves with the great evangelical impulses of their era, modeling their crusade on the pattern of Christian martyrdom—of indifference followed by a sense of

[89] "Mobs," *The Anti Slavery Papers of James Russell Lowell,* I:102.
[90] The Cincinnati *Republican and Commercial Register,* July 23, 1836; The Utica, New York, *Friend of Man,* February 15, 1840; and *The National Anti Slavery Standard,* July 5, 1856.

sinfulness and conversion, forgiveness of one's enemies, willingness to suffer, sacrifice of personal comfort and ambition, complete dedication to the cause. These men were sincerely convinced that they were doing God's work in campaigning against slavery, as the early Christian apostles had done God's work in propagating His word among the pagan. Thus the Executive Committee of the American Antislavery Society, in its *Fifth Annual Report* of 1838, believed deeply "that the enterprise which has been committed to their care, enjoys the favor of Almighty God. The seal which He has always set upon every successful and glorious reformation, He has suffered to be estamped upon this." And like their early Christian brethren, they expected the same persecution from the evil and unconverted.

By identifying themselves with the Christian martyrs the abolitionists added powerful ammunition to their arsenal. The folklore of martyrdom was already well developed among generations of Americans who had been brought up on Foxe's *Book of Martyrs,* the hardships of the Puritan colonists, the victims of the Boston Massacre, the travail of Valley Forge, and the death of Nathan Hale. By their constant insistence on being heard under any conditions, and through their well-publicized sufferings, this small group of abolitionists succeeded in merging their cause on the one hand with cherished American traditions of free speech and assembly, and on the other with the powerful Christian tradition of suffering for the right and moral. Eventually, those abolitionists who were first regarded by many as fanatical troublemakers came to be thought of, in some circles, at least, as self-sacrificing martyrs, able to say with St. Paul, "If God be for us, who can be against us?" In the hands of shrewd and able men, who knew the potency of this emotionally-loaded concept and who used it with the greatest sincerity, the martyr complex became an increasingly effective antislavery weapon.[91]

[91] For a thorough and incisive study of this aspect of abolitionism, consult Hazel C. Wolf, *On Freedom's Altar: The Martyr Complex in the Abolition Movement.* See also Louis Filler, *The Crusade Against Slavery,*

Mob cases in the Northern states were concentrated mostly in New England, New York, and Ohio, where the most powerful abolitionist societies operated. New England was dominated by the New England Anti Slavery Society, later the Massachusetts Anti Slavery Society. New York was the headquarters of the national group as well as of the city society, while the state society covered the Mohawk valley and the region south of Lake Ontario to Buffalo. Ohio had the Ohio Anti Slavery Society, and later the Western Anti Slavery Society.

The mob period in New England ran its course by 1838 without real violence. Intensive work by the abolitionists early in the decade—Samuel J. May in Vermont in 1834-1836, Henry B. Stanton in Rhode Island in 1835, and Amos A. Phelps in the general area in 1834—did much to accustom New England to abolitionism and to remove some opposition to it. Its most famous case was Boston's great mob of October 21, 1835, at the end of a tour made by the British abolitionist George Thompson through New England. Thompson left a trail of disturbance through Massachusetts,[92] and as the time for his arrival approached in Boston, where he was to speak before the Boston Female Anti Slavery Society, anti-British and antiabolitionist feeling ran high. Garrison's *Liberator* (published in the city) and his notorious aggressiveness had already made Boston acutely sensitive to the subject of slavery.

Fearing a mob, the trustees of New Jerusalem Church, which had been hired for Thompson's lecture, demanded a $20,000 deposit to cover possible damages. The owners of Julien Hall, a second choice, refused to rent to the Society at all. Early in

---

Chapter 3, "Abolitionists and Reformers." The relationship between abolitionism and contemporary evangelistic theology is well handled by Charles C. Cole, *The Social Ideas of the Northern Evangelists,* and Timothy L. Smith, *Revivalism and Social Reform in Mid-Nineteenth Century America.*

[92] Thompson was mobbed at Lowell, Concord, Haverhill, New Bedford, and Lynn; F. G. de Fontaine, *History of American Abolitionism,* 31; *The Liberator,* December 6 and 13, 1834; and S. G. Pickard, *Life and Letters of John G. Whittier,* I:145-148.

August a Faneuil Hall mass meeting was called to discuss ways and means of preventing Thompson's appearance, and in September Garrison found a gallows constructed in front of his home, with an attached placard reading "Judge Lynch's law."[93]

Thompson's arrival on October 21 touched off the spark. A mob, composed for the most part of the city's prominent citizens, after failing to find Thompson, seized Garrison, roped him, and paraded him through the streets until he was given sanctuary in the city jail.[94] This was the first important appearance of the "respectable mob" in New England, but others followed. Samuel J. May was mobbed five times in Vermont; at about the time of the Boston incident, he was prevented from speaking in Montpelier by a group led by a bank president and two colonels of state militia.[95]

Maine reported but two disturbances. A meeting was broken up in Bridgton in 1836, but the abolitionists prosecuted the mob leader (a local lawyer) and twelve companions, all of whom were fined $25 and costs. Not until 1844, however, when S. S. Foster and John Spear were attacked in Portland, did Maine have any significant difficulties over abolition.[96] Connecticut, the least hospitable of the New England states to abolition, was never thoroughly canvassed by agents. The appearance of an abolition lecturer was almost certain to touch off trouble, and the societies soon gave up any attempt to convert it.[97] New

[93] The Boston *Advertiser*, September 12, 1835.

[94] For accounts, see W. P. and F. J. Garrison, *William Lloyd Garrison*, II:1-37; *Niles' Register*, 49:145-146; S. G. Pickard, *op. cit.*, I:143-144; and especially the reminiscences of Garrison, Phillips, Parker, H. C. Wright, Higginson, and others in *Proceedings of the Anti Slavery Meeting Held in Stacy Hall . . . op. cit.* The abolitionist account of the affair is not trustworthy; for a later analysis, see R. B. Nye, *William Lloyd Garrison*, 84-88.

[95] W. H. Siebert, *Vermont's Antislavery and Underground Railroad Record*, 25, and the Buffalo *Spectator*, reprinted in the *Philanthropist*, April 21, 1837.

[96] *The Liberator*, August 20, 1836, and *The National Anti Slavery Standard*, February 27, 1845.

[97] Connecticut mobs were swift and effective. See the accounts of mobs at New Haven, *The Liberator*, April 16, 1833, and December 17, 1836; at Meriden, *ibid.*, November 10, 1837; and at Norwich, the New York *Emancipator*, June 7, 1838.

Hampshire recorded but one mild disturbance, in Newport in 1836; and Henry C. Wright reported the same year that when a mob threatened him in Bristol, Rhode Island, it was quickly put down by "respectable citizens" and the authorities.[98]

Massachusetts, however, was never fully pacified until the 'fifties. Whittier was mobbed at Newburyport, Concord, and Plymouth in the early 'thirties. C. C. Burleigh was attacked in Mansfield in October of 1836. Oliver Johnson and Amos Dresser were ejected from a Marblehead meeting in March, 1837. Stoneham, Massachusetts, reported a "respectable mob" the same month, and agent Graham reported another mild incident in Boston in April, 1837.[99] Abel Brown's lecture was dispersed by asafoetida in the stove at Northampton in 1843; Stephen Foster, Parker Pillsbury, Lucy Stone, and William Wells Brown were sharply handled in East Harwich in 1848; and the ubiquitous George Thompson touched off another series of minor disturbances in the spring of 1851 during his second Massachusetts tour.[100]

New York City experienced perhaps the worst disorders. Close and profitable connections with the slave states, and a fairly large and influential group of resident Southerners, combined to make the city an antiabolitionist stronghold. New York merchants regarded abolitionism as a threat to Southern trade relations; the fact that the names of the Tappans were linked to New York, which was also the headquarters of the American Anti Slavery Society, was highly embarrassing. It was not uncommon for business firms to insert notices in the newspapers assuring Southern customers that they held no sympathy with the abolitionists, and frequent resolutions of censure against them were passed at directors' meetings.[101]

---

[98] *The Liberator*, December 3 and October 29, 1836.

[99] *Ibid.*, October 22 and November 5, 1836, April 7 and March 31, 1837; the Cincinnati *Philanthropist*, April 28, 1837; and S. G. Pickard, *op. cit.*, I:148-155.

[100] *The National Anti Slavery Standard*, March 23, 1843; *The Anti Slavery Bugle*, September 15 and 22, 1848; the Springfield, Mass., *Republican*, February 17 and 19, 1851; *The National Anti Slavery Standard*, December 19, 1850; and the correspondence of H. C. Wright to *The Anti Slavery Bugle*, June 14, 1851.

[101] Philip S. Foner, *Business and Slavery*, 12-14, 160-162.

The organization of the New York City Anti Slavery Society on October 2, 1833, provided the occasion for the city's first conspicuous disturbance. On that date Leavitt, Green, Rankin, Goodell, Elizur Wright, and Lewis and Arthur Tappan intended to call a meeting at Clinton Hall to launch the city's first abolition society, but before the meeting the city was placarded by signs, signed "Many Southerners," which urged all citizens unsympathetic to abolition to break it up. Discretion led the abolitionists to change their meeting place to Chatham Street Chapel. A large crowd gathered at Clinton Hall on the appointed evening, however, and held an antiabolitionist meeting, addressed by General Robert Bogardus, F. A. Tallmadge of New York, and other prominent citizens. Resolutions affirmed that "our duty to our country, and to our Southern brethren in particular, renders it improper and inexpedient to agitate a question pregnant with peril and difficulty to the common weal," and at the conclusion of the meeting a portion of the crowd moved on Chatham Street Chapel. The abolitionists, however, had finished a few minutes before the arrival of the Clinton Hall group, who satisfied themselves by conducting a mock meeting burlesquing them.[102]

On July 8, 1834, a meeting of the American Anti Slavery Society at Chatham Street Chapel was invaded and broken up. Since the meeting was attended by free Negroes, the race question seems to have been at least partially responsible. According to the New York *Daily Advertiser*, the Sacred Music Society had hired the chapel for the same evening, and, upon arriving, found an abolitionist meeting in progress. Demands for the use of the hall, it was claimed, led to an attack by the Negroes upon members of the music society, joined by others from both camps. Lewis Tappan was stoned on the way home, but escaped injury.[103] On the evening of the 9th, crowds began to gather about the chapel again, on the strength of a rumored abolitionist meeting. When no abolitionists appeared, the

[102] F. G. de Fontaine, *op. cit.*, 26-27; *Niles' Register*, 46:111-112; and *The Abolitionist* I (November, 1833), 171-173.
[103] The New York *Daily Advertiser*, reprinted in *Niles' Register*, 46:357, and the New York *Commercial Advertiser*, July 8, 1834.

crowd broke into the chapel and held another antiabolitionist meeting. In an ugly mood, it next invaded the Bowery Theater and broke up a production of *Metamora* because of a rumor that the British stage manager had made anti-American remarks. The group next moved on to Lewis Tappan's home to sack it and burn the furniture in the street. Later, after the churches of Drs. Ludlow and Cox (believed to be abolitionists) had been damaged by the mob, barricades began to appear in the streets.

The next day the riot burst out with augmented violence. The Tappans' store was attacked, but police drove off the rioters, who then invaded the Negro section and wrecked three Negro churches, a Negro school, and about twenty Negro homes. As violence grew, Mayor C. W. Lawrence, after two proclamations, deputized several citizens and called out the militia. The riots gradually subsided. Although the members of the American Anti Slavery Society issued a flat denial of responsibility, Mayor Lawrence specifically declared them to be the cause of the disturbance, while several newspapers condoned the riots on the ground that abolitionists could neither merit nor enjoy any legal protection against mobs. The three-day riots evidently had the desired effect, for the extremist Richmond *Enquirer* thought them ". . . highly gratifying to the people of the South, as a strong, and indeed conclusive manifestation that the public sentiment of the north will itself suffice to put down that fanatical spirit of false philanthropy and real incendiarism."[104]

The riots of 1834 were the worst suffered by the city. Meetings of New Yorkers in 1835 and 1836 reaffirmed their determination "to frustrate and defeat the mischievous schemes of designing demagogues and deluded fanatics,"[105] but nothing happened until 1850, when the sixteenth anniversary meeting

[104] de Fontaine, *op. cit.*, 28-29; *Niles' Register*, 46:357-360; and Bayard Tuckerman, *William Jay and the Constitutional Movement for the Abolition of Slavery* (New York, 1893) , 55. The abolitionists, one newspaper said, intended to "mulattoize our posterity" by race amalgamation.

[105] *Niles' Register*, 48:232, and William Birney, *op. cit.*, 196. Birney believed that antiabolitionist activity was planned by a guiding committee located in New York, though his evidence is unconvincing.

of the American Anti Slavery Society at the Broadway Tabernacle was annoyed by a group led by Isaiah Rynders, a Tammany politician, and forced to disperse.[106] Both the New York *Globe* and *The Herald* urged the mobs on, *The Herald* saying, "The merchants, men of business, and men of property in this city should frown down the meeting of these madmen, if they would save themselves." Newspapers in general, however, decried the mobs and pointed out the danger to free speech.[107]

The abolitionists met less difficulty in outstate New York. The earliest and most determined attack on them occurred in October, 1835, as the state convention met in Utica. Before the convention, an antiabolitionist meeting led by Congressman Samuel Beardsley resolved that it was "the incumbent duty of every citizen to make use of all lawful and proper means to arrest the disgrace that would settle upon this city by the public assemblage of this convention." Fearing trouble, the state abolitionist committee advised adjournment of the first day's meetings, and Gerrit Smith, a wealthy resident of nearby Peterboro, offered his home as a meeting place. The abolitionists departed at five in the morning as a mob gathered to throw stones and mud, the same mob which later in the day sacked the offices of the Utica *Standard and Democrat,* an antislavery paper.[108] Theodore Weld's tour of western New York in 1836 met some violence, especially at Lockport and Troy, and a year

[106] John Jay Chapman, *William Lloyd Garrison,* 199-218; *The National Anti Slavery Standard,* May 30, 1850; the Salem *Anti Slavery Bugle,* May 18 and 25, 1850. See John G. Whittier's pessimistic letter in the *Bugle,* June 1, 1850, feeling that "the great battle for free speech and assembly" might have to be fought all over again.

[107] Foner, *op. cit.,* 28. For newspaper opinion in New York City, see *The Tribune,* May 9; *The People's Weekly Journal,* May 11; *The Sunday Mercury,* May 12; *The Sun,* May 8; *The Sunday Atlas,* May 12; and *The Journal of Commerce,* May 11. For other opinions, see the Cincinnati *Nonpareil and Herald,* the Cayuga, N. Y., *Chief,* the Niagara, N. Y., *Cataract,* the Syracuse *Star,* the Boston *Old Colony Reporter,* the Onondaga, N. Y., *Standard,* the Albany *Atlas,* and others in *The National Anti Slavery Standard,* May 23 and 30, 1850. *The Liberator,* September 30, 1853, reported interruption of a meeting at Metropolitan Hall, but it seems to have amounted to nothing.

[108] *Niles' Register,* 49:146-48, 162-63, 183.

later, S. L. Gould, an American Anti Slavery Society agent, was roughly handled in Poughkeepsie.[109] Upper New York state, where the societies were strongest, was fairly well pacified by 1838, and except for minor disturbances at the state convention of 1840 at Oswego, nothing serious was subsequently reported.[110] New Jersey, like Connecticut, was never thoroughly canvassed by the abolitionists because of practically insurmountable opposition. New Jersey's southern trade connections made it highly sensitive to discussions of slavery, and as late as 1848 the citizens of Newark, backed by the constable and the mayor, flatly warned abolition agents to stay out of the city.[111]

In Pennsylvania abolitionist strength was centered about Philadelphia, with areas of favorable sentiment in the northwestern counties bordering on the Western Reserve and in the southwestern counties along the Ohio River. Despite the strong Quaker and antislavery feeling in Philadelphia, however, there was also powerful opposition, most spectacularly confirmed by the famous Pennsylvania Hall riot and fire of 1838.

The Hall, built by subscription of $40,000 to provide a meeting place for various societies, opened on May 14, 1838. The Female Anti Slavery Society, which included pacifist, temperance, and feminist members as well as abolitionists, leased the building for May 16, and, after receiving several threats, petitioned the Mayor for protection.[112] The protection was obviously inadequate, for a mob burned the building to the ground

109 G. H. Barnes, *The Antislavery Impulse*, 85-86; *The Anti Slavery Record* II (July, 1836), 9-10; and *The Liberator*, May 11, 1840.

110 The Utica, N. Y., *Friend of Man*, February 5, 1840.

111 Letter of William Larison to *The National Anti Slavery Standard*, August 17, 1840.

112 Philadelphia had suffered a serious race riot, called the "passover riot," in 1834, which destroyed forty-five buildings; see *Niles' Register*, 46:313. Present at the 1838 meeting were Abby Kelly, Maria Chapman, the Grimké sisters, Lucretia Mott, Lewis Gunn, C. C. Burleigh, Garrison, Alvan Stewart, and others. Burleigh possessed a tremendous beard and cultivated a resemblance to pictures of Christ; since Garrison was bald, the appearance of the two on the same platform provided opportunities for hecklers, one of whom shouted, "Cut the whiskers off Christ and make a wig for Garrison!"

shortly after the meetings began and went on to attack the offices of Whittier's *Pennsylvania Freeman*, a Negro orphans' home, and a Negro school. The abolitionists' claim that police and firemen did not attempt to prevent the mob or to put out the fire seems to have support from contemporary newspaper accounts. Though the Philadelphia *Gazette* calculated the crowd at the impossibly high figure of 20,000 to 30,000, the report of the investigating jury fixed responsibility on "an orderly, welldressed assemblage of men, of whom not more than fifty seem at any one time to have taken an active part in the work of destruction."[113] The greatest factor in arousing violence, the press agreed, was the mingling of Negroes and whites at the convention.[114] At the same time a majority of editors condemned the action of the mob as a dangerous precedent. The Richmond *Compiler* thought "the event is to be regretted, but exhibits . . . a feeling worthy of Americans," while the Richmond *Whig* warned that "mob law . . . cannot be justified by any combination of circumstances." The Rochester, New York, *Democrat* warned that "No *moral* question can be put down by force."[115]

Combined with the death of Lovejoy in 1837 in Illinois, and the attacks on Birney in 1836 in Cincinnati, the burning of Pennsylvania Hall gave pause to leaders of opinion in the North. It occurred to many that though abolitionism and mobs might both seem to be evils, the latter might well be the more dangerous. Many agreed with William Ellery Channing, who had long deprecated the violence of abolitionist agitation:

Everywhere the excesses of the Abolitionists are used to palliate the persecution they suffer. But are they the only intolerant people in

[113] *Niles' Register*, 54:195, and the Hallowell, Maine, *Liberty Standard*, August 2, 1841. Complete accounts are found in *The History of Pennsylvania Hall, Which was Destroyed By A Mob; The Address of the Eastern Executive Committee of the State Anti Slavery Society to the Citizens of Eastern Pennsylvania;* and *The Emancipator*, June 7, 1838. See Whittier's poem, "Pennsylvania Hall," *Works* (Riverside ed., Boston and New York, 1888), VII:58.

[114] *Niles' Register, loc. cit.*

[115] Reprinted by *The Emancipator*, June 14, 1838, and *The Liberator*, June 29, 1838.

the country? Is there a single political party, which does not deal as freely in denunciation? Is there a religious sect, which has not its measure of bitterness? I ask, as before if fierce denunciation is to be visited with flames, where will the conflagration stop?[116]

After the destruction of Pennsylvania Hall, Pennsylvania recorded few disturbances over abolition, the majority of which apparently arose from anti-Negro feeling. Pittsburgh had already experienced a minor race riot in 1836, and in 1839 a Negro procession celebrating West Indian emancipation was attacked, a meeting-hall wrecked, and a church burned.[117] The Negro abolition lecturer Charles Remond was mobbed in Newtown, Pennsylvania, in 1845, and a mob invaded a feminist meeting held by Mary Grew and Lucretia Mott on June 15, 1851, to eject a free Negro who had attended.[118] Except for a mob led by the justice of the peace, which attacked Walker and Curtis of the Western Anti Slavery Society in Springfield, Pennsylvania, in 1848, no other important incidents involving antiabolitionist mobs in the state were reported in the antislavery press.[119]

Ohio's mob period was more intense and of longer duration than that of any other Northern state. Situated at the crossroads of the West, Ohio drew migration from New England, New York, Pennsylvania, the eastern slave states, and the western slave territory of Kentucky and Tennessee, giving it a composite population which ranged from the highly abolitionist Western Reserve area in its northeast to the pro-slave, Southern settled counties of the south and southwest along the Ohio River. Ohio also possessed two aggressive antislavery societies,

---

[116] W. E. Channing, *Remarks on the Slavery Question in a Letter to Jonathan Phillips, Esq.*, 80. When Philadelphia went through the anti-Irish riots in 1844, abolitionists quickly pointed out that their warnings of establishing a precedent of mob action against minorities in 1838 had gone unheeded; see "The Mob Triumph in Philadelphia," the Cincinnati *Weekly Herald and Philanthropist*, July 15, 1844.

[117] The Cincinnati *Repository and Commercial Register*, July 27, 1836, and D. L. Dumond, *Antislavery Origins of the Civil War*, 59.

[118] *The National Anti Slavery Standard*, March 20, 1845, and *The Anti Slavery Bugle*, June 28, 1851.

[119] *The Anti Slavery Bugle*, December 1, 1848.

the Ohio Anti Slavery Society, organized in 1836, and the Western Anti Slavery Society, which covered western Pennsylvania, Ohio, and parts of Indiana and Michigan after its organization in 1840. The unusual strength of the antiabolitionist opposition in Ohio stemmed from several sources. The river cities had close trade connections with the slave states of the upper South and the Mississippi valley, which would certainly be affected by a retaliatory Southern boycott. The proximity of Ohio made the state a haven for fugitive slaves, and Ohioans were aware of the ill-feeling that slave escapes, supposedly engineered by abolitionists, created in the South. It was also feared that emancipation might result in a flood of freed Negroes to add to the already sizeable black population of the state. The period of antiabolitionist activity, therefore, began in Ohio in the early 'thirties and persisted until the late 'forties, when public opinion began to show signs of shifting.

The earliest mobs in Ohio came in Cincinnati, where the Lane Seminary dispute of 1834, though it involved no mobs, indicated the temper of local opinion. Theodore Weld, the leader of the Lane group, toured Ohio as an agent of the American Anti Slavery Society in 1834 and 1835, and encountered strong opposition in many places; his letters listed Circleville, Oldtown, Chardon, Painesville, Zanesville, and Putnam as towns which produced mobs of varying degrees of strength.[120] In May of 1836 Birney was prevented from speaking by a Columbus mob. In the same year abolitionists at Blendon and Elliotville reported mobs, while in Zanesville in 1836 placards urged mob action "to rid ourselves of the disgrace of AMALGAMATION."[121] When the Ohio Anti Slavery Society convention chose Granville as its meeting place in 1836, a committee of Granville citizens, certain that trouble was imminent, asked the Society to stay away. James Thome, lecturing in a

[120] G. H. Barnes, and D. L. Dumond, eds., *The Letters of Theodore Weld, op. cit.,* Index, "Mob Violence."
[121] *Ibid.,* I:360-361, 258-259; D. L. Dumond, ed., *The Letters of James G. Birney,* I:324; and the Cincinnati *Philanthropist,* April 28 and August 5, 1837, and July 15, 1836.

schoolhouse two miles south of Granville before the convention, was driven away and the schoolhouse burned. When the convention finally met, the delegates were threatened by a large crowd (which had been partially recruited from St. Albans, Mount Vernon, and Newark), egged, clubbed, and finally driven out of town to a barn.[122] Birney's Cincinnati *Philanthropist* press was wrecked in July of 1836 by a mob which had the backing of the city's prominent citizens.[123] Mobs were also reported during 1836 in Circleville, Painesville, Marietta, Willoughby, St. Albans, Brimfield, New Lisbon, Mount Vernon, Middlebury, Grafton, and Mount Pleasant.[124]

The year 1837 found opposition to the abolitionists decreasing to some extent in Ohio, though several incidents were reported. Birney and Rankin were each mobbed in Dayton early in the year, and another case occurred at Miller, near Mount Vernon.[125] Marius Robinson, working through northern Ohio, was mobbed three times, not seriously, in the week of January 25, 1837. Later, in June, he was severely handled at Berlin, Ohio, near Akron, and was in ill health for some time afterwards.[126] Other cases, no doubt many of them, went unrecorded.[127] A lyceum discussion of abolition was twice broken up by gangs in November of 1838 in Barnesville, Ohio, the leaders affirming that "they had the sanction of the whole community—at least, of every respectable citizen of the place."[128] The next year the fourth annual meeting of the Ohio Anti Slavery Society, held at Putnam, was stoned by a mob from

[122] The Cincinnati *Philanthropist*, May 6, 1838; Dumond, *Birney Letters*, I:318-322, and R. S. Fletcher, *The History of Oberlin College*, I:239.

[123] *The Narrative of the Late Riotous Proceedings Against the Liberty of the Press in Cincinnati* (Cincinnati, 1836).

[124] Francis P. Weisenburger, *The Passing of the Frontier 1825-1850*, 372.

[125] Dumond, *Birney Letters, op. cit.*, I:375, and *The Philanthropist*, January 21, 1837.

[126] Letters of January 25 and June 13, Robinson correspondence, Western Reserve Historical Society, Cleveland. Robinson was later brought to court on charges of inciting a mob, but acquitted. At Granville, Ohio, in 1839 he was shipped out of town as a vagrant.

[127] See, for example, the letters concerning the experiences of Oberlin students in 1837, Fletcher, *op. cit.*, I:243-244.

[128] Letter of Eli Nichols to *The Philanthropist*, December 18, 1838.

Zanesville, which also burned two barns belonging to suspected abolitionists. The civil authorities of Putnam arrested and fined the mob leaders and crushed the movement completely.[129]

Though portions of Ohio were pacified by 1840, accounts of mobs dotted the decade, and opposition to the abolitionists did not cease in the Ohio river counties until nearly 1850.[130] Professor Fairchild of Oberlin was threatened at Martinsville in the early months of 1840, though he later expressed the opinion that the country near Wheeling was rapidly becoming safe for abolitionists.[131] Cincinnati remained hostile for some time; during the race riots of September, 1841, the press of *The Philanthropist,* then under the editorship of Gamaliel Bailey, was again destroyed.[132] At Sharon, thirteen miles from the city, an antislavery meeting was egged in April of 1841 by a group led by a tavern-keeper and the justice of the peace; in Cincinnati itself, in June, a mob attacked the home of John Burnett on suspicion of harboring fugitive slaves. Previously the Cincinnati delegation, returning from the state convention of abolitionists at Columbus, had been attacked by a mob at Dayton during a stop-over.[133] In 1843 an antislavery meeting at Cleves, near Cincinnati, was notified by a citizens' committee that its doctrines were "incendiary"; although some mob members attended the meeting with clubs, they did not use them. The last major outbreak in Cincinnati came in August of 1843, when the city underwent "Scanlan mob" riots, which began over rumors of fugitive slaves being sheltered in the city.[134]

Sporadic disturbances over abolition continued in other sec-

---

[129] *Ibid.,* June 11, 1839.

[130] Marius Robinson thought Hamilton and Licking Counties produced the most dangerous mobs in Ohio, while Harrison and Jefferson Counties produced the least. Letter of January 29, 1837, Robinson correspondence, Western Reserve Historical Society.

[131] *The Philanthropist,* March 10, 1840.

[132] *The Liberator,* September 24, 1841.

[133] *The Philanthropist,* February 3 and 17, April 28, June 30, 1841.

[134] *Ibid.,* March 11, August 1 and 9, 1843, and *The National Anti Slavery Standard,* March 29, 1856.

tions of the state. The Elyria, Ohio, *Atlas and Elyria Recorder* noted "a slight mob, not equal to the common run," in July of 1843, while in 1845 R. W. Greene, an agent, was beaten in Greene County and Stephen Foster stoned in Cadiz.[135] During 1846, Ohio Anti Slavery Society lecturers reported disturbances at Knoxville, Richmond, and Harrison. Meetings of the Western Anti Slavery Society were broken up by mobs at Savannah in Ashland County in 1847, and a group led by a Methodist deacon stoned one of the society's agents at Leesburgh in 1848. These were the last evidences of the dying opposition to abolitionists in Ohio.[136] The dogged efforts of the American Anti Slavery Society, the Ohio Anti Slavery Society, and the Western Anti Slavery Society, spread over nearly fifteen years of canvassing the state, eventually achieved results, and Ohio, like the other Northern states, allowed abolitionist societies and agents to proselytize freely.

West of Ohio the abolitionist societies did not begin intensive campaigns until after 1840, nearly at the close of the mob period, and cases of violence against them and their agents were few and scattered. The weekly reports sent in by agents of the Western Anti Slavery Society, operating in Ohio, Michigan, and Indiana, cited only a few minor incidents after 1845.[137] Indiana, with a relatively large Southern population, remained the least sympathetic of the western states toward abolition, and it is significant that it was also among the last of the Northern states to remove its "black laws." In 1839 the abolitionist press wryly remarked that its cause must be gaining in Indiana, since "men of property and standing have joined the mobocrats" who were suppressing discussion of the slave question, and as late as 1856 an antislavery meeting was broken

[135] *The Philanthropist*, April 7, 1845, and *The National Anti Slavery Standard*, August 17, 1843 and September 25, 1845.

[136] *The Anti Slavery Bugle*, July 3, 1846, November 12, 1847, and August 4, 1848. Frederick Douglass was stoned and clubbed in Columbus in July, 1850, but because of his alleged disparagement of the Constitution rather than for his abolitionism; *ibid.*, August 24, 1850, and *The National Anti Slavery Standard*, August 15, 1850.

[137] "Notes from the Lecturing Field," published weekly in *The Anti Slavery Bugle*, official organ of the Society, 1846-1855.

up in Jennings County.[138] The Indiana Anti Slavery Society was never strong, and though Arnold Buffum and Stephen Harding worked energetically in the 'forties to make it so, it never became an important agency in abolitionizing the state. In Michigan an early antislavery outpost was established in the Detroit area, with others at Adrian, Marshall, and Ann Arbor. Little interference with abolitionist speakers and meetings was reported.[139]

In Illinois, antiabolitionist sentiment was concentrated in the region south of Jacksonville, though "mobocratic exhibitions were likely to be encountered anywhere south of Peoria," according to one agent.[140] Proximity to slave territory, a fairly large Negro population, and Southern migration to Illinois tended to make the southern portion of the state strongly opposed to abolition, while the existence of strong abolition societies in the Galesburg-Alton area made clashes inevitable. The most serious of all, of course, was that which resulted in the death of Elijah Lovejoy in 1837.[141] Alton in 1841 still retained a citizens' committee to handle abolitionists, and a committee was empowered in 1843 by a Peoria meeting to inform the Peoria Anti Slavery Society that the organization of any antislavery society would be opposed, if necessary by force. Ignoring the warning, the abolitionists met to be dispersed by an orderly and determined mob, led by a candidate for judge, the sheriff, and a prominent lawyer. The citizens' committee went on to warn local papers to eschew abolition as "contrary to our interests and honor," and eventually forced one editor to leave town.[142]

---

[138] *The Massachusetts Abolitionist,* April 4, 1839, and *The Anti Slavery Bugle,* May 10, 1856.

[139] Walker and Treat of the Western Anti Slavery Society were threatened at Adrian in 1851 by citizens angry over their talk of disunion, never popular in the West; *The Anti Slavery Bugle,* February 15, 1851.

[140] W. T. Allan of the Illinois State Anti Slavery Society, in *The Philanthropist,* January 6, 1841. For the hardships and difficulties facing the Indiana abolitionist, see O. N. Huff, "Unnamed Heroes of Old Newport," *Indiana Magazine of History* III (1907), 133-43, and Etta French, "Stephen S. Harding, A Hoosier Abolitionist," *ibid.,* XXVII (Sept., 1931), 207-30.

[141] The Lovejoy case is discussed at length in Chapter IV.

[142] *The National Anti Slavery Standard,* April 14, 1843.

From the earliest phase of the controversy over slavery, the abolitionists were conscious of the close relationship between their cause and that of free discussion. Judge Jay in 1835 appealed to "every genuine republican to resist with energy and decision so palpable an outrage" as suppression of abolitionist liberty of speech, since it was a heritage common to all Americans.[143] Birney believed that the right to discuss slavery eventually involved the perpetuation of all free institutions, warning that "the salvation of the country now depends upon *our* living down and working down, these mobs." The Vermont Anti Slavery Society resolved that to allow any self-appointed group to suppress free discussion was "to acquiesce in the subversion of the fundamental principles of all freedom."[144] Abolition societies, in their announcements, resolutions, and constitutions, carefully quoted all of the constitutional guarantees of free speech and stressed the importance of keeping them inviolate.[145] Freedom of expression, it was maintained, was a basic minority right, not just for abolitionists, but for all Americans. "If it is surrendered," said Lewis Gunn, "we ourselves are slaves . . .; it lies at the foundation of all our other rights."[146]

The abolitionist cause therefore from the first stood upon firm moral ground by identifying itself with a fundamental democratic privilege. If free speech were slavery's greatest foe, in attacking slavery, the abolitionists were, in effect, preserv-

[143] Bayard Tuckerman, *op. cit.*, 74.

[144] Robert Price, "The Ohio Antislavery Convention of 1836," *Ohio Archaeological and Historical Quarterly* XLV (April, 1936), 186; Birney in *The Anti Slavery Record* II (July, 1836), 8, and II (April, 1836), 67-69; and W. H. Siebert, *Vermont's Antislavery and Underground Railroad Record*, 91. For similar remarks, see S. B. Treadwell, *op. cit.*, 128-127, 363-371; Gerrit Smith, *The Anti Slavery Almanac* (1837 ed.), 8-12; Harriet Martineau, *Society in America*, 18-20, 49-55; and Elizur Wright, Jr., in *The Quarterly Anti Slavery Magazine* I (July, 1836), 400-409.

[145] E. D. Preston, "The Fugitive Slave Acts in Ohio," *Journal of Negro History* XXVII (October, 1943), 453.

[146] Lewis Gunn, "The Right of Free Discussion," *The History of Pennsylvania Hall . . .*, *op. cit.*, 64. See also Gerrit Smith, in *The Legion of Liberty and the Force of Truth*, 105; N. P. Rogers, in *A Collection of Valuable Documents*, 377; and Wendell Phillips, *Speech at the Worcester Disunion Convention, January 15, 1857*, 4.

ing that fundamental right. Why was it, the abolitionists asked, that prison reform, prohibition of alcoholic beverages, women's rights, or any other reform could be preached without opposition, but that antislavery agitation was immediately to be put down? Mobs and gag-laws betrayed the essential weakness of the very cause they were meant to strengthen. If abolitionists were wicked men, and their cause wrong, why did not the proslavery faction allow them to condemn themselves out of their own mouths?[147]

The abolitionists pointed out that if free discussion were right, and that if slavery could not be maintained in the face of it, slavery must therefore be wrong. If slavery could not survive criticism, and if the right to discuss and criticize it freely were threatened by slavery's existence, the American people would have to choose between the two. "The contest," said Francis Jackson, "is therefore between liberty and slavery. If slavery cannot exist with free discussion—so neither can liberty breathe without it. Losing this, we too, shall not be freemen indeed, but little, if at all, superior to the millions we now seek to emancipate."[148]

The effect upon Northern opinion of the period of mob law was, as the abolitionists anticipated, largely sympathetic to their cause. The fact that suppression of free speech affected every man who held a stake in the American tradition assisted them greatly in enlisting support from non-abolitionists and neutrals. In putting down the abolitionists, it was argued, the North was establishing a precedent that could be invoked against any minority whose opinions did not meet the public favor. As Professor Follen of Harvard pointed out, "A mob excited against abolition now may excite another mob far more dangerous to others than it is to us. It is impossible to prescribe limits to lawless acts of popular violence."[149] Many in the North recognized the validity of the argument. The Ver-

[147] L. M. Child, *George W. Julian, Speeches on Political Questions,* 3 and J. H. Raymond, "A Plea for Free Speech," *Autographs for Freedom,* 245.

[148] *The Legion of Liberty and the Force of Truth, op. cit.,* 108.

[149] *The Liberator,* March 19, 1836.

mont *Watchman and State Gazette,* while admitting its disagreement with abolitionism, at the same time disapproved of "all measures to put down discussion by force," and a meeting in Lowell, Massachusetts, called to stir up opposition to abolition, ended by affirming the right of all abolitionists to be heard, and to resist "the imperious demands of Southern tyranny."[150] The Detroit Presbytery in 1836 went on record as favoring free speech for abolitionists as "a privilege no human government has a right to take away," and the Reverend Albert Barnes told the alumni of Hamilton College that "the most appalling danger that threatens our country is the threatened restriction of the right of free discussion."[151]

The death of Lovejoy, coupled with the attacks upon Garrison, Birney, and Pennsylvania Hall, and the increasing frequency of incidents involving abolitionist speakers and presses in the free states, shocked a great segment of opinion in the North into agreement with the abolitionist contention that a basic constitutional right was at stake in the controversy over slavery. Prominent men such as Webster, Channing, and Alexander Everett, lent their weight to the abolitionist side; and newspaper opinion, always sensitive of threats to free discussion, expressed the fear that mob action might become dangerously out of hand.[152] The Adrian, Michigan, *Expositor,* which was not an abolitionist newspaper, summarized the Northern reaction by saying:

We tell you, gentlemen, when you encourage such proceedings you are handling edged tools—you know not how soon such weapons

---

[150] Siebert, *op. cit.,* 27, and *Niles' Register,* 49:74-76.

[151] *The Philanthropist,* April 1, 1836, and January 6, 1837.

[152] See Webster, *The Anti Slavery Record* II (December, 1836), 155-156; Channing, *Slavery,* 165, his *Remarks on the Slavery Question . . . ,* and his open letter to Birney, *Works,* II:159-160; and A. H. Everett, quoted by Bayard Tuckerman, *op. cit.,* 82-83. For editorial comment see the editorials from various papers, especially the cool and well-reasoned editorial from the Salem, Massachusetts, *Landmark,* reprinted in *The Liberator,* January 3, 1835. Note also in *The Emancipator,* March 22, 1838, the report of the Committee on Internal Affairs to the Assembly of New York dealing with mobs.

may turn against yourselves. . . . We repeat, the liberty of speech and of the press must be respected, or you are violators of the very principles of that compact you profess so ardently to love.[153]

The end of the period of violence in the North came with the shift of public opinion after 1840. Though the abolitionists' right to free speech was never again seriously threatened in the North, they continued to warn the nation that until slavery was dead, free speech was never out of danger.[154] With all their faults of intolerance, intensity, fanaticism, and narrow single-mindedness, the abolitionists nevertheless laid claim to a principle without which the nation could not exist, and the attempt to suppress them in the North by denying them expression was bound to fail. There was too much at stake for the free states to risk willingly the traditional right of the citizen to express his opinion. To thousands of Northerners, the abolitionist contention that their cause and that of civil liberty were joined, seemed believable and logical.

The abolitionists from the start held every moral advantage. They were the martyrs, the oppressed and persecuted, the defenders of free speech and free criticism. When the abolitionists emerged as guardians of white liberties, as well as crusaders for those of blacks, their cause gained immeasurably in moral strength. The influence of the era of mob violence, and the threat to free discussion occasioned by it, was a significant factor in cementing support in the North for the antislavery movement.

[153] *The Anti Slavery Bugle*, February 15, 1857.

[154] The remarks of Joshua Giddings and Horace Mann in the House, reprinted in *The Anti Slavery Bugle*, July 10, 1852 and April 12, 1857 furnish excellent summaries of this argument. A famous case of the 'fifties was that of Theodore Parker, charged with a misdemeanor for a speech in Faneuil Hall against the fugitive slave law. Though never brought to trial, Parker published his defense, an exhaustive analysis of the development of free speech and free thought up to his time, as *The Trial of Theodore Parker . . . With the Defence.*

Abolitionism,
the Constitution, and
Natural Liberties

VI

THE SLAVERY ISSUE forced on the nation a growing realization of the need for establishing the meaning of the guarantees of liberty written into the Declaration of Independence and the Constitution. From the beginning of the controversy, it was recognized by both antislavery and proslavery elements that the two documents which lay at the foundation of the republic must be interpreted, one way or another, to settle the two great questions posed by slavery's existence—what was liberty and what was equality?

Neither the Declaration nor the Constitution themselves provided complete or specific definitions. None of the previous discussions and interpretations of them gave a conclusive answer to the problem specifically presented by slavery. Therefore men in the South and the North, after 1830, tried to clarify and re-evaluate the words *liberty* and *equality*. If slavery denied the natural right to liberty and equality postulated by the Declaration, the institution had no place in the American system. If it did not conflict with the Declaration, slavery was therefore a recognized part of the national pattern, to be protected, retained, and even extended. Similarly, if slavery had the sanction of the Constitution, it deserved recognition and protection under the terms of that document; whereas if it did not, slavery was illegal and unconstitutional. The problem of placing slavery in its proper relationship to the natural and constitutional rights and liberties of the nation thus became highly important to both pro- and anti-slavery forces.

The natural rights portion of the slavery argument developed first. Reference to slavery had been made in passing during the discussions of natural rights incident to the Revolution. In the process of justifying a war for independence on the grounds of natural rights and the consent of the governed, the question of the right of all men to liberty, including Negro slaves, was certain to arise. James Otis, pleading the colonists' cause in *The Rights of British Colonies* in 1764, and Arthur Lee of Virginia in his *Essay in Vindication of the Continental Colonies of America* in the same year, both mentioned the inherent right of slaves to liberty. When the colonists drew up their list of grievances against the Crown, they alluded to the natural rights argument in objecting to the royal disallowance of the slave trade acts, and Jefferson, both in the Virginia Convention of 1774 and the first draft of the Declaration, put it to similar use.[1]

---

[1] W. S. Jenkins' *Proslavery Thought in the Old South*, 22-47, and Alice Adams' *The Neglected Period of Antislavery*, ch. IV, furnish discussions of the natural rights philosophy in the South, while B. F. Wright, *American Interpretations of Natural Law*, is a general history of its applications in American history. For Jefferson's indictment of George III as a "Violator of the sacred rights of life and liberty" see A. A. Lipscomb and A. E. Bergh, *The Writings of Thomas Jefferson*, I:34. A good brief treatment of the role of Jefferson in the development of Southern liberal thought, is Clement Eaton's "The Jeffersonian Tradition of Liberalism in America," *South Atlantic Quarterly* XLIII (January, 1944), 1-10. Two excellent ex-

A few years later Tory writers pointed out inconsistencies between the Declaration and the existence of slavery, as did contemporary thinkers such as Anthony Benezet, Benjamin Rush, George Mason, George Buchanan, and William Pinkney of Maryland.[2] Thomas Paine, the great proponent of the natural rights philosophy, thought in 1775 that since slaves "are not convicted of forfeiting freedom, they have still a natural, perfect right to it," and many agreed.[3]

In the Northern colonies the natural rights philosophy, expounded by the revolutionaries, had profound effects upon public opinion in regard to slavery. Harvard students debated in 1773 whether or not the Negro possessed a natural right to liberty as white men did, while later in the decade the Massachusetts emancipation bills of 1776 and 1777 were based almost wholly upon the proposition that slavery was "contrary to the laws of nature" and to "natural and inalienable rights." The first antislavery petition, presented to Congress in 1793 and signed by Franklin among others, quoted the principle "equal liberty was the portion, and is still the birthright, of all men."[4]

Southern revolutionary leaders and political philosophers were also affected by the current popularity of the natural rights philosophy. Following the war, a flood of manumissions swept Virginia, the free Negro population mounting from less than 3,000 in 1782, to 13,000 in 1790, and to 20,000 in 1800. More than one slaveholder freed his slaves, as did John Pleasants in 1771, in the conviction that "all mankind have an undoubted right to freedom," or like St. George Tucker

---

positions of the proslavery point of view toward the Declaration of Independence and the natural rights school are William Gilmore Simms, "Miss Martineau on Slavery," *Southern Literary Messenger* III (November, 1837), 652-4; and James D. Holcombe, "Is Slavery Consistent with Natural Law?" *ibid.*, XXVII (December, 1858), 401-21.

[2] Merle Curti, *The Growth of American Thought*, 120, 137-38, 170-71.

[3] M. D. Conway, *The Works of Thomas Paine*, I:17. L. D. Turner, "Antislavery Sentiment in American Literature," *Journal of Negro History* XIV (October, 1929), 380-84, cites numerous similar quotations.

[4] Emory Washburn, "The Extinction of Slavery in Massachusetts," *Massachusetts Historical Society Transactions* XXXIV, 33-46, and *Annals of Congress, 1st Congress, 2nd Session,* 1239.

planned emancipation schemes based on Jeffersonian doctrines.[5]

The natural rights philosophy was well established in the United States by 1800, and the pattern set for the next phase of the controversy. The question of whether or not slavery violated the inalienable right of all men to liberty (and not white men only) and the pursuit of happiness took on a much greater urgency with the opening of the aggressive phase of the antislavery movement. Practically all the literature subsequently written in opposition to or in defense of slavery grew to some degree from varying interpretations of the natural rights concept as it related to the institution.[6]

The abolition movement from its earliest to its latest stage was rooted in the natural rights philosophy. The American Anti Slavery Society, in its first Declaration of Sentiments adopted in 1833, asserted that its aim was simply the practical realization of the preamble to the Declaration of Independence.[7] Two years later William Ellery Channing pointed out that the abolition argument rested wholly upon the Declaration, which "established the reality and sacredness of human rights, and that slavery is an infraction of them. . . ." The Liberty Party later incorporated much the same statement in its platform, and the political-action wing of the abolitionists chose the same principle for party politics.[8] The National Anti

[5] J. H. Russell, *The Free Negro in Virginia*, 61; Helen T. Catterall, *Judicial Cases Concerning Slavery*, I:105; and J. C. Ballagh, "Antislavery Sentiment in Virginia," *South Atlantic Quarterly* I (April, 1902), 113. In 1806 Virginia began to place legal restriction upon manumission to stem the tendency, and the Virginia legislature rejected Tucker's plan. James Birney senior freed his slaves in 1839 on the ground that slavery violated the Declaration of Independence, according to William Birney, *James G. Birney and His Times*, 360. See also Catterall, *op. cit.*, II:49, 67, and 149, and Beverly Munford, *Virginia's Attitude Toward Slavery and Secession*, 104-113, for other examples of natural rights antislavery sympathy.

[6] B. F. Wright, *op. cit.*, 211.

[7] *The Platform of the American Anti Slavery Society and its Auxiliaries*, 7.

[8] W. E. Channing, *Slavery*, 46; William Goodell, *A Full Statement of the Reasons . . . Offered to the Committee of the Legislature of Massachusetts*, 17; R. R. Gurley to J. G. Birney, D. L. Dumond, ed., *The Letters of James G. Birney*, I:57; Alice Adams, *op. cit.*, 18; Articles I, III, IX, and X in the

Slavery Convention reaffirmed the stand in 1857, saying, "The only abolitionism we promulgate . . . is embodied in the self-evident truths of the Declaration of Independence . . . and in the Golden Rule of the Gospel—nothing more, nothing less," while Garrison summarized it with the simple statement, "The people of this state profess to believe in the Declaration of Independence. That is my Abolitionism. Every man, therefore, who disclaims Abolitionism, repudiates the Declaration of Independence."[9] No single point of view was more consistently accepted by the various groups of abolitionists throughout the period, and none met more general support among them. The natural rights argument was a common ground upon which all antislavery men could agree, whatever their other differences.[10]

Man's natural rights, as interpreted by the abolitionists, derived from two sources, nature and God. The rights of man were natural in the sense that they were inherent in man by the fact of his existence, or "natural" in the sense that they were implanted in humanity by a God of nature. Thus the Presbyterian General Assembly denounced slavery as "a gross violation of the most precious and sacred rights of human nature," while the Michigan Anti Slavery Society resolved that "human beings have, by virtue of their existence, certain inalienable rights, which no being in the universe, not even God himself, can have a right to infringe, among which are life, liberty, and the pursuit of happiness."[11]

Liberty Party Platform and Goodell's call for a convention, Dumond, *op. cit.*, II:1048.

[9] *The National Anti Slavery Standard*, February 21, 1857, and Garrison's *The Abolitionists; a Speech at Cooper Institute, January 14, 1862* (n.p., 1862), 2.

[10] Garrison, Goodell, Parker, Birney, and others placed especial emphasis upon the natural rights theory. See Dumond, *op. cit.*, II:700; Theodore Parker, *A Letter to the People of the United States, Touching the Matter of Slavery*, 106-107; and Goodell, *Slavery and Antislavery*, 1. Lincoln's Alton and Springfield speeches are interesting interpretations of the Declaration; see Nicolay and Hay, *Abraham Lincoln, A History*, VI:170, 182-83.

[11] *The Anti Slavery Bugle*, March 3, 1856. See also Gerrit Smith and Horace Mann, quoted by B. F. Wright, *op. cit.*, 214-15, and Alexander Ross, *Recollections*, 7-8.

Others considered the rights in question to be God-given. The American Anti Slavery Society Convention stated in 1833 that "the right to enjoy liberty is inalienable. To invade it is to usurp the prerogative of Jehovah." Similarly, the Rhode Island Anti Slavery Society in 1836 believed natural rights to be divinely bestowed upon man, and that to infringe upon them was to transgress God's law. "God has given every man essential rights which the majority shall not violate," said another, and Benjamin Wade defined the Declaration of Independence as the first great antislavery document, "a declaration of Almighty God, that all men are created equal, and have the same inherent rights."[12] William Swaim of North Carolina held that "liberty is the inalienable birthright of every human being; and that God has made no difference in this respect between the *white and the black.*"[13] William Ellery Channing saw these human rights as "the gifts of God, and inseparable from human nature, of which slavery is the infraction." Garrison assumed as "self-evident truth, that the liberty of a people is a gift of God and nature. . . ."[14] Salmon P. Chase told the Senate that "Master and Slave, according to the principles of the Declaration of Independence, and by the law of nature, are alike men, and endowed by their Creator with equal rights . . .," while Theodore Parker defined life, liberty, and the pursuit of happiness as inalienable natural rights, divinely bestowed upon all men, white or black, in equal number and force, and therefore guaranteed by government.[15]

[12] B. F. Wright, *op. cit.,* 212; *Proceedings of the Rhode Island Antislavery Convention Held in Providence* . . . , 17-20, a long and careful analysis of the question; "Junius," *The Philanthropist,* June 16, 1837; and *The Congressional Globe, 31st Congress, 1st Session,* February 6, 1854, 339. William Goodell said in *The Anti Slavery Almanac* (1838 ed.), 7: "God has made out 'free papers' for every human being. Our fathers, in signing the Declaration of Independence, republished and endorsed them."

[13] *Address to the People of North Carolina on the Evils of Slavery.*

[14] W. E. Channing, *Slavery,* 11; and W. P. and F. J. Garrison, *William Lloyd Garrison,* I:200.

[15] S. P. Chase, *Speech in the Senate, February 3, 1854,* 37; Theodore Parker, *The Dangers from Slavery,* 1-3. See also Goodell, "Declaration and Exposé," *The American Anti Slavery Almanac* (1837 ed.), 30-32, and Charles Olcott, *Two Lectures on . . . Slavery and Abolition,* 26-27.

The advocates of slavery replied by choosing one of two alternatives—they either denied the existence of such natural rights as the abolitionists defined them; or they attempted to reconcile the institution of slavery with them by redefining them or explaining wherein slavery and natural liberty had no relationship under the circumstances.[16] In the latter case, they argued that human rights were not fixed, but varied in quality and quantity according to a scale based on education, intelligence, color, and so on. As individuals moved up the scale, their rights increased in number, but the number of people possessing and enjoying them necessarily diminished. A slave then was robbed of none of his natural liberties, but possessed the maximum number of rights commensurate with his capacity and position in society.

The right to liberty was "a privilege and a distinction belonging to white men"—a Negro, therefore, could hardly lose that which he did not have. "The truth is," wrote William Gilmore Simms, the Carolina author and critic,

that our rights depend entirely on the degree of obedience which we pay to the laws of our creation. All our rights, whether from nature or society—and these are the only two sources of rights known to us —result from the performance of our duties. Unless we perform our duties, we have no rights. . . . The man has no rights by nature, unless by a compliance with nature; as he would have no rights from society, unless by a compliance with its laws.[17]

Thomas Dew, writing in 1832 of the Virginia Debates, found slavery and nature's law quite compatible, while A. H. Stephens thought that natural rights were subject to modifications by the practical considerations of Southern society—the Negro might possess "natural and inalienable rights," but "stern necessity, bearing the marks of the Creator himself," might "interpose and prevent their full enjoyment." A writer in the Richmond *Examiner* removed the Negro from the whole natural rights tradition by declaring that

16 W. S. Jenkins, *op. cit.*, 121-23; also 214-15.
17 Simms, *op. cit.*, 653; A. Y. Lloyd, *The Slavery Controversy*, 263.

... the negro race is the result of a different act of the Creator than that which originated the Caucasian, and is consequently beyond the scope of those abstract axioms of the white race, which declare that all MEN have equal rights.[18]

A. T. Bledsoe came to the same conclusion, arguing that for the public good "no class of men can have a natural right to exercise a power which, in being entrusted to them, would be wielded for harm and not for good." R. W. Bailey agreed that, though men possessed natural liberty, it was not to be used in such a manner as "to endanger safety and propriety." John C. Hurd concluded that "natural law" was law only to the extent that it was recognized in courts of justice, and that when the will of the state was not in accord with the law of nature, the latter gave way to the former. Samuel Seabury identified natural and divine law as one, but believed the answer to the problem of obedience to both was to be found in the Bible, which sanctioned slavery.[19]

Attempts to reconcile slavery with the natural rights philosophy proved for the most part to be unsatisfactory, and the majority of pro-slavery thinkers found it simpler and more effective to jettison the natural rights theory entirely. Perhaps their greatest stumbling block was the clear enunciation of the principle written into the Declaration by the Virginian, Thomas Jefferson. Simms explained that "our excellent forefathers . . . were not in the best mood to become philosophers, however well calculated to approve themselves the best of patriots," and suggested that the phrase employed in the Declaration meant solely that Americans were equal to British subjects in rights; an anonymous "North Carolinian" argued that while

[18] Ruth Scarborough, *Opposition to Slavery in Georgia Prior to 1860*, 184; Richmond *Examiner*, quoted in *DeBow's Review* XI (October, 1851), 465.

[19] A. T. Bledsoe, *Essay on Liberty and Slavery*, 109; R. W. Bailey, *The Issue, Presented in a Series of Letters on Slavery*, 53; B. F. Wright, *op. cit.*, 218 ff. Thomas Dew's *Essay on Slavery* (Richmond, 1849) also attacked the doctrines of equality and natural rights; see Kenneth M. Stampp, "An Analysis of T. R. Dew's Review of the Debates in the Virginia Legislature," *Journal of Negro History* XXVII (October, 1942), 380-88.

it might be abstractly true, it was practically false.[20] J. H. Hammond thought the idea that all men are created equal "ridiculously absurd. . . . The phrase was simply a fine sounding one, significant of that sentimental French philosophy, then so current, which was destined to bear such sanguinary consequences."[21]

So consistent were the Southern attacks on the Declaration of Independence that Abraham Lincoln remarked in 1857 that it had been only a short time since

> our Declaration of Independence was held sacred by all, and thought to include all; but now, to aid in making the bondage of the Negro universal and eternal, it is sneered at and construed, and hawked at and torn, till, if its framers could rise from their graves, they could not at all recognize it.[22]

Others were less charitable toward the founding fathers, and Jefferson's reputation in particular suffered greatly at the hands of Southern commentators. His views, it was said, were the result of his fondness for French radicalism, his penchant for "strange eccentricities, quaint expressions, gleaming paradoxes, and sweeping assertions."[23] Direct denials of his principles and those of the Declaration were conventional after 1830. Thomas Cooper characterized the rights of man as "a great deal of nonsense. . . . Nothing can be more untrue; no human being ever was, now is, or ever will be born free." "Man has no inalienable rights," wrote another Southerner, "not even those of life, liberty, and the pursuit of happiness. . . . Instead of that 'glittering generality' which might serve as a motto for the wildest anarchy, the truth is that men and races of men have certain natural capacities and duties, and the right to use the one and discharge the other." George Fitzhugh, paraphrasing a famous Jeffersonian phrase, remarked that some

[20] Simms, *op. cit.*, 652-54; "A North Carolinian," *Southern Slavery Considered Upon General Principles*, 7.
[21] *The Pro-Slavery Argument*, 250.
[22] Roy P. Basler, ed., *Collected Works of Abraham Lincoln*, II:298.
[23] G. S. Sawyer, *Southern Institutes*, 208.

men "are born with saddles on their backs and others booted and spurred to ride them, and the riding does them good. They need the whip, the reins, the spur. . . ." James Holcombe felt that the Revolutionary generation accepted "those expositions of human rights embodied in the infidel philosophy of France . . . in a glow of generous enthusiasm," but that they were not really to be believed. "The celebrated declaration of Mr. Jefferson," he continued,

that he knew of no attribute of the Almighty which would take the side of the master in a contest with his slave, is so far from commanding the assent of the slaveholder of this generation, that the justice, the humanity, and the policy of the relation as it exists with us, has become the prevailing conviction of our people.[24]

Chancellor Harper reversed the argument by claiming that slavery was the natural state of man, and freedom "a forced and artificial state" for inferior men, a view later expanded by George Fitzhugh. William Gilmore Simms summarized the debate by explaining that distinction, not equality, was nature's law, and that only equality within the categories provided by nature constituted true freedom:

Democracy is not levelling—it is, properly defined, the harmony of the moral world. It insists upon inequalities, as its law declares, that all men should hold the place to which they are properly entitled. The definition of liberty is, the undisturbed possession of that place in society to which our moral and intellectual merits entitle us. *He is a free man, whatever his condition, who fills his proper place. He is a slave only, who is forced into a position in society below the claims of his intellect.*[25]

[24] Jenkins, *op. cit.*, 125; W. H. Holcombe, *The Alternative: A Separate Nationality or the Africanization of the South*, 5; Fitzhugh, quoted by Stampp, *The Peculiar Institution*, 420, with the same quotation appearing in *The Anti Slavery Bugle*, September 20, 1856, from the Richmond *Examiner*; James D. Holcombe, "Is Slavery Consistent with Natural Law?" *op. cit.*, 402-3.

[25] *The Pro-Slavery Argument*, 28; Fitzhugh, *supra cit.*, 71; Simms, *op. cit.*, 653. Simms continued his argument to point out that the slave in the South enjoyed far more equality than the free Negro in the North. The

In general, the denial of the natural rights philosophy, and with it the validity of the principles of the Declaration of Independence, became a common theme in proslavery literature after 1840.[26]

Closely related to the controversy over the natural right to freedom was the argument over equality.[27] Opposing views of the meaning of the Declaration's statement that "all men are created equal" were not new,[28] but the differences in Northern and Southern interpretations were intensified and widened by the abolitionists' exploitation of the issue after 1830. They made the nation conscious of the wide differences between equality in theory and practice by simply demanding for the slave that which the Declaration clearly stated was the right of all men.

The abolitionist interpretation of the equality clause of the Declaration was literal and unequivocal. William H. Seward believed the American democratic system "founded in the nattural equality of *all* men—not alone *American* men, nor alone all *white* men, but men of every country, clime and complexion are equal, not made equal by human laws, but born equal." The institution of slavery, abolitionists unanimously agreed,

---

freedman "contends for an equality with a people to whom he is morally and physically inferior, so that he provokes hatred and lives in a state of continual personal insecurity." The slave, living where no pretense is made of equality, is "regarded as filling his true place, and occupying his just position, and while he does so he does not offend, but meets with favor and acceptance"; 545.

[26] See Calhoun's incisive denial, R. K. Crallé, ed., *Works*, I:55-59; Jonathan Fletcher's review of Channing, *DeBow's Review* IX (July, 1850), 22-31; T. R. R. Cobb, "What is Slavery and Its Foundation in Natural Law," *An Historical Sketch of Slavery from the Earliest Periods* (Philadelphia, 1858), and R. L. Dabney, *A Defence of Virginia*, 241-65.

[27] T. V. Smith, *The American Philosophy of Equality*, especially chapter II, 35-84, is a good general discussion.

[28] Compare the 1818 constitution of Connecticut, ". . . all *men*, when they form a social compact, are equal in rights," and the 1819 constitution of Mississippi and Alabama, ". . . all *freemen*, when they form a social compact, are equal in rights." Quoted by T. V. Smith, *supra cit.*, 50. Between 1794 and 1829 antislavery societies held twenty-four conventions, each calling attention to the equality clauses of the Declaration.

contradicted this natural equality and destroyed it.[29] There were, however, differences of opinion among them as to what this equality of Negro and white men involved. One group believed it meant that "the men who are now slaves must be admitted to all the rights, privileges, and immunities, political, social, and religious, which belong to American citizens generally."[30] Another view, apparently more widely accepted, interpreted the term *equality* to mean that the Negro was "equally entitled to his life, his liberty, and the fruit of his toil," and not necessarily immediate social and political equality.[31]

The proslavery leaders replied either by denying the equality clause of the Declaration categorically, or by launching a counter-attack—that slavery was actually the only system which encouraged *true* equality. Jefferson's "nowhere accredited dogma" was merely "the natural result of the excited state of the public mind" during Revolutionary days, not to be interpreted as the abolitionists would have it.[32] The Declaration was not intended to apply to the Negro; had its framers so meant it, it would never have been signed by Southern slaveholders—the preamble simply stated that the signers sanctioned no royal or aristocratic class in the republic. "The doctrine of equality contained in it refers to the Anglo-Saxon race," resolved the Ohio Constitutional Convention of 1850,

[29] Seward, Cleveland speech, October 26, 1848, in G. E. Baker, ed., *The Works of William H. Seward*, III:293. The law of equality was "a divine law, which is written in the hearts and consciences of men," said Seward in *The Irrepressible Conflict*, 1. See also Joseph Tracy, *Natural Equality, A Sermon . . . at Montpelier*, for a judicious analysis of the question, and Richard Hildreth, *Despotism in America*, 96-107.

[30] *The National Anti Slavery Standard*, September 17, 1846.

[31] Owen Lovejoy of Illinois in the House of Representatives, 1859, quoted by *The National Era*, March 7, 1859. Abel Thomas, in a child's primer, *The Gospel of Slavery*, 1, phrased it: "Men differ in color, and stature, and weight . . . , but equal in rights are the great and the small, in sight of the God and Creator of all." Lincoln's analysis of the equality clause of the Declaration is interesting; see Nicolay and Hay, *op. cit.*, I:289 and V:35-41.

[32] Hammond, *The Pro-Slavery Argument, op. cit.*, 110, and T. R. R. Cobb, *op. cit.*, clxix.

a sentiment in which Indiana opinion concurred. "All (*White*) men are created equal," said the New York *Day Book,* emphasizing the italics, "and therefore entitled to equal rights," while the Washington *Union* said, "There is no equality among men except in the universal duty to obey the laws of God."[33]

By no stretch of interpretation, claimed the South, could the Declaration be construed to include Negroes in its definition of equality. Bishop Hopkins of Vermont termed the Jeffersonian doctrine "a manifest absurdity." William Gilmore Simms pointed out that men were born unequal, and that since their so-called inalienable rights were violated daily by laws passed for society's betterment, society recognized no such rights except within legal restrictions. Enslaving the Negro for the benefit of society was hardly a violation of a right to equality the Negro did not possess.[34] Pickens of South Carolina declared in the House that the Declaration embodied only "an abstract truth, but like other mere abstractions, it can have no actual existence," and James G. Birney, speaking of the Southern planters he had known, judged that the majority of them believed "the self-evident principle that *all men are created equal* is about as ridiculous nonsense as was ever published."[35]

Nature and experience, said the antiabolitionists, conspired to make a failure out of any attempt to gain equality for the Negro.[36] South Carolina courts decided in 1848 that "the long experience of very many of these United States . . . is, that the white Caucasian and the black African cannot live together upon terms of equality." The Richmond *Examiner* brushed

---

[33] Albert Beveridge, *Abraham Lincoln,* II:53, and (Calvin Colton) "A Northern Man," *Abolition A Sedition,* 121-123; H. C. Hubbart, *The Older Middle West, 1840-1880,* 48-49; prospectus of the *Day Book,* R. G. Horton, *A Youth's History of the Great Civil War,* Appendix; and the Washington *Union,* quoted by *The National Era,* May 1, 1851.

[34] W. H. Siebert, *Vermont's Antislavery and Underground Railroad Record,* 20, and *The Pro-Slavery Argument, op. cit.,* 259-60.

[35] Pickens' speech, *The Philanthropist,* February 9, 1836, and Birney to R. R. Gurley, Dumond, *op. cit.,* I:97.

[36] See W. S. Grayson, "Natural Equality of Man Treated as a Question of Philosophy," *DeBow's Review* XXVI (January, 1859), 29-43, and G. D. Shortridge, "Mr. Jefferson, The Declaration of Independence, and Freedom," *ibid.,* XXVI (May, 1859), 547-60.

aside the Declaration, since it was not the organic law of the Union and therefore was inapplicable to slavery; "The Union was not founded upon the Red Republican principle of the equality of all men, but upon the commonsense principle that the negro is a negro, and the white man is his superior and lord, by nature and by the providence of God."[37]

To prove the inequality of the black to the white race, the proslavery group called science to its aid. Respected scientists such as Dr. Joseph Nott of Mobile, Alabama, proved, after a battery of anthropological tests, that the Negro was a subordinate race, never intended by nature to be the equal of the white. Nott's book, *Two Lectures on the Natural History of the Caucasian and Negro Races,* published in 1845, was an invaluable source of quotations for proslavery writers over the next twenty years. "The plain and inevitable deduction is this," Nott wrote in one of many articles on the subject,

that the negro is a totally distinct and inferior animal and species of animal from the Caucasian; that the negro is the connecting link between man and the brute creation; that the negro is intended by nature for a similar dependence upon the Caucasian man, in which only the ox, the ass, and the horse fulfill the intent of their creation. . . .[38]

Nor was Nott alone in his deduction; Dr. Samuel G. Morton, Dr. John Bachman, George Combe the phrenologist, and the famed Harvard scientist Professor Louis Agassiz agreed with him in substance. The Negro was therefore a natural slave,

[37] Helen T. Catterall, *op. cit.,* II:405; *The National Anti Slavery Standard,* October 11, 1856; and *The National Era,* May 1, 1851.

[38] "The Negro Race," *DeBow's Review* XI (October, 1851) , 405. See also Nott's "The Slave Question," and "Statistics of the Southern Slave Population," *ibid.,* IV (November, 1847) , 287-91; "The Nature and Destiny of the Negro," *ibid.,* X (November, 1851) , 339-42; and "Reflections on the Census of 1840," *Southern Literary Messenger* IX (June, 1843) , 348. For a complete study of racial theories in early nineteenth-century America, see William Stanton, *The Leopard's Spots.* Agassiz's racial theories are summarized in Edward C. Lurie, *Louis Agassiz* (Chicago, 1960) , 143-44, 256-57, 260-62, 305-6. "The brain of the negro," wrote Agassiz, "is that of the imperfect brain of a seven month's infant in the womb of the white."

wrote Dr. Samuel Cartwright of New Orleans, and talk of equality among races utter folly. "Comparative anatomy discloses," said Cartwright, "history tells, chemistry proves, and the Bible reveals, that by a higher law than the union, the Constitution, or any other human enactments, the negro is a slave."[39] The claims of the abolitionists, wrote Nott,

the angry and senseless discussions on negro emancipation, which have agitated Christendom for the last half century, were commenced in ignorance, and the abolitionists have only become more angry and unreasonable, as facts have risen up against their theories.[40]

What, then, did the term *equality* mean to those who refused to include the Negro within the terms of the Declaration? It was determined, said the Washington *Union*, "by the varying influences of origin and caste, age, numbers, geographical position, and contact with other societies and communities." It was generally agreed that it implied an equality only among equals; it did not mean that all men were fit for any place in society, but rather only for that place to which they were entitled by their moral, intellectual, and physical resources. Since the Negro belonged to an inferior race, attempts to make him equal to a superior race were unthinkable perversions of true equality and did injustice to both Negro and white. This concept of equality was "a sounder philosophy than that of Thomas Jefferson, or his friends of the French

[39] "How to Save the Republic, and the Position of the South in the Union," *DeBow's Review* XI (August, 1851), 194. See also Cartwright's obnoxious essay, "Diseases and Peculiarities of the Negro Race," *ibid.*, XI (July, 1855), 69 ff. Two court cases gave legal recognition to the doctrine of racial inferiority, Pendleton vs. State (Arkansas) and Vinyard vs. Passalaigue (South Carolina); see Catterall, *op. cit.*, V:231 and II:405. Compare also William Tecumseh Sherman, "All the Congresses on earth can't make the Negro anything else than what he is; he must be subject to the white man . . . ," letter of July, 1860, quoted in Allan Nevins, *Ordeal of The Union*, I:510.

[40] "The Slave Question," *op. cit.*, 288. So thought more than a few Northerners, judging by the press; see the editorials in H. C. Perkins, *Northern Editorials on Secession* (New York, 1942), I:468, 471, 475, *passim*.

Revolutionary school," because it provided the only reasonable basis for a true republic—slavery led directly to "the establishment of a new system and a new civilization based on foundations of everlasting truth, the legal and political equality of the race, or of all those whom the Almighty Creator has himself made equal."[41]

First and most boldly developed by Calhoun, this doctrine of "a classified equality among equals" found its full expression in the Southern proslavery propaganda of the 'fifties. Where slavery did not exist, it was argued, menial tasks were performed by white citizens, and their degradation affected the entire class, dividing it into the rich and the inferior "freeborn poor." With an admittedly inferior class to perform society's drudgery, both rich and poor were equal within their own classes. Slavery produced in Southern white society "as nearly a perfect spirit of equality as can be expected or desired in the world."[42] It was thus "the cornerstone of our republican system," according to J. H. Hammond, while Toombs of Georgia wrote that "the perfect equality of the superior race, and the legal subordination of the inferior race, are the foundation on which we have erected our republican system."[43] The abolitionist claim for equality between white and Negro, founded in natural right and confirmed by the Declaration of Independence, was therefore contrary not only to science, law, nature, and experience, but was in effect an attack upon truly republican government itself.

The discussion of the meanings implicit in the Declaration

[41]W. S. Jenkins, *op. cit.*, 193-94. The Washington *Southern Press*, quoted by *The National Era*, February 13, 1851, and J. H. Van Evrie, *White Supremacy and Negro Subordination*, 422.

[42] Thomas Dew, *The Pro-Slavery Argument, op. cit.*, 261. See also Henry Wise, R. M. Johnson, T. R. R. Cobb, Jefferson Davis, and others, quoted by Jenkins, *op. cit.*, 173, 193-95. *The Anti Slavery Bugle* of November 16, 1850, quoted Tucker of Virginia: "No sir, without social organization there can be no civilization. . . . The Southern gentleman, studiously observing all possible courtesy in his deportment to the Negro, makes a gentleman of him, while he himself becomes more of a gentleman by his condescension. The man of Ohio has nobody below him but his hog."

[43] Quoted by Jenkins, *op. cit.*, 194, and T. V. Smith, *op. cit.*, 109.

of Independence carried less weight in the antislavery controversy than the argument over the Constitution, which, as Southerners pointed out, was the organic law of the land, whereas the Declaration, however one interpreted it, was not. Calhoun in his Senate resolutions of 1837 stated the Southern view of the Constitution and slavery in its clearest form: slavery was constitutional and to be protected by the Constitution; Congress had no right to interfere with it in the states or territories, was committed to protect it, and to suppress criticism of it or agitation against it. Abolitionists, faced with the problem of placing slavery in its proper relation to constitutional law, developed three contrasting views of the matter. Some agreed with the South that the Constitution sanctioned slavery, and contended that therefore the document was to be amended or disregarded. Others claimed that the Constitution quite clearly outlawed slavery, and that therefore the system was to be abandoned immediately as unconstitutional. Others thought the document neutral, neither for nor against slavery, which meant that slavery could be abolished quite simply by passing new legislation. The abolitionists never fully reconciled these three views, and their debates over them split the movement, sometimes seriously.[44]

The South maintained that the Constitution established slavery on a national basis. The Southern slave states had ratified the Constitution—implied evidence that the system was recognized at the time of ratification—and the several compromises reached by the Convention over slavery proved that the framers were well aware of its existence. The bill of rights applied only to those who had entered into that original compact—from which the Negro was excluded—and the rights involved in them were social and political rights not possessed by Negroes. The Constitution was therefore a proslavery doc-

[44] See the debate between Gerrit Smith and Edmund Quincy, and between Horace Mann and Wendell Phillips, *The Anti Slavery Bugle*, January 15, 1847, and March 3 to May 5, 1853. William Goodell, *Slavery and Antislavery, op. cit.*, chapter XLIX, summarizes the abolitionist points of view on the Constitution to 1852.

ument; interference with the slave system was a violation of Southern constitutional rights.[45]

To this, one group of abolitionists replied that the Constitution was in reality an antislavery document, and slavery therefore unconstitutional, illegal, and immediately to be abolished.[46] Worked out in the 'forties and fully developed in the 'fifties, this doctrine possessed certain advantages for the abolitionists in that it simplified many of the legal and political difficulties that might be involved in immediate abolition. The Liberty League, in nominating Gerrit Smith for president, adopted this principle in 1847, while in the West political conventions in Indiana, Illinois, and Wisconsin declared slavery unconstitutional in 1845.[47]

At the center of the argument that the Constitution forbade slavery was the contention that the Declaration, a prior document and one carrying within it the principles of the national government-to-be, was antislavery. The Declaration, which abolitionists considered as part of constitutional law, made slavery illegal; the Constitution did not specifically re-establish it. The single question at issue was, therefore, did the Constitution *implicitly* sanction it as an *existing* institution? Since slavery was abolished by the Declaration and thus had no legal existence in 1783, it was therefore manifestly impossible for the Constitution to sanction it.[48]

The whole point of the abolitionist argument rested on the

[45] "Slavery at the South," *DeBow's Review* VII (November, 1849), 384-85. Jenkins, *op. cit.*, 149, 157, summarizes the Southern argument.

[46] For summaries, see William Goodell, *Views of American Constitutional Law upon American Slavery;* N. P. Bailey, *Our Duty as Taught By the Aggressive Nature of Slavery* . . .; G. W. F. Mellen, *An Argument upon The Unconstitutionality of Slavery;* and Gamaliel Bailey, *The Anti Slavery Bugle,* February 24, 1843.

[47] T. C. Smith, *The Liberty and Free Soil Parties in the Northwest,* 99.

[48] Lysander Spooner, *The Unconstitutionality of Slavery.* "J. D. C." writing in *The Anti Slavery Bugle,* October 9, 1852, argued that since England had outlawed slavery in 1752, it was at the same time outlawed in all British colonies; that the Declaration abolished it a second time; that the Constitution did not legalize it; and that the non-importation clause implicitly abolished it once more, while the 1793 fugitive slave law neither legalized it nor was intended to apply to the whole system.

belief that the Declaration was an accepted portion of constitutional law, a point Goodell, Spooner, and others argued thoroughly and interminably. The Declaration, they claimed, laid the basis of American government; the Constitution itself rested upon it and was written in harmony with it.[49] Assuming that the Declaration, the Articles of Confederation, and the Articles of Association affirmed the natural right of freedom to every man, it was unthinkable that the Constitution would later deny it; the "due process" clause alone indicated that slavery was constitutionally illegal.[50] "One thing is certain," said Henry Ward Beecher, "that the Constitution was formed as a bona-fide instrument of liberty. Its framers never thought that it would be twisted into an instrument to build up slavery."[51]

Variations on this theme were common. Horace Mann believed that at most the Constitution simply "acquiesced" in slavery, but neither legalized nor protected it. Cassius Clay of Kentucky and S. J. May of Vermont thought it neither proslavery nor antislavery. Birney was of the opinion that the Constitutional Convention, interested primarily in forming a union, left the settlement of the slavery question for a later

---

[49] Spooner, *op. cit.*, 36-38; Goodell, *Views of American Constitutional Law* . . . , 134-142; Goodell, *Our National Charter for the Millions* (New York, 1864) ; Charles Sumner, "The Landmark of Freedom," *Recent Speeches and Addresses;* Beriah Green, *A Discourse in Commemoration . . . of Elijah P. Lovejoy,* 5; Gerrit Smith, *Substance of a Speech Made in the Capital of the State of New York; Speech of the Hon. John J. Perry of Maine in the House . . .; Speech of the Hon. Cydnor B. Tompkins of Ohio in the House . . .;* "Resolutions of the State Antislavery Convention of Illinois," *The National Era,* February 6, 1861; Joel Tiffany, *A Treatise on the Unconstitutionality of Slavery* . . .; S. P. Chase, "Address at the Southern and Western Liberty Convention at Cincinnati," in C. D. Cleveland, ed., *Antislavery Addresses of 1844 and 1845;* W. H. Seward, "The Basis of the American Constitution," in Julia Griffiths, ed., *Autographs for Freedom,* 201-207.

[50] N. P. Rogers, "The Constitution," *The Quarterly Anti Slavery Magazine* II (January, 1837), 145-63, and Salmon P. Chase to Birney, in Dumond, *Birney Letters, op. cit.,* II:806.

[51] Beecher to the American and Foreign Anti Slavery Society, 1851, in *The Anti Slavery Bugle,* June 7, 1851. Samuel J. May, *Recollections of the Anti Slavery Conflict,* said, 142-43, that antislavery societies sometimes distributed copies of the Constitution as good antislavery propaganda.

meeting that most certainly would have outlawed it; however, the rapid rise of cotton as a factor in Southern economics had made the abolition of slavery impossible when the time for decision arrived.[52] Others felt that the Convention, though recognizing the existence of the system, intended to make it unconstitutional after 1808; or that they did not intend it to spread but instead to die a natural death. Others believed that slavery violated the spirit of the Constitution, though not necessarily the letter.[53]

A small but important wing of the abolitionist movement in New England, including Garrison, Phillips, and Edmund Quincy, denounced the Constitution as a proslavery document and refused to recognize it as a legal instrument of government. Garrison, speaking at the New England Anti Slavery Convention in 1855, said:

We know that the people of the country never did make an anti-slavery Constitution. We affirm it to be a 'self-evident truth' that they have been morally incapable, through prejudice, hatred, and oppression, of adopting, designedly and purposely, a Constitution that should instantly emancipate every slave. . . . The Constitution of the United States is what the people meant it to be.[54]

Denouncing it as "a covenant with death and an agreement with Hell," Garrison and his followers labeled the Constitution an instrument of oppression and slavery.[55]

[52] *The Anti Slavery Bugle*, July 2, 1853; the Lexington, Kentucky, *True American*, June 24, 1845; S. J. May, "Slavery and the Constitution," *The Quarterly Anti Slavery Magazine* II (October, 1836, and April, 1847), 73-90, 226-38; and Birney, "Why Slavery is in the Constitution," Julia Griffiths, ed., *Autographs for Freedom, op. cit.*, 116-127. Birney believed that the "whole Constitution," properly applied, was an inherently antislavery document; see Dumond, *Birney Letters, op. cit.*, II:90.

[53] Anonymous, *Remarks on the Constitution by a Friend of Humanity, on the Subject of Slavery*, and "A Philadelphian," *Free Remarks on the Spirit of the Federal Constitution;* remarks of counsel, Commonwealth vs. Jenison (Pennsylvania), Catterall, *op. cit.*, IV:481; and Fuller of Massachusetts, quoted by Jenkins, *op. cit.*, 176.

[54] *The National Anti Slavery Standard*, June 16, 1855.

[55] Edmund Quincy's letter to Gerrit Smith, *The Anti Slavery Bugle*, December 25, 1846; the resolutions of the Rhode Island Convention of 1846, *ibid.*, December 11, 1846; speech of Wendell Phillips, *ibid.*, April 20,

This disagreement among abolitionists over the proper construction of the Constitution was of vital importance to the movement. If the Constitution were a neutral or an antislavery document, the most efficient and proper method of abolishing slavery was by political action, retaining the Constitution as an article of government but ensuring its proper interpretation by political means—a view adopted by the Liberty party and later by the Radical Abolitionists as meaning abolition by Federal action through Congress.[56] But if the Constitution were a proslavery document, it must, therefore, be by-passed or violated. The fundamental disagreement split the abolitionists into a political-action group and an anti-Constitution group, each distrustful of the other.[57] From it grew the disunion controversy and the "higher law" doctrine of nullification.

The disunionist position was relatively simple. If the Constitution permitted and protected slavery, the solution lay in dissolving the Union it created and establishing a new one with a new constitution. The Syracuse Anti Slavery Convention of 1855 declared:

We conceive slaveholding to be the annihilation of human rights, and we hold it to be the grand end and mission of Civil Government to *protect* human rights. . . . We accordingly declare and

---

1853. Oliver Johnson, *William Lloyd Garrison and His Times*, 334-38, summarizes Garrison's views on the Constitution. William Goodell replied to the Garrisonians in "The Constitution of the United States not a Pro-Slavery Document," *The Radical Abolitionist*, August, 1857, and in *The American Jubilee*, January, 1855.

[56] See Birney's letter to the Michigan Anti Slavery Convention, January 1, 1846, in Dumond, *Birney Letters, op. cit.*, II:990, and T. C. Smith, *op. cit.*, 99-100. *The National Anti Slavery Standard*, September 18, 1855, defined the Radical Abolitionists as "believers in Spooner's doctrine of the unconstitutionality of slavery and in the right of Congress to abolish it in the States."

[57] Note the resolution of the American Anti Slavery Convention at Syracuse in 1850, attempting to heal the breach: "Resolved, that we will not impeach the sincerity of any person's antislavery feeling . . . , either because on the one hand, of his belief, or on the other hand, of his disbelief, that the Federal Constitution is responsible for the existence of American slavery, or impotent to destroy it." *The Anti Slavery Bugle*, February 9, 1850.

maintain that there can be no legitimate Civil Government . . . that is not authorized, nay, that is not politically and morally bound to suppress slaveholding.[58]

A union based on a proslavery constitution was, in the opinion of the Cleveland *True Democrat*, "a mere League for the extension and perpetuation of human slavery," and therefore not worth maintaining.[59] Led by Garrison, Quincy, and Phillips, the anti-constitutionalist group grew to large numbers in the 'fifties. The American Anti Slavery Society and the New England Anti Slavery Society both adopted "No Union With Slaveholders" as a slogan, and the Michigan, Pennsylvania, and Massachusetts state societies followed them in passing disunion resolutions.[60] Phillips was especially indefatigable in preaching disunion, and the movement culminated in the Worcester and Cleveland disunionist conventions of 1857.[61]

Less direct was the position taken by the proponents of the "higher law" doctrine, who, after 1850, developed a different kind of constitutional argument. The principle itself, that a law higher than human enactments existed in the laws of God, was deeply ingrained in the American tradition.[62] Fairly early in the antislavery movement, use had been made of it by the religious objectors to slavery, men such as Wayland and Channing, who found in the laws protecting slavery a conflict with

[58] *The National Anti Slavery Standard*, July 14, 1855.

[59] Quoted by *The Anti Slavery Bugle*, February 23, 1850.

[60] *Ibid.*, October 30, 1852, June 11, 1853, and May 26, 1855.

[61] See Phillips' speeches to the American Anti Slavery Society, *The Anti Slavery Bugle*, June 3, 1854, and to the New England Anti Slavery Convention, *ibid.*, June 30, 1855; the speeches of Garrison, Quincy, and Phillips at the American Anti Slavery Society Anniversary of 1857, *ibid.*, May 23, May 30, and June 6, 1857; Quincy's editorial in *The National Anti Slavery Standard*, February 18, 1857; *The Proceedings of the State Disunion Convention* . . . (Boston, 1857); and the reports of the National Disunion Convention at Cleveland, *The Anti Slavery Bugle*, November 7 and 14, 1857. Disunion conventions met yearly in New England from 1854 to 1858.

[62] For a discussion of the history of the "higher law" doctrine, see Edward S. Corwin, "The 'Higher Law' Backgrounds of American Constitutional Law," *Harvard Law Review* XLII (December, 1928, and January, 1929), 149-85, 365-409. An excellent summary of the doctrine as developed by the New England theologians and reformers is Henry Steele Commager, *Theodore Parker*, Chapter X, "The Higher Law."

a superior law deriving from natural, divinely-bestowed rights.[63] When the abolitionists perceived the value of the principle, the argument over the Constitution and slavery shifted from a legalistic to a moral basis. Possibly the greatest factor in its development was the dispute over the constitutionality of the fugitive slave law of 1850, which, it was claimed, abridged the natural right of man to freedom and was therefore illegal— not by man-made standards, but by divine law. "To most Northern men the right of every man to his freedom is a self-evident truth," said James Freeman Clarke in explaining the growth of the "higher law" doctrine after 1850. "If told that the Constitution and the laws forbade helping a fugitive to escape, they appealed to 'the higher law', recognized by the greatest jurists as superior to human enactments."[64] From its application to the fugitive slave law, the abolitionists expanded the "higher law" argument to include the whole question of slavery's moral legality.

The *Declaration of Sentiments of the American Antislavery Convention* gave a comprehensive statement of the "higher law" theory in 1833, resolving

that all those laws which are now in force, admitting the right of slavery, are therefore, before God, utterly null and void; being an audacious usurpation of the Divine prerogative, a daring infringement on the law of nature, a base overthrow of the very foundations of the social compact, a complete extinction of all the relations, endearments, and obligations of mankind, and a presumptuous transgression of all the holy commandments; and that therefore they ought instantly to be abrogated.

Seward, speaking during the debate that followed Webster's seventh of March speech, enunciated the doctrine somewhat more succinctly: "The law of nations disavows such compacts; the law of nature, written on the hearts and consciences of men,

[63] W. E. Channing, "Remarks on the Slavery Question," *Works* V:19; Theodore Parker, *Address of the Committee Appointed by a Public Meeting, Held at Faneuil Hall, September 24, 1846* . . . , Appendix, 20-22; and William Bowditch, *Slavery and the Constitution*.

[64] James Freeman Clarke, *Antislavery Days*, 152.

repudiates them." Sumner, like Seward, found the origins of the "higher law" in nature, and was likewise convinced that slavery was a violation of it.[65] Others discovered its sources not in nature and nature's rights, but more directly in God. Said William Goodell:

There is nothing in the universe that can deserve the name or do the work of valid law but the commandment and the ordinance of the living God. . . . The practice of slaveholding, for this reason, can never be legalized, and all legislative or judicial attempts to sustain it are rebellion against God, and treason against all civil society.[66]

Synthesizing the two views, the argument from natural rights and the argument from divine precept, William Hosmer's book, *The Higher Law* (1852), provided the most complete and penetrating analysis of the theory produced during the period. The laws of God and nature, explained Hosmer, are identical, and government, in following one, must perforce follow the other. The individual conscience constitutes the highest tribunal of judgment; human legislation which contravenes it is therefore voided, and must be disobeyed. Since slavery deprives man of his most fundamental human right, it is therefore a violation of both natural and divine law—laws which sustain slavery are not laws in a higher sense, but outrages. "The fact that a law is constitutional amounts to nothing, unless it is also pure," said Hosmer. "It must harmonize with the law of God, or be set at naught by upright men."[67] Hosmer's interpretation be-

[65] *Congressional Globe, 31st Congress, 1st Session, Appendix,* 263, and E. L. Pierce, *Memoirs and Letters of Charles Sumner,* I:66-80. See also B. F. Wright, *op. cit.,* 222.

[66] In Julia Griffiths, ed., *Autographs for Freedom, op. cit.,* 116. Concerning the divine origins of "higher law," see R. S. Egleston, *Human Legislation Void When It Conflicts With the Law of God . . .;* the Reverend L. Smith, *The Higher Law, or Christ and His Law Supreme;* and W. W. Patton, *Conscience and Law.*

[67] William Hosmer, *The Higher Law,* 176. Compare Thoreau's "Resistance to Civil Government," *Works,* VI:356-58. An excellent summary of all the early moral, legal, and religious arguments relating to the doctrine is the anonymous *The Higher Law,* published by S. W. Benedict.

came standard among abolitionists as an argument against the constitutionality of slavery, a highly effective one in that it placed the controversy upon seemingly unimpeachable supralegal grounds.[68]

The "higher law" doctrine, as worked out by Hosmer, his predecessors and his successors, gave legal sanction to the nullification and disunion elements within abolitionist ranks. If laws sustaining slavery existed in the government and the Constitution, it was therefore necessary to withdraw support from the government and the Constitution. As Hosmer affirmed, "Men have no right to make a constitution which sanctions slavery, and it is the imperative duty of all good men to break it, when made. . . ."[69] By virtue of the "higher law," said Marius Robinson, the Constitution was "inoperative and void," while C. C. Burleigh believed that "every true lover of humanity is bound to refuse it obedience, and is bound to go on persevering in obedience to the higher law." So did the General Assembly of Connecticut go on record to the effect that since God's law was supreme, "no law contrary to His will is binding upon us."[70]

Others believed that the withdrawal of the free states from the Union was the only logical answer to a constitution which contradicted higher law. Joseph Treat defined government as "a voluntary society founded upon divine principles," dissoluble at the discretion of the individual in the event of gov-

[68] For typical expressions of this doctrine, see H. W. Beecher, in J. R. Howard, ed., *Patriotic Addresses,* 173; C. C. Burleigh to the New England Anti Slavery Society, *The Anti Slavery Bugle,* June 22, 1850; Edmund Quincy to the American Anti Slavery Society, *The National Anti Slavery Standard,* May 9, 1853; Gerrit Smith's Syracuse speech, *ibid.,* November 1, 1856; and the speech of Lawyer Riddle in the Oberlin-Wellington "rescue" case, in Jacob R. Shipherd, *History of the Oberlin-Wellington Rescue,* 45-47. The most authoritative rebuttal was that of the Reverend Moses Stuart of Andover, *Conscience and the Constitution;* see also the reply of the district attorney, Shipherd, *op. cit.,* 82-85.

[69] *The Higher Law,* 176. See also E. H. Gray, *Assaults upon Freedom.*

[70] *The Anti Slavery Bugle,* June 22, 1850, and July 12, 1851. See also the resolution of the Western Anti Slavery Society and the speech of George Sumner in Salem, Ohio, *ibid.,* September 26, 1850, and March 4, 1854.

ernment's violation of those precepts.[71] Reinforcing the already strong disunionist sentiments of the Garrison-Quincy-Phillips group who justified secession on grounds of natural rights, the "higher law" advocates thus arrived ultimately at the same conclusion. "If we cannot obey the Constitution without disobeying God," said William Bowditch, "we must secede to obey God's laws."[72]

The controversy over the natural and constitutional rights of men and Americans was of great importance in the history of the development of the civil liberties tradition. Historically, the controversy intensified the division between North and South by making sharply evident the differences in the fundamental concepts of right and law upon which the two social systems were built. The disagreement over the Declaration and the Constitution emphasized the differences and erased the similarities in the two societies; there was no longer even surface agreement on the meaning of such terms as *liberty, rights, equality,* or *natural law.* The argument meant that certain decisions had to be made. The Declaration of Independence was either a fundamental instrument of government, to be applied in practice, or it was nothing more than an abstract body of theory with little meaning to government or society. The Constitution either denied the natural rights of man by establishing and protecting slavery, or it did not. Clarification of issues long in *sub-rosa* conflict drew clear lines of cleavage and ranged North and South on opposite sides of the issue.

In another sense, by revealing the dichotomy between the implied theory of government underlying the Declaration and the practical application of it by the Constitution, the controversy brought into question, for the first time since the founding of the Republic, the real meanings of the documents themselves. Attack on and defense of slavery on theoretical grounds forced Americans to define the terms *liberty, equality,* and *natural rights,* terms of primary importance in any discussion of those civil rights which stemmed from them, or any

[71] *Ibid.*, April 6, 1849.
[72] *Ibid.*, December 8, 1849.

analysis of the governmental system which protected and controlled them. At the bottom of the controversy over civil liberties lay considerations of basic human, natural, and divine rights.

In addition, the development of these two widely divergent philosophies of individual rights and constitutional law made slavery a national rather than a sectional issue. Forced to deny the existence of natural rights, apparently forced to contradict divine law, the proslavery thinkers fostered the impression in the North that not only were the rights of black men involved in the slavery struggle, but the whole question of the rights of man. If the Constitution were really a proslavery document, and the "self-evident" truths of the Declaration were only meaningless generalities, then the nationalization of slavery seemed inevitable. By adopting as part of their platform the principles of the Declaration, and by shifting the argument against slavery to the grounds of natural and divine law, the abolitionists changed the tone of the controversy. Their movement became a crusade, not merely the struggle of a few men for the freedom of the blacks, but a great moral battle for first principles, for God and liberty, for the divine and natural rights of man.

Workmen and Runaways

VII

A BOLITIONISTS were still a minority at the outset of the Civil War, but while they had failed to make the North abolitionist, they had succeeded to a large extent in making it anti-Southern. By seizing upon issues designed to appeal to the general public, and by making a bid for support of key Northern elements, they managed with some success to capture the attention of important segments of public opinion. Two aspects of this conquest were the abolitionists' attempts to gain the sympathies of the laboring and mechanic classes, and their adoption of the cause of the fugitive slave. They did not obtain, in the end, either unanimous or organized backing from labor, although abolitionism eventually gained much from labor's secondary approval. In the second instance, by linking the plight of the fugitive to the civil liberties controversy and by making the issue part of a larger conflict over natural and constitutional rights, they were very successful indeed.

Both abolitionist and proslavery groups made strong bids for labor backing. In the North, the workingmen and mechanics, though they displayed little interest in the legal or philosophical phases of the slavery controversy, perceived dimly that its settlement might have powerful implications in their own struggle for social and political recognition. The abolitionist argued that the existence of a slave labor system periled their wage system, and that the competition of skilled and unskilled slave tended to depreciate the value of free labor. "Wage slavery" and chattel slavery were closely related in economic effect, and the former could not be successfully attacked until the latter was eradicated.[1] By pointing out the relationship between the two, and by holding up the threat that wage slavery might conceivably turn into chattel slavery or something similar, the abolitionists hoped to gain some kind of organized labor support.

In this campaign nearly the whole structure of the proslavery argument provided ammunition. The Southern argument that slavery was the best possible system for labor, the abolitionists reasoned, implied that slavery would be a distinct improvement over free labor in the Northern factory. Therefore, they warned the Northern workman, it was part of the slaveholder's plan to introduce it into Northern industry as they had in the South. If, as some Southerners believed, the laboring class was unfitted for self-government, the Northern laborer could thus best guard his political rights by helping abolish the system. If slaves were better off and more secure than wage laborers, as Fitzhugh and his predecessors suggested, the introduction of slavery into the North could be justified as a way of bettering the free laborer's lot.

It was not difficult to find intemperate quotations from the Southern press to impress the free workman with the designs of the Southern slaveholder upon him. The Republican party in 1856 distributed a reprint of a South Carolina paper which said, "Master and slave is a relation as necessary as that of parent and child, and the Northern states will yet have to in-

---

[1] George E. McNeill, *The Labor Movement,* 122. The most complete and careful treatment of abolition and labor is Bernard Mandel, *Labor: Free and Slave* (New York, 1956). See also D. L. Dumond, *Antislavery,* 352-54.

troduce it. Slavery is the natural state and normal condition of the laboring man, whether white or black."[2] The editor of the Charleston *Mercury* was quoted to the effect that no workman was wise enough to govern himself—or others—and another South Carolina paper believed that the great danger of free society was "a servile class of mechanics and laborers, unfit for self-government, and yet clothed with the attributes and powers of citizens."[3] Such statements, joined with the usual quotations from Leigh, McDuffie, Calhoun and Fitzhugh made out a damaging case. "Let the people of the whole country keep in mind," said Gamaliel Bailey, "that the Southern Democracy claims the right to enslave the *whole laboring population* of the country."[4]

More threatening to the laborer were reports in the abolitionist press emphasizing the substantial amount of agreement among certain Northerners with the Southern contention that slavery was the best of all labor systems. Solon Robinson of Indiana, a contributor to the New York *Agriculturalist* and an authority on farm labor problems, defended slavery as "a perfect labor system" and suggested its adoption throughout the nation.[5] A Cincinnati industrial meeting "expressed a decided preference for the relations of labor and capital in the slave states," while an Illinois editor admitted to a "full and decided preference in favor of slave labor in all agricultural business." The Salem *Register,* the Pittsburgh *Post,* and the New York *Herald* thought slaves better taken care of and happier than many white laborers, and in factory-conscious New Hampshire

[2] Quoted by James O'Neal, *op. cit.,* 169.

[3] The New York *Daily Tribune,* November 9, 1854, and G. M. Weston, *op. cit.,* 2. A writer in *DeBow's Review* explained that "Nature puts the ruling elements uppermost and the masses below and subject to those elements;" a strong labor class threatened the supremacy of the ruling elements, and if such a class ever gained "the political power of a country, it is in fact in a state of revolution, which must end in substantially transferring property to themselves." Cited by Mandel, *op. cit.,* 40.

[4] *The National Era,* January 24, 1856.

[5] "Negro Slavery at the South," *DeBow's Review* VII o.s. (September, 1849), 206-55, and VII o.s. (November, 1849), 379-89, and "Slavery," *The National Anti Slavery Standard,* April 11, 1850.

a debate was held on this very question. The New York *Day Book* advocated white slavery for those unable to support themselves.[6] Such opinions, though relatively few in number, reported the Boston *Telegraph,* were still numerous enough perhaps "to stimulate Northern capitalists to imitate the example of Southern slaveholders." The danger of a coalition of Northern industrialist with Southern planter was always kept before the workman by the abolitionist press.[7]

The appeal of the antislavery men to the laborer was threefold: first, they wanted to convince the Northern workman that the slavery system was the natural enemy of free labor; second, that slavery in the South restricted the market for Northern-manufactured goods, and thereby robbed him of wages; and third, that slavery excluded workers from Southern employment by reducing the need for free labor. In addition, whenever possible the abolitionist politicians pointed out that the Southern slaveholders consistently opposed such things as tariffs, homestead laws, and other legislation that accrued to the workman's benefit. To this end they pointed out that its very existence threatened the wage system. Garrison, in 1834, urged that the abolition of slavery was indispensable "to make labor respectable and the workingman respected."[8] Walt Whitman, editorializing in the Brooklyn *Eagle* in 1847, wrote that "Slavery is a good thing enough (viewed partially) to the rich —the one out of thousands; but it is destructive to the dignity and independence of all who work and to labor itself."[9] John Rankin told the mechanics of the North, "The laborers of the South are slaves, low, ignorant, and mean. Thus labor is associated with that which is mean and degraded. . . . Slavery not only tends to degrade the free laborer, but tends to depress

---

[6] *The Weekly Herald and Philanthropist,* April 8, 1844; *The Anti Slavery Bugle,* October 21, 1854; *Niles' Register,* 47:59-60; *The National Anti Slavery Standard,* February 21, 1850, quoting the Boston *Atlas,* and *The Anti Slavery Bugle,* November 21, 1854, January 6, 1855, and December 6, 1856.

[7] *The Anti Slavery Bugle,* January 6, 1855.

[8] *The Liberator,* December 30, 1834. The best exposition of the abolitionist appeal to the laborer is Mandel's, *op. cit.,* 226 ff.

[9] September 12, 1847.

him. The working of three millions without wages tends to reduce the price of labor." Missourian George Patterson wrote in 1852, "I have often thought that the working men, the mechanics and laboring men of the free states, act like fools in their opposition to abolition lecturers, when if those same white working men were in the slave states, they would be despised."[10]

The fact that similar arguments had been long current in the South made the abolitionist case stronger. In the border states, considerable opposition among workmen to chattel slavery had developed by the 1850's, and even the states where slavery was dominant reported labor troubles over the competition offered to whites by skilled slave labor.[11] All the facts, therefore, tended to show that the existence of slavery anywhere in the nation was dangerous to free labor. Slavery, the Rhode Island Antislavery Convention resolved in 1836, "blights the industry of the nation by making labor disreputable." Abolition would "give new activity to our shops and shipping." Garrison's *Liberator* assured the workman "steadier employment and most likely higher wages to all kinds of labor" by creating a new Southern market for Northern goods. "If the

[10] John Rankin, "Letters on Slavery, No. VIII," *The Philanthropist*, August 6, 1839. Patterson is quoted in Nevins, *Ordeal of the Union*, I:420-1. For similar discussions, see Giddings' Tremont Temple speech, in the Boston *Daily Whig*, July 3, 1848, and his Providence address, the Providence *Daily Tribune*, July 11, 1854; "Slavery and Free Soil," *The Anti Slavery Bugle*, October 6, 1848; the speech of Charles Durkee of Wisconsin in the House, *The National Era*, August 26, 1852; Francis P. Blair, "Letter to My Neighbors," *ibid.*, October 2, 1856; and the anonymous *Sons of Liberty in 1776 and 1856*, 7-9.

[11] Southern opinion of slavery as inimical to free labor is reported in *The Anti Slavery Bugle*, November 28, 1857; a debate in the Missouri House on the subject appears in the St. Louis *Christian Advocate*, May 19, 1858; other items include the Louisville *Examiner* and the Danville, Virginia, *Register*, quoted by *The National Era*, November 25, 1847, and September 6, 1849; "Slavery Degrades the Free Laborer," the Louisville *Examiner* reprinted in *The Anti Slavery Bugle*, June 2, 1848; and Cassius Clay's Lexington *True American*, *ibid.*, December 19, 1845. *The National Anti Slavery Standard*, July 5, 1849, and July 31, 1851, reported that the *Georgia Miscellany* had protested the training of slaves in the skilled trades, and that the Georgia Mechanics' Convention of 1850 had gone on record as opposing it.

free laborers will examine this part of the subject," concluded the abolitionists, "they will find that the abolition of slavery will greatly promote their interests, and that abolitionists are their friends, and slaveholders their worst enemies."[12]

Another aspect of the abolitionist appeal to the Northern workman was the threat of white slavery. If slavery were ever extended to the white man, the laborer was warned, he would be the first to be enslaved, since his was the weakest political and economic position in society. Such, it was claimed, was the actual intention of the slaveholding South, which, with the support of the powerful industrial interests of the North, was gaining dominance over the national government. William Goodell made one of the earliest of these accusations in 1836, when he told the Lunt Committee of the Massachusetts legislature that behind the Southern memorials protesting the abolitionists' use of the press there lay "a deep and foul conspiracy against the laboring people of the North. . . . The object of the South is to destroy the free labor of the North, and *reduce our laboring citizens to the moral and physical conditions of their slaves.*"[13] The statement was repeated many times in the 'thirties, buttressed by references to the developing proslavery argument.[14] Reviewing the Southern claim that slavery was a

[12] Rankin, "Letters on Slavery, No. VIII," *loc. cit.* The Rhode Island Convention and *The Liberator* are quoted in Williston Loftus, "Abolition and Labor," *Journal of Negro History* XXXIII (July, 1948), 257-8.

[10] William Goodell, *A Full Statement of the Reasons . . . Offered to the Committee of the Legislature of Massachusetts . . .*, 22. "Let the mechanic and workingman take a prospective view of the matter," commented Garrison in *The Liberator*, March 26, 1836. "Not far below the horizon of events, is that condition of things whose threatening aspect may even now be seen."

[14] *Proceedings of the Rhode Island Anti Slavery Convention . . .*, *op. cit.*, 39; Birney and Gerrit Smith, *The Philanthropist*, February 9 and June 10, 1836; Henry B. Stanton, *Remarks in Representatives' Hall . . .*, 58; "The Differences Between a Free Laborer and a Slave," *The Liberator*, December 1, 1837; *Address of the Eastern Executive Committee of the State Anti Slavery Society to the Citizens of Pennsylvania*, 11-12; David Root, *Sermon Delivered Before the Anti Slavery Society of Haverhill, Mass.*, 18-20; William Goodell, "Northern Laborers," and "To the Laboring People of the Free States," *The American Anti Slavery Almanac* (1839 ed.), 4-5, and *The Anti Slavery Lecturer*, No. 8 (August, 1839).

"positive good" for society, *The Emancipator* remarked in 1839:

> The inference irresistibly follows, that it could be no sin for the Northern capitalist to hold the Northern white laborer, without his consent, for a slave. . . . If the free white laborer of the North is "worse off" than the laboring slave of the South, and if this consideration makes it right and merciful to hold the Southern laborer as a slave, then righteousness and mercy not only permit but require that the white laborer of the North should likewise be held as a slave. . . . This has been done in Europe, and would be done in America if the aristocracy had the power. The struggle is between the antagonist principles of free and slave labor. They cannot much longer co-exist. One must prevail to the destruction of the other. The laborers of America will either be free or enslaved.[15]

Subsequent arguments directed at the Northern workman deviated but little from the pattern laid down during the 'thirties, and the abolitionist continued his appeal to the labor interests until the eve of the Civil War.[16] Although the abolitionist enterprise was designed to abolish chattel slavery, "yet the doctrine it advocates," the abolitionists maintained, "will benefit the laborer everywhere, for the interests of labor are one, and everything, which tends to elevate labor, and secure for it its just dues, must benefit those . . . identified with it."[17]

The laboring class was still too disorganized and too po-

[15] "What They Would Do If They Could," *The Philanthropist,* June 15, 1839.

[16] The Utica, N. Y., *Friend of Man,* February 12, 1840; "The Monstrous Alliance and Its Results," and "The Slaveholder and the Workingman," *The Philanthropist,* November 4, 1840; "The Workingman's Friend," and "Slavery and the Workingman," *ibid.,* July 30, 1842, and June 4, 1841; the speech of Wilson of New Hampshire in the House, *The National Era,* February 22, 1849, and "The Labor Question," *ibid.,* July 31 and August 21, 1851; *The Weekly Herald and Philanthropist,* June 10, 1844, and *The Anti Slavery Bugle,* September 11, 1852; *The American Jubilee,* March, 1835; "Slavery to be Made the Universal Condition of the Laboring Classes of Society," *The National Anti Slavery Standard,* October 11, 1856; "Something for Mechanics and Laborers to Think About," *The Anti Slavery Bugle,* October 18, 1856; Horace Greeley's editorial in the New York *Daily Tribune,* October 24, 1856; and William Goodell, "Judicial Blindness," *The Radical Abolitionist,* December, 1857.

[17] "Labor and Laborers," *The Anti Slavery Bugle,* March 26, 1847.

litically immature in the period preceding the Civil War to have a great deal of influence in the antislavery movement. In New England, especially, the workers tended to be antislavery partisans (the textile-mill girls were often rabidly abolitionist), but in New York, New Jersey, Pennsylvania, Ohio, and Illinois, a number of labor leaders felt that although the abolitionists were essentially right in their opposition to slavery, they agitated the question far too energetically and neglected other reforms.[18] Also, the Northern laborer, like the Southern poor white, realized that freeing the Negro might well result in the emigration Northward of a horde of cheap labor. Abolition carried with it the real threat of economic competition from the freedman, an argument the abolitionist generally disregarded.

On the other hand, a segment of Northern labor believed that the abolitionist stopped short of the real issue, and felt that the abolition of "wage slavery" must precede any other. "Down with all slavery, both chattel and wage," was a popular slogan in labor circles.[19] Basing their argument upon natural rights and equalitarian philosophy, labor Associationists such as George Ripley claimed that the abolition of chattel slavery was simply one minor part of the larger crusade for all workmen's rights, and that white wage slavery was to be abolished before black.[20] Land reformers, like George Evans, believed that although chattel slavery violated the Negro's right to per-

[18] Herbert Harris, *American Labor*, 59. The Boston *Pilot* noted that antislavery societies counted among their members some of New England's most respected factory-owners, whose "hearts were soft as butter towards the oppressed laborers of the South, but hard as flint towards a large portion of the white laborers" at home: Mandel, *op. cit.*, 94.

[19] For a complete exposition of this viewpoint, consult *The Slavery of Poverty, with a Plan for its Abolition*, Quarterly Pamphlet Number One of the "New York Society for the Abolition of All Slavery," and editorials from *The Phalanx*, in J. R. Commons, ed., *A Documentary History of American Industrial Society*, VII:207-209.

[20] See the extracts from *The Harbinger* and *The National Anti Slavery Standard*, and the argument between Ripley and Wendell Phillips, in Commons *supra. cit.*, VII:216-19, 220-22. Greeley, a labor reformer before he was an abolitionist, angered the antislavery men by his insistence upon the priority of Northern labor problems; see the essay on Greeley, and his letter to the Cincinnati Anti Slavery Convention, *ibid.*, VII:1-45, 211-16.

sonal liberty, wage slavery violated the more important right of a man to own land; equal rights to the soil must precede the abolition of Negro slavery, else the root of the evil would never be eradicated.[21]

In the main, organized labor remained relatively indifferent to abolitionism. The Northern workman was acutely aware of his own problems, and occasionally he pointed out to the antislavery reformer that charity might well begin at home. As one Irish Congressman explained it, "The only difference between the Negro slave of the South, and the white wage slave of the North, is that the one has a master without asking for him, and the other has to beg for the privilege of becoming a slave."[22] Labor and abolitionist groups might agree that both wage and chattel slavery were evil, but no practical agreement could be reached on how to cooperate for the abolition of either or both. But though laboring interests gave the abolitionist movement little assistance, the long campaign to convince the laborer of the rightness of the antislavery cause brought a good deal of support to the movement and materially strengthened it.

The proslavery Southerner made a similar bid for the support of labor in both North and South. On the one hand, he hoped to convince the Northern workman that it was to his advantage to keep slavery where it was, and on the other to persuade the Southern white workingman that he had a vital interest in keeping slavery as it was. His strongest argument, in both instances, was the appeal to race prejudice. Proslavery men in the North reminded the workman that, as the New York *Globe* pointed out, the abolition of slavery would "create inevitably a pinching competition between white labor and black labor," and as the freed Negro left the South, he "would contaminate the industrious and laboring classes of the North by a revolting admixture of the black element." In the same vein Henry Clay suggested to his friend, the Reverend Calvin Colton, that he write a pamphlet for distribution among Northern workmen, arguing that if the Negro were freed, he

[21] Evans' letter to Gerrit Smith, *ibid.*, VII:352-56.
[22] Mandel, *op. cit.*, 79.

would compete for jobs, lower the wage scale by working for less money, and reduce the white laborer to the "despised and degraded condition of the black man." In almost every Northern state, representatives of labor urged the introduction of laws prohibiting Negro migration into the state or restricting their employment, some of which passed.[23] In the South the appeal to the white laborer was much easier to frame and proved undeniably effective. To the poor white Southerner, slavery meant status; by assigning certain menial tasks to the slave, Southern society in return guaranteed social position to the poorest and most ignorant white. As Frederick Olmsted noted in his travels, the mass of the Southern poor whites could not be exceeded "in idolatry to slavery. . . . Their hatred of the Negro is proportionate to the equality of their intellect and character to his; and their regard for slavery to their disinclination to compete with him in a fair field."[24]

The Southern workman did not want the Negro as a social or economic competitor in the free labor market, and he needed little convincing of the folly of abolition. The major reason that Hinton R. Helper's book, *The Impending Crisis of The South: How to Meet It* (1857), was banned in the South was that it showed with some conviction that the overall effect of slavery on the free white laborer and farmer was bad, and that it might well have caused a good deal of labor unrest had it been allowed to circulate. At the same time, some slaveholders found it profitable, especially in the cities, to hire out those of their slaves who possessed marketable skills. In industries such as iron smelting and forging, for example, the majority of the workers in the entire South were slaves. Trades such as bricklaying, carpentering, and woodworking were in some Southern cities almost exclusively Negro, and slaves did a great deal of the work on the railroads, docks, and in the mines. After 1840 there were a number of

[23] Lofton, *op. cit.*, 275; Mandel, *op. cit.*, 66-68.

[24] *A Journey in the Back Country* (New York, 1860), 78. George Weston's article in the New York *Weekly Tribune*, February 9, 1856, "The Poor Whites of the South," is one of the best pieces of contemporary journalism on this subject.

experiments in the use of slave labor in factories; the operators of the Saluda Cotton Mills of South Carolina claimed that they saved about thirty percent in labor cost by using Negroes exclusively.[25]

The proslavery argument to the Southern white laborer, however, fell upon the prongs of a dilemma. The slaveholder could appeal to the workman for support on the basis that slavery gave the white man status and prevented Negro competition—yet at the same time the hiring-out system, the penetration of slaves into more and more skilled trades, and the claim that slavery was the best of all systems for factories as well as for farms clearly *did* make the Negro the white man's economic rival. It was impossible to tell the South, as Southern leaders did, that it needed industry, to tell the Northern industrialist that slavery provided the best and most tractable labor force, and not expect the workingman to put the two together.[26] It was equally hard to explain to the Southern mechanic how slavery insured that the Negro would be kept at menial and low-paid tasks, and at the same time to employ skilled slaves at an increasing variety of jobs. There was a great

[25] Ernest M. Lander, "Manufacturing in South Carolina 1815-1860," *Business History Review* XXVII (March, 1954) , 62; J. D. B. DeBow hoped to fill the South with such factories; see his *Industrial Resources of the Southern and Western States* (New Orleans, 1852) , I: 232; II: 122-127. Such demands for industrializing the South drew sharp opposition from slaveowning interests, and the conflict was one of increasing importance through the 'fifties; Philip G. Davidson, "Industrialism in the Ante-Bellum South," *South Atlantic Quarterly* XXVII (October 1928) , 405-25; and Leonard P. Stavisky, "Industrialism in Antebellum Charleston," *Journal of Negro History* XXXVI (July, 1951) , 302-23.

[26] William J. Grayson's popular rimed defense of slavery, *The Hireling and The Slave* (1856) , reminded employers everywhere that in the South
>No mobs of factious workman gather here,
>No strikes we dread, no lawless riots fear . . . ,
>No want to goad, no faction to deplore,
>The Slave escapes the perils of the poor.

A common argument was that slavery provided "perpetual peace between the warring elements" of labor and capital. "Harmonizing the interest betwixt capital and labor, Southern slavery has solved the problem over which statesmen have toiled and philanthropists mourned from the first existence of organized society," wrote one Southern leader; Stampp, *Peculiar Institution*, 421.

deal of conflict over this issue in the South throughout the 'forties and 'fifties. Mechanics' conventions passed resolution after resolution condemning the employment of slaves, and now and then workmen resorted to strikes and violence. The most publicized case involved the Tredegar Iron Works at Richmond, Virginia, where in 1847 the white laborers struck over the increased use of hired slaves. The millowners broke the strike simply by hiring more Negroes, but the number of protests over the practice grew rapidly in the South during the pre-war years.[27] Nevertheless, the argument from prejudice proved compelling. Whatever problems were raised by slavery in the Southern labor market, the poor white worker and mechanic threw in their lot with the proslavery elements, for reasons which Senator Charles James put quite bluntly. "Under the existing state of things," he said, "the poor white man will endure the evils of pinching poverty rather than engage in servile labor."[28]

The fugitive slave discussion, from the abolitionist point of view, involved such basic principles as personal freedom, freedom of transit, jury trial, and the integrity of the individual. In addition it possessed a strong humanitarian appeal, built on the sympathy of the average man for the escaped slave, pursued by slave-catchers and hounds in his race for freedom. A single runaway, taken in a Northern town by a Southern sheriff, could do more to excite antislavery feeling than a dozen societies; his capture gave concrete illustration of those

[27] Bernard Mandel, *op. cit.*, chapter II, "In the Lion's Den," cites the Richmond and other cases. In Wilmington, North Carolina, white masons pulled down houses built by slave labor, *The Anti Slavery Bugle* reported on September 5, 1857, while the Wake County, North Carolina, Workingmen's Association advised taxing slave labor and property, reported *The National Anti Slavery Standard* of December 27, 1859. *The National Era* of October 11, 1849, and August 31, 1854, reprinted editorials from the Jackson, Mississippi, *Mississippian*, The Norfolk, Virginia, *Argus and Democrat*, the Suffolk, Virginia, *Intelligencer*, the Spartansburg, South Carolina, *Express*, and the Charleston *Standard*, discussing the problem of white and skilled slave labor, indicating the scope of the problem in the slave states. See also T. M. Whitfield, *Slavery Agitation in Virginia, 1829-1832*, 119-23.

[28] Nevins, *Ordeal of the Union*, I:464.

evils of slavery long preached in the abstract. The legal right of the slaveholder to recapture his property in any state lent conviction to the abolitionist claim that slavery was to be extended through the Union by the "slavepower." Capturing a fugitive in a free state was but one step removed from bringing slaves into it, the abolitionists believed, there to hold them. After 1850, their contention that Southern slaveholders controlled the executive, judiciary, and legislative branches of the government, and intended to use them to promote their special interests, became more credible in the light of events. In the argument over fugitive slaves the proslavery element had Federal law on its side; the abolitionists, however, had moral and ethical support, as well as the great American sympathy for the underdog.

The original constitutional provisions for the return of escaped "persons held to service or labor" made no mention of color, nor did the fugitive slave law of 1793, since both were probably designed to allow the capture of runaway apprentices and servants as well as Negro slaves. The 1793 act made a clear distinction between fugitives from justice and from service; in the former case, the fugitive was to be surrendered on demand of the executive of the claimant state, while in the latter, the escaped person was surrendered upon claim of the party to whom the labor was due.[29] Based on the proposition that a slave was property whose possession was guaranteed by the Constitution, the 1793 law excited little opposition until the opening of the abolition movement.

Abuses, the abolitionists pointed out, were easily justified by the law, and the whole process of recovery violated the spirit of American justice. Especially noticeable was the fact that any slaveholder or his agent might enter a free state to seize a Negro, whether he was a fugitive slave, a manumitted one, one who had bought his freedom, or one who had always lived

[29] The claimant or his agent possessed power of arrest; oral or written evidence was then to be presented to any judicial officer of the Federal, state, or local government, whose magistrates were empowered to issue a certificate of transfer to the claimant's state. The Northwest Ordinance forbade slavery, but provided for the return of escaped slaves. See the discussion in Dumond, *Antislavery*, 305-25.

in a free state, and that the burden of proof lay with the Negro. Freedom, for a Negro, was difficult to prove; records were not always available, and testimony often untrustworthy. Arrest could be made before any presentation of evidence, no provision was made for a Negro's defense, no jury was called, and the judicial officer held the decisive power. A Negro, it was presumed under the law, was a slave unless satisfactory evidence was presented to the contrary.

Dissatisfaction with the Federal statute of 1793 appeared first in the eighteen-twenties. State laws tending to interfere with its operation were passed by Indiana in 1824, Pennsylvania in 1826, Connecticut in 1838, and New York in 1840.[30] The most consistent offenses against the law appeared in Illinois, Pennsylvania, Ohio, and New York, states which were either strongholds of colonization, or contiguous to slave states and therefore places of refuge for escaped slaves. The objections to the fugitive slave law were usually based upon moral or legal grounds. James G. Birney thought that the law of 1793 was not only "immoral, and inhuman," tending "to deny the truths of the Declaration of Independence," but illegal in the Northwest territory. The law of 1787, he argued, gave only the "original" slave states, not "new" slave states, the right to take fugitives from the territory; furthermore, the 1787 ordinance could have been altered only by common consent, which the 1793 act did not have.[31] Others called it a violation of the Constitution, common law, and moral law, meanwhile counselling resistance to it.[32]

Disturbances over the arrest or escape of slaves in the 'thirties testified to the growing importance of the issue. Vermont officially forbade any state court of record or any magistrate to consider the laws binding. Two Negroes were rescued from Pennsylvania jails by abolitionists in 1834; in both cases, Pitts-

[30] Allen Johnson, "The Constitutionality of the Fugitive Slave Acts," *Yale Law Journal* XXXI (December, 1921), 168.

[31] "Memorial to the Legislature of Michigan," and "Slavery in the Northwest," D. L. Dumond, *The Letters of James G. Birney*, II:720n., 724-25.

[32] R. S. Fletcher, *A History of Oberlin College*, I:396-400, summarizes Finney's views on fugitive slaves.

burgh courts convicted and fined the rescuers. James G. Birney was found guilty and fined under Ohio law for harboring an escaped slave in 1837, and a similar case that same year excited disturbance in New York City.

Cases involving assistance to fugitives (an offense at law in most Southern states) caused a good deal of Southern irritation. In 1837 the officers of the brig *Susan* allowed a Negro stowaway to escape at a Maine port. When the governor of Georgia asked their extradition, Governor Dunlap of Maine refused. Another extradition request, concerning three sailors on a New York ship who had helped a slave escape from Virginia, was refused by Governor Seward of New York in 1839. After several years of argument, the New York legislature passed a personal liberty law to assist fugitives; Virginia immediately retaliated by requiring inspection of all New York-bound vessels.[33] The "Negro seamen" act of 1820 in South Carolina brought protests from Northern states that free colored sailors were being robbed of their privileges and immunities by being forced to remain in jail while in port. The law was declared unconstitutional, but South Carolina still watched Northern crews closely to prevent them from giving help to slaves. One of the most widely publicized cases was that of Captain Jonathan Walker, a Massachusetts shipwright who helped some Negroes escape to the Bahamas when he was in Florida working in the coastal trade. He was caught in 1844, jailed (with bail set at the inordinately large amount of $10,-000) and kept shackled to the jail floor in Pensacola prison. He was convicted under Florida law, fined, and the letters "SS" for "slave stealer" branded on his right hand. Northern abolitionists paid his fine and Walker came North to serve as a traveling lecturer. Walker's "branded hand" became one of the most famous exhibits of the abolitionist argument; Whittier wrote a poem about it, and newspapers everywhere in the North carried accounts of Walker's trial and captivity.[34]

[33] Johnson, *op. cit.*, 168; *Niles' Register*, 50:423-24 and 52:117.

[34] *Niles' Register*, 27:242. Contemporary clippings of the Walker case are preserved in the Michigan Historical Collections, Ann Arbor. A memorial to Walker was dedicated in Muskegon, Michigan, after his death in that city in 1878.

Ohio, the center of the western abolitionists, naturally became a focal point of resistance to the fugitive slave act in the 'thirties. The passage by the Ohio legislature in 1838 and 1839 of drastic "black laws," partially aimed at preventing abolitionist slave-running, aroused a storm of protest and encouraged deliberate attempts to evade the law.[35] Abolitionists made a practice of forming vigilance committees to keep watch for Southern sheriffs and slaveholders' agents, and at times forcibly rescued escaped slaves from their custody.[36] Probably the most widely known early case of this type was the arrest and conviction in Kentucky in 1838 of John B. Mahan of Brown County, Ohio. Mahan, one of the founders of the Ohio Anti Slavery Society, was seized and taken to Kentucky for trial. By forfeiting a $1600 bond he was able to return to Ohio and was eventually acquitted, but not before his case had elicited widespread comment and a determination to nullify the fugitive slave laws by systematic violation.[37]

Calvin Fairbanks, an Oberlin graduate, was the center of another widely publicized case. Fairbanks, who ran slaves across the Ohio River from 1837 to 1845, was finally caught and served four years in jail, emerging in 1849. Apprehended in Indiana in 1851 for the same offense, he was kidnapped, taken to Kentucky, and sentenced in 1854 to serve fifteen years. He was finally pardoned in 1862. Alanson Work and George Thompson, two other Oberlin students, were involved in another famous fugitive slave case in Missouri. With James Burr, a Quincy, Illinois, abolitionist, they attempted in 1841 to help slaves escape from Missouri across the river into free territory. They were caught, jailed for two and a half months at Palmyra, Missouri, and finally tried. The court sentenced them to twelve years in the state prison; however, the governor of the state par-

[35] See the reactions of the Cincinnati *Philanthropist,* the organ of the Ohio Anti Slavery Society, September 17, 1839.

[36] *Ibid.,* November 20, 1838, October 8 and November 5, 1839. The Utica, N. Y., *Friend of Man,* October 30, 1839, noted the formation of similar committees in Massachusetts.

[37] J. B. Reed and H. R. Reeder, *The Trial of the Reverend John B. Mahan.*

doned them in 1845. During their time in prison, the three of them corresponded constantly with abolitionist societies and newspapers, until theirs became one of the most widely-publicized jail cells in Illinois.[38]

By 1840, the fugitive slave question was rapidly developing into a major national issue in the controversy over slavery. In New York the state law which allowed a slaveholder to retain property in a slave for nine months of residence was almost repealed. The Supreme Court of Ohio, in a significant decision, ruled in 1841 that if an owner voluntarily brought a slave into a free state, or permitted him to come, the slave was henceforth free.[39] But minor victories in the states had little effect upon the operation of the Federal law, and the abolitionists searched for a way to break the provisions of the 1793 act. The means was provided by the Prigg case, decided in Pennsylvania in 1842, which was generally understood to be the test case which might settle the fugitive slave controversy permanently.

In 1837 Edward Prigg, the agent of a Maryland slaveholder, seized a Negro woman who had escaped into Pennsylvania in 1832. Receiving little cooperation from local Pennsylvania authorities, Prigg took the woman and her children back to Maryland, failing to comply with a number of requirements of the Pennsylvania law of 1826 governing the return of fugitives. He was indicted and convicted of kidnapping in a Pennsylvania court; by an agreement between Pennsylvania and Maryland the case was taken to the Federal Supreme Court for settlement of the conflict between Federal and state laws.[40]

The Court's decision failed, however, to provide a final reso-

[38] George Thompson, *Prison Life and Reflections*, is an account by one of the prisoners. See also W. G. Burroughs, "Oberlin's Part in the Slavery Conflict," *The Ohio Archaeological and Historical Quarterly* XX (1911), 269-333.

[39] The Utica, N. Y., *Friend of Man*, October 16 and 23, 1839, and *Niles' Register*, 60:206. At the end of nine months under the New York law the slave was declared free if the master failed to renew his right of property by legal process.

[40] Joseph L. Nogee, "The Prigg Case and Fugitive Slavery," *Journal of Negro History* XXXIX (July, 1954), 185-206.

lution. The majority held that the Pennsylvania statute was void, since the power and obligation to enforce the 1793 law rested with the Federal government. On the other hand, the Court held that state authorities were not obligated to assist the Federal government in the administration of Federal law; in fact, states might even prohibit magistrates from giving assistance.[41] Thus while the decision affirmed the authority of the Federal government over fugitive slaves and supported the 1793 act, it provided at the same time an opportunity for abolitionists to block its enforcement by action in the states. The result was the passage of legislation in the Northern states designed to remove the legal resources of the state from support of the Federal law, or to hamper or circumvent it. Massachusetts, for example, specifically forbade all law officers to take part in enforcing the Federal law; copies of this statute, circulated in the South, caused quick protest, and similar acts by other free states resulted in a demand from the South for a tighter and more enforceable Federal law.

Northern sentiment, caught by the humanitarian appeal of the escaped slave, was receptive to the antislavery argument, and after 1845 the fugitive slave question became a valuable plank in the abolitionist platform. If slavery was a benevolent system, why did slaves run away? If slave-masters were kind and paternal, why did they hunt slaves with dogs and guns? If the Constitution protected the slave-catcher and his system, was it not proof that the Constitution was a proslavery document, and the Union founded upon it a false one? If the North believed that it had nothing to do with slavery, what about the slave-agent who invaded a Northern town to chain and transport a man to lifelong servitude, before the very eyes of helpless free men?[42] The vigilance committee of Boston injected an ominous note into the discussion—could you prove, before a

[41] For the entire decision, see Richard Peters, reporter, *Report of the Case of Edward Prigg against the Commonwealth of Pennsylvania.*

[42] "Southern Aggressions on Northern Rights," *The National Anti Slavery Standard,* November 24, 1842. *The Anti Slavery Bugle, The National Era, The National Anti Slavery Standard,* and other antislavery newspapers are filled with similar arguments during the 'forties.

justice, that you were not a slave, if the justice wanted to believe otherwise? Could not the fugitive slave laws be applied to white servants? In view of the existence of slaves who were ninety-nine percent white, the Boston committee saw some ominous portents for poor white men.[43]

Slave escapes were common, and court decisions, occurring almost yearly, gave the abolitionists plenty of opportunity to agitate the issue. A Negro named Latimer, taken in Boston, was declined the jury trial required by state law when the judge refused to issue a *habeas corpus* writ on the ground that the Prigg decision had rendered the state law void; abolitionists raised $400 and purchased Latimer to free him. Negro stowaways on Northern-bound vessels figured in two cases in 1846 in New York and Massachusetts. The arrest and conviction of three Ohioans in Virginia, in the celebrated "Parkersburg case," aroused feeling in Ohio, and disturbances over the apprehension of fugitives were reported as far west as Chicago.[44]

As Lovejoy had been the martyr for freedom of the press, so Charles T. Torrey became the martyr for the cause of the escaped slave. Torrey, a New England theological student, was an active member of the Massachusetts Anti Slavery Society and also a correspondent for New York and Boston abolitionist papers. When he attended a slaveholders' convention in Annapolis in 1842 he was manhandled and jailed, emerging from imprisonment as a dedicated abolitionist and champion of the fugitive slave. Well-known as a lecturer, he was also notorious in the upper South as a helper of escaped slaves. Apprehended in Baltimore in 1844 for aiding a slave escape, he was convicted and sentenced to prison; early in his term he developed tuberculosis, and as his health failed, abolitionists kept track of his gradual decline. Torrey wrote a number of letters to his friends which received wide press coverage, and his death in 1846 was, Garrison wrote, "nothing but slow, fiendish murder."[45]

[43] *Address of the Committee Appointed by a Public Meeting, Held at Faneuil Hall . . . ,* 6-7.

[44] *The National Anti Slavery Standard,* November 10 and 24, December 15, 1842.

[45] Hazel C. Wolf, *On Freedom's Altar,* 81-100, is a good account. Also, *The National Anti Slavery Standard,* January 16, 1845.

The Van Zandt case, argued by Seward and Chase before the Supreme Court in 1847, attracted nationwide attention. Van Zandt, after losing $1200 in damages to the owner of a slave he had helped to escape, appealed the judgment, and though his two lawyers were the best the abolitionists could provide, the Court ruled against him.[46] A minor riot in Washington in 1848 over escaped Negroes, and the pardon in 1849 of Calvin Fairbanks, who had served four years of a fourteen-year sentence for helping fugitives, gave the abolitionists further occasion for publicity. Yet, as the decade closed, the abolitionists had been unsuccessful in their attack on the fugitive slave acts. Attempts to secure favorable legal rulings had generally resulted in failure. Though most of the Northern states had modified their "black laws" and had loosened state laws governing the return of fugitives, the Federal statute remained impregnable. Public opinion as yet was not ready to accept or sanction extra-legal means of nullifying it, but the Compromise of 1850 soon gave the abolitionists a powerful propaganda weapon.

Among the measures passed in the fall of 1850 which made up the great "Compromise" was a new fugitive slave law, designed to remedy some of the defects of the old and to placate rising Southern resentment at the arguments over slavery in Congress. Intended as a concession to the South, the fugitive slave act of 1850 was really little compensation for the loss, under the terms of the entire Compromise, of Southern equality in the Senate and the end of the slave trade in the District of Columbia. Furthermore, any advantages accruing to the South under the new law were more than offset by the fact that it lent itself admirably to abolitionist propaganda. After 1850 the North underwent a change in its attitude toward slavery. The fugitive slave law of 1850 marked the first phase of this change. Later factors, such as the Dred Scott ruling and the Kansas troubles, intensified it and tended to confirm what the abolitionists claimed the 1850 Compromise really meant—the extension of slavery and "slavepower" domination of the Union.

The 1850 act provided that circuit courts should choose com-

---

[46] Chase's argument appears in S. P. Chase, *Reclamation of Fugitives from Justice.*

missioners to carry out the provisions of the fugitive slave law, possessed of concurrent jurisdiction with the district and circuit court judges and empowered to issue warrants to owners or owners' agents for the reclamation of fugitives. In the event of trial to determine the fugitive's status, the commissioner heard the evidence and granted a certificate allowing the owner or agent to remove him if the decision made him a slave—a commissioner's fee for deciding in favor of the claimant was $10, against, $5. The law forbade admission of testimony by the fugitive, required "all good citizens" to "aid in prompt and efficient execution of this law," and allowed officers to "summon bystanders to their aid."

The Compromise found some favor in the North, but the campaign waged by the abolitionists to discredit it far outweighed the efforts of Northern moderates to defend it. Webster's famous seventh of March speech in support of the Compromise expressed the view of the moderate elements in the North, but the time for compromise was nearly past.[47] Most conservative opinion agreed that the 1850 law, and obedience to it, were necessary to preserve the Union. The Detroit *Free Press* believed that "to repeal the fugitive slave law is to repeal the Union. To alter it is to alter the Union. To resist it is to destroy the Union."[48] Though some ministers preached obedience, in contrast to the "higher law" school of thought which counselled resistance, the "higher law" group exerted the greater influence and wider appeal.[49] "Come, come, we know better," wrote Boston divine Theodore Parker at the news of

[47] For abolitionist reactions to Webster's speech, see Whittier's "Ichabod," *Poetical Works*, IV:63-66, and the rebuttals of Phillips and Parker, *The Anti Slavery Bugle*, April 6 and 20, 1850. In defense of Webster, consult Claude M. Fuess, "Daniel Webster and the Abolitionists," *Proceedings of the Massachusetts Historical Society* LXIV (1932), 28-42.

[48] Quoted by *The Anti Slavery Bugle*, November 30, 1850. See also the Youngstown, Ohio, *Republican*, quoted in this issue, and *The Speech of Mr. Burns of Richland . . . in the Ohio Senate . . .* (Columbus, 1851).

[49] Moses Stuart of Andover and I. S. Smith of New York were among prominent divines in the North who refused to recognize the "higher law" argument. See the appraisal of Stuart in *The Anti Slavery Bugle*, March 15, 1851, and Smith's *The Religious Duty of Obedience to the Law* (New York, 1850).

the passage of the Compromise. "Men of New England know better than this. We know that we ought not to keep a wicked law, and that it must not be kept when the law of God forbids." The Worcester *Spy* put it more succinctly: "Congress has made the law. We claim the right to disobey it; a right guaranteed us by a higher law than the Constitution."[50] In effect, sentiment in favor of the 1850 fugitive slave law was disunited and sporadic; opposition to it was widespread and unified.

This fact was manifested almost immediately by numerous meetings of protest scattered throughout the Northern states and by fairly general editorial disagreement with that portion of the Compromise. Meetings of condemnation were reported from Illinois, Connecticut, New York, Ohio, Indiana, Massachusetts, Michigan, Iowa, and Delaware.[51] In Ohio seventeen were held in the month of October, 1850. "The excitement occasioned by the passage of the Fugitive Slave Law," wrote editor Oliver Johnson, "is becoming more intense with every hour. The papers are filled with discussions of the subject and with the proceedings of meetings held to denounce the law. We cannot pretend to notice one in fifty of these assemblages."[52] New York and Boston meetings were reported in the same month that a Pittsburgh assembly openly advocated disobedience to the law.[53] "Is there no Mason and Dixon's line to hold against slavery?" cried the Windham, Vermont, *Democrat,* "no standpoint for enemies of slavery outside the slave states? The passage of the Fugitive Slave Bill is a precursor of the tactics of the proslavery party of the Union." The Columbus, Ohio, *Standard*

[50] Parker is quoted in Henry Steele Commager, *Theodore Parker,* 207; and the Worcester *Spy* in Avery Craven, *The Growth of Southern Nationalism,* 147.

[51] *The National Era,* August 4, 1850, and *The Anti Slavery Bugle,* October 5, 1850, reprinted numerous editorials from these states attacking the law. The Sandwich, Canada West, *Voice of the Fugitive* carried reports of dozens of these meetings during 1851 and 1852.

[52] *The Anti Slavery Bugle,* October 12 and 19, 1850, November 9 and 16, 1850. Craven, *Southern Nationalism,* 152-54, is a useful summary of Northern rejection of the fugitive slave law of 1850.

[53] *The Anti Slavery Bugle,* October 12 and 19, 1850.

concluded gloomily, "Now we are all slavecatchers."[54] The reaction of the North to the 1850 act was distinctly unfavorable.[55]

The trend of public opinion was successfully seized upon by the abolitionists, and as a result more neutral thought in the North was swayed toward tolerance of or active sympathy with the antislavery doctrine by the act of 1850 than by any previous event since Lovejoy's death. To the abolitionists, the fugitive slave issue afforded a rallying point for all the divisions by which the movement was plagued. Political action men, disunionists, anti-Constitutionalists, non-voters, and non-resistant pacifists found it something on which all could agree, producing "a valuable tendency to unity and fraternization."[56]

The abolitionists immediately refused to consider the fugitive slave law, or any laws related to it, as a "compromise." The slavery question, said Seward in the Senate, "cannot be settled by this bill. Slavery and freedom are conflicting systems brought together by the union of the States, not neutralized or even harmonized. Their antagonism is radical, and therefore perpetual."[57] Far from being a compromise, said *The National Era,* this bill was an irritant; if the aim of its proponents had been to "create deep excitement in the free states, to extend agitation on the subject of slavery, to provoke into intense activity every latent feeling against their peculiar system . . . , they could not have devised a more effectual method." The country had been "drugged to death by compromises," said Gamaliel Bailey; the fugitive slave law was the last straw, and to call the scheme which included it a "compromise" was simply self-delusion.[58]

[54] *Ibid.,* October 5, 1850.

[55] Gamaliel Bailey, "The Agitation at the North," *The National Era,* October 24, 1850, and Henry Wilson, *The History of the Rise and Fall of the Slavepower in America,* II, Chapter XXV.

[56] Marius Robinson, *The Anti Slavery Bugle,* May 31, 1851.

[57] *Ibid.,* July 20, 1850.

[58] *The National Era,* October 10, 1850; also *ibid.,* March 25, 1852, and *The Anti Slavery Bugle,* February 9, March 9, and April 13, 1850, for editorials and speeches by Marius Robinson, William Jay, and Joshua Giddings. E. D. Preston, "The Fugitive Slave Acts in Ohio," *Journal of Negro History* XXVIII (October, 1943), 422-478, is a good study of western reactions to the controversy.

Having set themselves against the fugitive slave provisions of the Compromise, the abolitionists began a campaign to turn Northern opinion against it. The act was, they believed, contrary to "higher law," that moral law of God which was above and beyond constitutional, man-made law; therefore the act should not be obeyed. The choice lay between obedience to a man-made statute and transgression of the law of God, or obedience to a higher law than human legislation—a doctrine of nullification based on religious and moral reasons.[59] "Let no man tell you," said Joshua Giddings of Ohio in the House, "that there is no higher law than this fugitive slave bill. We feel that there is a law of right, of justice, of freedom, implanted in the breasts of every intelligent human being, that bids him look with scorn upon this libel on all that is called the law."[60] Chase, Charles Francis Adams, Parker, Samuel May, Horace Mann, Elizur Wright, and a host of others condemned the fugitive slave act as a violation of Christianity.[61] Judas Iscariot too, they pointed out, was merely fulfilling Roman constitutional obligations. The Common Council of Chicago attacked the law as "revolting to our moral sense and an outrage upon our feelings of justice and humanity"; while *The Free Presbyterian* thought it "made humanity a crime, submission to ruffian violence a virtue, and obedience to God an offense to be punished by fine and imprisonment."[62] Counselling open or covert resistance, the "higher law" doctrine, preached from dozens of pulpits and spread wide by the aboli-

[59] An interesting debate is that of the Reverend John C. Lord, *The Higher Law in its Application to the Fugitive Slave Bill* (Buffalo, 1851), and the Reverend W. C. Wisner, *A Review of Dr. Lord's Sermon on the Higher Law*. . . . Other discussions include that of the Reverend W. H. Furness, *A Discourse Occasioned by the Boston Fugitive Slave Case* . . .; the Reverend Leonard Withington, *Thanksgiving Sermon, Preached November 28, 1850* . . .; and Horace Mann, *Speech . . . on the Institution of Slavery, Delivered in the House of Representatives, August 17, 1852.*

[60] *Congressional Globe, 31st Congress, 2nd Session*, 15-16.

[61] An excellent summary of the "higher law" doctrine is contained in the reports of the Jerry Rescue Convention at Syracuse, *The Anti Slavery Bugle*, October 30, 1852.

[62] August Cochin, *The Results of Slavery*, 19; and Charles W. Mann, *The Chicago Common Council and the Fugitive Slave Law of 1850*; and *The Anti Slavery Bugle*, October 5, 1850.

tionist press, helped to effect a dramatic change of attitude toward slavery in the North.[63] Emerson's curt "I will not obey it, By God," summarized the reaction of many Northerners.[64]

While the "higher law" doctrine did not concern itself with the actual constitutionality of the fugitive slave law, that too was brought into question. Lack of jury trial for the accused, the use of unconstitutional tribunals of justice, the authorization of *ex parte* testimony, the prohibition of the *habeas corpus* —these were among the reasons given by abolitionists for questioning the law's legality.[65] Judges McLean and Flinn in Ohio ruled the law constitutional in an 1853 case, but a partial abolitionist victory was secured through a Wisconsin Supreme Court ruling that it was not.[66] No court decision really settled the matter until Taney and the Supreme Court attempted to do so in 1859.

Most appealing to the Northern public as an argument against the constitutionality of the law was the abolitionist contention that it violated the natural rights of life, liberty, and the pursuit of happiness—rights guaranteed to the Negro, it was assumed, by the Declaration and the Constitution. The Compromise was condemned as "an audacious violation of the first principles of Civil Liberty, the Common Law, the Constitution of the United States, and the Law of God."[67] Formal res-

[63] For explanations and discussion see W. W. Patton, *Conscience and Law* . . .; Asa Rand, *The Slave Catcher Caught in the Meshes of Eternal Law;* William Hosmer, *The Higher Law in its Relation to Civil Government;* S. J. May, "Obedience to the Fugitive Slave Law, Disobedience to God," *The Anti Slavery Bugle,* April 5, 1851; L. Smith, *The Higher Law* . . .; S. J. May, *The Fugitive Slave Law and its Victims;* Theodore Parker, *The New Crime Against Humanity* . . .; and R. S. Egleston, *Human Legislation Void When it Conflicts with the Law Of God.*

[64] Bliss Perry, ed., *The Heart of Emerson's Journals,* 256.

[65] Lysander Spooner, *A Defence for Fugitive Slaves,* and *An Essay on the Trial by Jury.* Similar arguments are expounded in Charles Stearns, *The Fugitive Slave Law Shown to be Unconstitutional, Impolitic, Inhuman, and Diabolical,* and T. H. Talbot, *An Argument on the Fugitive Slave Act.*

[66] *The Anti Slavery Bugle,* August 27 and September 3, 1853, and *Decisions of the Supreme Court of Wisconsin in the Cases of Booth and Ryecraft.*

[67] Anonymous, *The Fugitive Slave Bill,* 7.

olutions of antislavery groups denounced it as a "violation of man's natural right to personal security, personal liberty, and private property . . . ," which "strikes down some of the dearest principles upon which our fathers predicated their right to assert and maintain their independence," nor could the law be obeyed without "repudiating the doctrines of the Declaration of Independence."[68] "No Robbery of Man's Inalienable Rights Can Be Law," was the slogan of the first Jerry Rescue Convention, held in Syracuse to commemorate a successful slave escape of 1851.[69] A typical newspaper cartoon of 1851 showed an arrogant slaveholder, rope and fetters in hand, riding a bridled Daniel Webster toward a frightened Negro shielded by Garrison; behind stood a Temple of Liberty, flying a flag inscribed "All Men Are Equal."[70] As tension over the fugitive slave issue increased, abolitionists made appeals for deliberate violations of the act to test its legal standing in every state.[71] Joshua Giddings tried to revive the Revolutionary Sons of Liberty for the purpose of fighting it, and nearly ten thousand people attended a mass meeting in Cleveland's Public Square to hear speeches on "the Inalienable Rights of Man— Founded in Nature as Constituted By God, and Well Recited by our Fathers in the Declaration of Independence" in defiance of it.[72]

The 1850 Act not only endangered escaped slaves in the North, but, the abolitionist claimed, under its provisions free Negroes, legal citizens of Northern states, were liable to kidnapping and enslavement. The law placed the burden of proof upon the Negro, assuming that he was an escaped slave unless he could prove otherwise, and the news of its passage filled

[68] Resolutions of the Cleveland meeting, October 11, 1850, in W. G. Cochran, *The Fugitive Slave Law in the Western Reserve*, 98. Similar resolutions came from Norwalk, Painesville, Canfield, and Columbus.

[69] *The Anti Slavery Bugle*, September 25, 1852.

[70] A. Nevins and F. Weitenkampf, *A Century of Political Cartoons*, 71.

[71] A good summary is Horace Mann's *New Dangers to Freedom, and New Duties for Its Defenders*.

[72] J. R. Shipherd, *History of the Oberlin-Wellington Rescue*, 7, 257-59.

Northern Negroes with fear and gloom.[73] The case of James Hamlet of New York, a free Negro who was seized and taken South a week after the bill became law, seemed to indicate that the abolitionists' claims were not unfounded.[74] Complaints of kidnapping were common, and after 1850 such cases were well publicized by the abolitionist press. *The Anti Slavery Bugle,* as early as 1846, reported twenty-three cases for that year; it was believed that after 1850 the number doubled and tripled.[75] If a free black man could be taken into slavery under the 1850 statute, the future might see white men taken the same way. "The Fugitive Slave Law will be made to look small by the side of the next encroachment upon the Rights of Man," warned Garrison, and his warning was echoed by others.[76] "Now what is to prevent any black or white man from being snatched away from home and friends by such proceedings?" asked the Reverend J. L. DeSellers of Ohio. "We all know there are plenty of vilians (*sic*) who will swear false. . . ."[77] Though no authentic cases of white kidnappings were uncovered, and the reports of some of the Negro kidnappings are open to question, the abolitionist warnings no doubt still had some influence.

[73] *The National Anti Slavery Standard,* October 1, 5, and 10, 1850, carried accounts of the mass meetings of New York Negroes.

[74] Hamlet's freedom was purchased by contributions from New Yorkers; see the editorial by Edmund Quincy, *ibid.,* October 17, 1850.

[75] William Kittle, *Freedom versus Slavery in the United States,* 21-22, and *The Anti Slavery Bugle,* March 27, 1852. G. M. Stroud, *A Sketch of the Laws Relating to Slavery in the Several States . . . ,* 94, claims thirty kidnappings occurred in Philadelphia from 1825-27. See also John Hope Franklin, *From Slavery to Freedom,* chapter XVI on the status of the free Negro, and Earl W. Fornell, "The Abductions of Free Negroes and Slaves in Texas," *Southwestern Historical Quarterly* LX (January, 1957), 369-80, for illustrative cases.

[76] Garrison's remarks at the seventeenth anniversary of the American Anti Slavery Society, *The Anti Slavery Bugle,* May 31, 1851. See also Gamaliel Bailey in *The National Era,* August 28, 1851; editorials from *The Essex Freeman* and *The Wisconsin Free Democrat* in *The Anti Slavery Bugle,* March 27, 1852, and the two-column editorial, *ibid.,* April 17, 1852; and Edmund Quincy in *The National Anti Slavery Standard,* September 26, October 3 and 17, 1850.

[77] Sermon notes, Nessly Collection, Western Reserve Historical Society, Cleveland.

One of the most effective weapons possessed by the abolitionists in their campaign against the fugitive slave law was the appeal to the natural humanitarian sympathies of the average man. The press was filled with accounts of the trials and sufferings of fugitive Negroes; *The National Anti Slavery Standard* ran a weekly column called "The Hunt," and *The Anti Slavery Bugle* averaged three reports a week for several years. Henry Bibb, himself an escaped slave, published *The Voice of the Fugitive* from Sandwich, Canada West, an organ expressly devoted to the cause. Nor did the press lack for material. After 1850 nearly every year had its highly newsworthy case. Henry Long of New York was seized and remitted to slavery in 1850 after a brief court fight. William Crafts and his wife were apprehended in Boston, a few months after the 1850 law went into effect, amid considerable excitement.[78]

Widely publicized was the "Jerry Rescue" of 1851 at Syracuse, where a group of abolitionists broke into jail, rescued one Jerry McHenry who had been seized by a slave-agent, and sent him into Canada. The "rescuers" were arrested and released, but held a yearly anniversary meeting in Syracuse thereafter to celebrate their successful defiance of the statute.[79] The cases of Shadrach and Thomas Sims, both in Boston, of Johnson in Chicago, of William Parker in Philadelphia, of Sweitzer and Clarissa in Pennsylvania—all in 1851—added fuel to the fire. Other cases found news space each year, until the famous rendition of Anthony Burns in Boston in 1854 roused Northern sympathies to a high pitch from which they did not recede during the period.

Burns, a slave preacher from Richmond, escaped to Boston in 1854, where he was caught, jailed, and claimed by his master. Wendell Phillips, Theodore Parker, and T. W. Higginson at a public meeting urged resistance to the fugitive slave law, and

[78] *The National Anti Slavery Standard*, January 2, 9, and 16, 1851, and *The National Era*, November 7, 1850. The judge of the United States Circuit Court which sent Long into slavery was Andrew T. Judson, who prosecuted Prudence Crandall in the famous Connecticut school case in 1833.

[79] *The Anti Slavery Bugle*, October 11 and November 8, 1851.

afterwards an abolitionist vigilance committee stormed the jail and removed Burns, killing a United States marshal in the process. The court, however, ordered Burns restored to his owner, and in June of that year Burns was taken back to slavery, the Federal marshals protected by lines of armed troops ordered to the scene by the President of the United States. Few who watched the march down Boston's State Street, lined by silent, sullen crowds, ever forgot the case of Anthony Burns.[80]

The Glover case in Wisconsin provided a Western counterpart that same year. After a United States marshal arrested a Negro named Glover in Milwaukee, Sherman Booth, a local abolitionist editor, insisted on a trial so that the constitutionality of the fugitive slave law might be tested. When the judge refused to honor a writ of *habeas corpus* for Glover, Booth and a group of friends freed him from his cell and helped him to Canada, for which Booth himself was sent to jail. Booth was in and out of jail for the next several years, until finally in 1860 a group of abolitionists rescued him from imprisonment and he began a game of hide-and-seek with the courts. He was caught for the last time in late 1860, and again confined until March, 1861, when President Buchanan pardoned him.[81]

All in all, eighty-one important cases involving fugitive slaves can be identified among the hundreds that occurred during the period 1850 to 1860.[82] That the cumulative effect

[80] *The Anti Slavery Bugle*, March 1 and 8, and June 21, 1851; *The National Anti Slavery Standard*, April 24 and May 1, 1851; and *The National Era*, April 10, 1851. A full account of the Burns case is found in *The Anti Slavery Bugle*, June 3, 1854. See also Theodore Parker's eloquent *The New Crime Against Humanity*, W. I. Bowditch, *The Rendition of Anthony Burns*, and C. E. Stevens, *Anthony Burns, A History*. For recent estimates of the Burns incident, see Hazel Wolf, *op. cit.*, 105-7, and Samuel Shapiro, "The Rendition of Anthony Burns," *Journal of Negro History* XLVI (January, 1959), 34-51. The recollections of Austin Bearse, *Reminiscences of Fugitive Slave Days in Boston* (1880) are interesting and useful.

[81] *The National Era*, September 21, 1854, and the Cincinnati *Gazette*, February 11, 12, 13, 22, and 28, 1856. See also Wolf, *op. cit.*, 106-7.

[82] W. H. Siebert, *The Underground Railroad from Slavery to Freedom*, Appendix B.

upon Northern opinion was large was graphically illustrated by the impressions of a Cass County, Michigan, correspondent, who wrote to Oliver Johnson.

> You can remember how little antislavery feeling there was in this town when you lived West, but it has greatly changed since. . . . Our citizens side almost with entire unanimity in favor of the poor captives and fugitives, and there is deep feeling on the subject.[83]

The most concrete evidences of the shift of Northern public opinion were the state "personal liberty laws" passed after 1850, intended to rectify the violations of civil rights involved in the Federal statute. Before 1850, attempts had been made in some of the free states to hamper the operation of the Federal law of 1793 by passing legislation circumscribing its powers, or by setting up difficult rules for the recovery of escaped slaves. Pennsylvania, Indiana, Connecticut, Vermont, and New York had such personal liberty laws before 1840, while Massachusetts in 1837 made an effort to provide a jury trial for fugitives.[84] After the Prigg decision, Massachusetts, Pennsylvania, and Rhode Island made further changes in their laws, but similar attempts in New York and Ohio were unsuccessful.[85]

During the 'forties and the 'fifties, as the antislavery societies built up political strength, other laws appeared on Northern statute books. Designed to prevent kidnapping and to safeguard the rights of free Negroes, these not only failed to support the Federal act but in some cases directly contravened it. Most of them guaranteed *habeas corpus* and jury trial to fugitives, forbade the use of state and county jails for their detention, placed fines upon citizens assisting in their capture, and provided legal defense for the accused. Maine, Massachusetts, Pennsylvania, New York, Vermont, Wisconsin, New Hampshire, Connecticut, Michigan, Rhode Island, and New Jersey prohibited citizens or law officers from aiding in the execution

---

[83] *The Anti Slavery Bugle,* November 2, 1850.

[84] *The Liberator,* April 7 and 21, 1837. Ohio, however, tightened its own fugitive slave law in 1839.

[85] Henry Wilson, *op. cit.,* II:57-8.

of the Federal law. Maine, Massachusetts, Michigan, Vermont, and Rhode Island denied the use of public buildings for any purpose which might aid the master or his agent in capturing a slave. Maine, Massachusetts, Pennsylvania, Vermont, Wisconsin, New York, and Michigan provided defense for fugitives at public expense. Maine, Vermont, and New Hampshire declared a slave free if brought within their borders, while New Hampshire declared him unconditionally free in any state.[86]

These laws were not adopted without opposition,[87] but the fact that some were passed in all the free states except Ohio and Indiana indicated not only the growing strength of the abolitionists but the great effect of the fugitive slave controversy on the Northern attitude toward slavery. Justified as necessary safeguards to civil rights, the laws were not unreasonably regarded by the South as deliberate attempts to hinder recovery of fugitives and to abrogate the constitutional rights of the slaveholder.[88]

The fugitive slave law of 1850 gave a powerful impetus to the so-called "underground railroad." The British abolition acts made Canada a haven for fugitives, and since the personal liberty laws of many Northern states made recovery of them difficult, the railroad prospered in the 'fifties. Joshua Giddings, speaking in Congress, expressed the aim and temper of the underground escape route by saying, "The spirit which threw the tea into Boston harbor will set your infamous law at defiance. The spirit which overthrew the power of the British Crown will submit to no force that shall constrain them to comply with the odious provisions of this enactment."[89]

In such a spirit, disobedience to the Federal law became, to many, a patriotic act in defense of liberty, and a steady stream of escaped slaves ran through communities that twenty years

[86] Report of the Committee of the Virginia Legislature, 1860, quoted by W. G. Fowler, *The Sectional Controversy*, 201.

[87] See the list of nineteen Massachusetts newspapers which opposed the state personal liberty law, in the Cincinnati *Commercial*, January 5, 1861.

[88] Editorials from Southern newspapers reprinted in *The National Anti Slavery Standard*, December 12, 1851.

[89] The Sandwich, Canada West, *Voice of the Fugitive*, October 22 and November 5, 1851.

earlier might have mobbed abolitionists. The three main lines of the system ran from Missouri northeast across Illinois; from Kentucky and Virginia across Ohio and western Pennsylvania; and from Maryland and Virginia across eastern Pennsylvania, with the Ohio line carrying the heaviest traffic.[90] By 1851 it was boasted that a slave could be run from any border state to Canada in forty-eight hours, and invitations and instructions to slaves were issued by the press and antislavery societies.[91] The number of Negroes who escaped by this means is difficult to estimate; it is clear, however, that while the underground railroad probably did not appreciably weaken slavery, it strengthened antislavery feeling in the North by making the fugitive slave the object of compassion and by making those who assisted him popular heroes.

No trustworthy figures are available concerning the number of fugitive slaves who escaped northward, nor is it likely there ever will be. It is certain, however, that far fewer slaves escaped to freedom than either slaveholders or abolitionists claimed. According to the 1850 Census, for example, there were only sixteen runaways in South Carolina out of a total of 400,000 slaves; the Census of 1860 reported only 803 escapees in 1859 for the entire South. Contemporary estimates, which were likely to vary with the imagination of the estimator, ranged from hundreds to hundreds of thousands; even the most recent of 50,000 to 60,000 are probably far too high. Similarly, far fewer fugitives were recaptured in the North by Southern owners than the abolitionists claimed; the press coverage given to a relatively small number of well-publicized cases led both North and South to believe the actual problem was far greater than it was.[92]

[90] Studies of the underground railroad are W. H. Siebert, *op. cit.*, and William Breyfogle, *Make Free*. See also Benjamin G. Merkel, "The Underground Railroad and the Missouri Borders," *Missouri Historical Review* XXXVII (April, 1943), 271-86.

[91] The Sandwich, Canada West, *Voice of the Fugitive*, October 22 and November 5, 1851, and *The Anti Slavery Bugle*, April 10, 1852.

[92] See Allan Nevins, *Ordeal of the Union*, I:383-86, for a good discussion of the problem. A. B. Hart, *op. cit.*, 230, believes about seventeen hundred slaves escaped yearly, mostly through Ohio. Herbert Aptheker, *The Negro in the Abolition Movement*, 13, estimates two thousand a year for thirty

It is also possible that the underground railroad was never so widely accepted nor so effective as the public gave it credit for being. There were a number of antislavery sympathizers who disapproved of violating the law and gave only minimum assistance to the system; Northern Negroes, not white abolitionists, provided the greater part of the apparatus, except for a few famous instances such as Levi Coffin in Ohio. *Uncle Tom's Cabin,* which for the first time gave the "railroad" wide publicity in the escape of George and Eliza Harris, led to the tremendous popularity of "escape tales," some perhaps true, others more fiction than fact. The South accepted such stories at face value more often than not, and the abolitionists found the whole romantic concept of the secret, conspiratorial escape apparatus to be superb propaganda.[93]

The dissension between North and South over fugitive slaves culminated in the Dred Scott case of 1857,[94] which, in the opinion of abolitionists, was the next to the last act in the "great conspiracy." In it all the prophecies, made since the Compromise of 1850, seemed to come true. William Goodell thought it meant "another fetter is forged; another turn of the screw is in progress." Taney's opinion meant, he explained, that slaves might go anywhere with masters and state laws could not liberate them; that state laws abolishing slavery were

---

years. The Antislavery Society of Canada in 1852, however, fixed the number of fugitives then in Canada at more than thirty thousand, according to *The Anti Slavery Bugle,* April 10, 1852. But the Census of 1851, *ibid.,* September 13, 1851, showed more slaves had been manumitted (1314) than had apparently escaped (1017).

[93] Larry Gara, *The Liberty Line: The Legend of the Underground Railroad,* is responsible for a major re-evaluation of the underground railroad in recent scholarship. See also Gara's "The Underground Railroad: A Re-evaluation," *Ohio Historical Quarterly* LXIX (July, 1960), 217-30; "The Underground Railway, Legend or Reality?" *Proceedings of the American Philosophical Society* CV (1961), No. 3, 334-39; "Propaganda Uses of the Underground Railroad," *Mid-America* XXIII (July, 1952), 155-72. Gara concludes that the railroad was a "combination of fact and fancy . . . , far more important as a propaganda device than as an aid to fleeing slaves."

[94] B. C. Howard, *Report of the Decision of the Supreme Court . . . in the Case of Dred Scott vs. Sanford,* carried the full text. Vincent C. Hopkins, *Dred Scott's Case* provides a complete account.

now unconstitutional; and that all congressional acts barring the slave trade were set aside.[95] Marius Robinson agreed: "It makes slavery the primary law of the Union, the sustaining and defending of human chattelism the main object of the Constitution. It makes slavery lawful and constitutional, as well in Ohio and Massachusetts as in Oregon and Kansas. It has free scope everywhere. . . ."[96] Gerrit Smith recommended hanging Taney, and New Hampshire immediately passed an act to nullify the Court's ruling by granting citizenship to all Negroes and freedom to all slaves.[97]

The abolitionists were not alone in their attacks upon the Court's opinion in the case. The Senate of Pennsylvania protested it as having "no binding authority on a free people," and the New York State legislature censured it. Northern opinion, as reported in the newspapers, tended to agree that, in conjunction with the fugitive slave law of 1850, the ruling meant that slavery was nationalized, and that it was now a matter for Northern consciences as well as Southern. The New York *Tribune* believed "it brings us face to face with the great issue in the right shape"—only one more decision was needed to make slavery national and to nullify all state laws abolishing it.

The New York *Evening Post* thought that the decision "had changed the very blood of our constitution . . . , and has given our government a direction and purpose as novel as it is barbarous and humiliating." The New York *Courier and Enquirer* characterized it as "a concession or admission that the Government of this nation is with and in the institution of slavery"; and the New York *Commercial Advertiser* warned that "under that decision slaveholders *in transitu* might con-

---

[95] *The Radical Abolitionist*, April, 1857; also Goodell's "Constitutions and Facts vs. Judicial Opinions," The New York *Weekly Tribune*, March 21, 1857.

[96] *The Anti Slavery Bugle*, March 20, 1857. See also Robinson's editorials in the issues of March 14 and November 5, 1857.

[97] *Ibid.*, April 14 and June 27, 1857. Harold Schwartz, "The Controversial Dred Scott Decision," *Missouri Historical Review* LIV (April, 1960), 262-73, is a useful general treatment.

vert the Empire City into a slave mart."[98] The Albany *Journal*
called it "a mixed conspiracy" to give slavery "unrestricted
rights." In New England the Hartford *Press* and the Worcester
Spy thought "We are none of us now free," and wondered if
"enough liberty were left worth living for." In the West, the
Lansing, Michigan, *Republican* termed the opinion "a direct
denial of the Declaration of Independence," and the Wautoma,
Wisconsin, *Journal* thought that the issue was now evident to
every freeman—"Slavery everywhere in this nation, or slavery
nowhere in all our borders." The Milwaukee *Democrat* believed the liberty of all Americans at stake—"the Constitution
either guarantees liberty to all, or it guarantees liberty to
none."[99]

After the Dred Scott ruling, the connection between fugitive
slaves, human rights, and civil rights, was fully established.
Oberlin College students who snatched a Negro from the
custody of Federal officials at Wellington, Ohio, in 1858, were
treated during their brief imprisonment as martyrs to liberty
and quickly released. A crowd of thousands met in Cleveland's
Public Square, by the jail which held the "rescuers," to hear
and cheer speeches by Chase, Giddings, Spalding, and others
on the necessity of preserving not only Negro, but American
rights and liberties.[100] No clearer or more comprehensive state-

[98] *Ibid.*, April 4, April 18, and March 20, 1857; The New York *Tribune*,
March 7, 1857, and the New York *Times*, March 7-11, 1857.

[99] *The Radical Abolitionist*, May, 1857. See also the Portland, Maine,
Enquirer, the Kenosha, Wisconsin, *Telegraph*, the Fond du Lac, Wiscon-
sin, *Commonwealth*, and the New York *Examiner*, quoted in this issue.
An account of the abolitionist movement in Wisconsin is found in J. N.
Davidson, "Negro Slavery in Wisconsin," and "Negro Slavery and the
Underground Railroad in Wisconsin," *Parkman Club Papers*, Nos. 16 and
18, 131-222.

[100] See the speeches, the report of the trial, and the history of the case
in J. R. Shipherd, *History of the Oberlin-Wellington Rescue*. Oberlin had
been known since 1834 as a hotbed of abolitionism, and since 1837 as a
main station of the Ohio line of the underground railroad. The case
became a *cause célèbre* in the West. The report of the trial contains perhaps the most complete presentation of the constitutional and "higher
law" arguments made during the period. Thirty-seven Oberlinites, both
students and faculty, were indicted for violation of the Federal law. Defense Attorneys Spalding, Riddle, and Griswold took the ground that the

ment of the relationship was made than that of the defense counsel in one of the last important fugitive slave cases to be tried, that of Joseph Stoat of Illinois in 1859. Indifference to the liberties of others, said the defense, bred indifference to one's own; therein lay the danger.

The first step to the loss of peoples' liberties is to cease to prize them, and the first effort of those who desire to steal away a people's rights, is to infuse into the popular mind an indifference to all questions of right and freedom, to bring over it that cold and hard selfishness which regards nothing as important which does not affect the special personal comfort and welfare of the individual. . . . The people of the North are opposed to the fugitive slave act because they regard the provisions of this law as most dangerous to the rights of freemen . . . , and its execution is pregnant with dangers to the liberty of freemen.[101]

The fugitive slave question, agitated for more than thirty years by abolitionist and slaveholder alike, was a major factor in the growth of antislavery opinion in the North. Through an appeal to the humanitarian sympathies of moderate and neutral segments of the free-state population, it provided abolitionists with a potent propaganda weapon. The fugitive slave act of 1850 and the case of Dred Scott in 1857 provided abolitionists with seemingly irrefutable proof of what they had always suspected and of which they had repeatedly warned— that a slavepower conspiracy intended to gain control of the Federal government, reach into the states, and extend and perpetuate the system of slavery on a nationwide basis. This "conspiracy" threatened, said the abolitionists (and more than a few Northerners believed them), the natural, civil, and constitutional rights not only of Negroes, but ultimately those of every freeborn American.

law was unconstitutional and by reason of conflict with "higher law" should be disobeyed at any cost; see especially Riddle's address to the Supreme Court, 186-194, Attorney General Wolcott's brief in behalf of the State, 195-225, and District Attorney Belden's reply, 82-96.

[101] R. R. Hitt, reporter, *The Argument of E. C. Larned, Counsel for the Defence on the Trial of Joseph Stoat . . .*, 9, 13, 25.

The Great Slave Power Conspiracy

VIII

QUITE EARLY in the controversy over slavery the abolitionists made it clear that they considered their struggle to free the slave as part of a much greater contest against the machinations of a well-organized "Slave Power" plot to subvert American liberties. The slavery question, said William Goodell,

involves in it the question of the civil and political liberties of the nominally free . . . , the question of whether liberty shall be relinquished, for the security of slavery, or whether slavery shall be overthrown by the spirit of liberty. It is the question of whether civil government shall secure and protect human rights, or whether a ruthless despotism, displacing civil government (properly so called) shall be wielded by the Slave Power for the subjugation of freemen.[1]

"The Slave Power threat," echoed Garrison, "will never cease until slavery itself is outlawed."[2]

By thus fusing their cause with a broader one, the aboli-

---

[1] *Slavery and Antislavery*, 583-84.
[2] "The Abolitionists and their Relation to the War," *Pulpit and Rostrum*, No. 26.

tionists gained support from neutral and conservative Northerners. The exposure of a plot against American freedom naturally attracted more public attention than did the relatively academic question of the right or wrong of Negro slavery. Herein lay one of the reasons for the increasing success of the abolition cause as the controversy over slavery wore on. The abolitionists were aided in their campaign by two factors: the resurgent democratic, humanitarian, reform movement which swept the age, and the Southern refusal to allow any attempts at a critical examination of slavery. The age of Emerson and Jackson was an era of optimism about the future state of man and American society. Slavery, and the whole cluster of problems about it, did not fit into this framework. "What is a man born for," asked Emerson, "but to be a Reformer, a Remaker of what man has made?" And the institution of slavery, if ever any institution was, was ripe for reform. The abolition of the system was at first no more than another attempt to improve society; in time it absorbed more and more of the energies of those who, responding to the spirit of Emerson's query, hoped to put the finishing touches to the perfection of American institutions. Entangled with every phase of contemporary reform, from transcendental philosophy to women's rights, the issue of slavery in the brief space of thirty years became a central point on which reformers of every kind could unite.[3]

An important factor in turning Northern sentiment against the South (which could then be translated into sentiment against slavery) was the South's tendency to identify all antislavery opinion with the extremists. The South, as time passed, refused to allow consideration of its own problems even by Southerners, and its growing distrust and suspicion made discussion of vital issues as impossible with "fire-eaters" as with Garrisonians. The institution whose supporters could not permit discussion or criticism, and who showed themselves willing to sacrifice the most cherished traditional liberties in its defense, wrote its own doom.

In attacking the abolitionists, the South made the error of

[3] For a contemporary appraisal of abolition and other reforms, see Harriet Martineau's *The Martyr Age of the United States of America*.

attacking the rights of the Northern white man as well, and in so doing afforded the abolitionist an opportunity to present himself to the nation as the defender not only of Negro rights, but of freedom itself. All those liberties of speech, press, religion, assembly, and thought were, according to the Richmond *Enquirer,* "curses to the North" because they really led to "treason, polygamy, free love, vile superstition, and vile infidelities." *"You must take away these* liberties at the North," it warned, "or they will destroy private property, religion, marriage, nay, *government itself!"*[4]

The men who carried the burden in the beginning stages of the abolition movement saw that the great question at issue was not only the freedom of the black man but also that of the white.[5] Whittier, while editing the *New England Weekly Review* in 1830, called attention to the inconsistency of the slaveholder who "boasts of his republicanism and his love of liberty, and in the same breath defends in the abstract the accursed system of slavery." William Swaim, the North Carolina Quaker, wrote in the same year that slavery struck "at the root of our republican institutions, and . . . would overturn even our liberty itself."[6] The contradictions between what all Americans professed and what slavery did was evident to many others quite early in the antislavery crusade.

The violent reaction of the South to the opening cannonades of abolition confirmed the abolitionist belief that not only slavery, but the whole tradition of American civil rights was at stake. James G. Birney, one of the first to perceive the wider implications of the controversy, wrote from Kentucky to Gerrit Smith in 1835, "It has now become absolutely necessary, that Slavery should cease in order that freedom may be preserved

---

[4] *The Anti Slavery Bugle,* October 18, 1856.

[5] Garrison wrote, "The antislavery struggle was commenced primarily and exclusively with reference to the emancipation of the enslaved portion of the African race in our land; in it now are seen to be included the rights and liberties of all classes of people, without regard to complexion." *The Anti Slavery Bugle,* May 9, 1857; also Goodell, *op. cit.,* 408 ff.

[6] Alice Adams, *The Neglected Period of Antislavery,* 50; and William Swaim, *Address to the People of North Carolina on the Evils of Slavery,* 50.

to any portion of the land. . . ."[7] William Thomas, in that year, published a long analysis of the relationship of the abolition controversy to civil liberties, concluding that only by flying at once to their defense could the traditional rights of all Americans be preserved.[8] The American Anti Slavery Society warned the public, "We must all be free, or all slaves together," and William Jay, president of the New York City Anti Slavery Society, pointed out that though "we commenced the present struggle to obtain the freedom of the slave, we are compelled to continue it to preserve our own."[9]

To obtain help in the crusade to save American rights from the threat of proslavery suppression, abolitionists appealed to friends of liberty everywhere to "recognize each other as fellow-laborers, and learn consistency from their common enemy," to unite with the abolitionists against those "illiberal principles, the anti-republican tendencies," by which the proponents of slavery hoped "to modify our institutions and modes of life. . . ."[10] The yearly Anti Slavery Almanac gathered information on mobs, violations of free speech, and attacks on the press, printed articles concerning the dangers to civil liberties, doing much to keep the abolitionists conscious of their broader responsibility to the American public.[11] By 1838 the argument

[7] Dumond, ed., *The Letters of James G. Birney*, I:243. In May of 1835 Birney, already well-known in the East through his struggle for a free press in Kentucky, expressed the same sentiments in a speech to the American Anti Slavery Society in New York, giving voice for probably the first time to what became a favorite theme in that society's propaganda campaign; see William Birney, *James G. Birney and His Times*, 175.

[8] William Thomas ("Defensor"), *Enemies of the Constitution*, 104-22.

[9] "The Executive Committee of the American Anti Slavery Society to the American People," the Cincinnati *Philanthropist*, July 8, 1836, and Bayard Tuckerman, *William Jay and the Constitutional Movement for the Abolition of Slavery*, 80. See also the resolutions of the Ohio Anti Slavery Society, *The Philanthropist*, April 8, 1836; the speech of Gerrit Smith to the American Anti Slavery Society Anniversary, *ibid.*, June 10, 1836; "How Can It Be Done?" *The Anti Slavery Record*, September 1836, 10; and *The Proceedings of the Indiana Convention Assembled to Organize a State Anti Slavery Society, Held in Milton*.

[10] C. C. Follen, "The Cause of Freedom in our Country," *The Quarterly Anti Slavery Magazine* II (October, 1836), 65.

[11] In 1836 the *Almanac* carried full accounts of the Lane Seminary dis-

that the abolitionists were really an advance guard in the battle for every American's civil liberties, was a principle fully perfected, reaffirmed yearly by antislavery societies and constantly referred to by abolitionist speakers as an integral part of the attack upon slavery.[12] "It is no longer a question of slavery for the black man," cried agent Stanley Webb, "but of liberty for the white man," and abolitionists everywhere drummed the point home from press and platform for more than twenty years.[13]

Of the early abolitionists, James G. Birney and William Goodell were apparently the first to recognize the importance of this particular aspect of the antislavery argument. Birney, said his son, was convinced from the beginning that "the real question of the times was not negro slavery, but the preservation of liberty in what were called the free states."[14] Goodell,

---

pute; in 1837 it reprinted Gerrit Smith's Peterboro speech on free speech; in 1838 it reviewed the controversies over petition and the press, and carried two articles by Goodell on the threat of slavery to Northern freedom. In 1839 it carried two more long articles on the maintenance of white rights against the threat of slavery, and listed the voting records of Northern congressmen on all legislation pertaining to slavery and civil rights. The 1840 edition contained another voting list, three warning articles, and a list of anti-abolitionist mobs since 1834, pointing out how these affected free speech.

[12] See, for example, S. B. Treadwell, *American Liberties and American Slavery Morally and Politically Illustrated;* the Birney-Elmore correspondence and Birney's statement of the aims of the Liberty party, March, 1842, in Dumond, *Letters, op. cit.,* II:645-56; the article by A. G. Kir, *The Philanthropist,* April 9, 1839, and the resolutions of the various antislavery societies of Ohio and Indiana, *ibid.,* September 3, 1839.

[13] S. Webb, *Speech in the National Anti Slavery Convention, Held in Albany . . .,* 1. See also Joshua Giddings' 1842 speech, in Henry Wilson, *The History of the Rise and Fall of the Slave Power in America,* I:166; "What Slavery Has Done" and "Who is Free?" *The Anti Slavery Bugle,* October 24, 1845, and October 30, 1846; the letter of Cassius Clay, *ibid.,* July 5, 1851; Horace Greeley in the New York *Daily Tribune,* January 18, 1855; R. P. Spaulding at the Massillon Convention, Ohio, *The Anti Slavery Bugle,* September 2, 1856; William Goodell, "How the Oligarchy Rules," *The Radical Abolitionist,* December 26, 1857; the resolutions of the Cleveland mass-meeting, J. R. Shipherd, *The History of the Oberlin-Wellington Rescue,* 253; and Harriet Beecher Stowe, *Key to Uncle Tom's Cabin,* 398.

[14] William Birney, *op. cit.,* 231; also Dumond, *Letters, op. cit.,* I:364, 485, 564-67, and II:645-56.

beginning in 1838, developed the idea in a number of editorials and essays, leading to a long analysis in *Slavery and Antislavery* (1852), and another in *The American Slave Code in Theory and Practice* (1853). So too did such prominent early leaders as Gerrit Smith and Wendell Phillips.[15] Though some accused the abolitionists of deliberately fomenting violence in an effort to gain public sympathy and support,[16] the violence of their opposition and the trend of events tended to reinforce their case. It became by 1840 almost a matter of course to accept their warnings at face value. In the face of the proslavery argument and of recurrent mobs, "lynchings," and threats, said Edward Beecher, "the supporters of law and order saw that some organized, systematic effort was absolutely necessary to save their own liberties from the ruthless hands of unprincipled men."[17]

Slavery and liberty, the abolitionists contended, were absolutely incompatible; one must drive out the other, and unless slavery were defeated, the outcome of the clash was foreordained. Long before Seward spoke of an "irrepressible conflict" or Lincoln of a "house divided," Birney wrote in 1836, "If slavery live at the South, liberty must die at the North. There is no middle ground."[18] A Connecticut minister, a year later, saw "the elements of conflict and repulsion in fearful operation in this land of liberty. Slavery and freedom cannot long co-exist—one must destroy the other."[19] Nor could Ralph Waldo Emerson see how "a barbarous community and a civil-

[15] See Smith's "Free Discussion," *The American Anti Slavery Almanac*, 8-12. T. G. Helm's "Wendell Phillips and the Abolition Movement," *The Reformed Church Review* XX (April, 1916), 203-204, 206-211, contains an analysis of Phillips' interests in the abolition movement.

[16] Garrison's aim, said the *Boston Recorder* in 1835, was "to identify his cause with the cause of civil liberty, by making it necessary for all who defend civil liberty to defend him . . .," quoted by *The National Anti Slavery Standard*, November 3, 1855. Channing's *Slavery* (Boston, 1836), and Catherine Beecher's *Essay upon Slavery and Abolition* (Philadelphia, 1837), voiced similar suspicions.

[17] Henry Wilson, *op. cit.*, I:362.

[18] The Cincinnati *Philanthropist*, December 30, 1836.

[19] The Reverend Arthur Granger, *A Sermon Preached . . . in Meriden, Connecticut*, 5.

ized community can constitute one state. I think that we must get rid of slavery, or we must get rid of freedom."[20] Seward repeated the doctrine of irreconcilability many times,[21] and by the opening of the 'forties, the idea was a standard element of the abolitionist argument and remained so through the Civil War.[22]

Though the abolitionists could point to a long history of encroachment upon their own rights as proof of the incompatibility of slavery and liberty, even better evidence lay in the loss of the free white man's liberties in the slaveholding states. As early as 1836 the abolitionists, referring to the recent Southern legislation governing speech, opinion, and the press, claimed that the Southern white man to all practical purposes had completely lost his liberty of thought and expression; subsequent events simply added fresh proof.[23] Southern white men, who were in one sense slaves to the slavery system, could not "be regarded as a people in possession of civil, religious, and political freedom." A Southerner could not educate a slave, hire one if he needed labor, have one testify in court, or give one religious instruction; he could not move or free slaves

[20] Concord Address, *The National Anti Slavery Standard,* June 14, 1856.

[21] See his Cleveland speech of 1848, his Rochester speech of 1858, and his Dubuque speech of 1860, in G. E. Baker, ed., *The Works of William H. Seward,* III:295, IV:289-302, 372.

[22] Examples of its development over the years include: George Bancroft, "The Decline of Athens," *Literary and Historical Miscellanies;* "What Have The Free States to do with Slavery?" *American Anti Slavery Almanac,* 5-13; Horace Bushnell, *Discourse Delivered in North Church, Hartford* . . ., 5; G. E. Day, *The Dangers of Our Country* . . ., 14-15; editorials from the Ashtabula, Ohio, *Sentinel,* July 31, 1845, *The Charter Oak,* the *Massachusetts Spy,* reprinted in *The Anti Slavery Bugle* and *The National Era,* August 7, 1846, and June 10, 1847; Theodore Parker, *The Dangers from Slavery,* 3-5; "O. S. Freeman," *Letters on Slavery Addressed to the Proslavery Men of America;* C. F. Adams, *What Makes Slavery a Matter of National Concern?;* "The Irrepressible Conflict of Freedom and Slavery," *The National Era,* November 18, 1858; Carl Schurz, "The Doom of Slavery," in Frederic Bancroft, ed., *Speeches, Correspondence, and Political Papers of Carl Schurz,* I:121-31; and the Cincinnati *Commercial,* December 1, 1860.

[23] *Proceedings of the Rhode Island Anti Slavery Convention, Held in Providence on the 2d, 3d, and 4th of February, 1836,* 22-24, and "Slavery at War with Our Liberties," *The Liberator,* November 22, 1839.

without permission, speak against slavery, or write, listen to, or read antislavery opinion.[24] "It is not *negro* slavery alone from which the slave states need deliverance," remarked *The National Era*. "First, the whites must regain their lost rights."[25]

Some Southerners agreed that these charges had some foundation. An anonymous Virginian thought that slavery "cast a blighting shadow" over "the liberties of the Anglo-Saxon race," and that "in Southern states the non-slaveholding whites are no longer free, a padlock has been placed on their mouths . . . , and they enjoy less liberty than the subjects of many European monarchs."[26] Cassius Clay of Kentucky and later H. R. Helper of North Carolina warned the Southern white man that his traditional rights were gradually disappearing, and even *De-Bow's Review*, the staunchest of proslavery periodicals, once published an article decrying the appearance of "symptoms" dangerous to civil liberty in the South.[27] For the most part, however, if there were substantial numbers of Southerners who saw this kind of danger in the continuation of slavery, they found it the better part of discretion to keep quiet.

In the end the abolitionist claims were widely accepted in the North and implicitly incorporated in the principles of the Republican party. As the Chicago *Daily Democrat* decided in 1860, since the Slave Power had suppressed civil liberty in fifteen states of the Union, "Liberty, not Slavery, is henceforth

[24] William Goodell, *The American Slave Code in Theory and Practice*, 372. Chapter II is a detailed analysis of the restraints placed by slavery upon Southern whites.

[25] May 21, 1857. Other expressions of the same idea may be found in "Address to the People of the United States," the Cincinnati *Weekly Herald and Philanthropist*, June 25, 1845; Gerrit Smith, *Speech Made . . . in the Capitol of the State of New York;* Garrison's Abingdon speech, *The National Anti Slavery Standard*, July 25, 1850; G. M. Weston, "The Poor Whites of the South," *The National Era*, February 28, 1856; "Law and Liberty," *ibid.*, November 24, 1859; H. B. Stowe, "Poor White Trash," *Key to Uncle Tom's Cabin, op. cit.*, 365-381; and Richard Hildreth, *Despotism in America*.

[26] "A Virginian," *Slavery in Maryland*, 20-21.

[27] Clay's Cincinnati speech, *The National Era*, December 7, 1854, and H. R. Helper, *The Impending Crisis*, 360; "The South and Her Remedies," *DeBow's Review* X (January, 1851), 1-9.

to be the end of government."[28] When the Civil War came, abolitionists asserted it to be a war not merely to abolish slavery but to preserve free government against the forces of oppression, a struggle to prevent the establishment by the Slave Power of "an oligarchic, slaveholding despotism, to the extinction of all free institutions." The fight against slavery grew into a war for the preservation of civil liberty.[29]

While the abolitionists could point to a long chain of suppressions of the right to speak, print, and assemble, and to numerous attacks upon other constitutional and traditional liberties, it was not until 1845 that they discovered and developed an effective device to unite all their arguments under one common heading. Putting together the evidence, they concluded that there existed a secret conspiracy among Southern slaveholders to foist slavery upon the nation, destroy civil liberty, extend slavery into the territories (possibly to whites), reopen the slave trade, take control of the Federal government, and establish a ruling Southern aristocracy founded on a slave economy. As summarized by Charles Sumner in 1855, this conspiracy would make the North

. . . the vassal of an OLIGARCHY, whose single inspiration comes from slavery. . . . With a watchfulness that never sleeps, and an activity that never tires—with as many eyes as Argus and as many arms as Briareus—the SLAVE OLIGARCHY asserts its perpetual and insatiate masterdom.[30]

The importance of the threat of this "slave power" in shaping Northern and Western thought on the slavery question

[28] Quoted by H. C. Perkins, *Northern Editorials on Secession*, I:508.

[29] Garrison, "The Abolitionists and Their Relations to the War," *op. cit.*, 44-47. The British and French reformers tended to accept the abolitionist view; see F. M. Edge, *Slavery Doomed*, and August Cochin, *The Results of Slavery*.

[30] Charles Sumner, *The Antislavery Enterprise . . ., An Address to the People of New York*, 29-30. For historical treatments from the abolitionist point of view, see Henry Wilson, *The History of the Rise and Fall of the Slave Power in America*, and J. E. Cairnes, *The Slave Power*. A fascinating example is John Smith Dye, *History of the Plots and Crimes of the Great Conspiracy to Overthrow Liberty in America*, which accuses slaveholders of poisoning Harrison and Taylor and attempting to kill Jackson.

during the decades 1840 to 1860 is not to be underestimated. Repeated accusations, revelations of "proofs" and "plots," and apparently convincing evidence of recent history, combined to give authenticity to the abolitionist charge. The abolitionists, to perhaps a larger extent than many historians have believed, became identified in the popular mind as the sole defenders of the democratic tradition against the machinations of this dangerous, secret cabal. To the mechanic, immigrant laborer, farmer, and lower- and middle-class workman the appeal of the charge was especially strong, since these groups were already prone to doubt the motives of the rich and powerful.

The belligerence of the Southern faction in Congress seemed to lend further proof to these charges of "conspiracy." By 1858 a large segment of the populace in the North and West believed that unless the Slave Power was defeated by the abolition of slavery, the nation could no longer exist as a free republic. Lincoln's statement in 1858 that the nation could not exist half-free and half-slave, but would become one or the other, was meant, of course, literally; he voiced the fear of many Northerners that it might become a nation of slaves. As the threat of "black Republicanism" was used by the proslavery element to unify opinion in the South, so the impending menace of the Slave Power became an important factor in promoting and consolidating antislavery sentiment in the North.

Early in the abolitionist movement, certain of its leaders claimed to possess reliable evidence of the existence of such a conspiracy, although the term "Slave Power" to describe it did not come into general use until the 'forties. In 1836 the Anti Slavery Convention of Rhode Island resolved that the battle against slavery was actually a struggle against "an absolute despotism" which was "determined to stifle the discussion of inalienable rights" and to "invade the most sacred rights of American citizens."[31] A year later James G. Birney repeated the indictment, calling the slavery faction "a Despotism which has attempted to fetter the free mind of the North." In 1838

[31] *Proceedings of the Rhode Island Anti Slavery Convention . . ., op. cit.*, 30.

The Emancipator published "evidence" of an organized plot by slaveholders to overthrow the American government, and later in the same year John Quincy Adams cited proof of its existence.[32] The National Convention of Abolitionists, meeting at Albany in 1839, warned the nation that "the events of the last five or six years leave no room for doubt that the SLAVE POWER is now waging a deliberate and determined war against the liberties of the free states," a warning repeated more frequently by 1840, while in 1842 the citizens of Northampton, Massachusetts, petitioned Congress for relief from the "dictatorship" of the Slave Power.[33]

J. G. Palfrey of Massachusetts, distinguished scholar and one-time editor of *The North American Review,* condemned the Southern "political power" as "an active oligarchy" that had, since 1793, "maintained its terrible ascendancy." The opinions of men such as Palfrey and Adams were highly regarded in the North, and other respected men joined them in their warnings.[34] By 1845 the constantly reiterated admonitions of the abolitionists had begun to take effect, and from that date on, Northern opinion was appreciably colored by the acceptance of the belief that a Southern Slave Power conspiracy against the rights of the free states undoubtedly existed.[35]

[32] The Cincinnati *Philanthropist,* June 7, 1837, and November 27, 1838; *The Emancipator,* February 6, 1838.

[33] Birney, "To the Citizens of the United States," and "Letter to the American Anti Slavery Society," *The Philanthropist,* September 17, 1839 and May 11, 1840; Joshua Leavitt, "The Political Power of Slavery," *ibid.,* November 18, 1840; William Goodell, "The Ascendancy of the Slave Power," the Utica, N.Y., *Friend of Man,* September 2, 1840; anonymous, "The Slave Power," *The Massachusetts Abolitionist,* February 6, 1840; and *The Liberator,* May 20 and 27, June 3, 1842.

[34] Henry Wilson, *op. cit.,* II:200. See Palfrey's *Papers on the Slave Power, First Published in the Boston Whig;* Adams' North Bridgewater address in *The Anti Slavery Bugle,* March 10, 1848; and also Theodore Parker's speech to the American Anti Slavery Society, *The National Anti Slavery Standard,* June 22, 1848; Josiah Quincy, *The Nature and Power of the Slave States* . . . (Boston, 1856) ; and Joshua Giddings, *Speeches in Congress* (Boston and Cleveland, 1853) , 243 ff.

[35] Wilson, *op. cit.,* II:189, placed the beginning of the Mexican War as the date after which "reflecting men" saw "some malignant and potent agency at work. . . . They called it the Slave Power."

The Great Slave Power Conspiracy

What was the Slave Power, and from what did it arise? One abolitionist called it "that control in and over the government of the United States which is exercised by a comparatively small number of persons, distinguished from the other twenty millions of free citizens, and bound together in a common interest, by being owners of slaves."[36] Definitions agreed that it was fundamentally "an aristocracy constituted and organized on the basis of ownership of slaves."[37] Economically, said Gamaliel Bailey, it was based "on the associated wealth of a class of slaveholding monopolists, who constitute about a sixty-sixth part of the population of this country," while Henry Wilson, using different terms, called it "the *political influence* of slavery . . . , the influence that results from the holding of four million men as property . . . , the holding of them by law, and the desire to extend and perpetuate it."[38] Its roots lay in the institution of slavery, which naturally "developed and gratified the most intense spirit of personal pride, a love of class distinctions, and the lust of dominion. Hence arose a commanding power, ever sensitive, jealous, proscriptive, dominating, and aggressive. . . ."[39] This aristocracy was founded upon these principles: that slavery is not a moral wrong, that it is a right possessed by the slaveholder, that he holds the right of property in man, that slavery is legal, and that it is constitutional.[40] Its power in the South rested upon such things as uneven representation in state legislatures, the slaveholders' control of educational and opinion-forming media, and their monopoly of the South's economic system and supplies.[41]

[36] Anonymous, *Five Years' Progress of the Slave Power*, 2.

[37] *Facts for the People*, February 1, 1856.

[38] The Cincinnati *Weekly Herald and Philanthropist*, September 16, 1844, and Henry Wilson, *The Aggressions of the Slave Power*, 16.

[39] Henry Wilson, *The History of the Rise and Fall of the Slave Power*, *op. cit.*, I:2. See also Gamaliel Bailey in *The Philanthropist*, June 2, 1837: "This despotism has arisen from lax notions of human rights; and Southern slavery is the school in which these notions have been acquired."

[40] William Goodell, "The Philosophy of the Slaveholding Supremacy," *The American Jubilee*, January and March, 1855.

[41] "Southern Unanimity," *Five Years' Progress of the Slave Power*, *op. cit.*, Chapter XI.

The abolitionists also charged that the Slave Power threat was intensified by an approaching coalition of a Southern slaveholder and Northern capitalist, through "religious or denominational fellowship, or commercial cupidity, or constant intermarriage, or political alliance, or social affinity, or complexional prejudice, or rather, through all these combined."[42] The Rhode Island Convention of 1836 thought it mattered little "whether the Aristocracy of the North and the slaveholder of the South have *literally* combined . . . , or whether they are drawn to act in concert by the operation of moral affinities or identities of interest. . . . It is sufficient to know *the fact* that they do act together, and so act that liberty is not only endangered but outraged."[43] Marius Robinson pointed out that "the spirit of slavery is not confined to the South. . . . Its exhibitions are the same, whether North or South." Gamaliel Bailey in 1839 believed it increasingly clear that Northern interests had entered into "an atrocious bargain with slaveholders," and defined the Slave Power as "not only the actual slaveholding community, but the slaveholding spirit, which, fostered by prejudice and interests, pervades the whole Union."[44] Cassius Clay defined the issue as lying "between the slaveholding aristocracy of the South and the large shipping merchants and cotton dealers of the North on the one hand, and the great non-slaveholding masses of the whole Union on the other."[45]

The tendency grew to include in the "conspiracy" not only slaveholders, but Northern commercial and manufacturing in-

[42] Garrison, in *The Anti Slavery Bugle*, May 9, 1857. See also "The Alliance with the Northern Money Power," in *Five Years' Progress of the Slave Power, op. cit.,* 25-31.

[43] *Proceedings of the Convention, Held in Providence . . .,* 30. Evidence of a coalition between Southern and Northern autocrats, pp. 31-37, cites the various mobbings of abolitionists, Northern acquiescence to demands for stifling the abolition press, anti-abolition sentiment of Northern commercial interests and churches, the threat to academic freedom, etc.

[44] Letter of June 15, 1837, Robinson correspondence, Western Reserve Historical Society; *The Philanthropist*, January 22, 1839; *The Liberator,* October 23, 1840.

[45] *The Anti Slavery Bugle*, July 5, 1851.

terests, until by 1850 the term "Slave Power" meant, as Wendell Phillips strikingly phrased it, an alliance of "the Lords of the Lash and the Lords of the Loom," and the fight against it became a battle against conservatism, aristocracy, and the power of capital in Ohio and Massachusetts as well as in South Carolina.[46] "The wealth of the North and the wealth of the South," cried *The Anti Slavery Bugle*, "are combined to crush the liberal, free, progressive spirit of the age."[47]

After the Compromise of 1850, the Slave Power became the primary object of abolitionist attack. John Rankin believed that "the slave power has already seized upon the General Government, and has overthrown the rights of the free States, and made the citizens slave citizens. . . . The struggle between the slave and the free institutions is for existence. They are antagonistic principles and cannot exist long together—one or the other must fall."[48] In Congress the charge was endlessly repeated, and abolitionist speakers and editors gave tongue throughout the land. *"The South is thoroughly in earnest,"* wrote William Goodell. "She is no land of *shams*. There is reality, terrible reality, there. The South has one object in view, and never loses sight of it for a single hour."[49]

[46] Speech to the American Anti Slavery Society, *The National Anti Slavery Standard*, June 14, 1859.

[47] *The Anti Slavery Bugle*, November 9, 1850, and William Goodell, *The Rights and Wrongs of Rhode Island*. For similar warnings, see Bayard Tuckerman, *William Jay and the Constitutional Movement for the Abolition of Slavery*, 80; William Goodell (?), "Letter from the Executive Committee of the New York Anti Slavery Society," *A Collection of Valuable Documents*, 71-2; *Proceedings of the Indiana Convention . . . to Organize a State Anti Slavery Society;* "How Can It Be Done?" *The Anti Slavery Record* II (September, 1836), 1-11; C. C. Follen, "The Cause of Freedom in our Country," *Quarterly Anti Slavery Magazine* II (October, 1836), 65; S. B. Treadwell, *op. cit.*, 103; Thomas Morris, *Speech . . . in Reply to the Hon. Henry Clay*, 5-8; and Gamaliel Bailey, "Tendencies of the American People," *The National Era*, June 26, 1851.

[48] *The Anti Slavery Bugle*, December 4, 1852.

[49] *The American Jubilee*, June, 1854. For other warnings, see the remarks of Washburne of Maine, Fessenden of Maine, and Blair of Missouri, reprinted in *The Radical Abolitionist*, April, 1858; Josiah Quincy, *Addresses Illustrative of the Nature and Power of the Slave States;* Seward's Detroit speech, "The Slaveholding Class Dominant in the Republic," *The National Era*, February 5, 1857, and his Albany speech, *ibid.*, October 25,

The aggressions of this Slave Power were closely charted by the abolitionist press and the events of the period 1840 to 1858 were interpreted (and sometimes twisted) to illustrate the development of a great plot by that Power to seize control of the nation. The first great opportunity for the abolitionists came with the problems of Texas annexation and the Mexican War. Many Southerners felt that control of Texas was vital to slavery's existence, and equally as many Northerners denounced its annexation as a proslavery scheme. Successful annexation (justified by Calhoun on the grounds that it was "necessary to preserve domestic institutions," and that slavery in Texas was "essential to the peace, safety, and prosperity" of the slaveholding states) convinced the abolitionists that the subsequent Mexican War was the logical result of the expansionist policies pursued by the Slave Power.[50] From that point on, they claimed, "Slavery became the controlling element in American politics."[51]

After the Mexican War, abolitionists contended that the Slave Power had similar designs on Cuba and Central America, for "consolidating the whole into a vast slave empire, in which were only two classes, *Masters* and *slaves*."[52] The great "perils

---

1855; Sumner's Faneuil Hall speech, "The Slave Oligarchy," *The Anti Slavery Bugle*, November 17, 1855; G. W. Julian, "The Strength and Weakness of the Slave Power," *ibid.*, June 6, 1852; C. B. Tompkins of Ohio, *Speech in the House of Representatives*, April 24, 1860; Goodell, "The Great Conspiracy," *The Radical Abolitionist*, April, 1858; Gamaliel Bailey's editorials, "The Influences to which Congress and the Chief Executive are Subjected," "A Dark Conspiracy," "The Privileged Class," and "Despotism," *The National Era*, November 21, 1850, June 19, 1851, December 20, 1855, and March 13, 1856; and the Reverend Frederick Frothingham, *Discourse . . . at Portland, Maine*, and "The Influence of the Slave Power," *Liberty Tract Number 3*.

[50] For abolitionist interpretations of the Mexican War, see Henry Wilson, *op. cit.*, II:7-30; "Slaveholding Rule," the Cincinnati *Weekly Herald and Philanthropist*, November 25, 1846; "This Hour," *The National Anti Slavery Standard*, July 20, 1848; Lowell's *Biglow Papers, First Series, Works*; and S. C. Phillips, *An Address Upon the Annexation of Texas . . .*; John D. P. Fuller, "The Slavery Question and the Movement to Acquire Mexico," *Mississippi Valley Historical Review* XXI (June, 1934), 31-48.

[51] Frederick Frothingham, *Discourse . . . at Portland, Maine*, 11.

[52] Marius Robinson, notes for speeches, Western Reserve Historical Society.

of the day," listed by *The True Democrat* in 1851, were the annexation of Cuba and Santo Domingo and the extension of slavery into New Mexico, Utah, and California.[53] During Pierce's administration, Walker's "filibuster" government in Nicaragua was recognized amid Southern applause for his reestablishment of slavery in that country, and there was Southern talk of its eventual annexation. This, added to the assistance given the insurrectionist Lopez in Cuba (which resulted in the indictment of the governors of Louisiana and Mississippi), provided enough evidence to make such warnings plausible. Southern leaders themselves furnished additional proof by frequent references to the desirability of extending slavery southward, and quotations to this effect were widely reprinted in the Northern press. Governor Adams of South Carolina thought that since slavery "has exalted the white race itself to higher hopes and purposes, it is perhaps the most sacred obligation that we should give it the means of expansion . . . ," and the Charleston *Mercury*, speaking of Mexico and Central America, thought it probable that "in the future the Anglo-Saxon race will . . . occupy and absorb the whole of that splendid but ill-peopled country and to remove, by gradual process, the worthless mongrel races that now inhabit and curse the land."[54]

In Congress Giddings accused the South of an effort "to meanly and piratically steal Cuba, in order that the chains of slavery . . . (*might*) be more securely riveted upon her bondsmen," while the Ostend Manifesto of 1854, bluntly recommending the purchase of Cuba, seemed to indicate a fixed timetable for the extension of the Slave Power through the Caribbean and Central America.[55] Mexico, it was also charged,

[53] *The Anti Slavery Bugle*, July 19, 1851.

[54] Nevins, *Ordeal of the Union*, II:519; Charleston, S. C., *Mercury*, February 28, 1860.

[55] See "Annexation of Cuba," "The Projected Invasion of Cuba," and "The Cuban Plot Not Relinquished," *The Anti Slavery Bugle*, April 13, 1849, and June 1 and 29, 1850; *The Richmond Penny Post*, quoted *ibid.*, September 23, 1854; and the New Orleans *Delta* and the remarks of Mason of Virginia, *The National Era*, November 20, 1856 and January 6, 1853, for examples of the Cuban controversy.

was the next objective of the slavery extensionists, who hoped that by fomenting revolution, northern Mexico might break off to form another Texas.[56] The conversion of California and the West to slave territory was assumed to be the second phase of the Slave Power's master plan—the admission of California as a free state was hailed as a resounding victory over the plot.[57]

The complete indictment against the Slave Power was impressive, and, if one accepted abolitionist logic, unanswerable. In the 'forties, Joshua Giddings listed ten proofs of its existence and its strength: the fugitive slave law of 1793; the Creek and Negro troubles in Florida in 1815; the Seminole War; the maintenance of slavery in the District of Columbia; the refusal to recognize Haiti; the attempts to recapture fugitive slaves from Canada; the suppression of petitions in the House after 1836; the attacks on free speech and press, and the controversy over the mails; the extension of slavery into the Southwest; and the agitation for the re-opening of the slave trade.[58] Seward, in 1855, added the Missouri Compromise, the annexation of Texas, the war with Mexico, the Kansas struggle, and the Compromise of 1850.[59] The Dred Scott affair afforded more proof, and by 1858 a substantial number of Northerners were ready to agree with the Cincinnati *Daily Commercial* that "There is such a thing as THE SLAVE POWER. It has marched over and annihilated the boundaries of the states.

[56] *The Anti Slavery Bugle*, September 3, 1855 and March 13, 1852, and *The National Era*, August 7, 1851.

[57] See "A New Slave State on the Pacific," *The Anti Slavery Bugle*, December 8, 1849, and December 13, 1851; "The Slaveholding Scheme—Mutilation of California," and "Slavery and California," *The National Era*, December 12, 1850, February 19 and 26, March 11, and April 15, 1852; and *The American Jubilee*, November, 1854.

[58] J. R. Giddings, *The Rights of the Free States Subverted*.

[59] Albany speech, in *Facts for the People*, November 1, 1855. See also the evidence cited by Henry Wilson, *op. cit.*, I:30, 50-56, 120-23, 148-52, 339-43, *et seq.*, and *Wideawake Papers, Number 3*. Probably the most detailed analysis of the "Slave Power conspiracy" is in *Facts for the People*, February 1, March 1, and April 11, 1856.

We are now one great homogeneous slaveholding community."[60]

The aim of the Slave Power, maintained the abolitionists, was threefold: to re-open the slave trade; to extend the institution of slavery throughout the entire nation and beyond; and to remove from the free white man those constitutional and traditional guarantees of liberty which stood in the way of the control over the middle and lower classes by a privileged aristocracy of slaveholder and capitalist.[61] Successful realization of all these, they warned, was not far in the future.

Southern agitation for a renewal of the slave trade, especially after 1850, gave rather convincing corroboration to the first claim. The failing slave economy led many Southerners to advocate the repeal of the laws forbidding the importation of slaves. Texas delegations to the commercial conventions held annually in New Orleans voted by a heavy majority in 1856, 1857, 1858, and 1859 to begin the importation of African slaves. It would be a work of "philanthropy and patriotism" to "take black barbarians and make good Christians of them," the delegation resolved, but strong opposition from Texas churches prevented carrying the resolutions further. In South Carolina and Louisiana powerfully-organized minorities among the slaveholders seemed to be on the verge of success in re-opening the trade in 1859, while eighteen prominent Mississippians that year pledged themselves to purchase 1000 African Negroes, to encourage some ready entrepreneur. The *Wanderer*, under Captain Corrie, actually did bring four hundred and twenty

[60] The Cincinnati *Daily Commercial*, March 12, 1857. See also Oliver Johnson, *William Lloyd Garrison and His Times*, 380-81; Marius Robinson, *The Anti Slavery Bugle*, November 5, 1857; William Goodell, *The Radical Abolitionist*, April 1, 1857; and the editorial opinions reprinted *ibid.*, May, 1857.

[61] For the complete indictment, see Chapter IV, "Preparation Made for Future Movement," *Five Years' Progress of the Slave Power, op. cit.*; there was assumed a general plot "to defeat the spirit of liberty in the free states . . . and to convert our American republic into an odious aristocracy," and specifically a plot to make slave states of New Mexico and Utah, divide California into a free and a slave state, divide Texas into four new slave states, and to take over Mexico, Santo Domingo, Yucatan, and Nicaragua as slave territory.

slaves from Africa to the United States in December of 1858 and sold them; the *Clotilde,* in 1859, brought one hundred and sixteen, probably the last ever to be imported. Though proposals to re-open the slave trade were favored only by a minority in the South the abolitionists were quick to seize on them as evidence that the Slave Power intended to entrench itself even more firmly by thus bolstering the institution upon which it rested.[62] In 1854 the Charleston *Mercury* and the Charleston *Standard* both pointed out the inconsistency of the Federal government's stand in accepting slavery as an institution and yet outlawing the means by which it was supported, and two years later Governor Adams of South Carolina made strong representations in his annual message for the revival of the trade.[63] In the years following, demands became stronger and more frequent, a marked contrast to the Southern attitude of twenty years earlier and a good illustration of how completely the South had committed itself to the defense and maintenance of slavery.[64] The abolitionist press kept careful count of Southern requests for the re-opening of the slave trade and constantly warned Congress of the new and more potent Slave Power that would result from a repeal of the laws of 1808.[65]

[62] "Extraordinary Proofs of the Grand Conspiracy," The New York *Emancipator and Free American,* March 16, 1853; Harvey Wish, "The Revival of the African Slave Trade in the United States," *Mississippi Valley Historical Review* XXVII (March, 1941), 569-88; W. J. Carnathan, "The Proposals to Reopen the Slave Trade," *South Atlantic Quarterly* XXV (1926), 410-30; Earl Fornell, "Agitation in Texas for Reopening the Slave Trade," *Southwestern Historical Quarterly* LX (October, 1956), 245-59. *DeBow's Review* for 1857-59 is filled with discussions of this issue.

[63] *The Anti Slavery Bugle,* July 18, 1854, and December 6, 1856, and the New York *Daily Tribune,* November 9, 1854.

[64] The New Orleans *Delta,* reported *The Anti Slavery Bugle,* May 16, 1857, suggested indentured Negro "coolie" labor; the proposed "African Labor Importation Association" to be formed in Mississippi, *ibid.,* February 27, 1858, was another subterfuge. A Louisiana proposal to import 2500 Negro "apprentices" failed by but two votes in the state legislature, reported *The Radical Abolitionist,* April, 1858. See also the debate in the Georgia senate, the Savannah *Republican,* November 23, 1858; and the remarks of Daniel Lee of Georgia, *The National Era,* March 10, 1859.

[65] *The National Era,* July 20, 1854, April 1 and 7, 1859; *The American Jubilee,* February, 1855; and *The Anti Slavery Bugle,* March 27, 1858. The

More spectacular was the abolitionist claim that the Slave Power intended to legalize the institution of slavery through all the states of the Union. As early as 1844 Gamaliel Bailey exposed "a deliberate plot . . . to sustain the slavery of this country against the advancing civilization of the age, and to extend it over almost illimitable regions," an indictment frequently levelled in subsequent years. A statement attributed to Toombs of Georgia that he would some day call the roll of his slaves on Bunker Hill gained wide publicity.[66] During the 'fifties the accusation commonly formed a part of almost every abolitionist argument, until anti-extension became, by way of the Republican party, a cardinal principle in Northern political thought.[67]

Difficult to establish, but tremendously effective as a propaganda device, was the claim that the Slave Power intended gradually to subvert white liberties until some form of white slavery became nationwide policy. Since slavery, ran abolitionist logic, was founded upon a violation of a fundamental tenet of free government (that all men are born free and equal), it therefore by the simple fact of its existence threat-

---

Wanderer and *Echo* cases received close coverage in the abolition press as forerunners of a Southern attempt to evade existing laws against the trade. William Goodell's scrapbook for 1856, in the Oberlin College Library, contains many clippings from Southern newspapers expressing favor of the slave trade with Goodell's marginal notations.

[66] *The National Era*, August 23, 1855; *The Anti Slavery Bugle*, September 15, 1855; *Facts for the People*, September, 1855, and *The National Anti Slavery Standard*, December 20, 1856.

[67] For examples, see J. E. Cairnes, *op. cit.*, 60-63; the Columbus *Ohio State Journal*, quoted by *The Anti Slavery Bugle*, March 28, 1857; the Wautoma, Wisconsin, *Journal*, November 18, 1856; William Goodell in *The American Jubilee*, July and November, 1854; Trumbull of Ohio, *The Radical Abolitionist* II (August, 1856), 2; Horace Mann, *Appendix to the Congressional Globe, 32nd Congress, 1st Session*, August 23, 1852, 1076; Seward's Albany speech, *Facts for the People*, December 1, 1855; Sumner's "The Anti Slavery Enterprise . . .," *The Anti Slavery Bugle*, May 26, 1855; the letters of C. H. Delano and J. U. Root, Giddings correspondence, Ohio State Archaeological and Historical Society Collections, August 22, 1847, and August 11, 1851; and Nicolay and Hay, *Abraham Lincoln; A History*, I:215-16, 240, 611-12. For the adoption of the anti-extension principle by the Republican party, see the files of *The Radical Abolitionist* for 1857 and 1858.

ened free government and was the first step toward despotism.[68] Shortly after the beginning of the aggressive phase of abolition, abolitionists in the North recognized the appeal of the charge, made use of it, and continued to develop it. Birney believed in 1835 that "the contest is becoming—has become—one, not alone of freedom for the blacks, but of freedom for the white," and a year later William Chaplin pointed out that "all history, experience, and observation teach that if we tamely acquiesce in perfidy and outrage practised upon innocent sufferers, we, ourselves, shall sooner or later become their victims."[69] By 1850 the belief was current in antislavery circles that the Slave Power intended to undermine the liberties of the white freeman. Warnings after that date were clear and frequent. "The mere discovery of a grand plot against our liberties and the hopes of mankind is worth a thousand times more than it has cost," said the abolitionists, "and till the whole conspiracy is crushed, there will be work enough for any Anti Slavery Society."[70]

The proslavery argument after 1820 furnished what seemed to be demonstrable proof of the existence of a Slave Power plot to destroy white liberties. In order to defend slavery, its advocates were often forced to question or abandon certain cher-

[68] "O. S. Freeman" (Edward Coit Rogers), *Letters on Slavery*, 63.

[69] Dumond, ed., *The Letters of James G. Birney*, *op. cit.*, I:243, and *The Legion of Liberty and the Force of Truth*, 136. See also the Birney letters, *supra cit.*, I:363, 485, 565, 654-56.

[70] "How Can It Be Done?" *The Anti Slavery Record* II (September, 1836), 10. The subsequent development of the idea may be traced in: "To the Citizens of the United States," *The Philanthropist*, September 17, 1839; Thomas Morris, "To the Pennsylvania Hall Committee," *ibid.*, June 26, 1838; William Goodell, "Slavery Endangers Our Liberties," *The Anti Slavery Lecturer* I (August and September, 1839) ; "The Slavepower Conspiracy Against Civil Rights," the Cincinnati *Weekly Herald and Philanthropist*, June 25, 1845; the letter of Joshua Giddings, *The Anti Slavery Bugle*, October 17, 1845; the letter of Cassius Clay, *The Weekly Herald and Philanthropist*, June 18, 1845; *The Substance of a Speech Made by Gerrit Smith, in the Capitol . . .*, 21; William Goodell, *Slavery and Antislavery*, 583-84; Goodell, editorial, *The Radical Abolitionist*, December 26, 1857; resolutions of the Western Antislavery Society, *The National Anti Slavery Standard*, September 20, 1856; Carl Schurz' St. Louis speech, in Frederic Bancroft, *op. cit.*, I:121-31; and the speech of John B. Alley of Massachusetts, January 26, 1861, *Congressional Globe 36th Congress 2nd Session*, I:584 ff.

ished principles of the American tradition, or to deny the relevance of much of the American experience. If proslavery men "advocated principles which are utterly and irreconcilably opposed to the principles of liberty," they could not, it seemed to the abolitionists, "fail to promote a universal and eternal reign of despotism."[71] In addition, the South evolved a new theory of slavery, a counterattack which boldly asserted slavery to be a "positive good," not simply a defensible system but the best and soundest foundation for stability and progress, whereas freedom, in the usual sense, was little more than a danger to the human race.[72] Certain elements of the "positive good" school of thought adapted themselves admirably to abolitionist use.

Slavery, said the proslavery element of the South, had natural, historical, and moral justification. B. W. Leigh, at the Virginia Constitutional Convention of 1829, was of the opinion that "there must be some peasantry, and as the country fills up there must be more."[73] Governor McDuffie of South Carolina was more definite in his annual message for 1835:

If we look into the elements of which all political communities are composed, it will be found that servitude in some form is one of the essential constituents. No community has ever existed without it, and we may confidently assert, none ever will. In the very nature of things, there must be classes of persons to discharge all the different offices of society, from the highest to the lowest.[74]

[71] William McMichael, *Slavery and Its Remedy*, 132.

[72] Discussions of the "positive good" argument and its development may be found in W. S. Jenkins, *Proslavery Thought in the Old South*, 48-107; A. Y. Lloyd, *The Slavery Controversy*, 126-264; and Virginius Dabney, *Liberalism in the South*, 68-72. Illuminating contemporary discussions are found in E. N. Elliott, ed., *The Pro Slavery Argument*; Governor McDuffie's message to the South Carolina legislature in 1835, the New Richmond, Ohio, *Philanthropist*, January 1, 1836; Governor Bagley's message to the Alabama legislature, *Niles' Register*, 59:233-34; speech of Bayly of Accomack to the Virginia House of Delegates, February 15, 1838, reprinted in *The Philanthropist*, December 17, 1839; and the letter of the Rt. Rev. W. H. Barnwell of Charleston, S. C., in *The National Anti Slavery Standard*, June 29, 1848.

[73] Quoted by William Goodell in *The Anti Slavery Lecturer*, No. 8, August, 1839.

[74] The New Richmond, Ohio, *Philanthropist*, January 1, 1836.

Calhoun in 1836 called slavery "a universal condition," and Negro slavery simply "one modification" of it, while Chancellor Harper in 1837 thought that "the exclusive owners of property . . . ought to be the virtual rulers of mankind," and that "it is as much the order of nature that men should enslave each other as that animals should prey upon each other."[75]

Another principle of the "positive good" argument rested upon the accusation that free society, "that little experiment made in a corner of Western Europe," had failed dismally.[76] "Modern free society," said the New Orleans *Delta*, in an editorial endlessly reprinted by the abolitionists, "as at present organized, is radically wrong and rotten. It is self-destroying, and can never exist happily and normally, until it is qualified by the introduction of some principle equivalent in its effect to the institution of slavery."[77] "Free society," repeated the Richmond *Enquirer*, "in the long run is an impracticable form of society; it is everywhere starving, demoralized, and insurrectionary . . . , cowardly, selfish, sensual, licentious, infidel, agrarian and revolutionary."[78] George Fitzhugh's *Sociology for the South, or Free Society a Failure*, which appeared in 1854, concluded the development of the argument for the superiority of a slave system over a free; it became a valuable and vast source of quotations for abolitionist warnings against the machinations of the Slave Power.[79]

[75] Quoted by Goodell, *supra cit.*, and James O'Neal, *The Workers in American History*, 169.

[76] The Richmond *Enquirer*, quoted by *The National Era*, August 9, 1855. "Then we will invade the North," continued The *Enquirer*, "where a similar experiment is *making*, not made."

[77] *The National Anti Slavery Standard*, November 8, 1856, and *The National Era*, November 27, 1856. Abolitionist editors usually failed to print the rest of the quotation, which read, "We do not mean that the whites, or the laboring portion of them, should hold the relation of slaves. Far from it. We would have them liberated from real bondage, poverty, and want, to which free society exposes them."

[78] *The Anti Slavery Bugle*, October 18, 1856. See also "The Blessings of Slavery," the Richmond *Examiner*, October 15 and 23, 1856.

[79] See the review by *DeBow's Review* (July, 1855), 29-38. For the reception of the book in the South, see the Charleston *Mercury*, July 5, 1858; the Richmond *Enquirer*, January 19, 1856; the New Orleans *Picayune*,

The adoption by the South of the thesis that free society was a failure led directly to the contention that slavery was highly superior to it as an institution. It was, said the proslavery thinkers, the best system for the laborer, providing a security and benevolence lacking in a free competitive labor market. "Make the laboring man the slave of one man instead of the slave of society," remarked the Richmond *Enquirer*, "and he would be far better off." J. H. Hammond of South Carolina thought that actually "the whole hireling class of manual laborers and 'operatives' as you call them are essentially slaves." Northern employers, he suggested, " should become the owners of their laborers and as such be compelled to clothe and feed them decently, while in the West the public lands should be parcelled out in great estates and tilled by the landless poor bound in perpetuity to the soil." Senator Downs of Louisiana, in the same vein, challenged the opponents of slavery "to prove that the white laborers of the North are as happy, as contented, or as comfortable as the slaves of the South."[80] George Fitzhugh's *Cannibals All!,* in 1857, became the standard Southern expositor of the thesis, which remained a permanent principle in the proslavery argument.[81]

The assertion that the institution of slavery was the best labor system naturally produced a correlative claim that it was likewise most advantageous for the employer. Calhoun believed that under slavery it was impossible "that . . . conflict can take

---

September 19, 1858; and the New Orleans *True Delta*, May 27, 1859. A good reply to Fitzhugh is that of Gamaliel Bailey, "The Failure of Free Society," *The National Era*, August 16, 1855.

[80] Quoted by *The Anti Slavery Bugle*, September 20, and October 18, 1856. The Columbia, S. C., *Times*, quoted *ibid.*, January 20, 1855, and the Franklin, Louisiana, *Planters' Banner*, quoted in *The National Anti Slavery Standard*, May 10, 1849, come to similar conclusions.

[81] See also *The Pro-Slavery Argument, op. cit.,* 52-53. For Northern replies, see the Lynn *Record*, quoted in *The Liberator*, July 16, 1841; "White Slavery and Black Slavery," *The Weekly Herald and Philanthropist*, December 2 and 9, 1846; "Free and Slave Labor," *The National Era*, March 16, 1848; and S. B. Treadwell, *op. cit.,* 438-66. A conclusive treatment of this argument is Wilfrid Carsel, "The Slaveholder's Indictment of Northern Wage Slavery," *Journal of Southern History* VI (November, 1940), 504-21.

place between labor and capital," whereas T. R. R. Cobb pointed out that no solution to this conflict was so simple and effective as slavery, for "by making the laborer himself capital, the conflict ceases, and the interests become identical."[82] Strikes, the Southerners repeated, never occurred under slavery, while the labor troubles of the North showed "that the freedom of the laboring classes is dangerous to the welfare of society, and that the peculiar institutions of the North are inferior to those of the South."[83] Adoption of slavery in the Northern factory system, it was argued, would end the division between laborer and employer and result in greater security for both.[84]

In the same manner some Southerners claimed slavery's superiority over free society as a foundation for an enduring and truly republican government. Calhoun called slavery "the most solid and durable foundation on which to rear free and stable institutions." Hammond explained that it was actually "the cornerstone of the republican edifice" since it prevented "the ignorant, poor and therefore untrustworthy and unstable portion of the population from exercising political influence."[85] Robert Barnwell Rhett believed slavery to be "the conservative feature of Republican government—history furnishes no instance of a lasting republic where it did not exist," and the Richmond *South* agreed that it was "one of the best securities of real freedom."[86] The history of Northern free society, "marked for seventy years by a horrid alternation of famine and revolution," proved its inadequacy as a political system; in the South "the tyranny of the numerical majority" could not

[82] R. K. Crallé, ed., *The Works of John C. Calhoun*, III:180, and T. R. R. Cobb, *An Historical Sketch of Slavery . . .*, ccxiv.

[83] *The Anti Slavery Bugle*, August 10, 1850, and January 19, 1856.

[84] "A Citizen of Virginia," *The Union Past and Future*, 38.

[85] Crallé, *op. cit.*, II:362, and *DeBow's Review* VII (October, 1849), 296. For a further development of the idea, see M. Estes' *A Defence of Negro Slavery as It Exists in the United States*, 168-72. Birney's long analysis of this argument, which he called "the South Carolina doctrine of aristocracy," in *The Philanthropist* for March 18, 1837, traces it from Sir Robert Filmore through Leigh, Pickens, and McDuffie to Calhoun, its chief expositor.

[86] *The Anti Slavery Bugle*, July 26, 1851, and the Richmond *South*, July 8, 1858.

exist under slavery, and if republican government were to endure, it must perforce have its roots in slavery.[87]

The "positive good" thesis furnished the abolitionists with ample evidence of the danger facing Northern freemen. If slavery was a positive good, and the superior political, economic, and social system that the South claimed it to be, it seemed reasonable to expect that the next step would be an attempt to impose it upon the nation at large for the nation's own good. "Common sense," said Birney in 1836, "will soon teach those who are disposed to think or reason at all, that slavery must not be advocated in any manner or degree, unless . . . it be a blessing, and necessary to the well-being of society."[88] The course of the proslavery argument vividly carried out his prediction.

Basing their claims upon evidence provided by intemperate statements emanating from proslavery radicals, the abolitionists believed the real objective of the Slave Power was the extension of slavery to white men. Francis P. Blair accused the Southern slaveholder of desiring "the enslavement of the dependent class of the free white population"; Seward, in a speech at Rochester in 1858, was of the same opinion, and Doolittle of Wisconsin repeated the charge in Congress.[89] Certain aspects of the Southern argument encouraged such accusations. As one Southern paper pointed out, "The laws of the slave states justify the holding of white men in bondage. . . . Differences of race, of lineage, of language, of habits, and customs, all tend to render the institution more durable. . . ."[90]

It was easy, said the abolitionists, to take one more step, to show that if slavery were the best system for inferior races, it was also the best for inferior classes, regardless of race. The

[87] The Richmond *Enquirer*, quoted by *The National Era*, August 9, 1855, and "A Citizen of Virginia," *op. cit.*, 36-42.

[88] *The Philanthropist*, July 29, 1836.

[89] Blair, "The Influence of Slavery upon the Non-Slaveholding People of the South," *The Anti Slavery Bugle*, October 11, 1856; G. E. Baker, ed., *Works of W. H. Seward*, IV:289-292; and Doolittle, *Appendix to the Congressional Globe, 36th Congress, 1st Session*, January 3, 1860, 98, 103.

[90] *The National Anti Slavery Standard*, October 11, 1856. In William Goodell's scrapbook in the Oberlin College Library, this clipping bears the marginal comment in Goodell's hand, "Irish? German?"

Richmond *Enquirer,* in 1856, explained this with bone-chilling clarity in an editorial that was endlessly quoted in the Northern press and even inserted in the *Congressional Globe*:

> Until recently the defence of slavery has labored under great difficulties, because its apologists were merely apologists, took half-way ground. They confined the defence to mere *negro slavery,* thereby giving up the slavery principle, admitting other forms of slavery to be wrong, and yielding up the authority of the Bible, and of the history, practices, and experience of mankind.—Human experience, showing the universal success of slave society, and the universal failure of free society, was unavailing to them, because they were precluded from employing it, by admitting slavery in the abstract to be wrong. The defence of mere negro slavery involved them in still greater difficulty. The laws of all the Southern states justified the holding of white men in slavery, provided that through the mother they were descended, however remotely, from a negro slave. The bright mulattoes, according to their theory, were wrongfully held in slavery.
>
> The line of defence, however, is changed now, and the North is completely cornered, and dumb as an oyster. The South now maintains that slavery is right, natural, and necessary. It shows that all divine and almost all human authority justifies it. The South further charges, that the little experiment of free society has been, from the beginning, a cruel failure, and that symptoms of failure are abundant in our North. While it is far more obvious that negroes be slaves than whites—for they are only fit to labor, not to direct—yet the principle of slavery is in itself right, and does not depend on difference of complection.[91]

George Fitzhugh, speaking of England but with implied American applications, suggested that "The only way to permanently and efficiently remedy the complicated evils (*of poverty*) would be to enslave the whole of the people of England who have not property." The Richmond *Examiner,* pointing out that slaves in Biblical times were not Negroes, believed that "confining the jurisdiction of slavery to that race would be to weaken its

[91] Quoted by G. M. Weston, *Who Are and Who May Be Slaves,* 2; *The Radical Abolitionist,* October, 1857; and *The Anti Slavery Bugle,* October 11, 1856.

scriptural authority. . . . Slavery black or white is necessary."[92] Such statements were tirelessly quoted in the abolitionist press, and in conjunction with a few cases at law in the South involving white slavery, were no doubt worth the wide publicity they received.[93]

At an early stage in the antislavery controversy the abolitionists recognized that although Negroes were slaves in the South, the institution of slavery was not based on color—in fact, they reasoned, qualities far more important than complexion could be employed as pretexts for enslavement. Neither the Constitution nor the fugitive slave law of 1793 made any clear distinction between white and black slaves; slavery was a matter of condition, not of color, and the child followed the legal status of the mother under slavery.[94] If a person who was 99.99 percent white could, through the status of the mother, be made a slave upon claim of the mother's owner, the next step was an easy one to take.[95] The fugitive slave laws, and the Prigg and Dred Scott rulings tended to strengthen the argument. If there was no distinction between white and black slavery, and if a slaveholder possessed the right to pursue a slave into any state, he might kidnap and claim ownership of a white person.[96]

[92] *The Anti Slavery Bugle*, November 3, 1855, and September 20, 1856. The New York *Day Book* agreed with Fitzhugh that the children of the poor should be sold into slavery, according to *The Radical Abolitionist*, October, 1857. The established New England custom of "selling the poor" for labor seems to have escaped the notice of the abolitionists.

[93] White slave cases were reported in *The Anti Slavery Bugle*, February 19, 1847, February 25, 1858, and October 9, 1857; in *The National Era*, August 5, 1849, November 16 and December 7, 1854, and June 9 and September 15, 1859; in *The National Anti Slavery Standard*, August 2, 1849, and in "White Slavery in the United States," *Anti Slavery Tract Number 2*.

[94] *Proceedings of the Rhode Island Anti Slavery Convention . . .*, op. cit., 25; William Goodell, *The Anti Slavery Lecturer* I (August and September, 1839) , and *The Radical Abolitionist* II (June, 1857) , 96.

[95] "White Slaves," *The Philanthropist*, November 12, 1839. Frequently cited was the case of Sally Miller, or Salome Muller, of Louisiana, whom a jury could not decide was legally black or white, but who had been held as a slave for twenty-five years. The case is fully reported in *The Anti Slavery Bugle*, February 25, 1848.

[96] See Greeley on the Prigg decision, the New York *Tribune*, March 12, 1842; Frederick Frothingham on the fugitive slave law of 1850, *The National Anti Slavery Standard*, June 28, 1856; the *Illinois State Journal* on the Dred Scott case, quoted by Craven, op. cit., 386; and *The Speech of*

"The truth is," said the abolitionists, "the law of Southern slavery does not prescribe any color, or race, for either masters or slaves, and in point of fact, the institution does not rest upon distinction of race at all." The only reason for using pigmentation to vindicate Southern slavery was that the Negro, who by reason of his condition could be made a slave, happened to have a different color.[97] Legally, therefore, there was nothing to prevent the extension of slavery to whites, and such, it was presumed, was the intent of the Slave Power.[98] If white slavery were justified legally, it was also justified, according to the implications of the proslavery argument, by Biblical, moral, and natural right. "If slaveholding be a natural right," reasoned William Goodell, "then all men have a right to be slaveholders, and to make slaves of all whom they can overpower and control." If slavery, it was argued, was based upon "the right of the stronger class to enslave the weaker . . . , where is the man," asked the abolitionists, "who may not at any moment become a slave?"[99] As James Russell Lowell's Yankee commentator "Ezekiel Biglow" pointed out,

> Wy, it's jest ez clear ez figgers,
>   Clear ez one an' one make two,
> Chaps thet make black slaves o' n——s,
>   Want to make wite slaves o' you.[100]

The abolitionists made an especial effort to convince Northern immigrant groups of the stake they held in the consequent

John Hutchens of Ohio, Delivered in the House of Representatives, May 2, 1860, 4-5.

[97] G. M. Weston, *op. cit.,* 2, and *The Philanthropist,* July 29, 1836. See also G. M. Stroud, *A Sketch of the Laws Relating to Slavery in the Several States . . .,* Chapter I, and "An American," *America's Misfortune, A Practical View of Slavery,* for detailed discussions of slavery laws and color.

[98] Garrison to the American Anti Slavery Association Anniversary, *The Anti Slavery Bugle,* June 2, 1855.

[99] *The American Jubilee,* March, 1855, and *The Speech of the Hon. Sidney Edgerton of Ohio, Delivered in the House . . .,* February 29, 1860, 4. See Lincoln's lucid analysis of this question, Nicolay and Hay, *op. cit.,* I:178-79.

[100] Lowell, *The Biglow Papers: First Series,* 1848.

defeat of the Slave Power conspiracy to rob them of their freedom. The Massachusetts Anti Slavery Society, for example, resolved at a Faneuil Hall meeting in November of 1843 that "American slavery is the deadliest foe of the rights of labor; and therefore . . . , ought to be the object of special indignation and alarm to the hardworking Irish emigrant."[101] The rise of nativism in politics, beginning with the Native American party and culminating in the Know-Nothing movement of the 'fifties, gave the abolitionists a chance to join slavery and nativism as related dangers to the foreign-born; the Know-Nothing party, some of the antislavery leaders maintained, was merely the Slave Power plot in its political phase. The immigrant, therefore, must for his own interests cleave to the abolitionist cause, else as the Cincinnati *Freeman* phrased it, "What security have the Germans and Irish that their children will not, within a hundred years, be reduced to slavery in this land of their adoption?"[102] The Slave Power intended to enslave the immigrant by making servitude a prerequisite to citizenship, and by then denying him citizenship.[103]

Evidence to substantiate the "plot" against the immigrant was somewhat scanty. The Richmond *Whig*, it is true, did say that one of the advantages of slavery was that it excluded "a populace made up of the dregs of Europe," (a jab at New York and Boston) and the Raleigh, North Carolina, *Register* and the Lynchburg *Virginian* both expressed the fear that foreign immigration was inimical to slavery. But for the most part the

---

[101] *The National Anti Slavery Standard,* January 4, 1844.

[102] Quoted by *The Anti Slavery Bugle,* August 30, 1856. See also, for the abolitionist stand on nativism, "The New Party and Slavery," *The National Era,* November 16 and 23, 1854; "The Fruit Beginning to Appear," *ibid.,* July 12, 1855; "Fugitive Slaves, Free Negroes, and Naturalized Citizens," *ibid.,* June 30, 1859, and a letter from George Julian, *ibid.,* November 30, 1855; and J. G. Fee, "The South and Know nothingism," *ibid.,* March 22, 1855; and "Nativism" and "Native Americanism," *The Weekly Herald and Philanthropist,* October 23, November 26, and December 4, 1844. The most politically-minded of the abolitionist editors, Bailey of *The National Era* frequently reprinted items from Know-Nothing papers to prove his point, as in the issues of November 30, 1854, and November 29 and December 3, 1855.

[103] William Goodell, *The American Jubilee,* January, 1855.

abolitionists were forced to rely on statements from the Know-Nothing press to substantiate their case. The provisions of the Nebraska bill denying citizenship to aliens in the territory for five years, and the anti-foreign riots that accompanied nativistic politics, were seized upon as proof of the Slave Power's connivance against foreign minorities.[104]

The German press especially found a good deal of affinity with the abolitionists. The New York *Staatzeitung* and *Abend Zeitung, Der Freie Presse von Indiana,* the Milwaukee *Volksfreund, Corsair,* and *Newsbode,* the Cleveland German monthly *Atlanti,* the Albany *Freie Blatter,* the Philadelphia *German National Gazette* and *Turnzeitung,* the Illinois *German Tribune,* the Cincinnati *Freeman, Hochwachter,* and *Turnzeitung,* and other papers like them adopted an antislavery, free-soil stand, while the influence of men such as Carl Schurz and C. C. Follen turned many immigrants to the abolitionist cause.[105] The National Convention of German Turners in 1855 went on record as opposing slavery and its extension into free territory, while the Germans of Chicago, Milwaukee, St. Louis, and Cincinnati, according to *The Ohio Columbian,* were overwhelmingly abolitionist in sympathy. But the Northern German population, though deeply concerned with the abolition and secession issues, was at the same time more directly interested in homestead bills and labor legislation, and though sympathetic to the antislavery groups, by no means gave the support for which the abolitionists hoped.[106]

[104] *The Philanthropist,* January 27, 1837; the Richmond *Whig,* September 17, 1856; "The Nebraska Bill," *The National Era,* March 16, 1854; "The Louisville Mob," *ibid.,* August 16, 1855; "The Mob Triumph in Philadelphia," *The Weekly Herald and Philanthropist,* July 15, 1844; and "Mobs and Their Causes," *ibid.,* August 2, 1844.

[105] Items in *The National Era,* July 28 and December 22, 1853, December 13, 1855, and January 17, 1856; in *The Anti Slavery Bugle,* December 15 and 29, 1855; and in *The Massachusetts Abolitionist,* August 15, 1839. Perhaps the clearest exposition of slavery's threat to the immigrant is Schurz' Springfield, Mass., speech of January 4, 1860, reprinted in *The National Era,* February 2, 1860.

[106] The Mobile and Charleston Turners seceded from the national organization after the 1855 convention; see the account of the controversy in *The National Era,* December 20, 1855, and January 17, 1856. *The Ohio*

It was not the abolitionist warning of the threat to the liberties of the foreign-born, but other factors, primarily economic and political, which enlisted their support in the antislavery cause. The abolitionist campaign to convince the immigrant of the threat of white slavery must be written off as largely a failure, and after 1856 and the decline of Know-Nothingism, little more was said about it.

The abolitionist contention that there existed a Slave Power conspiracy which threatened the existence of personal and civil liberty, and even republican government itself, helped materially to mold Northern opinion during the years of the slavery controversy. As the Southern charge that abolitionists were conspiring to foment revolt, miscegenation, and social disorder tended to unify certain classes of the South in support of slavery, so did the abolitionist accusation tend to enlist support of certain Northern classes for the antislavery movement. "Where will it end?" asked the august *Atlantic Monthly,* assuredly not an abolitionist journal, in 1857:

Mighty events are at hand, even at the door; and the mission of all will be to fix Slavery firmly and forever on the throne of this nation. Is the success of this conspiracy to be final and eternal? Are the States which name themselves, in simplicity or irony, the Free States, to be always the satrapies of a central power like this?[107]

In some ways the "great Slave Power plot" overshadowed the importance in the public mind of "the abolitionist plot," by identifying the slaveholder with a greater conspiracy of infinitely more dangerous designs. Then, too, the abolitionist claim tended to discredit the proslavery argument by discovering in it broadly sinister implications, and by carrying its logic to the ultimate absurdity. The "Slave Power Threat" helped to widen the schism between proslavery and antislavery men

---

Columbian is quoted *ibid.,* December 13, 1855. The German population in the South, however, consistently supported slavery; see Andreas Dorpalen, "The German Element and the Issues of the Civil War," *Mississippi Valley Historical Review* XXIX (June, 1942), 55-76.
[107] "Where Will it End?" *Atlantic Monthly* I (1857), 22-46.

by making it more difficult than before to be neutral toward or tolerant of slavery or its extension.

The issue, as the abolitionist saw it, admitted of no compromise. Identifying their cause with the greater cause of freedom, and with the interests of large and unorganized special groups such as laborers or immigrants, the abolitionists considered themselves to be (and convinced others that they were) the sole remaining protectors of civil and political rights. The "Slave Power Threat" personified the proslavery argument, made it vivid and concrete, and dramatized the controversy into a contest between the forces of good and evil, of freedom and repression, of democracy and aristocracy. When war came, it was justified by the abolitionists and many others as the final defense against the assaults of the Slave Power on traditional American liberties. The South waged war, it was said, ". . . not against Abolitionism or Republicanism, *per se,* but against free institutions and the democratic theory of government universally."[108] Had it not been for their alertness and courage, the abolitionists said, "We should have had a nation in which were only two classes, *masters and slaves.* The antislavery people contributed to enlighten the people in regard to the villainous purposes and character of slavery . . . , and educated and awakened the people to vigilance to preserve their own liberties."[109]

Was there a Slave Power conspiracy, and were the abolitionists correct in ascribing to it the evil designs which formed so large and important a part of their propaganda? In the sense of the term as used by Wilson, Goodell, Bailey, Garrison,

· [108] Anonymous, *Southern Hatred of Free Institutions,* 10.

[109] Marius Robinson, undated lecture notes, Western Reserve Historical Society, Cleveland. Abolitionists always contended that the credit for arousing the North to the threat of slavery to freedom, and for unifying the North in the struggle against it, belonged to them. See H. W. Beecher's address of October 29, 1865, in *Patriotic Addresses,* 717 ff.; Wendell Phillips' Boston speech, *The National Anti Slavery Standard,* May 19, 1853; and his "Public Opinion," in *Speeches, Letters, and Lectures,* 52; and Joshua Giddings' scrapbook for 1856, in the Ohio State Archaeological and Historical Collections, in which he listed the contributions of the abolitionists to national security.

and others—a secret and highly organized group with conscious aims of imposing restrictions upon traditional liberties—the "Slave Power conspiracy" had no real existence. The South was never so completely unified as the antislavery press claimed. There was Southern disagreement upon such issues as Texas annexation, the Mexican War, the Wilmot Proviso, the 1859 Compromise, and the Kansas question.[110] Yet there was agreement among Southern leaders that slavery was a good system, probably the best, and that it should be retained and possibly extended. Certainly the events of the period 1830 to 1860 showed that in preserving and extending slavery the South was willing to infringe upon basic civil and personal rights. The Calhoun-Fitzhugh school of thought, that slavery was "a positive good," was something more than a defense of slavery; it was also a counterattack on free institutions.[111] While the "conspiracy" of which the abolitionists warned was no doubt an alliance of common economic and political interests, its inherent threat seemed to the times more than idle. The alliance itself was motivated by and founded upon the cardinal principle of slavery—the master principle—and the abolitionists were perhaps not wholly wrong in believing that its continued existence jeopardized the American tradition.

[110] See C. S. Boucher, *"In re* that Aggressive Slaveocracy," *Mississippi Valley Historical Review* (June-September, 1921), 13-80.

[111] See R. N. Current, "John C. Calhoun, Philosopher of Reaction," *The Antioch Review* (Summer, 1943), 223-34. It should not be forgotten that the South believed, to a large extent, that there was also a Northern "conspiracy," or at least a community of Northern opinion, bent on destroying Southern institutions and substituting a tumultuous, levelling free society which violated the whole spirit of Southern civilization. See the summary by Howard K. Beale of the rival conspiracy theories, "What Historians Have Said About the Causes of the Civil War," *Theory and Practice in Historical Study* (New York, 1946), 58-60.

A Final Estimate

THE ABOLITION CRUSADE was successful, of course, not simply because it managed to merge antislavery with civil liberties. Many other factors—ideological, political, and economic, were involved—yet it is plain from a study of the period that the abolition movement became inextricably bound up with the preservation of civil liberties, and that the relationship strengthened it and helped mobilize Northern opinion on its side. The controversy over slavery and civil liberties assisted, certainly, in turning anti-Southern into antislavery sentiment.

The abolitionists were, it is true, not above using civil rights as a stalking horse (as in the petition strategy), or playing on public sympathies (as in the numerous fugitive slave cases), or making the most of the opportunities that Southern extremism offered. But they were ready, always, to place their cause above all else. Weld and Stanton facing mobs, Birney risking security and property, Garrison accepting a lifetime of excoriation and abuse, the Tappans spending their fortune, hundreds of nameless lecturers, agents, and slaverunners risking discouragement, discomfort, disapproval, possibly injury and prison—all this is not to be dismissed as opportunism. They were obsessed with the idea that all men should be free.

Whether their labors were mistaken or ill-advised is not the question. The point is that they all were sincerely concerned with the preservation of freedom in their struggle to end slavery.

There were naturally large numbers of moderates both below and above the Ohio River who frowned upon both abolition radical and proslavery extremist. A majority of Northerners disapproved of the fanaticism of the Garrisonians, as certainly a large number of intelligent Southerners disagreed with the Ruffin-McDuffie-Hammond-Fitzhugh school of thought. The stereotype "abolitionist" no more represented the median of Northern opinion than the stereotype "slavocrat" represented the South. But while the average Northerner might disapprove of what Elijah Lovejoy thought and did, he believed implicitly in his right to think and do it, for he and Lovejoy possessed that right in common. The moderate Southerner might dislike the absurdities that emanated from the "positive good" apologists, and at the same time fiercely maintain the slaveholder's right to protect and retain his property, his economic system, and his distinctive civilization, for it was his civilization too. There were principles at stake on both sides.

The inevitable result of the argument between abolitionists and their opponents was to make not only Negroes, but rights, the point of conflict. The insistence upon the moral and legal right of a minority to speak and be heard, with full protection from suppression or interference, became in time nearly as important to the controversy as the abolition of the slave system. The net effect was to gain for abolition a body of supporters who thought less of the wrongs of the slave than of the rights of the white man   which helps to explain the contention of Lincoln and Seward that the Republican party was founded to protect white men, not black. The antislavery movement flourished under persecution. The abolitionists, and those in the North whose sympathies led them to see slavery as a threat to freedom, eventually united to protect those rights, basic to a democracy, by abolishing slavery.

Bibliography of Sources

I. General Studies, Biographies, and Collections

Adams, Alice D. *The Neglected Period of Anti-Slavery*. Boston, 1908.
Aptheker, Herbert. *Negro Slave Revolts in the United States*. New York, 1939.
Aptheker, Herbert. *The Negro in the Abolition Movement*. New York, 1941.
Aptheker, Herbert. *American Negro Slave Revolts*. New York, 1943.
Barnes, G. H. *The Antislavery Impulse*. New York, 1933.
Bassett, J. S. *Anti-Slavery Leaders of North Carolina*. Baltimore, 1898.
Bassett, J. S. *Slavery in the State of North Carolina*. Baltimore, 1899.
Beale, H. K. *A History of the Freedom of Teaching in American Schools*. New York, 1941.
Beardsley, Frank G. *A Mighty Winner of Souls: Charles G. Finney*. New York, 1937.
Birney, William. *James G. Birney and His Times*. New York, 1890.
Bodo, John. *The Protestant Clergy and Public Issues, 1812-1848*. Princeton, N.J., 1954.
Bone, W. P. *A History of Cumberland University, 1842-1935*. Lebanon, Tennessee, 1935.
Breyfogle, William. *Make Free: The Story of the Underground Railroads*. Philadelphia, 1958.
Burgess, J. W. *The Middle Period, 1817-1858*. New York, 1897.
Campbell, Mary Emily R. *The Attitude of Tennesseans Toward the Union*. New York, 1961.
Carpenter, J. T. *The South as a Conscious Minority, 1789-1861*. New York, 1930.
Carrington, Henry B. *Theodore Weld and a Famous Quartette*. Boston, 1904.
Catterall, Helen T. *Judicial Cases Concerning American Slavery*. Washington, 1929.

Chafee, Zechariah, Jr. *Freedom of Speech*. New York, 1920.
Chapman, John Jay. *William Lloyd Garrison*. New York, 1913.
Chester, Giraud. *Embattled Maiden: The Life of Anna Dickinson*. New York, 1951.
Cheyney, E. P. *Freedom of Inquiry and Expression*. Philadelphia, 1938.
Clarke, James Freeman. *Anti-Slavery Days*. New York, 1884.
Cochran, W. C. *The Fugitive Slave Law in the Western Reserve*. Cleveland, 1920.
Cole, Charles C. *The Social Ideas of the Northern Evangelists*. New York, 1954.
Coleman, J. W. *Slavery Times In Kentucky*. Chapel Hill, 1940.
Commager, Henry Steele. *Theodore Parker*. Boston, 1947.
Commons, John R., ed. *A History of Labor in the United States*. New York, 1921.
Cooley, H. S. *Slavery in New Jersey*. Baltimore, 1896.
Craven, Avery O. *Civil War in the Making, 1815-1860*. Baton Rouge, 1959.
Craven, Avery O. *The Coming of the Civil War*. New York, 1942.
Craven, Avery O. *Edmund Ruffin, Southerner*. New York, 1932.
Craven, Avery O. *The Growth of Southern Nationalism*. Baton Rouge, 1953.
Cromwell, Otelia. *Lucretia Mott*. Cambridge, Massachusetts, 1958.
Cutter, James E. *Lynch Law*. New York, 1905.
Dabney, Virginius. *Liberalism in the South*. Chapel Hill, 1932.
Del Porto, Joseph. *A Study of the Antislavery Journals* (unpublished doctoral dissertation, Michigan State University, 1953).
Dillon, Merton L. *Elijah P. Lovejoy, Abolitionist Editor*. Urbana, Illinois, 1961.
Dodd, W. E. *The Cotton Kingdom*. New Haven, 1919.
Donald, David. *Lincoln Reconsidered: Essays on the Civil War Era*. New York, 1956.
Drake, Thomas E. *Quakers and Slavery in America*. New Haven, 1959.
Dumond, D. L. *Antislavery Origins of the Civil War*. Ann Arbor, 1939.
Dumond, D. L. *Antislavery: The Crusade for Freedom in America*. Ann Arbor, 1962.
Dumond, D. L., ed. *The Letters of James G. Birney*. New York, 1938.
Dumond, D. L. and Barnes, G. H., eds. *The Letters of Theodore D. Weld, Angelina Grimké Weld, and Sarah Grimké*. New York, 1934.
Dunn, Jacob P. *Indiana: A Redemption from Slavery*. Boston and New York, 1891.
Dunn, Jacob P. *Slavery Petitions and Papers*. Indianapolis, 1894.
Eaton, Clement. *Freedom of Thought in the Old South*. Durham, 1940.
Eaton, Clement. *The Growth of Southern Civilization, 1790-1860*. New York, 1961.
Elkins, Stanley. *Slavery: A Problem in American Institutional and Intellectual Life*. Chicago, 1959.

Filler, Louis. *The Crusade Against Slavery*. New York, 1960.

Fine, Nathan. *Labor and Farmer Parties in the United States, 1828-1928*. New York, 1928.

Fladeland, Betty. *James Gillespie Birney: Slaveholder to Abolitionist*. Ithaca, 1955.

Flanders, R. B. *Plantation Slavery in Georgia*. Chapel Hill, 1933.

Fletcher, Robert S. *A History of Oberlin College*. Oberlin, Ohio, 1943.

Floan, Howard R. *The South in Northern Eyes, 1831-1861*. Austin, Texas, 1958.

Foner, Philip. *Business and Slavery*. Chapel Hill, 1941.

Foner, Philip, ed. *The Life and Writings of Frederick Douglass*. New York, 1950-52.

Fox, Early L. *The American Colonization Society, 1817-1840*. Baltimore, 1919.

Franklin, J. H. *The Free Negro in North Carolina, 1790-1860*. Chapel Hill, 1943.

Franklin, J. H. *From Slavery to Freedom: A History of the American Negro*. New York, 1947.

Friedel, Frank. *Francis Lieber: Nineteenth Century Liberal*. Baton Rouge, 1948.

Furnas, J. C. *Goodbye to Uncle Tom*. New York, 1956.

Gara, Larry. *The Liberty Line: The Legend of the Underground Railroad*. Lexington, Kentucky, 1961.

Gill, John. *Tide Without Turning: Elijah P. Lovejoy and the Freedom of the Press*. Boston, 1959.

Graham, Shirley. *There Was Once a Slave: The Story of Frederick Douglass*. New York, 1947.

Green, F. M. *Constitutional Development in the South Atlantic States, 1776-1860*. Chapel Hill, 1930.

Hamilton, J. G. deR. *Benjamin Sherwood Hedrick*. Baltimore, 1910.

Harris, Herbert. *American Labor*. New Haven, 1938.

Harris, N. D. *The History of Negro Servitude in Illinois*. Chicago, 1904.

Hart, Albert B. *Slavery and Abolition*. New York, 1906.

Harveson, M. E. *Catherine E. Beecher*. Philadelphia, 1932.

Herbert, Hilary. *The Abolition Crusade and its Consequences*. New York, 1912.

Hesseltine, W. B. *A History of the South*. New York, 1936.

Hickok, C. T. *The Negro in Ohio, 1802-1870*. Cleveland, 1896.

Hofstadter, Richard, and Metzger, Walter. *The Development of Academic Freedom*. New York, 1955.

Hopkins, Vincent. *Dred Scott's Case*. New York, 1951.

Hoss, Elijah Embree. *Elihu Embree, Abolitionist*. Nashville, 1897.

Hume, John F. *The Abolitionists*. New York, 1905.

Jenkins, W. S. *Pro-Slavery Thought in the Old South*. Chapel Hill, 1935.

Johnson, G. G. *Antebellum North Carolina*. Chapel Hill, 1937.

Ketring, Ruth A. *Charles Osborn in the Anti-Slavery Movement*. Columbus, Ohio, 1937.

Knight, Edgar W., ed. *A Documentary History of Education in the South Before 1860.* Five volumes. Chapel Hill, 1949.

Lader, Lawrence. *The Bold Brahmins: New England's War Against Slavery.* New York, 1961.

Lefler, Hugh T. *Hinton Rowan Helper: Advocate of a White America.* Charlottesville, Virginia, 1935.

Lefler, Hugh T. *A History of North Carolina.* Two volumes. New York, 1956.

Lien, A. J. *Privileges and Immunities of the Citizens of the United States.* New York, 1913.

Litwack, Leon. *North of Slavery: The Negro in the Free States, 1790-1860.* Chicago, 1961.

Lloyd, A. Y. *The Slavery Controversy, 1831-1860.* Chapel Hill, 1939.

Loomis, Willard D. *The Antislavery Movement in Ashtabula County, Ohio, 1834-1854.* Cleveland (unpublished dissertation, Western Reserve University).

McDougall, M. G. *Fugitive Slaves, 1619-1865.* Boston, 1891.

McGregor, J. C. *The Disruption of Virginia.* New York, 1922.

McNeill, George E. *The Labor Movement.* New York, 1887.

Macy, Jesse. *The Anti-Slavery Crusade.* New Haven, 1919.

Malin, James C. *The Nebraska Question, 1852-54.* Lawrence, Kansas, 1953.

Mandel, Bernard. *Labor: Free and Slave.* New York, 1955.

Mann, C. W. *The Chicago Common Council and the Fugitive Law of 1850.* Chicago, 1903.

Martin, Asa E. *Anti-Slavery in Kentucky Prior to 1850.* Louisville, 1918.

Mellon, Matthew T. *Early American Views on Negro Slavery.* Boston, 1934.

Merritt, Elizabeth. *James Henry Hammond, 1807-1864.* Baltimore, 1923.

Mooney, Charles C. *Slavery in Tennessee.* Bloomington, Indiana, 1957.

Moore, Glover. *The Missouri Controversy.* Lexington, Kentucky, 1953.

Muelder, Hermann P. *Fighters for Freedom: The History of the Antislavery Activities of Men and Women Associated with Knox College.* New York, 1959.

Munford, Beverly B. *Virginia's Attitude Toward Slavery and Secession.* New York, 1909.

Nevins, A. and Weitenkampf, F., eds. *A Century of Political Cartoons.* New York, 1944.

Nye, Russel B. *William Lloyd Garrison and the Humanitarian Reformers.* Boston, 1954.

O'Neal, James. *The Workers in American History.* New York, 1921.

Osterweis, Rollin G. *Romanticism and Nationalism in the Old South.* New Haven, 1949.

Perkins, H. C. *Northern Editorials on Secession.* New York, 1942.

Perry, Bliss, ed. *The Heart of Emerson's Journals.* New York, 1926.

Phillips, U. B. *American Negro Slavery.* New York, 1918.

Phillips, U. B. *Life and Labor in the Old South*. Boston, 1929.

Pierce, B. L. *Public Opinion and the Teaching of History in the United States*. New York, 1926.

Polk, William M. *Leonidas Polk, Bishop and General*. New York, 1915.

Quaife, M. M. *The Doctrine of Non-Intervention with Slavery in the Territories*. Chicago, 1910.

Quarles, Benjamin. *Frederick Douglass*. Washington, D. C., 1948.

Reilley, E. C. *The Early Slavery Controversy in the Western Reserve*. Cleveland, 1940 (unpublished dissertation, Western Reserve University).

Reuter, E. B. *The American Race Problem*. New York, 1938.

Rice, Madeleine H. *American Catholic Opinion in the Slavery Controversy*. New York, 1944.

Richardson, J. D. *Messages and Papers of the Presidents*. Washington, D. C., 1896.

Ritchie, William. *The Public Career of Cassius M. Clay*. Nashville, 1934.

Roberts, Joseph C. *The Road from Monticello*. Durham, North Carolina, 1941.

Rogers, Lindsay. *The Postal Power of Congress: A Study in Constitutional Expansion*. Baltimore, 1916.

Russel, R. R. *Economic Aspects of Southern Sectionalism, 1840-1861*. Urbana, Illinois, 1924.

Russell, John H. *The Free Negro in Virginia, 1619-1865*. Baltimore, 1913.

Savage, W. S. *The Controversy over the Distribution of Abolition Literature*. Washington, D. C., 1938.

Scarborough, Ruth. *Opposition to Slavery in Georgia Prior to 1861*. Nashville, 1933.

Seitz, Don C. *Horace Greeley*. Indianapolis, 1926.

Sellers, James B. *Slavery in Alabama*. University, Alabama, 1950.

Sherwin, Oscar. *Prophet of Liberty: The Life and Times of Wendell Phillips*. New York, 1958.

Siebert, W. H. *The Mysteries of Ohio's Underground Railroads*. Columbus, Ohio, 1951.

Siebert, W. H. *The Underground Railroad from Slavery to Freedom*. New York, 1938.

Siebert, W. H. *Vermont's Anti-Slavery and Underground Railroad Record*. Columbus, Ohio, 1937.

Simkins, Francis B. *The South Old and New*. New York, 1947.

Simms, Henry H. *A Decade of Sectional Controversy, 1851-1861*. Chapel Hill, 1942.

Skipper, Otis. *J. D. B. DeBow: Magazinist of the Old South*. Athens, Georgia, 1958.

Smiley, David L. *Lion of Whitehall: The Life of Cassius M. Clay*. Madison, Wisconsin, 1962.

Smith, T. V. *The American Philosophy of Equality*. Chicago, 1927.

Smith, Theodore C. *The Liberty and Free Soil Parties in the Northwest*. New York, 1897.

Smith, Theodore C. *Parties and Slavery.* New York, 1906.
Smith, Timothy L. *Revivalism and Social Reform in Mid-Nineteenth Century America.* New York, 1957.
Stampp, Kenneth M. *The Peculiar Institution: Slavery in the Antebellum South.* New York, 1956.
Stanton, William R. *The Leopard's Spots: Scientific Attitudes Toward Race in America, 1815-1859.* Chicago, 1960.
Steiner, B. C. *The History of Education in Connecticut.* Washington, D. C., 1893.
Stephenson, Gilbert T. *Race Distinctions in American Law.* New York, 1910.
Sydnor, Charles S. *The Development of Southern Sectionalism.* Baton Rouge, 1948.
Taylor, Orville. *Negro Slavery in Arkansas.* Durham, North Carolina, 1958.
Thomas, Benjamin P. *Theodore Weld: Crusader for Freedom.* New Brunswick, New Jersey, 1950.
Thornbrough, Emma Lou. *The Negro in Indiana.* Indianapolis, 1957.
Trexler, H. A. *Slavery in Missouri, 1804-1865.* Baltimore, 1914.
Tuckerman, Bayard. *William Jay and the Constitutional Movement for the Abolition of Slavery.* New York, 1893.
Tyler, Alice F. *Freedom's Ferment.* Minneapolis, 1944.
Tyler, W. S. *A History of Amherst College.* New York, 1895.
Waite, Frederick C. *Western Reserve University; The Hudson Era.* Cleveland, 1943.
Weeks, Stephen B. *Southern Quakers and Slavery.* Baltimore, 1896.
Weisenburger, F. P. *The Passing of the Frontier, 1825-1850.* Columbus, Ohio, 1941.
Weld, Ralph H. *Slavery in Connecticut.* New Haven, 1935.
Wharton, Vernon L. *The Negro in Mississippi, 1865-1900.* Chapel Hill, 1947.
Whipple, Leon. *Our Ancient Liberties.* New York, 1927.
White, Laura A. *Robert Barnwell Rhett, Father of Secession.* New York, 1931.
Whitfield, T. M. *Slavery Agitation in Virginia, 1829-1832.* Baltimore, 1930.
Wiltse, Charles M. *John C. Calhoun, Nullifier.* Indianapolis, 1949.
Wiltse, Charles M. *John C. Calhoun, Sectionalist.* New York, 1951.
Wise, John S. *The End of an Era.* Boston, 1900.
Wish, Harvey. *Southern Sketches.* Charlottesville, Virginia, 1938.
Wolf, Hazel C. *On Freedom's Altar: The Martyr Complex in the Abolition Movement.* Madison, Wisconsin, 1952.
Woodburn, J. A. *Higher Education in Indiana.* Washington, D. C., 1891.
Woodson, Carter G. *The Education of the Negro Prior to 1861.* New York, 1915.
Wright, Benjamin F. *American Interpretations of Natural Law.* New York, 1931.
Wright, James M. *The Free Negro in Maryland, 1634-1860.* Baltimore, 1916.

Bibliography of Sources

II. Articles

Addington, Wendell. "Slave Insurrections in Texas," *Journal of Negro History* XXXV (October, 1950), 408-34.

Apthcker, Herbert. "Militant Abolitionism," *Journal of Negro History* XXVI (October, 1941), 438-45.

Bailey, Hugh C. "Alabama's Political Leaders and the Missouri Compromise," *Alabama Review* IX (April, 1956), 120-35.

Ballagh, J. C. "Antislavery Sentiment in Virginia," *South Atlantic Quarterly* I (April, 1902), 107-17.

Bassett, John S. "Suffrage in the State of North Carolina 1779-1861," *Annual Report of the American Historical Association for the Year 1895*, 271-95.

Boucher, C. S. "*In re* That Aggressive Slaveocracy," *Mississippi Valley Historical Review* VIII (June, 1921), 13-80.

Bowen, A. L. "The Antislavery Convention Held in Alton, Illinois, October 26-28, 1837," *Journal of the Illinois Historical Society* XX (October, 1927), 337-56.

Bradford, S. Sydney. "The Negro Ironworker in Antebellum Virginia," *Journal of Southern History* XXV (May, 1959), 194-207.

Bridges, Hal. "D. H. Hill's Anti-Yankee Algebra," *Journal of Southern History* XXII (May, 1956), 220-22.

Burroughs, W. G. "Oberlin's Part in the Slavery Conflict," *Ohio Archaeological and Historical Quarterly* XX (1911), 269-83.

Carnahan, W. J. "The Proposal to Reopen the Slave Trade," *South Atlantic Quarterly* XXV (1926), 410-30.

Carr, J. W. "The Manhood Suffrage Movement in North Carolina," *Trinity College Historical Society Papers* XI (1915), 47-78.

Carsel, Wilfrid. "The Slaveholders' Indictment of Northern Wage Slavery," *Journal of Southern History* VI (November, 1940), 504-21.

Cole, A. C. "Lincoln and the American Tradition of Civil Liberty," *Illinois State Historical Society Journal* XIX (October 1926-January 1927), 102-14.

Corwin, E. S. "The 'Higher Law' Backgrounds of American Constitutional Law," *Harvard Law Review* XLII (December 1928-January 1929), 149-85, 365-409.

Craven, A. O. "The Coming of the War between the States, An Interpretation," *Journal of Southern History* II (February-November, 1936), 303-23.

Craven, A. O. "Poor Whites and Negroes in the Antebellum South," *Journal of Negro History* XV (January, 1930), 14-26.

Crowell, J. W. "The Aftermath of Nat Turner's Insurrection," *Journal of Negro History* V (April, 1920), 208-35.

David, C. W. A. "The Fugitive Slave Law of 1793," *Journal of Negro History* IX (January, 1924), 18-23.

Davidson, J. N. "Negro Slavery in Wisconsin," and "Negro Slavery and the Underground Railroad in Wisconsin," *Parkman Club Papers* (Nos. 16, 18), Milwaukee, 1896.

Davidson, Philip. "Industrialism in the Antebellum South," *South Atlantic Quarterly* XXVII (October, 1928), 405-25.

Dillon, Merton L. "The Failure of the American Abolitionists," *Journal of Southern History* XXV (May, 1959), 159-78.

Dodd, W. E. "Freedom of Speech in the South," *Nation* 84 (April 25, 1907), 383-84.

Dorpalen, Andreas. "The German Element and the Issues of the Civil War," *Mississippi Valley Historical Review* XXIX (June, 1942), 55-66.

Durden, Robert F. "J.D.B. DeBow: Convolutions of a Slavery Expansionist," *Journal of Southern History* XVII (November, 1951), 441-62.

Eaton, Clement. "Censorship of the Southern Mails," *American Historical Review* XLVIII (January, 1943), 266-80.

Eaton, Clement. "Class Differences in the Old South," *Virginia Quarterly Review* XXXIII (Summer, 1957), 357-63.

Eaton, Clement. "A Dangerous Pamphlet in the Old South," *Journal of Southern History* II (February-November, 1936), 323-35.

Eaton, Clement. "The Freedom of the Press in the Upper South," *Mississippi Valley Historical Review* XVIII (March, 1932), 470-87.

Eaton, Clement. "The Jeffersonian Tradition of Liberalism in America," *South Atlantic Quarterly* XLIII (January, 1944), 1-10.

Eaton, Clement. "Mob Violence in the South," *Mississippi Valley Historical Review* XXIX (December, 1942), 351-71.

Eaton, Clement. "The Resistance of the South to Northern Radicalism," *New England Quarterly* VII (June, 1935), 215-31.

Eaton, Clement. "Slave Hiring in the Upper South," *Mississippi Valley Historical Review* XLVI (March, 1960), 663-78.

Evans, Robert. "Some Economic Aspects of the Domestic Slave Trade," *Southern Economic Journal* XXVII (April, 1961), 329-38.

Ezell, John S. "A Southern Education for Southrons," *Journal of Southern History* XVII (August, 1951), 303-28.

Fishback, M. M. "Illinois Legislation on Slavery and Free Negroes, 1818-1865," *Transactions of the Illinois Historical Society* (1904), 414-32.

Fornell, Earl W. "Agitation in Texas for Reopening the Slave Trade," *Southwestern Historical Quarterly* LX (October, 1956), 245-49.

Fornell, Earl W. "Abductions of Free Negroes and Slaves in Texas," *Southwestern Historical Quarterly* LX (January, 1957), 369-80.

Frasure, C. M. "Charles Sumner and the Rights of the Negro," *Journal of Negro History* XIII (April, 1928), 1-24.

French, Etta R. "Stephen Harding, A Hoosier Abolitionist," *Indiana Magazine of History* XXVII (September, 1931), 207-30.

Fuess, Claude. "Daniel Webster and the Abolitionists," *Proceedings of the Massachusetts Historical Society* LXIV (1932), 29-42.

Fuller, John D. P. "The Slavery Question and the Movement to Acquire Mexico, 1846-48," *Mississippi Valley Historical Review* XXI (June, 1934), 31-48.

Galbreath, C. D. "The Antislavery Movement in Columbiana

County," *Ohio Archaeological and Historical Quarterly* XXX (1921), 370-76.

Gara, Larry. "Propaganda Uses of the Underground Railroad," *Mid-America* XXIII (July, 1952), 155-72.

Gara, Larry. "The Underground Railroad: A Re-evaluation," *The Ohio Historical Quarterly* LXIX (July, 1960), 217-30.

Gara, Larry. "The Underground Railway: Legend or Reality?" *Proceedings of the American Philosophical Society* CV (1961), No. 3, 334-39.

Griffin, Clifford. "The Abolitionists and the Benevolent Societies," *Journal of Negro History* XLIV (July, 1959), 195-217.

Griffin, Richard W. "Poor White Laborers in Southern Cotton Factories," *South Carolina Historical Magazine* LXI (January, 1960), 26-40.

Grim, P. R. "The Reverend John Rankin, Early Abolitionist," *Ohio Archaeological and Historical Quarterly* LIV (July, 1937), 215-57.

Harrison, Lowell. "Thomas Roderick Dew, Philosopher of the Old South," *Virginia Magazine of History and Biography* LVII (October, 1949), 390-405.

Helderman, L. C. "A Social Scientist of the Old South," *Journal of Southern History* II (May, 1936), 158-74.

Helm, T. G. "Wendell Phillips and the Abolition Movement," *Reformed Church Review* XX (April, 1916), 196-227.

Hesseltine, W. B. "Some New Aspects of the Proslavery Argument," *Journal of Negro History* XXI (January, 1936), 1-15.

Hirsch, Leo. "New York and the Negro, from 1783-1865," *Journal of Negro History* XVI (October, 1931), 382-474.

Huff, O. N. "Unnamed Heroes of Old Newport," *Indiana Magazine of History* III (1907), 133-43.

Johnson, Allen. "The Constitutionality of the Fugitive Slave Acts," *Yale Law Journal* XXXI (December, 1921), 161-82.

Julian, G. W. "The Rank of Charles Osborn as an Anti-Slavery Pioneer," *Indiana Historical Society Publications* II (1891), No. 6.

Lander, Everett M. "Manufacturing in South Carolina, 1815-1860," *Business History Review* XXVII (March, 1954), 62-71.

Lofton, John. "The Enslavement of the Southern Mind, 1775-1825," *Journal of Negro History* XLIII (April, 1958), 132-39.

Long, Byron R. "Joshua Reed Giddings, A Champion of Political Freedom," *Ohio Archaeological and Historical Quarterly* XXVIII (January, 1919), 1-47.

Ludlum, R. P. "Joshua R. Giddings, Radical," *Mississippi Valley Historical Review* XXIII (June, 1936), 49-60.

Lyons, A. A. "Religious Defense of Slavery in the North," *Trinity College Historical Society Papers* (Durham, 1919), No. 13.

McCarron, Anna. "The Trial of Prudence Crandall for the Crime of Educating Negroes in Connecticut," *The Connecticut Magazine* XII (1908), 225-32.

McKibben, Davidson. "Negro Slave Insurrections in Mississippi, 1800-1865," *Journal of Negro History* XXXIV (January, 1949), 73-91.

Mabry, W. A. "Antebellum Cincinnati and its Southern Trade,"

American Studies in Honor of William Kenneth Boyd (Durham, 1940), 60-86.

Martin, Ida M. "Civil Liberties in Georgia Legislation, 1800-1830," *Georgia Historical Quarterly* XXXXV (December, 1961), 329-44.

Mason, Vroman. "The Fugitive Slave Law in Wisconsin, with Reference to Nullification Sentiment," *Proceedings of the State Historical Society of Wisconsin* (Milwaukee, 1895).

Mead, E. O. "The Underground Railroad in Ohio," *Church Historical Society Papers* X (1899).

Merkel, Benjamin G. "The Abolition Aspects of Missouri's Antislavery Controversy, 1819-1865," *Missouri Historical Review* XLIV (April, 1950), 232-54.

Merkel, Benjamin G. "The Underground Railroad and the Missouri Borders," *Missouri Historical Review* XXXVII (April, 1943), 271-86.

Miles, Edwin A. "The Mississippi Slave Insurrection Scare of 1835," *Journal of Negro History* XLII (January, 1951), 48-60.

Moore, George Ellis. "Slavery as a Factor in the Formation of West Virginia," *West Virginia History* XVII (October, 1956), 5-9.

Morris, Richard. "The Measure of Bondage in the Slave States," *Mississippi Valley Historical Review* XLI (September, 1954), 219-40.

Morrow, Ralph E. "The Proslavery Argument Revisited," *Mississippi Valley Historical Review* XLVIII (June, 1961), 79-95.

Nixon, Herman C. "DeBow's Review," *Sewanee Review* XXXIX (1931), 54-61.

Nixon, Herman C. "J.D.B. DeBow, Publicist," *Southwestern Review* XX (1934-35), 212-22.

Nogee, Joseph L. "The Prigg Case and Fugitive Slavery," *Journal of Negro History* XXXIX (July, 1954), 185-206.

Owen, T. M. "An Alabama Protest Against Abolitionism in 1835," *Gulf States Historical Magazine* II (July, 1903), 30-41.

Perkins, H. C. "The Defense of Slavery in the Northern Press on the Eve of the Civil War," *Journal of Southern History* IX (February-November, 1943), 501-32.

Phillips, U. B. "The Central Theme of Southern History," *American Historical Review* XXXIV (October, 1928), 30-44.

Preston, Emmett D. "The Fugitive Slave Acts in Ohio," *Journal of Negro History* XXVII (October, 1943), 422-78.

Price, Robert. "The Ohio Antislavery Convention of 1836," *Ohio Archaeological and Historical Quarterly* XLV (April, 1936), 180-92.

Quarles, Benjamin. "Sources of Abolitionist Income," *Mississippi Valley Historical Review* XXXII (June, 1945), 63-87.

Rammelkamp, C. H. "Illinois College and the Antislavery Movement," *Illinois Historical Society Proceedings* (1908), 192-203.

Rammelkamp, C. H. "The Reverberations of the Slavery Conflict in a Pioneer College," *Mississippi Valley Historical Review* XIV (March, 1928), 447-61.

Russell, Robert R. "The Economic History of Negro Slavery," *Agricultural History* XI (1937), 308-21.

Bibliography of Sources

Russell, Robert R. "The General Effects of Slavery upon Southern Economic Progress," *Journal of Southern History* IV (February, 1938), 34-54.

Savage, W. S. "Abolitionist Literature in the Mails, 1835-1836," *Journal of Negro History* XIII (April, 1928), 150-85.

Schmidhauser, John R. "Judicial Behavior and the Sectional Crisis of 1837-1860," *Journal of Politics* XXIII (November, 1961), 615-41.

Schwartz, Harold. "The Controversial Dred Scott Decision," *Missouri Historical Review* LIV (April, 1960), 262-73.

Shanks, C. L. "The Biblical Antislavery Argument of the Decade 1830-40," *Journal of Negro History* XVI (April, 1931), 125-32.

Shapiro, Samuel. "The Rendition of Anthony Burns," *Journal of Negro History* XLIV (January, 1959), 34-51.

Shilling, D. C. "The Relation of Southern Ohio to the South During the Decade Preceding the Civil War," *Quarterly Publications of the Historical and Philosophical Association of Ohio* VIII (1913), No. 1.

Simms, H. H. "An Analysis of Abolition Literature, 1830-40," *Journal of Southern History* VI (August, 1940), 368-439.

Small, Edwin and Miriam. "Prudence Crandall, Champion of Negro Education," *New England Quarterly* XVIII (December, 1941), 506-39.

Smiley, David L. "Cassius M. Clay and John G. Fee: A Study in Southern Antislavery Thought," *Journal of Negro History* XLII (July, 1957), 211-13.

Smith, T. V. "Slavery and the American Doctrine of Equality," *Southwestern Political and Social Science Quarterly* VII (March, 1927), 333-52.

Southall, E. P. "Arthur Tappan and the Antislavery Movement," *Journal of Negro History* XV (April, 1930), 162-98.

Stampp, Kenneth. "The Fate of the Southern Antislavery Sentiment," *Journal of Negro History* XXVIII (January, 1943), 10-22.

Stavisky, Leonard. "Industrialism in Antebellum Charleston," *Journal of Negro History* XXXVI (July, 1951), 302-33.

Strong, Sydney. "The Exodus of Students from Lane Seminary to Oberlin in 1834," *Papers of the Ohio Church History Society* IV (1893), 1-16.

Sydnor, C. S. "The Free Negro in Mississippi before the Civil War," *American Historical Review* XXXII (July, 1927), 769-88.

Sydnor, C. S. "The Southerner and the Laws," *Journal of Southern History* VI (February, 1940), 3-24.

Thompson, W. G. "Eleutherian Institute," *Indiana Magazine of History* XIX (June, 1923), 110-20.

Tolbert, Noble J. "Daniel Worth: Tarheel Abolitionist," *North Carolina Historical Review* XXXIX (July, 1962), 284-305.

Tremain, Mary. "Slavery in the District of Columbia," *University of Nebraska Seminar Papers* (April, 1892), No. 2.

Turner, L. D. "Antislavery Sentiment in American Literature," *Journal of Negro History* XIV (October, 1929), 371-493.

Walsh, A. C. "Three Antislavery Newspapers Published in Ohio

Prior to 1823," *Ohio Archaeological and Historical Quarterly* XXXI (1922), 172-211.

Weeks, S. B. "Antislavery Sentiment in the South," *Publications of the Southern Historical Association* II (April, 1898), 87-131.

Weeks, S. B. "The History of Negro Suffrage," *Political Science Quarterly* IX (December, 1894), 671-703.

Weisenburger, F. P. "Charles Hammond, The First Great Journalist of the Old Northwest," *Ohio Archaeological and Historical Quarterly* XLIII (October, 1934), 340-427.

Whateley, G. C. "The Alabama Presbyterian and His Slave," *Alabama Review* XII (January, 1960), 40-51.

Williams, Irene. "The Operation of the Fugitive Slave Law in Western Pennsylvania, 1850-1860," *Western Pennsylvania Historical Magazine* IV (January, 1921), 150-61.

Wilson, Harold. "Basil Manly, Apologist for Slavery," *Alabama Review* XV (January, 1962), 38-54.

Wilson, Janet. "Early Antislavery Propaganda," *More Books: Bulletin of the Boston Public Library* XX (February, 1945), 31-52, XIX (November, December, 1944), 343-61, 393-406.

Wish, Harvey. "American Slave Insurrections before 1861," *Journal of Negro History* XXII (July, 1937), 299-321.

Wish, Harvey. "The Revival of the African Slave Trade in the United States," *Mississippi Valley Historical Review* XXVII (March, 1941), 569-88.

Wish, Harvey. "The Slave Insurrection Panic of 1856," *Journal of Southern History* V (February-November, 1939), 206-91.

Woodward, C. Vann. "The Antislavery Myth," *American Scholar* XXXI (Spring, 1962), 312-28.

Woolfolk, George R. "Planter Capitalism and Slavery: The Labor Thesis," *Journal of Negro History* XLI (April, 1956), 103-17.

Wormley, G. S. "Prudence Crandall," *Journal of Negro History* VIII (January, 1923), 72-80.

Zorn, Roman J. "The New England Antislavery Society: Pioneer Abolition Organization," *Journal of Negro History* XLIII (July, 1957), 157-76.

III. Newspapers, Periodicals, and Series Publications

A. NEWSPAPERS

The New York *Radical Abolitionist*. (Formerly also the *Anti-Slavery Examiner* and *The American Jubilee*.)

The New York *National Anti Slavery Standard*.

The New York *American Anti-Slavery Reporter*.

The New York *Weekly Tribune*.

The New York *Evening Post*.

The Boston *Liberator*.

The Boston *Emancipator*.

The Boston *Massachusetts Abolitionist*.

Bibliography of Sources

The Boston *Abolitionist*.
The Boston *Morning Post*.
The Boston *Advertiser*.
The Cincinnati *Philanthropist*. (First four months published from New Richmond, Ohio. Title changed to *The Weekly Herald and Philanthropist* in 1843).
The Cincinnati *Gazette*.
The Cincinnati *Repository and Commercial Record*.
The Cincinnati *Journal*.
The Washington, D. C., *National Era*.
The Salem, Ohio, *Anti Slavery Bugle*.
The Utica, New York, *Friend of Man*.
The Hallowell, Maine, *Liberty Standard*.
The Concord, New Hampshire, *Herald of Freedom*.
The Whitesboro and Honeoye, New York, *Christian Emancipator*.
The Cleveland *Liberalist*.
The Philadelphia *Pennsylvania Freeman*.
The Baltimore *Sun*.
The Wheeling *Tri-Weekly Gazette*.
The Wheeling *Intelligencer*.
The Charleston *Mercury*.
The Richmond *Enquirer*.
The Richmond *Examiner*.
The Detroit *Advertiser*.
The Sandwich, Canada West, *Voice of the Fugitive*.

B. SERIES AND PERIODICAL PUBLICATIONS

Niles' Register.
DeBow's Review.
Human Rights.
The Anti-Slavery Record. 1835-37, New York.
The Slave's Friend. 1836, New York.
The Quarterly Anti-Slavery Magazine. 1835-37, New York.
The Liberty Bell. 1839-46, 1847-58, Boston.
The American Anti-Slavery Almanac. 1836-40, 1832-44, Boston.
The Anti-Slavery Examiner. 1836-45, New York.
Anti-Slavery Tracts. 1855-56 o.s., 1860-62 n.s., New York.
Liberty Tracts. 1843, 1852, Boston.
Liberty Tracts. 1848 (?), New York.
The New England Anti-Slavery Tracts. n.d., Boston.
Facts for the People. 1842-44, 1853-56, Cincinnati, Washington.
The Liberty Almanac. 1847-49, New York.
The Legion of Liberty and the Force of Truth. 1840-44, New York.

IV. Reports, Proceedings, Platforms, of Societies

Annual Report of the American Abolition Society, 1856, 1858.
Annual Report of the American and Foreign Anti-Slavery Society, 1847-53.

Annual Report of the American Anti-Slavery Society, 1834-39, 1855-61.
Annual Report of the Anti-Slavery Society of Lane Seminary, 1834.
Annual Report of the Massachusetts Anti-Slavery Society, 1836-53.
Annual Report of the New England Anti-Slavery Society, 1833-55.
Annual Report of the New York City Anti-Slavery Society, 1833.
Annual Report of the Ohio Anti-Slavery Society, 1835-40.
Annual Report of the Indiana Anti-Slavery Society, 1838.
Annual Report of the Maine Anti-Slavery Society, 1839-40.
Annual Report of the New England Anti-Slavery Convention, 1836, 1838.
Annual Report of the New York State Anti-Slavery Society, 1835-36.
The American Anti-Slavery Society, Declaration of Sentiments, 1833, 1835.
The American Anti-Slavery Society, Platform of the Society and Its Auxiliaries, 1855, 1860.
The Lane Seminary Anti-Slavery Society, Preamble and Constitution, 1834.
The New York City Anti-Slavery Society, Address to the People of New York City, 1833.
The Ohio State Anti-Slavery Society, Letter from the Executive Committee, 1838.
Proceedings of the American Anti-Slavery Society, 1833, 1853, 1863.
Proceedings of the Annual Meetings held in 1854, 1855, and 1856, the Massachusetts Anti-Slavery Society.
Proceedings of the New England Anti-Slavery Convention, 1834, 1836.
Proceedings of the First Annual Meeting, New York State Anti-Slavery Society, 1836.
Proceedings of the Ohio State Anti-Slavery Convention, 1835.
Proceedings of the Rhode Island State Anti-Slavery Convention, 1836.
Proceedings of the Massachusetts State Disunion Convention, 1857.
Proceedings of the Anti-Slavery Meeting held in Stacy Hall, Boston, 1855.
Proceedings of the Constitutional Meeting at Faneuil Hall, Boston, 1850.
Proceedings of the Anti-Fugitive Slave Law Meeting . . . in Syracuse, 1851.
Proceedings of the Meeting held at Broadway Tabernacle . . ., 1856.

V. Contemporary Books, Biographies, Collections

Adams, Charles Francis, ed. *The Memoirs of John Quincy Adams.* Philadelphia, 1876.
Adams, Josiah Quincy. *A Memoir of John Quincy Adams.* Boston, 1858.
Adams, Nehemiah. *A Southside View of Slavery.* Boston, 1855.
Bacon, Leonard. *Slavery Discussed in Occasional Essays from 1833-1846.* New York, 1846.
Baker, G. E., ed. *The Works of William H. Seward.* New York, 1853.

Bancroft, Frederic, ed. *Speeches, Correspondence, and Political Papers of Carl Schurz.* New York, 1913.

Bancroft, George. *Literary and Historical Miscellanies.* New York, 1855.

Barre, W. L., ed. *The Speeches and Writings of Thomas F. Marshall.* Cincinnati, 1858.

Bearse, Austin. *Reminiscences of Fugitive Slave Days in Boston.* Boston, 1880.

Beecher, Catherine. *An Essay Upon Slavery and Abolitionism.* Philadelphia, 1837.

Beecher, Charles. *The Autobiography and Correspondence of Lyman Beecher.* New York, 1865.

Beecher, Henry Ward. *Patriotic Addresses.* New York, 1887.

Benton, T. H., ed. *Abridgement of the Debates of Congress,* New York, 1847-61.

Blanchard, J., and Rice, N. *A Debate on Slavery.* Cincinnati, 1859.

Bledsoe, Albert T. *An Essay on Liberty and Slavery.* Philadelphia, 1856.

Bowditch, William I. *Slavery and the Constitution.* Boston, 1849.

Bourne, George. *Slavery Illustrated in its Effects Upon Women and Domestic Society.* Boston, 1837.

Brown, William H. *An Historical Sketch of the Early Movement in Illinois for the Legalization of Slavery.* Chicago, 1865.

Buell, Walter. *Joshua R. Giddings.* Cleveland, 1882.

Bush, George. *Aphorisms on Slavery and Abolition.* New York, 1855.

Cairnes, John E. *The Slave Power: Its Character, Career, and Probable Designs.* New York, 1862.

Carey, Henry C. *The Slave Trade, Domestic and Foreign.* Philadelphia, 1853.

Carpenter, S. C. *The Logic of History.* Madison, Wisconsin, 1864.

Chambers, William. *American Slavery and Color.* London, 1861.

Channing, William Ellery. *Slavery.* Boston, 1836.

Cheever, George B. *God Against Slavery.* New York, 1857.

Child, Lydia M., ed. *George W. Julian, Speeches on Political Questions.* New York, 1872.

Christy, David. *Cotton is King.* Cincinnati, 1855.

Cleveland, C. D. *Anti-Slavery Addresses of 1844 and 1845.* Philadelphia, 1867.

Cobb, Howell. *A Scriptural Examination of the Institution of Slavery in the United States.* Perry, Georgia, 1856.

Cobb, Thomas R. R. *An Historical Sketch of Slavery from the Earliest Periods.* Philadelphia, 1858.

Cochin, August. *The Results of Slavery.* Boston, 1863.

Coffin, Joshua. *An Account of Some of the Principal Slave Insurrections.* New York, 1860.

Coffin, Levi. *Reminiscences.* Cincinnati, 1876.

Colton, Calvin. *Abolition a Sedition.* Philadelphia, 1839.

Colton, Calvin, ed. *Speeches of Henry Clay.* New York, 1857.

Colton, Calvin, ed. *The Works of Henry Clay.* New York, 1904.

Shambaugh Library

Crallé, Richard, ed. *The Works of John C. Calhoun*. New York, 1853-57.

Dabney, R. L. *A Defense of Virginia*. New York, 1867.

Davis, Jefferson. *The Rise and Fall of the Confederate Government*. New York, 1881.

DeBow, J. D. B. *The Industrial Resources, etc., of the Southern and Western States*. New Orleans, 1853.

DeBow, J. D. B. *The Interest in Slavery of the Non-Slaveholder*. Charleston, 1860.

de Fontaine, F. G. *The History of American Abolitionism*. New York, 1861.

Dye, John Smith. *History of the Plots and Crimes of the Great Conspiracy to Overthrow Liberty in America*. New York, 1866.

Edge, F. M. *Slavery Doomed*. London, 1860.

Elliott, Charles. *The Bible and Slavery*. Cincinnati, 1859.

Elliott, E. N., ed. *Cotton is King, and The Pro-Slavery Argument*. Augusta, Georgia, 1860.

Estes, Matthew. *A Defense of Negro Slavery as it Exists in the United States*. Montgomery, Alabama, 1846.

Fee, John G. *The Autobiography of John G. Fee*. Chicago, 1891.

Fitzhugh, George. *Sociology for the South*. New York, 1854.

Fletcher, John. *Studies on Slavery, in Eight Easy Lessons*. Natchez, Louisiana, 1852.

Flower, F. A. *History of the Republican Party*. Springfield, Illinois, 1884.

Fowler, W. G. *The Sectional Controversy*. New York, 1865.

Fulton, John, ed. *The Memoirs of Frederick A. P. Barnard*. New York, 1896.

Garrison, W. P. and F. J. *William Lloyd Garrison*. Boston, 1894.

Giddings, Joshua R. *History of the Rebellion: Its Authors and Causes*. New York, 1864.

Giddings, Joshua R. *Speeches in Congress*. Boston and Cleveland, 1853.

Godwin, Parke. *Political Essays*. New York, 1856.

Goodell, William. *Slavery and Anti-Slavery*. New York, 1852.

Goodell, William. *Views of American Constitutional Law, in its Bearing on American Slavery*. Utica, New York, 1844.

Goodell, William. *Our National Charters: for the Millions*. New York, 1864.

Greeley, Horace. *A History of the Struggle for Slavery Extension or Restriction in the United States*. New York, 1856.

Greeley, Horace. *The American Conflict*. New York, 1864-66.

Greeley, Horace, ed. *The Writings of Cassius Marcellus Clay*. New York, 1848.

Griffiths, Julia, ed. *Autographs for Freedom*. Boston, 1853.

Grimké, Frederick. *The Nature and Tendency of Free Institutions*. Cincinnati, 1848.

Harris, Alexander. *A Review of the Political Conflict in America*. New York, 1876.

Haviland, Laura. *A Woman's Life Work*. Chicago, 1889.

Helper, H. R. *The Impending Crisis of the South: How to Meet It.* New York, 1859.

Hildreth, Richard. *Despotism in America.* Boston, 1840.

Horton, R. G. *A Youth's History of the Civil War.* New York, 1867.

Hosmer, William. *The Higher Law in its Relations to Civil Government.* Auburn, New York, 1852.

Hundley, D. R. *Social Relations in our Southern States.* New York, 1860.

Hurd, John C. *The Law of Freedom and Bondage.* Boston, 1858-62.

Jay, William. *An Inquiry into the Character and Tendencies of the American Colonization and the American Anti-Slavery Society.* New York, 1835.

Jay, William. *A View of the Action of the Federal Government in Behalf of Slavery.* New York, 1839.

Jay, William. *Miscellaneous Writings on Slavery.* Boston, 1853.

Johnson, Oliver. *William Lloyd Garrison and His Times.* Boston, 1881.

Jones, J. Elizabeth. *The Young Abolitionists.* Boston, 1848.

Kimball, John C. *Connecticut's Canterbury Tale.* Hartford, 1888.

Lincoln, William S. *The Alton Trials.* New York, 1838.

Livermore, George. *An Historical Research Respecting the Opinions of the Founders of the Republic on Negroes.* Boston, 1862.

Lovejoy, J. C. and O. *Memoir of the Reverend Elijah P. Lovejoy.* New York, 1838.

Lowell, James Russell. *The Anti-Slavery Papers of James Russell Lowell.* Boston, 1902.

McMichael, William. *Slavery and Its Remedy.* Pittsburgh, 1856.

Mann, Horace. *Slavery: Letters and Speeches.* Boston, 1851.

Marsh, L. R., ed. *The Writings and Speeches of Alvan R. Stewart on Slavery.* New York, 1860.

Martineau, Harriet. *The Martyr Age of the United States of America.* Newcastle upon Tyne, 1840.

Martineau, Harriet. *Society in America.* London, 1837.

Matlack, Lucius C. *Anti-Slavery Struggle and Triumph in the Methodist Church.* New York, 1881.

Matlack, Lucius C. *The History of American Slavery and Methodism from 1780 to 1849.* New York, 1849.

May, Samuel J. *Some Recollections of Our Anti-Slavery Conflict.* Boston, 1869.

Mellen, G. W. F. *An Argument on the Unconstitutionality of Slavery.* Boston, 1841.

Moore, G. H. *Notes on the History of Slavery in Massachusetts.* New York, 1866.

Morris, B. F. *The Life of Thomas Morris.* Cincinnati, 1856.

Mumford, Thomas J. *Memoir of Samuel J. May.* Boston, 1873.

Noel, Baptist W. *Freedom and Slavery in the United States of America.* London, 1858.

Nott, Samuel. *Slavery and the Remedy.* Boston, 1859.

Parker, Theodore. *The Trial of Theodore Parker.* Boston, 1855.

Paulding, J. K. *Slavery in the United States.* Philadelphia, 1856.

Phelps, Amos A. *Lectures on Slavery and its Remedy*. Boston, 1834.

Phillips, Wendell. *Speeches, Lectures, and Letters*. Boston, 1870.

Pickard, S. G. *The Life and Letters of John Greenleaf Whittier*. Boston and New York, 1894.

Pierce, Edward L. *Memoirs and Letters of Charles Sumner*. Boston, 1893.

Pierpont, John, ed. *A Collection of the Newspaper Writings of N. P. Rogers*. Concord, New Hampshire, 1847.

Powell, Aaron. *Personal Reminiscences*. New York, 1899.

Robinson, John Bell. *Pictures of Slavery and Anti-Slavery*. Philadelphia, 1863.

Ross, Alexander. *Recollections and Experiences of an Abolitionist*. Toronto, 1875.

Ruffin, Edmund. *Slavery and Free Labor Compared*. Washington, 1853.

Sanborn, F. B. *The Life and Letters of John Brown*. Boston, 1891.

Sawyer, George S. *Southern Institutes*. Philadelphia, 1859.

Seabury, Samuel. *American Slavery . . . Justified by the Law of Nature*. New York, 1861.

Shipherd, Jacob. *History of the Oberlin-Wellington Rescue*. Boston, Cleveland, and New York, 1859.

Shumway, A. L. and Brower, C. D. *Oberliniana*. Cleveland, 1883.

Smith, Gerrit. *Sermons and Speeches*. New York, 1861.

Smith, Gerrit. *Speeches in Congress*. New York, 1855.

Smith, William A. *Lectures on the Philosophy and Practices of Slavery*. Nashville, 1856.

Spooner, Lysander. *The Unconstitutionality of Slavery*. Boston, 1847.

Stevens, Charles E. *Anthony Burns, A History*. Boston, 1856.

Stowe, Harriet B. *Key to Uncle Tom's Cabin*. London, n. d.

Stroud, George M. *A Sketch of the Laws Relating to Slavery in the Several States of the United States*. Philadelphia, 1856.

Sumner, Charles. *Recent Speeches and Addresses*. Boston, 1856.

Sunderland, LaRoy. *Anti-Slavery Manual*. New York, 1837.

Sunderland, LaRoy. *The Testimony of God Against Slavery*. Boston, 1835.

Tanner, Henry. *An Account of the Life, Trials, and Perils of the Reverend Elijah P. Lovejoy . . .* Chicago, 1881.

Tappan, Lewis. *The Life of Arthur Tappan*. New York, 1871.

Thomas, Abel C. ("Iron Gray") *The Gospel of Slavery: A Primer of Freedom*. New York, 1864.

Thomas, William. ("Defensor") *The Enemies of the Constitution Discovered . . .* Utica, New York, 1835.

Thompson, George. *Prison Life and Reflections*. Oberlin, Ohio, 1847.

Thompson, George, and Breckenridge, Robert J. *A Discussion on American Slavery*. Boston, 1836.

Treadwell, S. B. *American Liberties and American Slavery Morally and Politically Examined*. New York, 1839.

Vallandigham, Clement L. *Speeches, Arguments, Addresses, and Letters*. New York, 1864.

Van Evrie, J. H. *White Supremacy and Negro Subordination.* New York, 1868.

Wayland, Francis, and Fuller, Richard. *Domestic Slavery Considered As A Scriptural Institution* . . . New York, 1845.

Webb, Samuel (?). *History of Pennsylvania Hall, Destroyed by a Mob* . . . Philadelphia, 1838.

Weld, Theodore, *American Slavery As It Is.* New York, 1839.

Weld, Theodore. *The Bible Against Slavery.* Pittsburgh, 1864.

Weston, George M. *Progress of Slavery in the United States.* Washington, 1857.

Weston, George M. *Who Are and Who May Be Slaves in the United States: Facts for the People.* n.p., n.d.

Wheeler, Jacob. *A Practical Treatise on the Law of Slavery.* New Orleans, 1837.

Wigham, Eliza. *The Anti-Slavery Cause in America and Its Martyrs.* London, 1853 (?).

Willey, Austin. *A History of the Anti-Slavery Cause in State and Nation.* Portland, Maine, 1886.

Wilson, Henry. *History of the Rise and Fall of the Slave Power in America.* Boston, 1872.

Wolfe, Samuel L. *Helper's Impending Crisis Dissected.* New York, 1860.

A Collection of Valuable Documents. Boston, 1836.

America's Misfortune: A Practical View of Slavery. Buffalo, 1856.

The Higher Law. New York, 1851.

The Sons of Liberty in 1776 and 1856. New York, 1856.

Selections from the Speeches and Writings of Prominent Men in the United States on the Subject of Abolition and Agitation. New York, 1851.

VI. Speeches, Sermons, Pamphlets

Adams, Charles Francis. *What makes slavery a question of national concern.* Boston, 1855.

Adams, John Quincy. *Letters . . . to his constituents.* Boston, 1837.

Adams, John Quincy. *Speech . . . upon the right of the people . . . to petition . . .* Washington, 1838.

Address of the Executive Committee of the State Anti-slavery Association to the Citizens of Eastern Pennsylvania. Philadelphia, 1838.

Allen, George. *Resistance to slavery every man's duty.* Boston, 1847.

Alston, William J. *The slavery question.* Washington, 1850.

An Ancient Landmark, or the Essential Element of Civil and Religious Liberty . . . Watertown, Connecticut, 1838.

Bailey, Rufus. *The Issue, presented in a series of letters on slavery.* New York, 1837.

Bailey, N. P. *Our duty as taught by the aggressive nature of slavery.* Akron, 1855.

Barrows, Elijah P. *A view of the American slavery question.* New York, 1836.

Beecher, Edward. Narrative of the riots at Alton . . . Alton, Illinois, 1838.

Beecher, Lyman. Address at Miami University, September 29, 1835. Cincinnati, 1835.

Beecher, Lyman. The ballot-box a remedy for national crimes. Boston, 1838.

Bingham, John A. The assault upon Senator Sumner . . . Washington, 1856.

Birney, J. G. Correspondence between F. H. Elmore and James G. Birney. New York, 1838.

Birney, J. G. Letter on colonization . . . New York, 1838.

Birney, J. G. Letter to Ministers and Elders. New York, 1834.

Birney, J. G. Narrative of the late riotous proceedings against the liberty of the press in Cincinnati. Cincinnati, 1836.

Birney, J. G. The American churches, the bulwarks of American slavery. Newburyport, Massachusetts, 1842.

Bissell, William H. The slave question. Washington, 1850.

Bliss, Philemon. Citizenship: state citizens, general citizens. Washington, 1858.

Botts, John M. The past, present, and future of our country . . . Washington, 1860.

Bourne, George. Man-stealing denounced . . . Boston, 1834.

Bowditch, William I. The rendition of Anthony Burns. Boston, 1854.

Brisbane, W. H. Speech . . . delivered before the Ladies Anti-Slavery Society of Cincinnati. Hartford, 1840.

Brown, A. Y. Address on the progress of the United States. Nashville, 1860.

Brownlow, W. G. and Pryne, A. Ought American slavery to be perpetuated? Philadelphia, 1858.

Burns, S. Speech in the Ohio State Senate . . . Columbus, 1851.

Burritt, Elihu. A plan of brotherly cooperation of the North and South. New York, 1856.

Bushnell, Horace. A discourse on the slavery question. Hartford, 1839.

Bushnell, Horace. Politics under the law of God. Hartford, 1844.

Bushnell, Horace. The census and slavery . . . Hartford, 1860.

Calhoun, John C. Speech . . . on the slavery question . . . Washington, 1850.

Carey, Matthew. Letters on the Colonization Society . . . Philadelphia, 1832.

Channing, W. E. The duty of the free states . . . Boston, 1842.

Channing, W. E. A letter to James G. Birney . . . Boston, 1837.

Channing, W. E. Remarks on the slavery question . . . to Jonathan Phillips, Esq. Boston, 1839.

Chase, Salmon P. Speech in the Senate, February 3, 1854. Washington, 1854.

Chase, Salmon P. The reclamation of fugitives from justice. Cincinnati, 1847.

Cheever, Henry T. A tract for the times . . . New York, 1859.

Child, David Lee. The despotism of freedom. Boston, 1833.

Child, Lydia M. Anti slavery catechism. Newburyport, Massachusetts, 1836.

Christy, David. African colonization . . . Cincinnati, 1854.

"Citizen of Georgia." Remarks on slavery. Augusta, Georgia, 1835.

"Citizen of Virginia." The Union past and future. Charleston, South Carolina, 1850.

Corwin, Thomas. Speech on . . . the state of the Union . . . Washington, 1861.

Corwin, Thomas. Speech . . . in the House of Representatives . . . Washington, 1860.

Day, George E. The dangers of our country . . . Boston, 1842.

DeBow, J. D. B. The interest in slavery of the non-slaveholder. New York, 1860.

Decision of the Supreme Court of the State of Wisconsin in the cases of Booth and Ryecraft. Milwaukee, 1856.

Doolittle, James R. The Calhoun revolution: its bases and progress. Washington, 1860.

Dresser, Amos. The narrative of Amos Dresser, with Stone's letters from Natchez, New York, 1836.

Duncan, Alexander. Remarks . . . on the right of petition, delivered in the House of Representatives . . . Washington, 1844.

Duncan, James. A treatise on slavery . . . New York, 1840.

Dye, John Smith. History of the plots and crimes of the great conspiracy . . . New York, 1866.

Edgerton, Sidney. Speech . . . in the House of Representatives, February 29, 1860. Washington, 1860.

Egleston, R. S. Human legislation void when it conflicts with the law of God . . . Cleveland, 1856.

Extracts from Remarks on Dr. Channing's Slavery. Boston, 1836.

Fisher, Ellwood. Lecture on the North and the South . . . Cincinnati, 1849.

Fisher, George E. The church, the ministry, and slavery. Worcester, n.d.

Five Years' Progress of the Slave Power. New York, 1852.

Foster, E. B. A North-side view of slavery. Concord, New Hampshire, 1856.

Foster, S. S. The brotherhood of thieves, a true picture of the American church and clergy. Boston, 1843.

Foster, S. S. The rights of white men vindicated . . . Washington, 1858.

Frothingham, Frederick. The significance of the struggle between liberty and slavery. Boston, 1855.

Furness, William II. A discourse occasioned by the Boston fugitive slave case. Philadelphia, 1851.

Garrison, W. L. The abolitionists; a speech at Cooper Institute. n.p., 1862.

Garrison, W. L. The new reign of terror. New York, 1860.

Garrison, W. L. Southern hatred of . . . the people of the North and free institutions. Boston, 1862.

Garrison, W. L. Thoughts on African colonization. Boston, 1832.

Giddings, J. R. A letter upon the duty of anti-slavery men in the present crisis . . . Ravenna, Ohio, 1844.

Giddings, J. R. The moral responsibility of statesmen. Washington, 1854.

Giddings, J. R. The rights of the free states subverted . . . n.p., 1844.

Goodell, William. Address at the Macedon convention . . . Albany, 1847.

Goodell, William. Address . . . at the New York State Liberty Convention . . . Albany, 1845.

Goodell, William. An account of the interviews which took place . . . between a committee of the Massachusetts Anti-Slavery Society and the committee of the legislature . . . Boston, 1836.

Goodell, William. A full statement of the reasons which were in part offered to the committee of the legislature . . . Boston, 1836.

Goodell, William. Come-outerism: the duty of secession from a corrupt church. New York, 1845.

Goodell, William. The rights and wrongs of Rhode Island. Whitesboro, New York, 1842.

Goodloe, Daniel R. Inquiries into the causes which have retarded the accumulation of wealth and increase of population in the Southern states. Washington, 1846.

Goodloe, Daniel R. The South and the North . . . Washington, 1849.

Goodloe, Daniel R. The Southern platform . . . Boston, 1858.

Gray, E. H. Assaults upon freedom. Shelburne Falls, Massachusetts, 1854.

Green, Beriah. A discourse in commemoration of the martyrdom of Elijah P. Lovejoy . . . New York, 1838.

Green, Beriah. Sketches of the life and writings of James Gillespie Birney . . . Utica, New York, 1844.

Green, Beriah. Things for Northern men to do. Whiteside, New York, 1836.

Grimké, Angelina. Letter to Catherine E. Beecher . . . Boston, 1838.

Gunn, Lewis. Address to the abolitionists . . . Philadelphia, 1838.

Hall, Marshall. Two-fold slavery of the United States . . . London, 1854.

Hammond, J. H. Remarks . . . on the question of receiving petitions for the abolition of slavery . . . Washington, 1836 (?).

Hammond, S. H. Freedom national—slavery sectional. Washington, 1860.

Hancock, John H. The North and the South: the crisis before us. New York, 1856.

Higginson, T. H. The new revolution. Boston, 1857.

Hitt, R. R. Argument of E. C. Larned, counsel for the defense on the trial of Joseph Stoat . . . Chicago, 1860.

Hodges, C. E. Disunion our wisdom and our duty. New York, 1855.

Holcombe, W. H. The alternative: a separate nationality or the Africanization of the South, n.p., 1860.

May, Samuel J. A catalogue of anti-slavery publications in America. n.p., 1836 (?).

Morris, Thomas. Speech . . . in the Senate, February 6, 1839 . . . New York, n.d.

Motley, John Lothrop. The causes of the American Civil War. New York, 1861.

"New England Man." An attempt to demonstrate the practicability of emancipating the slaves . . . n.p., 1825.

"North Carolinian." Southern slavery considered on general principles. New York, 1861.

Olcott, Charles. Two lectures on the subject of slavery and abolition. Massillon, Ohio, 1838.

Parker, Theodore. Address of a committee appointed by a public meeting, held at Faneuil Hall . . . Boston, 1846.

Parker, Theodore. An address delivered before the New York City Anti-Slavery society . . . New York, 1854.

Parker, Theodore. The dangers from slavery. Boston, 1854.

Parker, Theodore. The effect of slavery on the American people. Boston, 1858.

Parker, Theodore. A letter to the people of the United States . . . Boston, 1848.

Parker, Theodore. The new crime against humanity . . . Boston, 1854.

Parker, Theodore. The present aspect of slavery in America . . . Boston, 1858.

Parker, Theodore. The relation of slavery to a republican form of government . . . Boston, 1858.

Palfrey, John G. Papers . . . on the slave power. Boston, 1846.

Palfrey, John G. Speech . . . on the political aspects of the slavery question. Washington, 1848.

Patton, William. The American crisis, or the true issue, liberty or slavery? London, 1861.

Patton, William. Conscience and law. New York, 1850.

Patton, William. Slavery and infidelity. Cincinnati, 1856.

Perry, John. Freedom national, slavery sectional . . . Washington, 1856.

Peters, Richard. Report of the case of Edward Prigg against the Commonwealth of Pennsylvania . . . Philadelphia, 1842.

"Philadelphian." Free remarks on the spirit of the Federal Constitution. Philadelphia, 1819.

Phillips, S. C. Address upon the annexation of Texas . . . Boston, 1845.

Philipps, Wendell. The Constitution a pro-slavery compact. New York, 1856.

Phillips, Wendell. The philosophy of the abolition movement. New York, 1860.

Phillips, Wendell. Speech . . . at the Worcester Disunion convention, Boston, 1857.

Pillsbury, Parker. The church as it is. Boston, 1847.

Plumer, William. Freedom's defence; or, a candid examination of Mr. Calhoun's report on the freedom of the press . . . Worcester, Massachusetts, 1836.

"Publicola." The present aspects of abolitionism. Richmond, 1847.

Quincy, Joseph. Addresses illustrative of the nature and power of the slave states . . . Boston, 1856.

Rand, Asa. The slave-catcher caught in the meshes of eternal law . . . Cleveland, 1852.

Rankin, John. Letters on American slavery. Boston, 1833.

Reeder, H. R., and Reid, J. B. The trial of the Reverend John B. Mahan . . . Cincinnati, 1838.

Remarks on the Constitution by a friend of humanity. Philadelphia, 1836.

Reese, David. Letters to the honorable William Jay. New York, 1835.

Rice, Nathan L. Lectures on slavery. Chicago, 1860.

Root, David. Sermon . . . to the anti slavery society of Haverhill, Mass. . . . Andover, 1836.

Ruffner, Henry. Address to the people of West Virginia . . . Lexington, Virginia, 1847.

Seward, W. H. The dangers of extending slavery. Washington, 1856.

Seward, W. H. The irrepressible conflict. Albany, 1860.

Sherwood, Lorenzo. The great question of the times exemplified in the antagonistic principles involved in the slaveholders' rebellion . . . New York, 1862.

Slade, William. Speech . . . on the right of petition . . . January 18 and 20, 1840 . . . Washington, 1840.

Slade, William. Speech . . . on the abolition of slavery and the slave trade in the District of Columbia . . . Washington, 1837 (?).

Slavery of Poverty, with the plan for its abolition. New York, 1842.

Smith, Gerrit. The crime of the abolitionists. Peterboro, New York, 1835.

Smith, Gerrit. Substance of a speech made in the capitol of the State of New York . . . Albany, 1850.

Smith, L. The higher law. Ravenna, Ohio, 1852.

South Vindicated from the Treason and Fanaticism of the Northern Abolitionists. Philadelphia, 1836.

Southern Hatred of Free Institutions. Boston, 1862.

Southern Notes for National Circulation. Boston, 1860.

Spear, Samuel T. The law-abiding conscience and the higher law conscience. New York, 1850.

Spofford, Ainsworth R. The higher law tried by reason and authority. New York, 1851.

Spooner, Lysander. A defense for fugitive slaves . . . Boston, 1850.

Spooner, Lysander. An essay on the trial by jury. Boston, 1852.

Stanly, Edward. Speech . . . exposing the causes of the slavery agitation. Washington, 1850.

Stanton, Henry B. Remarks in Representatives Hall . . . before the committee of the House of Representatives . . . Boston, 1837.

Stearns, Charles. The fugitive slave law shown to be unconstitutional, impolitic, inhuman, and diabolical. Boston, 1851.

Stone, Thomas T. The martyr of freedom. Boston, 1836.

Stringfellow, Thornton. Slavery, its origin, nature, and history . . . New York, 1861.

Stuart, Moses. Conscience and the Constitution. New York, 1850.

Sumner, Charles. The barbarism of slavery. Washington, 1860.

Sumner, Charles. A lecture on the anti-slavery enterprise . . . New York, 1855.

Sumner, Charles. Speech . . . on his motion to repeal the fugitive slave bill . . . Washington, 1852.

Swaim, William. Address to the people of North Carolina on the evils of slavery. Greensboro, North Carolina, 1830.

Tappan, Lewis. Address to the non-slaveholders of the South on the social and political evils of slavery. New York, 1833 (?).

Thacher, George. No fellowship with slavery. Meriden, Connecticut, 1856.

Tiffany, Joel. A treatise on the unconstitutionality of slavery. Cleveland, 1849.

Tompkins, Cydnor B. Slavery: what it is, what it has done, what it intends to do. Washington, 1860.

Tracy, Joseph. Natural equality, a sermon at Montpelier . . . Windsor, Vermont, 1833.

Trafton, Mark. The disturbing element in the body politic. Washington, 1856.

Trial of Reuben Crandall, M. D., carefully reported and compiled . . . Washington, 1836.

Trial of Reuben Crandall, M. D., charged with publishing seditious libels . . . New York, 1836.

Van Dyke, Henry. The character and influence of abolitionism. New York, 1860.

"Virginian." Slavery in Maryland. Baltimore, 1846.

Washburne, Israel. The politics of the country. Washington, 1856.

Watterson, Henry. George Dennison Prentice: a memorial address. Cincinnati, 1870.

Webb, J. Watson. Slavery and its tendencies. Washington, 1856.

Webb, Samuel. Speech in the National Anti-slavery convention, held at Albany, August 1, 1839. Philadelphia, 1840.

Weld, Theodore D. A Statement of the reasons which induced the students of Lane Seminary to dissolve their connection with that institution. Cincinnati, 1834.

Weld, Theodore D. The power of Congress over the District of Columbia. New York, 1838.

Wilson, Henry. The aggressions of the slave power. Washington, 1860 (?).

Wilson, James. Speech . . . on the political influence of slavery. Washington, 1849.

Wisner, W. C. A review of Dr. Lord's sermon of the higher law . . . Buffalo, 1851.

Withington, Leonard. Thanksgiving sermon, preached Nov. 28, 1850. Newburyport, Massachusetts, 1851.

Wright, Elizur, Jr. The sin of slavery and its remedy. New York, 1833.

Index